A Chance to Win

A Complete Guide to Physical Training for Football

Mike Gentry, Ed.D., CSCS, MSCC
Head Strength and Conditioning Coach
Virginia Tech

Tony Caterisano, Ph.D., FACSM, CSCS*D
Professor of Health and Exercise Science
Furman University

With foreword by Frank Beamer
Head Football Coach, Virginia Tech
2000 NCAA Div. I-A Coach of the Year

SP
SPORTS PUBLISHING
L.L.C.

www.SportsPublishingLLC.com

ISBN: 1-58261-955-7

Front cover photo of Michael Vick by Doug Pensinger/Getty Images.
Front cover photo of gym by Thomas M. Bailey.
All interior photos by Thomas M. Bailey.

Publishers: Peter L. Bannon and Joseph J. Bannon Sr.
Senior managing editor: Susan M. Moyer
Acquisitions editor: Bob Snodgrass
Developmental editors: Dean Miller and Elisa Bock Laird
Art director: K. Jeffrey Higgerson
Dust jacket design: Heidi Norsen
Project manager: Jim Henehan
Imaging: Kenneth J. O'Brien
Photo editor: Erin Linden-Levy
Vice president of sales and marketing: Kevin King
Media and promotions managers: Jonathan Patterson (regional),
        Randy Fouts (national), Maurey Williamson (print)

Printed in United States of America

Sports Publishing L.L.C.
804 North Neil Street
Champaign, IL 61820

Phone: 1-877-424-2665
Fax: 217-363-2073
Web site: www.SportsPublishingLLC.com

"I was not that strong when I got to Virginia Tech but I realized that training hard was important in staying injury free and developing as a player. I really exploded strength and speed wise under the direction of Coach Gentry. In two years my bench went up 50 pounds and I squatted 515. My vertical jump increased from 34.5 inches to 41 inches, and my forty time went from 4.42 to 4.25 while gaining 18 pounds of body weight!"

Michael Vick
All-Pro QB of the Atlanta Falcons
1st Draft Pick of 2001 NFL Draft
Virginia Tech Super Iron Hokie

"Virginia Tech football teams are always well prepared and well conditioned. When playing against them, they are always strong, physical, and powerful. When the game is over, win or lose, your players know they have been in a game. Mike Gentry is truly one of the best strength coaches in America. Year in and year out, Mike's strength and conditioning program has the Hokie players competing to be the best."

Al Johnson, M.S., CSCS, Director of Strength and Conditioning for Football
The Ohio State University
2002 NCAA National Champions

"There is no question about the value and importance of weight training as an ingredient to winning. We are very fortunate to have Mike Gentry running our strength and conditioning program."

Frank Beamer, Head Football Coach
Virginia Tech
Associated Press Coach of the Year–2000

"I have known Mike Gentry for nearly 20 years and have had the privilege of coaching players who have come from his program. His players have always been extremely advanced in their knowledge of lifting technique, work habits and commit themselves physically through strength and conditioning.

"Coach Gentry is an innovator; his programs are cutting edge in their scientific basis, yet he has long understood what is tried and true and what never changes in the training of football players.

"I advise every coach and player interested in maximizing their physical potential to not only buy this book but to also diligently adhere to the principles so convincingly presented by Coach Gentry."

Johnny Parker
Director of Strength and Conditioning
2003 Super Bowl Champion Tampa Bay Buccaneers
NFL Strength Conditioning Coach for over 20 Years
Three-Time Super Bowl Champion

"No need to look around anymore for a quality, no-nonsense, back-to-basics strength and conditioning manual for football. Mike Gentry has written one for all of us to use. There are no 'bells and whistles' in his book, *A Chance To Win*. There is, though, plenty of great, functional information for producing and training better football players. It will be a privilege and advantage for me to own this book."

Kevin Yoxall, MS, CCS, MSCC
Director of Strength and Conditioning
Auburn University

"Mike Gentry has established himself as one of the premier strength and conditioning coaches in the world."
Dr. Greg Shepard, President—Bigger, Faster, Stronger

"Whether you are a high school coach with a limited knowledge of strength and conditioning or an expert strength coach with all of the right degrees and certifications, this book is for you. This program, which has been proven through time-tested scientific principles, not gimmicks, will maximize your athletes' potential. It provides one with the tools to build a progressive program when working with the beginner as well as the advanced lifter, including the multi-sport athlete. I strongly recommend adding this wealth of information to your coaching library."

Julian Kaufman, M.Ed., CSCS
Head Strength and Conditioning Coach/Defensive Coordinator
Rockmart High School, Georgia

To our children, Christopher "Bo" Gentry, Ellie Caterisano,
and Mike Caterisano, for the inspiration they provide every day
that motivated us to write this book.

CONTENTS

Foreword

The Virginia Tech Football program has enjoyed a consistent level of success over the past few seasons, appearing in bowl games in each of the last 13 years. This strong tradition of success can be attributed to the fact that the Virginia Tech program has remained relatively stable. Stability and a strong tradition lead to consistency, and when you can be consistent in how you perform on Saturday, that's what gives you a chance to win.

A key component to consistent success is to have a top-level strength and conditioning program. There is no question about the value and importance of weight training as an ingredient to winning. Since 1987, we have been very fortunate to have one of the best strength coaches in the nation, Mike Gentry, running our program. Under his leadership, the Virginia Tech strength and conditioning program has established a fine tradition. With Mike's leadership, the program has developed average athletes into good athletes and good athletes into great athletes. Many players, such as Jarrett Ferguson and John Engelberger, came into the Tech program as walk-on athletes and ended up as high draft picks in the NFL. A big part of their transition was due to the improvements they experienced under the watchful eye of Coach Gentry. His level of knowledge and ability to motivate players are key factors in these and many other players' growth as athletes. In addition to developing the players physically, a good strength and conditioning program helps develop a player's self-discipline, to help that athlete realize his full potential. The younger players see the upperclassmen's intensity and strong work ethic, which motivates everyone to work hard to be the best.

A strength coach at any level can gain insight into developing and improving his strength and conditioning program by reading, and implementing the concepts outlined in this book. The authors share a combined 40-plus years of knowledge and experience in strength and conditioning, ranging from cutting-edge scientific theory to practical application in the weight room. Topics include not only the development of strength, speed, power and agility, but also chapters on conditioning, nutrition, and motivation. I believe that you will find this book to be a valuable resource that can provide up-to-date information on the physical preparation necessary for success on the football field.

Frank Beamer
Head Football Coach
Virginia Tech

Preface

About the Authors

In 1980 Mike Gentry, a high school football coach in Black Mountain, North Carolina had aspirations to become a college strength and conditioning coach and set out on a new career path. Gentry was a dedicated powerlifter and spent much of his spare time reading everything he could get his hands on related to the development of power and strength. The strength coaching profession was just beginning to gain popularity among some of the bigger college programs. He headed to The University of North Carolina–Chapel Hill and convinced the head strength coach, Paul Hoolihan, to hire him as a graduate assistant. Gentry enrolled in a master's degree program at UNC and picked up a part-time teaching assistantship as a weight-training instructor. During this time he became friends with another graduate student, Tony Caterisano, who was also a dedicated student of resistance training, specifically from the scientific research approach. They soon developed a strong friendship and became training partners during that year.

The following year Tony Caterisano left UNC to pursue his Ph.D. in exercise physiology at the University of Connecticut. Mike Gentry moved up to a full-time assistant strength coach position at UNC, but the two friends stayed in touch and shared information gained in both the laboratory and weight-room settings. Gentry later went on to become the head strength coach at East Carolina University and Caterisano, upon completing his degree became a professor of exercise science at Furman University. The story would probably have ended here except that both Gentry and Caterisano shared an unquenchable thirst for knowledge in the area of strength and conditioning.

They stayed in close contact throughout the years as Gentry left ECU and became the head strength coach for Virginia Tech. Caterisano, who had been trained as an academician, became the head wrestling coach at Furman and turned that winless program into a Southern Conference contender. Gentry, who had made great strides in helping the Virginia Tech program gain national prominence, pursued and earned his doctorate in education. Thus the theorist became the practitioner and the practitioner became the theorist. Twenty-plus years later they are comfortable in both worlds—the research lab and the weight room. This book represents what they have learned about strength and conditioning during all of those years on the field and in the classroom.

A Chance to Win

Vince Lombardi once said, "Winning isn't everything, it's the only thing." Wherever football is played, every fan, coach, and player would agree that it all comes down to the simple fact that everybody wants to win. But who is willing and able to do what it takes to win? Many successful coaches in the game today put it a different way "… we just want to give our guys a chance to win…" After all, as coaches, we can't control the breaks of the game, the bounce of the ball, or the way every close call by an official will go. Instead, each coach can only prepare his players for the best possible chance for success on the field. The coaches who can do this consistently are the ones who are most likely to give their players the greatest chance for success. It is all about preparation. Preparation includes a wide range of factors, from the teaching of basic skills to the development of strategies and game plans. But within this range, one of the most important parts of that preparation involves developing the physical abilities, often referred to as *athleticism*, in the players through a sound strength and conditioning program. That is why these men wanted to write this book.

Many coaches believe that athleticism is a God-given gift an athlete is born with or will simply never have. To some extent it is true that some athletes are endowed with greater levels of natural talent, physical maturity, and skill than others. However, each player has an athletic potential that can be maximized, giving each player a higher degree of athleticism through a well-designed strength and conditioning program. The strength and conditioning program in this book can give a team an edge that may make the difference between success and failure on the field.

Who Should Read This Book?

This book has been prepared to provide guidance to anyone who takes on the responsibility of developing a sound training program specifically for football players. It starts with the basics. Even someone with a limited background can successfully develop an effective training program for a player of any age and experience level. This book provides the underlying concepts in easy-to-understand terms, while it explains a systematic program for physically developing a football athlete.

Experienced strength and conditioning coaches can also use this program to coach athletes at an advanced level, giving them new insights into workout designs in their programs. This book offers no shortcuts or gimmicks, only time-tested methods of resistance training that have helped players at every level improve. It is the goal of this book to provide information for athletes, coaches, and parents on a practical and scientific approach for developing the right strength and the right conditioning program for football.

Acknowledgments

This book represents a lifetime goal that Mike Gentry and I have aspired to since the earliest days of our careers. How far we have come in those careers, as well as the attainment of the goal of writing this book, would not have been possible without the support and influence of many people. At the risk of failing to mention all of them, for that would require far more pages than our publisher would allow, I would like to mention a few.

First and foremost I would like to recognize the steadfast support of my family, especially the support of my wife, Margaret Rose Caterisano, whose unfaltering belief in me and helpful comments have made this whole project possible; my parents, Richard P. and Margaret A. Caterisano, for all their faith in me throughout the years.

I would also thank those who have guided me in my formal education: Dr. Andy Yiannakis for giving me my initial opportunity to pursue graduate work at UConn, and Drs. Thomas Sheehan, John Billing, Bob McMurray, and Earl Horner for their valuable guidance throughout my graduate studies. I would be remiss not to mention probably the greatest influence in my academic career, Dr. David N. Camaione, my mentor and good friend, whose valuable advice has served me well.

A common theme throughout this book is the emphasis on matching the theory with the practice. Many people have played a role in shaping both of these. I greatly appreciate the influence of many scientists who have served as my role models and taught me much through personal interaction as well as through their published works. I would like to thank Drs. Bill Kraemer, Andy Fry, and Mike Deschenes, who are not only great scientists, but also great people. Also, Dr. Vladimir Zatsiorsky, whom I have never met, but whose theories of strength training I have studied and heartily embrace. I also must thank the coaches and lifters who have influenced me: Gary Baldwin, who introduced me to the value of resistance training, and Dino Costanzo whose love of powerlifting and enthusiasm have motivated me to compete. My high school wrestling coach, Armand Cacciatore, the best coach I ever knew, showed me the art of coaching through his excellent example.

Finally, I would like to thank those individuals who have had a direct role in writing this book. Thanks to Dr. Larsen Bowker, ex-Virginia Tech varsity tennis coach and English professor, for his painstaking reviews and candid comments that greatly improved the quality of this text. I must also thank Jim Coffey, associate professor of speech communications at MCC, and Bill Caterisano of ColorCentrics Corp., for their helpful guidance in organizing this book, and Dr. Matt Feigenbaum for his reviews and valuable comments. A special thanks to Gayle Pyfrom for her skilled artwork in preparing some of the figures, as well as Thomas M. Bailey for his skillful photography. A big thanks to coach Frank Beamer for writing the foreword, and to the Virginia Tech Hokies for their fine example of an outstanding college football program.

Tony Caterisano

Acknowledgments

I am living a blessed life to be able to follow the career path I have chosen and to realize the long time goal of co-authoring this book. I thank God for all the blessings and opportunities he has provided me.

My parents, Irene and Roy Gentry, have always been supportive and great encouragers of my endeavors. Thank you.

Some of the coaches who were very influential to me include: Paul Hoolihan who gave me the opportunity to get started on this career path while a graduate student at the University of North Carolina, and Ed Emory former head football coach at East Carolina University, who gave me the chance to become the youngest head strength and conditioning coach in the country at the time. Coach Emory taught me the necessary work ethic and the will to win it takes to be successful at the Division I level.

I would like to also thank coach Art Baker, former head football coach at East Carolina University, whose integrity and faith provide a great example for all.

I would like to especially thank coach Frank Beamer, head football coach at Virginia Tech, who has made my job for the last 16 years the best collegiate strength and conditioning position in the United States. His character, organization, and support without micromanagement are rare qualities.

I have been fortunate that athletic directors Dr. Ken Karr, Dutch Baughman, David Braine and Jim Weaver have all seen the value of a quality strength and conditioning program for athletics and have supported the development of the program at both East Carolina University and Virginia Tech.

The opportunity to realize a lifelong academic goal was made possible by the support and encouragement of Virginia Tech faculty members Dr. Richard Stratton, Dr. John Burton and Dr. Larson Bowker. They may have seen more in me than I saw in myself.

I would like to also thank Mrs. Lisa Marie for all her help in the production of this book. Her willingness to work beyond the call of duty never goes unnoticed. I would like to thank Judi McBride for her encouragement and moral support throughout this project.

I also acknowledge the hard work and influence of trusted strength and conditioning assistants Chris Durrand, David Pratt, James Dunn, Scott Bennett, Sonny Sano, Jim Whitten, and Dr. Jay Johnson. I appreciate each of you.

Most importantly, I would like to thank the countless number of players at East Carolina University and Virginia Tech who have believed and "sweated blood" in the pursuit of excellence. You have been a constant source of inspiration to me. Thank you.

Mike Gentry

Introduction

What Is Athleticism and Why Is Developing It Important?

Athleticism is a general term we use to describe a combination of four basic conditioning goals: Strength, power, speed, and agility. In the next chapter we will specifically define these components so the reader can understand the importance of each, and how each component relates to the other three. While watching an outstanding football player perform at his best level, an experienced coach can see that each of these four basic components is essential to optimal performance on the field. Each component must be developed in the athlete based on prioritized training goals, at the appropriate time of the season, to have maximum carry over to the game.

It is impossible to train an athlete to maximize all four components at the same time. Instead, it is critical that the strength and conditioning program address each component at the appropriate time. The term **target adaptation** describes the specific results the coach will seek in each training phase, based on which component of developing athleticism holds the highest priority (Fleck & Kreamer, 1997). How we determine which target adaptation is most important is based on a number of factors, which will be discussed later in this book.

The Reality of Strength and Conditioning for Football

Before we get into specific approaches to strength and conditioning for football players, let's talk about some things that many successful coaches already know to be true. It is clear that the greater the natural ability of an athlete, the higher the potential for success. This is why recruiting at the collegiate level is so important. The best NCAA Division I programs bring in the best athletes possible and then try to develop those athletes into better players through improving mental and physical skills. Unfortunately, at some institutions, not as many individuals playing

will be the best natural athletes, so improving athleticism is even *more* crucial with players that are less than the cream-of-the-crop recruits. This often means that a coach must invest time in players who may not be starters at a critical position today, but may be starters later on. The bottom line is this—the difference between a successful and an unsuccessful football program is often how well each coach prepares, both mentally and physically, every athlete in his program.

All of us who've coached at any level appreciate some of the problems and dilemmas that coaches face year in and year out. Perhaps you are fortunate and have an ideal training facility with a full staff of assistant coaches, but the reality is that most strength coaches experience certain difficulties in administering a good strength and conditioning program. The following are the most frequently asked questions compiled from high school and college football coaches over the years of our interaction with them at various clinics and presentations:

How do I keep up with the latest training techniques, and with so many canned programs out there, how do I know which ones are the best for my players?

Even if I find the right training techniques (i.e., specific lifts, plyometrics, speed and agility drills, and conditioning exercises), when and how do I work these into the training routine?

Given the broad array of maturity and experience levels of players (especially at the middle and high school levels), how do I create a program that is safe and effective for each of them?

Many of the best high school players are multi-sport athletes playing other sports in the winter and spring seasons. How do I develop a program to serve them since they have a very limited off season?

My school has very limited resources and our weight training facility is underfunded. How do I develop a program with limited resources?

With so many players to train during the off season it is difficult to give each player the attention that they need to perform lifts with proper technique. How do I solve this man-power problem and get qualified people to help teach and supervise players?

We consider it important, if not vital, to answer these questions as directly and specifically as we can in the ensuing chapters of this book.

In our opinion, football coaches are some of the most dedicated and often underappreciated professionals in our education system. If you count the number of hours a football coach puts in each year, it is clear that many are overworked. Unfortunately, this leads to some coaches resorting to a one-size-fits-all approach to weight training and conditioning, which is usually based on tradition rather than science. At best, this yields some positive gains in strength and size among inexperienced players. The consequences of this approach, however, might not be the *best possible* results especially for an advanced athlete who requires a more specific program for optimum improvements. In the worst-case scenario, the results of such a hit or miss program can lead to overtraining, injury, and poor performance on the field.

At the high school level, coaches are also charged with developing a training program for a fairly unique population—the high school athlete, with some youngsters barely out of puberty and others virtually full-grown adults. We must remember that the high school years are critical to skeletal growth and overall physical development. What works well for one freshman offensive lineman may not work so well for another, based on maturity and development, even though they play the same position. Remember, some high school players are at a stage in their athletic career where *any* resistance training will increase their strength. You could literally dump a pile of large rocks in a field and get the players to move the pile around three days per week and, over time, you will see some gains in strength. But the question remains, are those players gaining the maximum amount of strength gain possible? Are athletes who lift weights using a standard body builder magazine program getting the best potential results? How does training in the weight room affect the way a player performs on the football field? The one-size-fits-all approach may work for some, but not for the players you count on the most.

Finally, football players at all levels come into a program with a wide range of skills, experience and natural ability. Some players are well acquainted with weightrooms. In some cases this can be a negative factor, if improper lifting techniques have been ingrained in their motor patterns. Others players have no experience and an over zealous weight training program carries a high risk of injury (Caine et al., 1992; Jones et al., 2000).

Some high school football players are multi-sport athletes who play a different sport every season. This means that they not only have a very short and limited off season, they may also be getting conflicting information from other coaches. Thus, the dilemma—how does the strength coach design a safe and effective strength and conditioning program for such a wide variety of athletes? How can he supervise a large number of athletes and be assured that they are performing the lifts correctly? Is it practical or even possible to custom design a conditioning program for each athlete? How do the activities performed during weight training and conditioning translate into better performance on the field? We believe that we can provide details and specific answers to these questions.

There Are a Lot of Books out There on Conditioning for Football. What Makes This One Unique?

This book is different because we offer a unique approach to the subject of strength and conditioning. It combines both the scientific research and practical application through decades of experience in the lab and in the weight room. Most importantly, the concepts presented in this book are based on a rigorous, field-tested program that has been adapted to serve the player regardless of his level of experience and physical maturity.

Our approach is based on Virginia Tech's football strength and conditioning program, which bridges the gap between resistance-training research and the practical application in the weight room. As of this writing, Virginia Tech has earned 13 postseason bowl bids in the last 13 years. The success of this football team is linked to its strength and conditioning program, whose success is based on the philosophy of teaching basic movements before allowing an athlete to perform the more complicated lifts and exercises.

The Virginia Tech approach is modeled after the old USSR/Eastern European principles of the 1960s, 1970s and 1980s. The USSR and Eastern Europeans dominated the world arena in many Olympic sports, especially in strength-power-type events. So, how did the Eastern Bloc accomplish such feats? A conversation with Sergei Beliaev, CEO of Super Sports Systems and former USSR national cycling team coach, provides some interesting insight into this question. According to Beliaev, the typical response of most U.S. coaches was "the Soviets are all on steroids…" yet rarely did these athletes test positive for substance violations (of course the rival coaches then simply attributed this fact to superior masking agents). What the American coaches failed to recognize was the strength of the Soviet system for combining research and coaching as a key element of their success. Unlike the American system, where exercise science researchers typically work independently and often in direct competition with one another, the Soviet researchers worked together. They pooled their data toward the common goal of improving athletic performance and winning gold medals. In the U.S., researchers seek publications and compete for grants,

often keeping their data and ideas to themselves for fear that another lab will publish similar studies. There is often a sense of competition between coaches and researchers in the U.S. rather than cooperation. With the Soviets, the ultimate reward was based on medal counts as a tool for promoting nationalism and showing the superiority of the Soviet way of life. The Soviet coaches worked together with the exercise scientists to field test and apply their theories. There was no gap between the scientists and the coaches as there is in America.

In addition, the Soviets were firm believers in coaching athletes to learn basic movements prior to teaching them complicated sport-specific skills. For example, Soviet wrestlers often engaged in gymnastic and tumbling programs to develop spatial awareness. By developing a feel for where their bodies are in space, they could better master the complex throwing and takedown techniques that eventually won gold medals in international competition.

Many of the principles related in this book are taken from these field-tested Soviet theories. We stress teaching lifting movements, which eventually leads to good technical form in executing the more complicated lifts and exercises. Most of these principles have been tested in the Virginia Tech strength and conditioning program, and the evidence of their effectiveness is shown by success on the field. What also makes this program unique is that we have discovered a way to counteract the one-size-fits-all approach to resistance training program design. By emphasizing proper progression and programming you can provide a progressive approach to teaching the resistance-training techniques in each of the major core lifts. For example, many coaches include Olympic lifts such as the power clean in their training regimen. The lift is very technical and proper technique is essential for the right target adaptation and, more importantly, the prevention of injury. As you will see in subsequent chapters, we break this lift down into preliminary lifts and basic movements.

These preliminary lifts are effective and safer lifts for less experienced players, yet they teach skills that are essential for moving up the levels of the lift. For the power clean, the first level would be a shoulder shrug, followed by an upright row, and then by simple jump shrug. These lifts could be performed by your most inexperienced lifters and would serve the dual role of improving their strength and power while teaching their muscle memory to perform the basic movements of the power clean.

The next level would introduce a high pull that involves key hip motions related to the clean. As the player progresses and ingrains these movements into his motor patterns, he will be ready for the third level, which would be the hang clean. Eventually, as you invest time in preparing the young athlete with the basic movements, the full power clean is easily taught. The key is to patiently bring each athlete along at his own pace so he is working at the appropriate level of experience and physical maturity. Although this may seem like an impractical approach of designing customized programs for each player, we will show you how to group your athletes based on maturity, experience, and performance.

How to Use This Book

For an athlete, coach, or parent to get the most out of this book, it is important that they read and understand the theories behind our methods. It might be tempting to simply skip these theoretical sections, move to the sample programs, and adapt them to your particular athletes. However, you'll get the most out of the program if you read all chapters and get to know not only *how* we designed the program, but *why* we designed it the way we did. In fact, it is probably a good idea for the coach to teach his players the underlying theories so that *they* understand the reason for the program's design.

We will present the background information, using analogies and real-life comparisons to aid the reader in understanding concepts and how they apply to the actual workouts. We want to avoid turning this into a college-level exercise physiology textbook, requiring a medical dictionary to look up every other word, so we have purposely tried to avoid excessive jargon. In the next chapter we will look at the science, which describes the basic concepts and background information on how the training system works.

The basic concepts covered in the first few chapters serve as a reference source for developing each component of the overall programs. We will provide information needed to create programs, along with guidelines and examples for implementing the program. On this latter point, we feel that there is as much art as there is science when putting a program into action and getting the best results from your time and effort. This is why we have included a chapter on training motivation. Chapter 9 will cover sample programs for various levels of experience and provide appropriate progressions for each lift to match each player's natural level of maturity and skill.

References

Fleck, S.J. and W.J. Kraemer, *Designing Resistance Training Programs 2nd ed.*, Human Kinetics Publisher, Champaign, IL. 1997.

The Science of Physical Performance and Athleticism

The Four Components of Athleticism: Strength, Power, Speed, and Agility

What exactly makes one player more athletic than another? Is it something that can be coached or are great athletes born rather than made? To answer these questions we must look not only at research studies, but also common practices of the players and coaches who work to improve themselves every day. Whenever a coach sees the *overlap* of theory and practice, he can be sure that there is good information regarding sound training principles. Based on our experience, we have observed that athleticism is something that *can* be developed and improved within each player's genetic limitation. To achieve optimum performance that carries over to the game, we must understand the relationship among four basic factors that make a difference in the athletic ability of a football player. The four components of athleticism are: 1) strength and increased lean body mass, 2) power, 3) speed and acceleration, and 4) quickness and agility.

Strength is defined as the capacity to generate a maximum amount of force through muscle contraction with no time limits. This time factor becomes very important in distinguishing the difference between strength and power. In addition, improving the athlete's body composition, which refers to the ratio of body fat to lean muscle, is an important part of the strength acquisition process. An important form of strength for any athlete, but especially a foot-

ball player, is what is commonly termed **core strength**. This describes the strength that can be generated by large muscle groups located in the hips, thighs, and torso that stabilize the body, which can affect performance on the field and help prevent injuries.

Think of core strength as the foundation of a building. A good building contractor would never build an expensive house on a cheap, substandard foundation. If he did, damage would occur at the weakest point, the foundation, which would be very expensive to repair and weaken the entire structure. Lack of core strength is the most prevalent cause of poor athletic performance and can cause chronic injuries (Caine et al., 1992; Jones et al., 2000). Core strength and a large amount of lean body mass with a minimal fat mass are important prerequisites for power. Many of the lifts and plyometric techniques used to acquire power are based on maximized strength and a balanced, stable muscle system.

Football is a game of power involving repetitive, explosive bursts of physical activity throughout the game. *Power* is defined as the ability to generate the greatest amount of force in the shortest period of time. In untrained individuals research shows that increasing strength alone results in an increase in power (Stone et al., 2000). One might assume this to be true with well-trained individuals. However, the idea that a high level of strength automatically results in a high level of power is often not the case.

A recent study that compared leg strength as measured by the squat and power clean to leg power as measured by vertical and long jump tests among a group of collegiate football players found the relationship between the two to be weak (Caterisano, 1999). The results showed that some of the strongest athletes didn't have the best vertical jumps. This is due to the fact that the subjects tested were college-level players who had already established good basic core strength. It demonstrates that the relationship between power and strength is not always proportional (Stone, et al., 2000; Cronin et al., 2000), due to a principle called *explosive strength deficit*, which we will discuss later in this chapter (Zatsiorsky, 1995).

Speed is the application of power, usually most relevant to sprinting, but also related to hand speed and foot speed in a game situation (Phelps, 2001). For example, power applied to the technique of running results in improved running speed. A player can become a faster runner if he develops increased leg power and applies it to proper running mechanics (see Chapter 4). In addition we believe that there is a distinct difference between maximum running speed and acceleration. Acceleration may be a bigger asset in a football game than maximum speed.

Finally, *agility* is the application of speed to an open-skill type of sport like football. Here the athlete is required to change direction very quickly, accelerate and decelerate. Research suggests that unless speed training includes multiple changes of direction, straight speed work does not have a direct carryover to agility (Young et al., 2001; Wojtys et al., 1996). Coordination, speed, flexibility, and a quick reaction time are the basic precursors of agility and they can be developed to improve agility. Strength, power, speed, and agility are the essence of athleticism and separate

the successful athlete from the unsuccessful athlete out on the football field. Developing them with systematic conditioning is the goal we believe will improve your program.

It is clear that the development of agility is the ultimate goal of every strength and conditioning program once the playing season is underway, but it is critical that the other three components of athleticism must be targeted in the proper order to build the foundation for an ideal strength and conditioning program. Again let's think of this as similar to building a house. The roof of the house is very critical because it protects us from the elements such as rain, snow, heat and cold. In fact we often use the metaphor "providing a roof over our heads…" to describe providing shelter for our family. Yet, who would begin building their house by building the roof first? It would make no sense to finish the roof and then try to figure out how to incorporate a foundation, a frame, and the walls. Unfortunately many strength and conditioning programs are designed with little or no consideration to the importance of the foundation. We believe and our research demonstrates that strength and good body composition are initially the highest priority and then, once established, the priority shifts to the development of power. Once power is maximized the training emphasis is focused on speed improvement and then followed by improving agility.

Probably the best way to visualize this is to look at it as if it were a pyramid (see Fig 2.1). Increased strength and body composition improvements (the base) sets the stage for increasing power. Power is then built on this base of strength because there are time limitations inherent in generating power. There is a difference between generating maximum force when given all the time required (i.e., lifting a heavy object slowly) and the amount of force one can generate in a *limited time*. When training for power, one is able to use only a small percentage of the one repetition max-

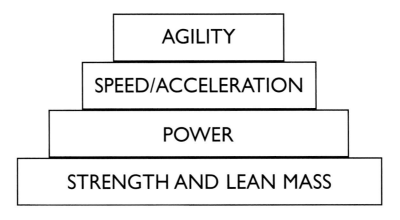

Fig. 2.1

imum (1 RM) because the velocity of the lift is critical. It only makes sense that getting the 1 RM higher through strength training results in an athlete being able to use a heavier weight for power training.

Once maximum power is developed, the athlete must learn to apply power using specific mechanics related to football and develop speed. This could be as simple as running fast or as complex as the techniques

for pass rushing stunts among defensive linemen, which require both hand speed and foot speed. The next step is to translate that speed into a performance in a game situation where the player must react and respond to the actions of his opponent. This would require agility, which includes the ability to react, change directions, accelerate, decelerate, and adjust to the situation on the field.

Why Do We Train in Cycles?

Why not work on all four components of athleticism in the same practice or workout? There is an old Chinese saying that answers this question—"It is an unwise hunter who chases two rabbits!" This is to say that one cannot place the same priority on all four components because, like our unwise hunter you will end up without a rabbit. The goal of training each component may not have as much carryover to the actual performance on the field. Strength is important as the foundation of power, speed, and agility, but it doesn't necessarily determine which player prevails on the field. No one is going to spot your team X number of touchdowns because your players can bench press more than your opponent's players. So, training for a 1 RM bench press may not be as valuable in a game as training your offensive linemen to use their upper body and hands to *explosively* engage the defensive linemen in a pass-blocking situation, which would require power and speed. Of course you must maintain basic strength throughout the year. What we are saying is that training for maximum strength will take a lower priority at certain times of the year and higher priority during other phases. This concept is called **specificity of training** and applies to performance on the football field. The ultimate goal is to develop a form of specificity called *transfer specificity*, which describes how well what the player does in the weight room carries over to what the player does on the field (Fleck & Kraemer, 1997; Pearson et al., 2000).

At this point one might ask, "Why not do the workouts that have the greatest transfer specificity all year round?" Why deviate from the specificity principle at all? This is where one must consider two factors. First, there is a relationship between all four components. A training program must address all four throughout the year but prioritize the most important component based on the proximity of competition (i.e., off season, preseason, or in-season). The second

factor is that, doing the same workouts with little variety is a sure path to both physical and psychological staleness, resulting in fewer gains in the target adaptation. Additionally, you increase the risk of overtraining and injury among your players by doing the same basic workouts. Overuse injuries are especially prevalent under conditions where the same repetitive movements are preformed week in and week out. Lack of variation can lead to tendonitis and stress fractures. Herein lies the problem—how does a coach design workouts that are specific and have the greatest carryover to the playing field, yet incorporate enough variety in the workout to the avoid problems previously mentioned? The answer is in properly cycling the training by using **periodization**. Periodization involves dividing the training into cycles in which target adaptations are prioritized based on where the training cycles fall relative to competition (Stone, et al., 1982; Fleck, 1999). In other words we always maintain each of the four components of athleticism (strength and body composition, power, speed, and agility) throughout the year but based on *priorities*, will put more emphasis on the component that serves our ultimate goals on the football field.

Periodization is an Eastern European concept designed to develop a balance between specificity and variation in a workout plan. It is based on the assumption that every sport has a season in which peak performance is the bottom line. During the off season (the period of time furthest from competition) and even during the preseason (the period of time immediately preceding competition), the athlete can concentrate on exercises and training goals that are the foundation of performance goals.

Vladimir Zatsiorsky, a former Russian exercise scientist now a professor at Penn State, uses two terms to describe this (Zatsiorsky, 1994). *Delayed transmutation* is defined as using lifts and other exercises that are not as muscle specific as your primary lifts during the off season. *Delayed transformation* is defined as using training loads (number of sets, number of repetitions per set, number of workouts per week, and the amount of resistance or intensity of each exercise) that are not as specific to your sport during this off season period.

An example of how this might apply could be in training an offensive lineman in the weight room. In offensive line plays such as pass blocking, the athlete must block his opponent in an all out effort for approximately seven seconds (the maximum amount of time needed for the quarterback to throw the ball). In this case strength, power, and speed are more important than muscular endurance and aerobic capacity. However, in the off season rather than working with heavy weights and short explosive exercises, which use many large muscle groups together, the coach may defer specificity (this is where the term *delayed* comes in because you are deferring the end results until later). The coach includes some aerobic work in the lineman's training routine to lose body fat and improve body composition. He may have this athlete do more isolation of muscle such as the triceps and quadriceps of the thigh to work some of the weak links in his blocking techniques. The coach may also

increase the number of sets and repetitions, and reduce the resistance in the weight workout to induce greater muscle hypertrophy to increase lean body mass. This would not be a good training routine if the athlete had to play in a game that week, but in the off season the athlete can afford to lose some performance capability, especially if it will pay off later in the season.

In addition to adding variety to the year-round training of an athlete, cycling the training also provides the needed rest for optimal recovery and restitution. The training process requires that we overload muscles and literally tear down muscle proteins in a workout. It is like remodeling your house. If you want to increase the size of your living room, you have to first tear down the existing walls. Only then will you be able to enlarge the room by building new walls. When we apply this example to training football players, it is important to note that the rest period leads to the adaptation (results) we are seeking. Just as it would be unwise to destroy the entire house just to remodel one room, we must be careful not to overstress our athletes and retard the recovery process. This will be discussed further in Chapter 3.

Strength and Lean Body Mass Development—The Balance Between Intensity and Volume Serves as the Foundation for Power

Strength was earlier defined as the maximum amount of force one can generate in an unlimited amount of time. There are many factors that determine strength relative to how much force a human can generate in a given muscle. Some of these factors are a matter of structure and leverage. Because this depends on body type and genetic endowments related to arm length, leg length, and body proportion, it is a factor that cannot be changed through a training regimen. Most of us would prefer to be tall and perfectly proportioned, but few of us are genetically programmed to be so.

Another strength determining factor is the rate of firing of a muscle cell known as **rate coding**, which describes the absolute amount of neural stimulation of the muscle cell. Increases in neural stimulation can increase the force generated by the muscle cell itself. During muscle contractions that require low levels of force, the firing frequency is low. As greater force is required, the frequency of neural stimulation increas-

es, increasing the amount of force generated by the muscle cell. But rate coding may play a big role in power development, based on how quickly force is developed. This will be discussed when we address power development in this chapter.

The factors related to strength, especially in large muscles, which *can* be affected by exercise will be the focus of the remainder of this section. Muscle size and neuromuscular factors have been proven to be adaptable components of strength. You want **training effects** that are the physical changes within the muscles as a result of exercise and that allow muscles to generate a greater amount of force.

To fully understand this, a little bit of the anatomy and physiology of the muscle cell and nervous system that supports it needs to be reviewed. We want the reader to be able to visualize what is taking place in the muscle during a given task. Before we start, let's define two important terms—intensity and volume. **Intensity**, when used in the context of strength training, simply refers to the amount of resistance or weight lifted. Thus, the heavier the weight, the higher the intensity. **Volume** is a bit more complicated. Basically, it reflects the number of repetitions and number of sets of repetitions a lifter does in a given workout. It may also be dependent on the time between sets and the number of different exercises done in a workout, as well as the number of workouts per week. Volume can be increased by doing more repetitions, more sets, taking less time between sets, doing more exercises per body part, or by doing more workouts per week (Fleck & Kraemer, 1997). Stating the obvious, as the intensity in a lifting program increases, the volume of work must decrease because most people can't lift a heavy weight as many times as they can lift a light weight. How intensity and volume affect the muscle changes will be discussed at the end of this section.

To understand how muscle cells adapt to exercise requires some basic understanding of the muscle cell itself. Muscle cells are unique to other cells in the body for two reasons: 1) they are the only cells that contract or shorten; and 2) unlike other cells that have only one nucleus, muscle cells have several nuclei. This latter point may not seem all that important, but research theory suggests it is the key to adaptation of muscle tissue to training. The way muscle cells contract is complicated, but at the risk of oversimplification can be boiled down to the following sequence of events.

First, some form of nerve stimulation signals the muscle to contract. This neural stimulation can be voluntary or purposely initiated from the higher levels of the brain, initiated from some more basic level of the brain such as the medulla (i.e., heart muscle), or can be due to some reflex at the spinal column level. Regardless of its origin, the effect on the muscle cell is to initiate a series of chemical changes to occur resulting in a muscle contraction. The actual physical components of this contraction are tiny protein filaments called Actin and Myosin, which connect and pull against each other thereby shortening the muscle cell. This shortening achieved by the contractile proteins Actin and Myosin sliding over each other (often referred to as *the twitch*) does not take place instantly, but depending on the muscle fiber type can occur over a wide range of time. This is *fast twitch* muscle fiber that can reach maximum force very quickly while *slow twitch* fibers take a relatively longer time to reach full contraction. The trade-off is that the fast twitch muscle cells fatigue much more quickly than the slow twitch cells, which have a very high endurance capacity.

It would be misleading to leave the impression that there are only these two distinct types of muscle cells. In reality consider these two types as the extreme ends of a spectrum, with other muscle cells along this continuum having varying degrees of twitch speed and endurance capability. The closer to the fast twitch end of the spectrum, the faster the twitch and force production but less resistance to fatigue (they fatigue quicker). The closer we get to the slow twitch end, the less the force production and the greater the resistance to fatigue (they can contract for a longer period of time). Some people think that a slow movement always uses slow twitch and that a rapid movement only uses fast twitch muscle cells, but as we will see, this is not always the case.

It is important to understand that a muscle cell, when it contracts, is an all-or-nothing proposition. A muscle cell either contracts completely to a point often to a point of full force or doesn't contract at all. If someone handed a person a raw egg, how does he hold the egg in his hand without crushing it? How does a person control the amount of force generated by a muscle if the muscle cell itself can only contract maximally? The answer is that we don't actually activate all of the muscle cells in a given muscle during a muscle contraction. We only use the appropriate number of muscle cells for the given level of force needed to complete a task.

Let us use the biceps as an example. If a person flexed his arm without any type of weight in his hand, he would only use a small percentage of the total number of muscle cells in that biceps muscle. If he did the same movement with a 10-pound dumbbell, he would recruit slightly more muscle cells. Adding another 10 pounds for a total of 20 pounds would require slightly more muscle cell activation, and so on. Eventually, that person would reach his maximum ability to overcome the weight (one repetition maximum or 1 RM). Even with a 1 RM, he would not recruit *all* of the muscle cells, because doing so could potentially produce forces that would damage the muscles and tendons. Fortunately, we have protective structures called the **Golgi tendon organs** that detect excessive strain on the muscles and tendons and prevent all of our muscle cells from being activated at once.

At this point it becomes clear that the muscle cell requires a critical link with the nervous system to function. Each nerve requires a source of stimulation that tells that muscle cell to either contract or relax. But because there are so many muscle cells in a given muscle, many of which serve the same function and are stimulated by the same level of force production, several muscle cells will *share* a common nerve supply. Thus muscle cells that share the same fiber type and threshold of activation (based on how much force is required in a given task) are grouped together to form what is called a motor unit (Enoka, 1995). Think of this as being similar to the lighting system in a large gymnasium in which you have maybe 40 separate lights controlled by four light switches. Each light switch controls 10 lights. The light switch has only an on or off position, so that turning the switch to the on position causes all 10 lights to be activated at once. If you only needed minimal light in the gym, you could just turn on one light switch, illuminating only 10 of the 40 lights. As you needed more light you could activate more rows of lights to increase the illumination in the gym. With the muscle, these motor units are recruited in such a way that groups of muscle cells are activated as a unit (see Fig. 2.2). As an athlete requires a greater force production in the muscle he would activate or recruit more motor units, just as turning on more lights causes a high degree of illumination in our previous example.

As previously mentioned, the motor units are composed of similar fiber types and cells that share a common threshold of activation, usually based on the amount of resistance or the volume of work. The sequence of how these motor units are activated (a term we call *motor unit recruitment*) is very specific, first to the amount of force one is trying to generate to overcome a given resistance, and then based on fatigue (Erim et al, 1996; Zatsiorsky, 1995; DeLuca & Erim, 1996). When we lift relatively light weights, we recruit what are referred to as **low threshold motor units**. These are groups of muscle cells that share a common nerve supply and are characterized by being small in size, and very fatigue resistant. An example of recruitment of these low threshold motor units would be flexing the biceps with no resistance. If you think about this movement, one could repeatedly perform this action for several minutes given the low demand of the task. This demonstrates that fatigue resistant quality of those motor units. If we add a small amount of resistance to the task, let's say a 10-pound dumbbell, we would recruit a few more **higher threshold motor units** to produce enough force to overcome the new level of resistance. These additional motor units would be slightly larger and thereby would produce a slightly larger amount of force per muscle cell, but the trade-off would be that these higher threshold motor units would fatigue more quickly than the low threshold motor units recruited with zero added

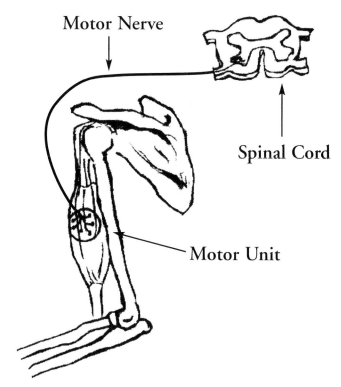

Fig. 2.2

resistance. As we add more and more weight to our example, we would recruit more motor units of a higher threshold (see Fig. 2.3—the area within the circle represents all of the motor units in a given muscle. The shaded area represents that portion of the muscle that is actually active at a given resistance level). Those high threshold motor units would be progressively larger and able to produce more force, as they would become less similar to slow twitch muscle fiber and more akin to fast twitch muscle cells. Think of the difference between slow twitch and fast twitch muscle as being more of a spectrum or continuum with a gradual difference than a black-and-white difference (see Fig 2.5). Of course we would see the trade-off. As the higher threshold motor units were recruited, what we gain in force production we lose in endurance capabilities.

Eventually as we keep adding weight to this biceps muscle, we would reach a limit of maximum force production that would be limited by two factors: 1) the Golgi tendon organ that protects the muscle and tendon and 2) the cross-sectional size of the muscle cells recruited. In other words we would not recruit all of the motor units in a given muscle, only those that our Golgi tendon organ deems safe (some scientists believe that through long-term training the Golgi tendon organ can be reset to allow recruitment

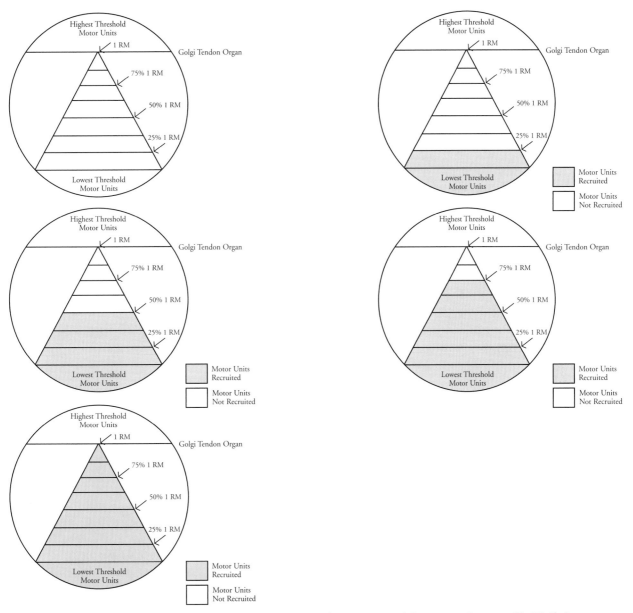

Fig. 2.3 With a single repetition, as percent of one repetition maximum (1 RM) increases more high threshold motor units are recruited.

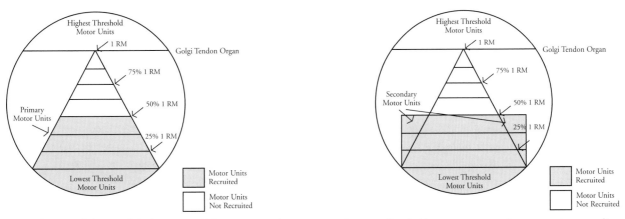

Fig. 2.4 With multiple repetitions as primary motor units fatigue, secondary motor units of the same threshold are recruited to maintain repetitions.

of higher threshold motor units). It should be apparent that to increase the maximum force a muscle can generate—also known as strength—we must activate and increase in size each of the individual cells that make up the high threshold motor units. We call this process **muscle hypertrophy** and in this case, we are trying to increase the size of the highest threshold motor units in order to increase maximum strength.

Increasing lean body mass is best achieved by a slightly different approach. As we stated earlier, lifting a weight that is less than maximal will recruit lower threshold motor units than lifting a maximum weight. The trade-off is that these motor units, although not as large and not as purely fast twitch as higher threshold motor units, will have a greater resistance to fatigue. Thus, we can perform more repetitions with lighter weights. If we just do a few repetitions with a sub-maximal weight, we will not see any significant hypertrophy because we fail to meet one of the three important criteria for inducing hypertrophy, which we will soon discover in this section. If, however, we perform exhaustive sets of repetitions (otherwise known as **high volume training**), we will not only exhaust these lower threshold motor units, but also recruit additional motor units of the same threshold (Zatsiorsky, 1995; Christova & Kossev, 1998; Miller, et al., 1996). Remember it takes more weight to recruit higher threshold motor units so these are *of the same threshold* as the motor units recruited initially. These additional motor units are termed *secondary* motor units and are brought in as the muscle attempts to maintain force production despite fatigue among the *primary* motor units, which were recruited when the set of repetitions began. This approach will result in a higher absolute number of motor units recruited and pushed to exhaustion, and ultimately will be best for increasing muscle size. The research also suggests that doing high volume training increases levels of human growth hormone, which was one of those anabolic (muscle building) hormones mentioned earlier (Kraemer et al.). Looking beyond the research, we observe that most competitive body builders use this high volume approach in preparing for contests. Remember, wherever we see an overlap of science and practice we get a clearer picture of what really is effective regarding training adaptations.

Figure 2.4 illustrates the effect of high volume training on motor unit recruitment.

Muscle Hypertrophy

All things being equal, a larger muscle cell produces a greater amount of force than a smaller muscle cell. Thus the primary goal of resistance training is to target the right muscle cells and stimulate them to grow larger. Three basic conditions must be met in order to induce muscle hypertrophy: 1) recruit specific muscle cells (motor units); 2) push those muscle cells to a point of fatigue; and 3) allow those muscle cells to recover and rebuild (Zatsiorsky, 1995). Given what we have just discussed about motor unit recruitment, it should be clear that very few muscle cells are recruited or activated in movements with no resistance.

Resistance amounts will determine how much of a given muscle we actually use based on recruiting higher threshold motor units. It is critical to understand that if we don't recruit the maximum level of motor unit threshold, we don't see any adaptation in those motor units. Lifting less than maximum weights would then recruit lower threshold motor units and only these motor units would have the potential for development. It may seem like a no-brainer to state that in order to get your one repetition maximum to increase you have to lift heavy weights, which is ultimately true. However, it is not a good idea to lift maximum weights all year round due to risk of injury and overtraining.

Recruiting the motor units does not, by itself, automatically induce muscle hypertrophy. The second criteria or requirement for stimulating growth is to push that motor unit to a point of physical failure or fatigue. This fatigue results in the destruction of the small contractile proteins in the individual cells due mainly to a protein-destroying hormone called **cortisol**. Destroying the proteins will set the stage for rebuilding. Again, think of it as a remodeling project in your home. If you want to increase the size of your living room, you must first tear down a wall or two as the first step. Only then can you enlarge the floor space and eventually rebuild new walls enclose your larger room. The factor that is critical here is that you don't tear down too many walls, causing the house to collapse, which is like overtraining syndrome, to be discussed in Chapter 6. To relate this back to muscle, we must target certain levels of motor unit threshold by lifting an appropriate amount of weight, but then push that motor unit to a point of just enough fatigue to get the cortisol to break down the muscle proteins.

A key factor here is that the lower threshold motor units are fatigue-resistant, so that it takes more repetitions and sets (volume) to push them to that level of fatigue. The highest threshold motor units are very easy to fatigue. Some motor units, such as those used in the one repetition maximum, fatigue after only one repetition. Others, in the lower threshold will not fatigue even though they are recruited. In order to promote hypertrophy in the low threshold motor units, one must do exhaustive numbers of sets and repititions. Although this high volume training plays a role in the eventual acquisition of strength, it has a direct effect on muscular endurance.

The final component of the muscle hypertrophy process is the rebuilding of the proteins and addition of more proteins as the body tries to adapt to the challenge created by overloading the muscle. This of course, requires rest. Think about the word *rest*—restitution, restoration—the process of rebuilding what has been damaged. In our home remodeling example, it is like replacing the torn-down walls with new and better walls. Thus, any well-designed program for promoting muscle hypertrophy must have just the right amount of rest incorporated in the training cycles to achieve this ultimate goal. Too much workout volume and intensity may even be worse than not enough, because once overtraining occurs the body must recover longer (almost like recovering from an injury) before it can start the muscle hypertrophy process again. At the deepest levels of overtraining, this may take months of recovery. Think of this as demolishing the entire house just to remodel the living room. Just as in the muscle breakdown process where cortisol is the primary hormone, there are key hormones in the rebuilding process as well. Two major hormones of protein building are testosterone and human growth hormone (also known as somatotropin). These hormones control the rate of protein re-synthesis and must be present for recovery to occur.

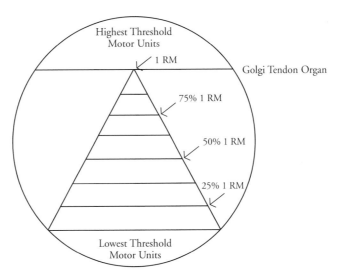

Fig. 2.5

Power and Explosive Strength Deficit

In physics, power is defined as work divided by time. In applying this to athletic performance, it really means how much muscular force can an athlete generate in such activities as throwing the ball, blocking, tackling, and running within the limitations of time. The game of football requires the ability to be fast and explosive. It is a game of speed and quickness, often dependent upon which player gets that half a step on his opponent, which quarterback has the quickest release while passing the ball, which lineman hits with explosive force before he is hit, and the list goes on. As we said earlier in the chapter, power does have a component involving absolute strength. However, strength is not necessarily the only determinant of power.

Published studies conducted at Furman University involved a large number of varsity football players to see how the relationship between strength and power compared. We had players perform one rep maximum trials on the back squat and the power clean, and then compared those results to their performance on vertical and long jump tests using statistical correlation methods. The results were surprising because we saw virtually zero correlation between the lifting performances and the jumping results. That is, the strongest players, as measured by the squat and power clean, were not necessarily the players with the greatest vertical jump. At first we thought that body weight might have been a factor, thinking that the strongest players may have been the heaviest players, required to move a greater mass in the jumping test. But when strength was corrected for body weight, there was no change in the results (Caterisano et. al., 1999). By digging deeper into the literature we found that this phenomenon could be explained by a concept termed *explosive strength deficit* (Zatsiorsky, 1995).

Explosive strength deficit is the relationship between how much force a muscle can generate in an unlimited amount of time versus how much force one can generate in an activity in which time limitations exist (see Fig. 2.6). Take the action of sprinting as an example of time limitation. In sprinting, a person's foot, with each stride, is only in contact with the ground for mere tenths of a second. The faster they sprint, the shorter the period of foot to ground contact. This means that the time for generating force becomes less and less. It may seem that this is no problem if an athlete is strong, except for the fact that it takes a relatively long period of time for a muscle to reach maximum force (i.e., several tenths of a second). It is only a portion of the full potential force generated by the muscle that is possible to be generated during that foot to ground contact time. Some athletes are better at getting a greater percentage of their potential maximum force generated than others and thereby have a smaller explosive strength deficit. In addition, we now know that through speed-specific training we can reduce this explosive strength deficit by training the muscle to generate force faster.

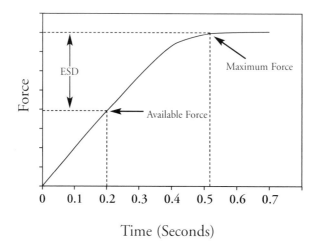

Fig. 2.6   Time (Seconds)

Figure 2.7 shows two athletes with distinctly different levels of strength and power. Player A can generate a maximum force in a 400 pound 1 RM leg press, while player B generates a 380 pound 1 RM leg press. But notice that it takes player B longer to reach maximum (.52 seconds) than player A (.35 seconds). In an actual sport performance, such as jumping, where the feet are in contact with the ground for only a relatively short period of time (.2 seconds), it is clear that player A can generate more force at that time limit. Thus his vertical jump is higher than player B because his explosive strength deficit is smaller.

The good news is that through proper velocity specific training, player B can reduce his explosive strength deficit and improve his power, resulting in a higher vertical jump.

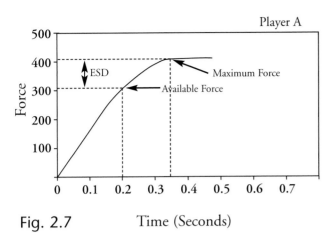

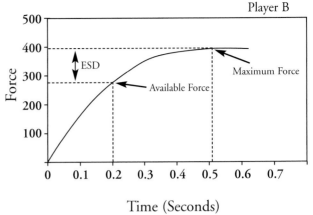

Fig. 2.7   Time (Seconds)

Speed—Applying Power to Technique

Being able to accelerate and run fast is probably one of the most valuable skills for any position in football. Some young athletes possess the natural ability to run fast, so speed development doesn't seem to be as important as it is with a player who lacks that ability. The truth is that both naturally fast and slow football players can improve speed through proper training. In addition, there is a big difference between developing maximum speed verses developing maximum acceleration. In the game of football, maximum acceleration may be even more important than maximum speed. The development of running speed will be addressed in Chapter 4 when we look at running programs. It is very important, however, to recognize that running speed is not the only type of speed essential for developing athleticism in football players. Other types of speed, such as foot quickness and hand speed can be of paramount importance, especially for offensive and defensive linemen.

Regardless of the type of speed, we must recognize that speed is based on power. It is that limited time element, where an athlete must generate as much force as possible that is one of the critical components of speed development. In addition, the mechanics (often referred to as *biomechanics*) of speed development are of equal importance. You could be coaching a player with great natural strength and power, the precursors to speed, but if that player doesn't apply that power with proper running mechanics, he will not run faster. What many coaches don't understand is that running is a skill that can be improved just like throwing a football or blocking and tackling. Yet how many coaches actually *teach* their players how to run in practice? Chapter 4 will cover basic techniques for developing skills associated with speed development specific to foot quickness, hand speed, and other forms of speed, and provide drills for reinforcing those skills.

Agility—Changing Direction in an Open-Skill Sport

Football is categorized as an open-skill sport because of the ever-changing nature of the movement within the sport. What a player does during any play and more importantly how he moves is dictated by the situation. He must respond, react, and usually change direction, either based on a specific play or based on how his opponent responds to that play. Compare this to a closed-skill sport, such as track, where the athlete performs based on a fixed environment. He prepares his starting blocks and runs on a track in his own lane to the finish line. The track doesn't move, the finish line doesn't move, and his

environment never changes from meet to meet (100 meter will always be a consistent distance in each race if he stays in that event).

In football, the athlete is often successful if he can respond and adjust to the changing situation as a play develops. This requires the ability to accelerate, decelerate, and change direction at critical points during a play. An obvious example is a defensive back covering a receiver who is trying to get open. It may not be as obvious in the case of an offensive lineman pass blocking. What often is a critical factor in the latter example is whether one athlete, the offensive lineman or the defensive lineman, is more capable of getting into a superior position during the play than his opponent. If the offensive lineman can't establish a strong, balanced blocking stance, the defensive lineman will prevail. On the other hand, if that defensive lineman is agile enough to turn the corner on the offensive lineman and place him in an off-balanced position, the defensive lineman will prevail. In either case, it boils down to agility.

Agility can be viewed as applying speed, accelerating, decelerating, changing direction, maintaining balance, and maximizing power while the environment around you continues to change. Many coaches believe that agility drills are the most effective way to develop these skills, which is essentially true. The key to maximizing the results of these drills, however, is to make sure that the foundations for agility (strength, power, and speed) are in place. Thus, the timing of when the agility drills outlined in Chapter 4 are incorporated into the training cycle is of critical importance and addressed in Chapter 3.

The Role of Physical Conditioning in Player Preparation

As most football coaches know, developing athleticism in their players is just one part of a football player's physical preparation. Another aspect of this preparation is physical conditioning. A physical conditioning program should prepare players to have the stamina needed to play at their highest level of physical performance for the duration of a game. This is especially true for players who play both offense and defense, as well as in games where players are involved in long offensive drives (on both sides of the ball). Many coaches believe in the more is better approach to physical conditioning, feeling that the harder the team works, the more successful they will be on the field. They may feel that doing too much running and physical training won't hurt, and it is better than putting a team out on the field that is out of shape. Unfortunately, this approach can be counterproductive on two levels.

First, too much volume and the wrong type of conditioning could end up being non-specific to the performance on the field, meaning little payoff for the time and effort expended in practice during the game. For example, the coach who has his players engage in high volume aerobic conditioning will see little carryover to performance on the field. Not only would this approach be ineffective, it may also create a negative hormonal imbalance in the player. More specifically, it results in too much **cortisol** breakdown of protein in the muscle, and not enough **testosterone,** the muscle-building hormone, and could decrease both strength and muscle mass (Fry & Kraemer, 1997).

Second, by incorporating too high of a volume of work in practice the players may be overtrained in the game situation, resulting in poor performance. In fact, many coaches mistake the symptoms of overtraining (to be discussed in Chapter 3) with a team being out of condition due to under training. Unfortunately, the erroneous remedy is to work the team harder, which only makes matters worse, when the team really needs to rest.

Does this mean that aerobic conditioning has no place in preparation for football? Actually, there may be some situations in which aerobic training, such as jogging, riding a stationary bike, etc., may play a role in the overall conditioning goal. For example, the coach may have a player who has a body composition that is overly fat, which could have a negative effect on speed and agility. The aerobic pathway of metabolism is the only way to target the goal of losing body fat since fat can only be metabolized in the presence of oxygen (the word *aerobic* literally means "with oxygen"). Hence, for a player with a high percentage of body fat, the highest priority may be to help him lose fat. The caution here is that too much aerobic activity may actually have a negative effect on strength gains. The good news, however, is that there are ways to gradually incorporate more interval-type training into this type of athlete's training cycles as he loses body fat, which will eventually result in his participation in the mainstream training of the rest of the players.

The most important role of the conditioning program is to stimulate adaptations in the players that allow an-all out effort on every play of the game in which he participates. Often this will vary from position to position, but the coach can group players by position demands and target the most appropriate conditioning program to serve that group of athletes. The conditioning program should closely mirror the energy system used by a player in the game. In general, football could be described as repeated bouts of high intensity activity with short rest intervals, involving the so-called anaerobic energy systems. This includes energy stored in the muscle, albeit short lived in duration, as well as the energy that can be transferred from a chemical process called **anaerobic glycolysis**. Anaerobic glycolysis is a fancy term for breaking down stored carbohydrates without oxygen available. The downside of providing energy to the muscle this way is that a by-product called **lactic acid** is also produced, which contributes to fatigue (Kraemer & Fleck, 1982). The good news here is that we can condition our players to chemically neutralize this lactic acid and hold off fatigue in the muscle through a proper conditioning program. Details about conditioning for football will be discussed in Chapter 5.

References

Caine, D., S. Roy, & K.M. Singer. "Stress changes of the distal radial growth plate: A radiographic survey and review of literature" *Am. J. Sports Med.* 20(3): pg. 290-298 1992.

Caterisano, A., C.W. Brown, L.P. Thurmond, D.R. Perkins, K. Linn, & E. A. Shortridge. "The Relationship Between Lower Body Strength and Power in Resistance Trained Athletes." *Medicine & Science in Sport and Exercise*, vol. 31, no. 5, May 1999.

Christova, P., & A. Kossev. "Motor unit activity during long-lasting intermittent muscle contractions in humans" *Eur. J. Appl. Physiol.* 77(4): pg. 379-387, Mar 1998.

Cronin, J.B., P.J. McNair, & R.N. Marshall. "The role of maximal strength and load on initial power production" *Med. Sci Sports Exerc.* Vol. 32, no. 10 pg. 1763-1769, 2000.

DeLuca, C.J., & Z. Erim. "Common drive of motor units in regulation of muscle force" *Trends Neurosci.* 17(7): pg. 299-305 Jul. 1994.

Enoka, R.M. "Morphological features and activation patterns of motor units" *J. Clin. Neurophysiol.* 12(6): pg. 538-559, Nov. 1995.

Erim, Z., C.J. DeLuca, K. Mineo, & T. Aoki. "Rank-ordered regulation of motor units" *Muscle Nerve* 19(5): pg. 563-573 May 1996.

Fleck, S.J. "Periodized Strength Training: A Critical Review" *Jour. Strength Cond. Res.* 13(1) pg. 82-89, 1999.

Fleck, S.J., & W.J. Kraemer. *Designing Resistance Training Programs* 2nd ed. Human Kinetics Publisher, Champaign, IL. 1997.

Fry, A.C., & W.J. Kraemer. "Resistance exercise overtraining and overreaching: Nueroendocrine responses" *Sports Medicine*, 232(2): pg 106-129, 1997.

Jones, C. S., C. Christensen, & M. Young. "Weight Training injury trends" *Phys. Sportsmed.* 28(7) July 2000.

Kraemer, W.J., & S.J. Fleck. "Exercise Physiology Corner; Anaerobic Metabolism and its Evaluation" *NSCA Jour.* Vol.4, no. 2, pg.20-21, 1982.

Kukulka, C.G., & H.P. Clamann. "Comparison of the recruitment and discharge properties of motor units in human brachial biceps and adductor pollicis during isometric contractions" *Brain Res. Vol.* 219, pg. 45-55, 1981.

Miller, K.J., S.J. Garland, T. Ivanova, & T. Ohtsuki. "Motor-unit behavior in humans during fatiguing arm movements" *J. Neurophysiol.* 75(4): pg. 1629-1636, Apr. 1996.

Pearson, D., A. Faigenbaum, M. Conley, & W.J. Kraemer. "The National Strength and Conditioning Association's Basic Guidelines for the Resistance Training of Athletes" *NSCA Jour* Vol.22, no. 4 pg. 14 –27, Aug. 2000.

Phelps, S.M. "Speed Training" *NSCA Jour.* Vol. 23 No. 2 Pg. 57-58 Apr. 2001.

Stone, M.H., D. Collins, S. Plisk, G. Haff, & M.E. Stone. "Training Principles: Evaluation of Modes and Methods of Training." *NSCA Jour* Vol. 22 No. 3 Pg. 65 – 76, 2000.

Stone, M.H., H. O'Bryant, J. Garhammer, J. McMillan, & R. Rozenek "A Theoretical Model of Strength Training" *NSCA Jour.* Vol.4, no. 4 pg. 36-39, 1982.

Wojtys, E.M., L.J. Huston, & S.D. Bastain. "Neuromuscular adaptations in isokinetic, isotonic, and agility training programs" *Am. J. Sports Med.* Vol. 24(2) pg. 187-196, 1996.

Young, W.B., M.H. McDowell, & B.J. Scarlett. "Specificity of Sprint and Agility Training Methods" *Jour. Strength Cond. Res.* 15(3) pg. 315-319, 2001.

Zatsiorsky, V., *Science and Practice of Strength Training*, Human Kinetics Publisher, Champaign, IL. 1995.

Developing Training Cycles

General Philosophy of Training Cycles

As mentioned in Chapter 2, there are a good number of sound reasons for a football coach to train his athletes using training cycles. They allow the coach to prioritize goals based on what is most important at any given time during the year. Cycling allows a coach to keep the workouts specific to the particular training goal, yet allows for enough variety in the workouts to keep them interesting to the players and avoid the mental and physical staleness earlier identified as **accommodation**. Because this book is dedicated to training a wide range of athletes, we would be remiss if we did not consider training cycle development relative to the different sub-groups of players on any given football team. For this reason, we will describe the general philosophy of training cycles for each of three sub-groups: beginner, intermediate, and advanced players.

It will be helpful to identify the criteria on which each sub-group is based: physical maturity, experience in the weight room, and subjective performance data.

These criteria provide a helpful starting point for the coach in placing each athlete in an appropriate grouping. Certain intangible characteristics, based on your judgment as the coach, should also play a role in categorizing your players. You may have an athlete who possesses some characteristics, but not all the characteristics required for placement in a given group. He may possess good physical maturity but have no experience in the weight room. This is where *your* judgment based on personality traits such as mental toughness and the ability to learn quickly (*coachability*, mental alertness, etc.) become the deciding factors. It is always best to err on the side of placing a player in a beginner group rather than placing him in a group that is too advanced. You can always move a player up once he proves that he can handle a more basic lifting and drilling group, but moving back to the beginning can be awkward and counterproductive.

Periodization

The key to sound program design is to maintain a systematic and consistent workout regimen, which targets the high priority training adaptations (specificity) while providing enough variety to avoid accommodation. This is best achieved through **periodization**, which simply means manipulating training loads (volume, frequency, and intensity), exercise selection, and rest periods in order to achieve a balance between consistency and variety. This is achieved through training cycles lasting anywhere from three to five weeks, targeting high priority goals determined by the time frame of your team in the competitive season that change in a systematic way as your priorities change.

Periodization cycles can be broken down into four distinct cycles:

The hypertrophy or preparation phase—This phase is characterized by relatively high-volume and low-intensity training that is often the least sport specific. The number of repetitions will be high (i.e., in weight lifting, greater than eight to 10 repetitions) and/or the number of sets will also be high (i.e. in weight lifting, greater than four to five sets). Naturally because the volume of training must be high, the resistance used must be relatively low. The goal of this cycle is to induce maximum muscle hypertrophy by recruiting lower threshold motor units but pushing them to a high level of exhaustion. This acts as the basic foundation of subsequent cycles by increasing the cross-sectional size of the muscle cells, establishing good circulation of blood flow to the muscle and establishing good lifting and/or drilling technique through low-intensity workouts (low weight, slow speed, low impact).

The strength or first transition phase—This phase is characterized by relatively moderate-volume and moderate-intensity training that is often more sport-specific than in the preceding cycle. With the reduc-

tion of volume (i.e., in weight lifting around five to six repetitions in three to four sets), the intensity can be elevated meaning more resistance, faster speeds, and high-impact drills. The strength, or first transition cycle, is designed to target higher threshold motor units and more sport-specific lifts and drills, as well as increasing overall strength by recruitment of the high threshold motor units.

The strength-power or competition phase—This phase is characterized by relatively low-volume and high-intensity training that is often the most sport specific. The number of repetitions will be low (i.e., in weight lifting equal to or less than three to four repetitions) and/or the number of sets may also be high or low (depending on the time of year). Because the volume is reduced, the intensity can be elevated with more resistance, faster speeds, and high-impact drills. Because football is primarily a strength-power sport, the highest specificity is achieved in this cycle. This cycle is often used for preseason training.

The unload or second transition (active rest) phase—This phase is one of low volume and low intensity. It is primarily included at points throughout the overall training system to prevent overtraining. It provides enough overload stimulus to the muscle to maintain strength, power, speed, and agility, while allowing the body to recover and restore itself. One-week unload cycles are often alternated between each of the above three cycles previously described to maximize recovery without losing ground (the scientific term for this is *detraining*).

Periodization for the Beginner

The beginner group will be made up of those players who lack physical maturity or experience in the training mode (i.e., weight room, plyometric drills, etc.). Physical maturity should be based on what the coach perceives as development though puberty. Look for the physical signs such as facial hair, a deepening voice, a higher level of muscularity, etc. Certain physical performance scores will also indicate physical maturity, such as a player being able to bench press a weight equal to his body weight or squat one and one-half the equivalent of his body weight. Bottom line: the coach must determine if a player is closer to being a child than an adult. This is especially true with high school players, because high school

age is a point of transition from childhood to adulthood. However, the coach must be careful not to stigmatize the players who fall in this category by making the player feel bad about the fact that he is physically maturing at a slower rate than some of his teammates. Quite often the so-called late bloomer ends up having a big growth spurt and could end up being next year's star. The last thing the coach wants to do is place players at a mental disadvantage of low confidence and low self-esteem. This can be avoided by giving the beginner group a code name (i.e., red team or blue team) that is not value laden and does not suggest that this group is in any way inferior to the other two groups.

In addition to physical maturity, the amount of experience the player has in resistance training is an important consideration. This should take into account the number of years of weight training experience and the quality of that experience. If a player has been lifting weights for two years in his basement, he may have enough experience if his father, who happens to be an avid weightlifter, has worked with him. If, on the other hand, the player has lifted with no guidance other than an issue of some muscle magazine, he may need to unlearn bad habits and be retrained in good habits. This would warrant his inclusion in the beginner group despite a training history.

The general goal of the beginning training cycle is to develop the basic movements of more complex lifts and drills while still providing a useful training regimen. Its focus is teaching and probably requires a higher level of supervision. A college psychology professor used to say that in training rats it typically took 30 trials to teach a rat to perform a simple task, but it took 300 trials to get that rat to unlearn the first task and relearn a different task. The same probably holds true for humans. Once we learn the neurological pathways to perform physical movements they become ingrained in our **kinesthetic memory** (muscle memory).

It may seem counterproductive to spend more time with the beginner groups given the fact that they are performing simpler lifts and drills. Working extensively with the beginner group will actually make it easier over a year, because the advanced groups will have fewer bad habits to correct as they come up. We recognize that the supervision of the weight room can become a logistical nightmare, so we will address some strategies for dealing with this problem later in that chapter.

The more specific goals of working with a beginner group can be broken down within each athleticism component. Depending on where in the off season, preseason, or in-season the training cycle falls, the beginner program will have the following characteristics:

Strength and lean body mass development—Even though the coach may manipulate the training loads every three to five weeks by changing the volume (sets and reps) and intensity (absolute amount of weight on the bar), the beginning program will tend to use low to moderate volumes with lower absolute amounts of weight on the bar. Thus, even in the lowest-volume/highest-intensity cycles, the repetition numbers never get lower than six to eight repetitions with a weight that can be lifted at least that number of times with good technical form.

The higher volume training would use even lighter weights and higher repetition numbers (10 to 12) but a lower number of sets (two to three) and fewer lifts per workout.

The lifts would be low-resistance preparation exercises, performed on weightlifting machines, and a few of the basic lifts using barbells. This is especially important with regard to preparation lifts that help develop basic movements for more complex lifts.

All lifts would be whole-body-type lifts, using several joints (compound lifts) rather than isolation lifts.

Training frequency for this group would be from two to three days per week, allowing maximum recovery between workouts (at least 48 hours between sessions).

Power development through plyometric training—Use mostly first level plyometric drills (see Chapter 4) that are low intensity and low volume. This would include rope jumping, dot drills, hops, standing long jumps, and standing vertical jumps. These help build power and coordination.

Other power exercises include explosive box stepups and skip variations (speed and power skipping) can be introduced once players gain mastery of first level plyos.

The volume will start out relatively low. Volume is measured by the number of sets of drills as well as the number of foot contacts. According to Dr. Donald Chu (considered to be a leading authority on plyometric program design) in his book *Jumping Into Plyometrics*, 60 to 100 foot contacts is considered low volume.

The frequency of this type of training should range from one to three days per week, depending on the amount of strength maintenance work that is also included in a given week. Remember that even though the power drills hold a higher priority, the basic strength exercises must be maintained at least twice per week.

Speed, acceleration, and agility development—With the beginner it is an ideal time to teach running mechanics (see Chapter 4). This would include running mechanics drills such as arm drills, as well as posture emphasis and leg mechanics drills such as ankling, A marches, and A skips.

Teach the player to relax while maintaining good mechanics. This can be taught by having the player focus his attention on certain physical cues: avoiding clenching the fists as you sprint; keeping the lower jaw relaxed and avoiding clenching your teeth; forcefully exhaling to avoid holding your breath.

Periodization for the Intermediate-Level Player

Usually, after a year of the beginner program described above, the average player will be ready to move up to the intermediate program, assuming that his physical maturity is keeping pace with his age. If the player has been through your beginner program, there is a good chance that he has been prepared to progress to the more sophisticated exercises outlined below. If the player has not been through your instruction but is, in your judgment, ready to start at the intermediate level, it might require some remedial work to get him up to the proper level of preparation. This is why it doesn't hurt to start an inexperienced beginner at the beginning level, even though he has a high level of physical maturity. Like the beginner program, the general training philosophies are listed by component.

Strength and lean body mass development—The training loads (volumes and intensity) will be more in line with normal periodization cycles, with each cycle lasting three to five weeks. The high-volume cycle will include volumes as high as five sets of 12 repetitions and occasionally three sets of 20 repetitions with relatively low weights.

The high intensity can include volumes of three to five repetitions with fairly high percentages of the one repetition maximum (up to 85 percent of 1 RM).

At this level more of the free weight versions of exercises are performed focusing on multi-joint lifts (compound lifts). The focus of teaching is to lead up to the higher velocity lifts.

Frequency will increase to three to four days per week, with a split routine in which different body parts are emphasized on different days.

Power development through plyometric training—The first level plyometric exercises such as dot drills, rope skipping, and speed ladder will be used daily as a warmup/lead-up routine prior to the more advanced plyometric and other non-plyometric workouts.

Once the lead-up drills are completed, the second level and modified third level drills will be introduced and incorporated into the workout. This would include bounding, cone jumps, low-hurdle jumps, and low-height box jumps with no weight added. The intensity of these drills is based on the height of the jumps and bounds, so the height should start out low and progress up to moderate levels.

The volume of plyometric training for this group should range between 100 to 150 foot contacts per workout in the off season, to 150 to 300 foot contacts in the preseason when power training takes a higher priority.

The coach should also introduce non-weighted upper-body plyometric exercises such as clapping pushups (see Chapter 4).

The frequency of plyometric training will be two days per week for the intermediate group.

Speed, acceleration, and agility development—The running mechanics drills must be reviewed and maintained in the intermediate level player. This would include the fast arm and A series drills described in Chapter 4.

Acceleration should be emphasized using the acceleration ladder (stick drill) described in Chapter 4, with time spent on proper starts.

At this point some of the over speed drills such as downhill running can be introduced as well as simpler programmed agility drills outlined in Chapter 4.

Speed, acceleration, and agility drills should be incorporated into the weekly routine two days per week.

Periodization for the Advanced-Level Player

We strongly recommended that a player spend a significant amount of time in the intermediate program before moving to the advanced program. This would probably be at least a full year. The coach should think of this as a long-term investment in the player because the lifting and drilling techniques learned in the beginner and intermediate level programs set the stage for the player learning the proper techniques in the more advanced level lifts. In Chapter 4 the lifts should include all advanced (three barbell code) lifts and for some of the players who have mastered those lifts, the collegiate level lifts (four barbell code). You will notice that this level will require more program variety from cycle to cycle.

Strength and lean body mass development—The majority of the weight training work will be performed with free weights. Free weights allow development of important stabilizer muscles needed for transferring strength to open skills used in playing the game. For this reason we also recommend sticking to multi-joint and full body lifts, with isolation lifts (using only one joint) used for working on weaknesses or injury-prone areas.

The lifts will also utilize a wide variety of lifting speeds (high-velocity lifts using low weights and low-velocity lifts using heavy weights), with a big emphasis on strength/power exercises such as the Olympic-style lifts.

Providing variety is extremely important at this level and can be done primarily through changing the training loads often. This is achieved by manipulating volume and intensity as often as every three weeks and changing the exercises. In order to keep the program as stable as possible, it is best to change the assistance lifts more often than the basic lifts.

Workouts should be designed to be short and intense, keeping the workout time to around one hour. By using a split routine, three to five days per week, where different muscle groups are trained on different days, all of the important lifts can be accomplished in this time frame.

Depending on the time of year, sport-specific exercises should be emphasized as the season approaches in order to get the best carryover to performance on the field. During the year, your program must include remedial exercises, which target weak-nesses and injury-prone areas should be given a high priority among certain athletes.

Power development through plyometric training—Beginning and intermediate plyometric exercises should be practiced occasionally, particularly as a lead-up to advanced plyometrics.

In advanced level plyometrics, the drills will be more sport specific and use multi-directional drills performed at fast speeds. This includes all of the box jump variations (lateral, multidirectional, weighted, etc.) as well as depth jumps. It is recommended that a player be able to squat with at least one and one-half times his body weight before engaging in depth jumps.

With all box and depth jumps, the *rate of amortization* (time it takes to make the transition from the downward movement to the upward movement) should be as short as possible. As the coach supervises these drills, he should encourage players to minimize the amount of time their feet are in contact with the floor.

The volume of plyometric training for this group should range between 120 to 200 foot contacts per workout in the off season, to 150 to 450 foot contacts in the preseason when power training takes a higher priority. With this higher volume per workout the plyometric training should be performed only one to two days per week.

Upper-body plyometrics, such as medicine ball throws, should also be included for upper-body power development.

Speed, acceleration, and agility development—The advanced level players should spend more time engaged in flexibility development as an important component to speed and agility. Chapter 6 addresses the development of flexibility through both static and dynamic stretching exercises. This includes sport-specific exercises such as groin stretches, shoulder stretches, hamstring muscle stretches, and, particularly for quarterbacks, core rotational stretches.

Among the advanced level players, it is still important to review running mechanics. Drills such as A series, fast legs, and arm drills can be incorporated into the warmup routine.

Emphasis should be placed on acceleration, especially as the season approaches. This includes acceleration ladder as well as resistive running (weighted sleds, uphill/stadium runs, and sand runs) and over speed drills (downhill running, elastic cord running, etc.).

For agility, rotating three to four different drills emphasizing change of direction should cycle through the entire arsenal of agility drills. These can be programmed with a set patterns or performed as reaction drills in which the player responds to a coach's visual or verbal cue. Also included in this rotation would be tennis ball and crazy ball reaction drills to develop agility.

Training Phases

Ideally, the most effective way to prepare for football competition is through a year-round program of strength and conditioning. This may not seem feasible in the real world with student-athletes participating in a wide variety of sports, extracurricular activities, and a normal social life. With proper planning and the right perspective, it is possible to develop a doable program. It requires that you keep the time commitment reasonable and the player feeling he can work your training regimen into his full schedule. Understanding the ultimate goal of each training phase and prioritizing the workouts serves that goal. This includes not only the resistance-training portion of the workout, but the conditioning aspect as well.

In order to manage the training design, we have divided the year up into three distinct training phases. The off season starts shortly after the conclusion of the last game of the year and runs up to the beginning of the preseason phase. This typically covers the time that players are still in school. We say the off season begins shortly after the last game, since a period of active rest is a good idea immediately following the season. This active rest period is two to three weeks in which the player can recover from the aches and pains accumulated over the course of the season and get a mental break from competition. The player will most likely be more enthusiastic about the off season training if allowed some time to himself. The preseason is a period immediately following the off season that usually encompasses the summer months when the player is out of school. The in season is the time between preparation for the first game and the final game of that particular year.

In the case of a 10-week regular season, the preseason would be the eight to 10 weeks of summer prior to the season and the off season would be about 20 or so weeks prior to the preseason, including two to three weeks dedicated to active rest. This would only be true for the single-sport athlete who plays only football. For multi-sport athletes, the off season is either much shorter, as in the case of a player who plays only two sports per year or may be nonexistent as in the case of the three-sport athlete. In the latter case, the three-sport athlete really only has a preseason and a long in-season phase. We will address coping with the multi-sport athlete later in this chapter.

The bottom line in programming strength and conditioning is to match the training goal to each phase, and prioritize the training regimen so that you target the most important adaptation of that particular phase. The next phase then builds on the target adaptation of the previous phase and so on. Keep in mind that you must also maintain whatever adaptation occurred in the previous phase rather than completely abandoning the hard-earned physical development. For example, if the ultimate goal of the off season is to gain maximal strength, the program will emphasis strength development exercises as a high priority. If the priority changes to speed-specific training in the preseason in order to develop maximal power, the program must be adjusted to accommodate that target adaptation. A good program will not, however, abandon strength development in the preseason. Instead, some will be used to at least maintain the strength gains of the off season. This is also true for the in-season training phase.

Off-Season Training

The most important goal of the off-season training in one phrase is to train each player to be bigger, leaner and stronger as the number-one priority. The majority of the training effort will be in pursuit of that goal. This means that weight training, in which the volume and intensity are cycled, tends toward a higher volume, lower intensity to promote gains in muscle size. Cycles of higher intensity weight training will be rotated periodically to provide variety to the workouts and avoid accommodation. In addition, the conditioning program should preserve lean body weight. This requires a relatively low volume of conditioning activity. Because the competitive season is far off, it is not as important to have the players in top physical condition, especially if it compromises the lean body mass gains that hold a higher priority in this phase.

Some power, speed, and agility drills will be performed, but only as a lead-up to the next phase of training. This phase is an ideal time to review proper running mechanics for all levels of players. Keep in mind that this training phase allows for the incorporation of good quality rest for the players. Because muscle building is a high priority, resting the players rather than pushing them with too much conditioning volume is very important and highly recommended.

Preseason Training

The best way to sum up the general goals of this training phase is to prepare the player for more sport-specific training and conditioning. The priority shifts from gaining maximal strength to increasing maximum power, speed, and agility. This means more velocity-specific resistance training that capitalizes on the strength gains of the off season program, while still maintaining basic strength. The number of strength exercises are cut back as well as the number of sets and reps, but the training intensities, based on lifting heavier weights is emphasized. The balance of the weight training is geared toward velocity-specific lifts for developing power and plyometric training. In addition, speed and agility training should mirror the same types of situations the player will experience in the game. Both programmed and reactive agility drills specific to playing position eventually become high priority in order to prepare the player for his up-coming season.

The conditioning program will also take a higher priority during the preseason with higher volumes and a shorter rest period between sprints in interval training. This is when players perform the most work volume with the least rest during this short training phase.

In-Season Training

The best way to summarize the in-season phase of training is to say that the goal is to maintain the strength, power, speed, agility, and level of conditioning gained in the off season and preseason. The biggest mistake a coach can make in the in-season training is trying to improve the strength and conditioning level of the players. This will most likely have a counterproductive effect on the way the athletes play in the game, because overtraining usually occurs when players are pushed too hard physically during the season. If the players are not prepared by the time the season starts, you need to re-evaluate your off season and preseason programs.

Having said this, consider that the second biggest mistake among coaches is to completely abandon the training program once the season starts. These coaches erroneously assume that daily practices will maintain the performance gains developed in the off and preseasons. Actually, unless some form of strength and power maintenance program is incorporated into the weekly practice schedule, those hard-earned performance gains will slowly deteriorate. These components, strength and power, are the foundation of athleticism, and the overall performance on the field will slowly dwindle without them. The timing of such a decrease in athletic performance could not be worse, because the end of the season (i.e., playoffs, postseason bowl) is often the most important time to have a team ready to compete.

The highest priority during in-season training should be to maintain strength and power without overtraining the athletes. Speed and agility would not actually have to be addressed beyond what each position coach would require in daily drills performed during practice. The key to accomplishing strength and power maintenance is to bring the players into the weight room twice per week (preferably early in the week to allow sufficient recovery prior to the game) and perform a moderate number of sets of low-volume, high-intensity weight training to maintain strength, and a moderately low volume of velocity-specific exercises such as plyometrics to preserve power. These would include just the core exercises using multi-joint lifts and drills.

When we examine the detraining process (training adaptations that are lost due to reduction or complete cessation of the exercise stimulus), we see that the initial losses of strength are not due to muscle **atrophy** (a reduction of the size of a muscle) as we once thought. Instead, the initial strength losses occur due to what are commonly referred to as **neuromuscular factors**. These involve the changes in the nerve and muscle connections that allow us to generate maximum force. The good news is that by stimulating these neural pathways two days per week, we maintain them and won't lose any significant level of strength. In addition, stimulating the muscle two times per week not only tends to maintain the muscle hypertrophy gained in the off season and preseason, but given the growth and maturity dynamics especially in the high school-aged player, probably leads to increases in strength. The key is that we don't want to push the players too hard to maximize strength at the expense of being prepared to play in the games.

The Multi-Sport Athlete

The problems associated with designing a program for the multi-sport athlete is probably more common at the high school or perhaps the Division III college level than the Division I, level where athletes tend to specialize in one sport. The multi-sport athlete, especially those who participate in a different sport each season, poses the greatest challenge to the strength and conditioning coach in designing off season phases. Typically the multi-sport athlete is going to be one of the better natural athletes and usually will be highly motivated. This can work in your favor because the small amount (volume) of in-season training that this athlete performs will probably be of sufficient quality to have a positive impact on his athletic performance. The key is to get the other coaches in the non-football sports to buy into the in-season training program. The only way to do this effectively is to get him to see the win-win potential that exists; the fact that his off season athlete is your in-season athlete (and vice versa), and both of you want him to be prepared. You can also use this as an opportunity to get the other coaches organized so that the weight training and conditioning program is well supervised. It's the old "I'll help you, if you'll help me" situation that can be beneficial to every athlete in your school and each sports program.

The first step in accommodating a multi-sport athlete is to organize all of the coaches in an educational institution to develop a universally beneficial strength and conditioning program. This can only be done if each coach feels that all sports are on an even footing in the training program. There can be no major sports and minor sports, nor one sport being more important in the training facility than another attitude. This should go beyond paying lip service to an all-sports-are-equal attitude, it must be established by actions and policy. The director of athletics must buy into the idea and lead the way in establishing fair and equal policies so that all sports, including women's teams, are equal partners. Without a prevailing attitude of cooperation among all of the coaches, the system won't work. If everyone is willing to cooperate, think of the potential for an excellent strength and conditioning program, one in which the supervision level is high, yet the burden of administration is shared by many, which keeps the time commitment of each coach to a minimum.

The second step is to educate each coach so that they see the benefits that can be derived from a sound strength and conditioning program. By doing this you are assured of reducing the conflicting information that athletes often receive when coaches in other sports contradict the training methods you are promoting. This requires leadership and education on the part of the head football coach, and/or strength coach in order to earn the respect of the other coaches in your school. The fact that you chose to buy and read this book is a good indication of your commitment to stay abreast of the latest training techniques available.

We recommend that you seek membership in the National Strength and Conditioning Association (NSCA), or similar organization, because these groups provide monthly publications on current strength and conditioning methods for all sports. Membership information is posted on their web site at www.nsca.com. In addition, they offer certification as a Certified Strength and Conditioning Specialist (CSCS), which can help add a sense of legitimacy to your role as the leader in organizing the strength and conditioning program at your school. By passing along your knowledge and expertise to coaches of other sports, they will see you as a partner in their quest for building a program and help you in supervising. Offering in-service training sessions for coaches several times per year is a good way to develop a consistent and effective group of strength coaches.

The cooperation among all coaches in an athletics department has the added bonus of presenting a united front when requesting funding for training equipment. For many programs, lack of facilities and equipment is a major snag in developing a sound strength and conditioning program. Perhaps you can convince the athletics director to take a certain amount of money each year off the top of the athletics budget to develop and maintain the resistance training facility.

A third step that may or may not be feasible in your particular school is to try to establish a weight training class that can be offered to all students in the school to fulfill physical education requirements. There may be qualified physical education teachers who can teach this or you may be able to teach it, especially if you demonstrate an expertise by gaining certification. The advantage to such a program, especially for the multi-sport athlete, is that the in-season training can be done well before formal practice times and not interfere with practice times. It is also a good opportunity for developing good student support for the sports program if administered correctly. This means paying attention to the non-athletes in the class as well as the athletes, in order to get the students to identify with your program in a positive way. This is also an effective way to recruit new players from the student body.

Once your training program is organized and established, training the multi-sport athlete is simply a matter of developing the usual target adaptations in the summer (preseason) and maintaining them throughout the year by a long in-season program. The preseason program will not be essentially different from the rest of the team, except that a slightly greater emphasis will be placed on developing strength, and less on power speed and agility. The assumption here is that while the athlete is participating in other sports once football is over, he is applying his strength gains to sport-specific power as well as gaining speed, quickness, and agility through his participation in that sport. The in-season training is designed to maintain what is gained in the summer and, perhaps, improve strength through natural growth and maturity.

If the coaches of other sports in your athletics department resist your attempts to organize, the alternative strategy is to work with each coach individually and get as many on board as possible. Perhaps by doing so, the coaches who initially resisted your attempts to develop a universal program might join in when they view the success gained within the smaller group of coaches who cooperate.

At the high school level, you might also identify a few parents who have weight-training experience to work with you program and act as supervisors and volunteer strength coaches. This not only helps solve your supervision concerns but can also lead to better support and understanding from among players' parents. Just be careful to only allow parents who are willing to discuss their training philosophies beforehand and then make sure that their training philosophy is compatible with yours. Some in-service training sessions would be wise to make sure your volunteers are on the same page. We also recommend that you or one of the assistant coaches be present whenever a parent volunteer is assisting in the training of your players to monitor his or her behavior.

In the case of a college-level program that lacks the personnel needed to adequately cover the weight-training facility, a potential source of manpower could be found through an internship program. If your institution has a physical education department (which may go by another name such as health and exercise science, kinesiology, sports studies, etc.), meet with the department chair and explore the possibility of developing a program where students (both undergraduate and graduate) intern in your program. It is a win-win situation because the student gains valuable experience as well as academic credit, while you get the extra supervision needed to run a quality program.

The academic department also gets FTEs, which are used by most state institutions to determine funding for departments based on the number of courses offered and the number of students enrolled. Thus the department can accommodate more students without added faculty commitment.

Overtraining—Diagnosis and Prevention

One of the reasons we cycle the strength and conditioning program is to avoid overtraining. Rest and recovery are the payoff phases of any strength and conditioning program. If you do not allow for the recovery to take place, you are jeopardizing your players' chances for maximal gains. This can have an especially devastating effect if it occurs during the season and players enter the game without adequate recovery. We commonly refer to this lack of recovery as *overtraining*.

Overtraining results from too high of a training load (volume, intensity, and frequency of training), and inadequate rest between workouts, or some combination of these. The difference between an ideal training routine and one that results in overtraining cannot be clearly defined. A given training load and rest period for one athlete may result in optimum gains, while the same training load and recovery may push another athlete into a state of overtraining. The key to managing overtraining for the football coach is being aware of the signs of overtraining and looking carefully, every day for these signs in every player. The following are some of the most observable and common signs of overtraining:

Performance symptom—Decreases in physical performance (strength, power, and speed) despite regular adherence to workouts. This would include the inability to reach previously attained standards (1 RM, 40-yard dash times, etc.)

Performance symptom—Loss of coordination and/or digression in skill development to a point where the player makes previously corrected mistakes and mental errors.

Psychological symptom—Player displays symptoms of depression and general loss of enthusiasm (apathy toward activities that he usually enjoys).

Psychological symptom—Emotional instability and lack of concentration (especially if schoolwork takes a rapid decline in a normally strong student).

Autoimmune system symptoms—Increased susceptibility to illnesses, colds, and allergies. This includes swollen lymph glands, slow healing to minor cuts and scrapes, etc.

Physiological symptoms—Rapid and unexplained weight loss despite the athlete attempting to maintain normal body weight and a loss of appetite.

Sleep-related symptoms—Insomnia or the inability to get a good night of sleep or waking up tired despite a normal eight hours of sleep.

From Kreider, Fry and O'Toole in their book entitled *Overtraining in Sport* (1998, Human Kinetics Publishing, Champaign, Ill.).

Dealing with Overtraining

The best way to deal with overtraining is to try to prevent it from occurring in the first place. The football coach must carefully plan the workout regimens, allowing sufficient unload cycles, to keep the total stress in the player's life at a manageable level. He must try to consider the total stress in the player's life, even outside of his role as an athlete. Young men must cope with a variety of stressful situations including the demands of school work, social and family problems, lifestyle choices such as amount of sleep, dietary factors, and so on. It may be impossible to adjust the workouts for many of these variables, but some can be managed. It may be as simple as timing the unload week to coincide with a heavy exam period in school. Making sure that players understand the importance of getting to bed early and how high-quality sleep is a key component of the recovery process. Educating your players about proper dietary habits based on information we have provided in Chapter 7.

The most important coping strategy for dealing with the problem of overtraining is early identification. The reason for this is that there are many levels or degrees of severity of chronic overtraining. Some mild forms can be corrected with a few days of rest. More severe forms can take months of rest to overcome. The more extreme cases can be devastating to a player's performance if it occurs as the competitive season begins, because he may not recover until the end of the season.

The cure, once the coach suspects overtraining in a player, is obvious—good quality rest. Depending on the training phase, this might involve total rest (giving the player a couple days off) or if the symptoms of overtraining are not too severe, putting in one or two unload weeks into the training routine. This may be done on an individual basis, if you feel that it is an isolated case, or can be done with the entire team if you suspect that a mistake was made in designing the program and the entire team is at risk.

Teaching the Lifts and Drills from Beginner to Advanced

Teaching the Lifts and Drills from Beginner to Advanced

So far we have outlined our approach to strength and conditioning for football players and offered a few basic concepts of the physiology behind our approach. We will now describe specific lifts and drills, which have been grouped according to the four basic components of athleticism outlined in the previous chapter. Within each grouping we will present these lifts and drills in a progression. Keep in mind that the greatest challenge of developing a strength and conditioning program for any football player is the wide range of physical maturity, natural ability, and training experience that each athlete brings into the program. We have coded each lift or drill according to the appropriate level of difficulty, but remember that an elementary lift can still benefit an experienced lifter within a properly planned program. For the weight lifting exercises we use a barbell symbol to denote the degree of difficulty with one barbell indicating the beginner level, two barbells an intermediate level, three barbells an advanced level, and four barbells a collegiate level lift (see Fig. 4.1).

To be effective it is essential that the coaches evaluate each athlete based on objective data from testing, as well as subjective information, or how each coach judges the player's level of maturity and preparedness. Based on this, it is important to develop a program that groups players among other participants who are of the same level of physical performance. When in doubt always be conservative and place a player in a beginning group. You can always advance him later if he shows that he is capable of working with a more advanced group. This not only ensures that players

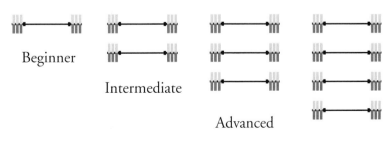

Beginner

Intermediate

Advanced

Collegiate Level*

*Note that collegiate level lifts would only be appropriate for high school players who were highly experienced in advanced level lifts.

work at the appropriate level of a lift or drill, as well as an appropriate training load (intensity and volume), but also provides an intrinsic source of motivation for each player as they work hard to move up levels of training. You can even use an incentive program (i.e., t-shirts) to motivate your players in this regard.

The first step in evaluating which exercises are appropriate is to establish a system of testing. There are many philosophies on testing. Some coaches believe in testing several times per season; others believe that fewer tests per season is better. Tests serve not only to help the coach evaluate players, but also to determine the effectiveness of your program. As mentioned earlier, the test itself serves as a source of motivating players, a topic that will be covered in greater depth in Chapter 8. In our opinion, it is sufficient to test players at the beginning and end of each training phase, which includes off season, preseason and in-season (keeping in mind that the beginning of each phase is the end of the phase that comes before it). Table 4.1 shows the basic tests that should be done at all testing sessions and the performance parameters that each test assesses. A detailed description of each test will be included in this chapter.

Each lift and drill is broken down into its components and the critical coaching points of each are highlighted. These coaching points are important not only to insure that the activity is targeting the proper performance goal, but also to minimize the chance of injury. A qualified coach, volunteer, or parent, who is aware of the procedure, should strictly supervise each group of lifters and watch for the critical coaching points of each exercise. It is essential to conduct some orientation sessions with your assistants to familiarize them with each lift and drill and to make sure that everyone is on the same page when it comes to the content of what they are teaching.

One last point about teaching these lifts and drills: It is very important to emphasis the details of the lifting or drilling techniques. The smallest error can lead to major problems, especially with the more advanced lifts. The progressions are designed to teach the players important basic movements in the elementary versions of the exercises that will carry over to the more advanced version of the lifts and make the teaching those lifts that much easier. Investing the time with the younger, less experienced lifters will pay off later as they advance.

Test	Performance tested	Number of trials
40-yard dash	Acceleration and speed	Have three coaches time each trial and average the time from three stopwatches. Take the best of the three trials.
10-yard dash	Acceleration	Electronically timed is ideal but if not available same as the 40-yard.
Vertical jump	Lower body power	Best of three trials
Skinfold test (Jackson-Pollack protocol or waist-to-hip ratio test)	Body composition percentage fat	Most consistent measure of three trials
1 RM bench press	Upper-body strength	Best lift within five trials
1 RM squat or leg press*	Lower-body strength	Best lift within five trials
Two-hand medicine ball throw	Upper-body power	Best of three trials
20-yard shuttle run (pro agility)	Agility and quickness	Best of three trials
Sit and reach test	Flexibility	Best of three trials

Table 4.1   *Depends on level of experience and physical maturity

Basic Testing

Testing is an important component in this program because it not only allows coaches to assess the players and place them in the appropriate groupings, but also provides feedback to tell them about the effectiveness of the training regimen. A good testing program also provides information that is useful in helping players set goals, motivates players to give good efforts because they know their performance will be evaluated, and may also be useful in allowing a coach to determine a player's aptitude for playing a certain position, based on natural talent. It is therefore critical that proper testing be conducted in a formal session to guarantee that the tests are objective, reliable, and valid.

Objectivity simply means that the person testing has no influence on the test result. For example, if a player were testing his best friend and wanted to create a bias in his favor, a good objective testing procedure should prevent this. Every test condition must be the same for all players and must be the same from test to test.

The validity of the tests refers to whether the test actually assesses what it is supposed to measure. An example of lack of validity would be weighing players to determine body composition (percentage of body fat). Although a person's body weight may have an indirect relationship with the percentage of body fat, weighing a player does not tell us how much of that weight is fat and how much is lean body weight.

Reliability measures whether the test is consistent from measurement to measurement. With this last point, if you test everyone in the 40-yard dash on grass and in cleats on the preseason test, you must test everyone on grass and in cleats on the in-season test to preserve reliability. If you test them in running shoes on an all-weather track, you will not be able to compare the results and see the effectiveness of the program because the change in the performance may be due to running surface variability.

The tests we recommend have been documented to be both valid and reliable in the research literature, if done properly. Often you will get the best validity and reliability in testing if you allow athletes to practice the tests in a *familiarization session*. This minimizes the *learning effect* so that rather than testing how quickly skills are learned, you are testing the true performance potential of the player. In addition, a standard warmup routine should precede all testing sessions. Be sure to do the exact same warm-up for all testing to avoid problems with reliability, because an extra stressful warmup could affect the results of some of these tests.

1) 10-yard dash and 40-yard dash—acceleration and maximum speed

Equipment needed—Suitable running surface, stopwatch (to 1/100 second), cones and marking materials such as chalk. Electronic timing (typically using laser technology) is an ideal, albeit expensive, option for good reliable and valid speed and acceleration testing. This is especially true for testing the 10-yard dash, where the margin for timing errors is great.

The test can be run on any acceptable surface (all-weather track, cinder track, grass, artificial turf) but you must be sure that the surface is consistent from test to test. This is especially true if weather is a factor as in the case of a grass surface.

• Measure and mark distance using cones and chalk lines. Three timers are off to one side and should straddle the finish line.

• Have athlete assume either a standard ready stance or a stance specific to their position. You may also use starting blocks if available, but be sure athletes have a chance to familiarize themselves with starting from blocks or you may be testing starting block skills rather than acceleration and maximum speed.

• Give the ready command to prepare the runner and the timers (some players might prefer a go command, but this is optional). All three timers start their stopwatches on the first movement by the athlete (either hand or foot). Each stops the watch once any body part of the player crosses the finish line. Electronic timing (as shown on the previous page) is the more accurate way to conduct this test, especially in the 10-yard dash.

• Allow athletes sufficient recovery between trials and repeat for a total of three trials. Take the average of the three stopwatches as the trial time. Record the best trial time out of three trials.

2) Vertical jump—lower-body power

Equipment needed—tape measure, sufficiently high vertical wall, rectangular chalkboard, with inch markings, chalk or Vertec™ vertical jump tester.

Assuming a limited budget you can construct a valid vertical jump testing station by bolting a rectangular chalkboard (minimum 2 ft. x 4 ft.) lengthwise on any vertical wall of sufficient height (any wall in a gymnasium will work). The board should be at least six feet from the floor, and the floor should be clear of any obstructions.

• Have the player chalk his fingertips. Standing at a right angle to the wall with the chalked hand closest to the wall, the player to stretches and reaches as high on the chalkboard as possible with his feet flat on the floor.

• Re-chalk the hand and have the player assume a crouch position and prepare to jump. The player may move his arms and flex his legs just prior to the jump, but he must not move his feet (no shuffle step) just prior to the jump.

• The player jumps as high as possible and touches the highest point possible on the chalkboard with the chalked hand.

• The coach then measures the distance between the upper and lower chalk mark (placing the tape at the top of each mark) and records this measure in inches.

- The best of three trials is the final score.

or

- If you have a Vertec™ vertical jump tester, you can use the following protocol. Have the player stand under the Vertec™ with both arms and stretched. Lower the Vertec™ until the middle fingers of the extended hands touch the lowest vane.

- Have the player assume a jumping ready position similar to the chalkboard method. Remember he can swing his arms and flex his legs but cannot move his feet prior to the jump (no shuffle step).

- The player then jumps as high as possible and slaps as high on the row of vanes as possible with both hands.

- You can then move all vanes at and below the highest vane slapped out of the way, and the player can attempt a second trial. Once the second trial is complete, you will again move any vanes displaced and a third attempt is performed.

- Following the third trial, the vertical jump score is calculated by counting the number of vanes displaced by the player, with the distance between blue vanes being one inch and the distance between blue and white vanes being half of an inch.

3) Skinfold assessment or waist-to-hip ratio—to estimate percentage of body fat and monitor body composition

Equipment needed—tape measure and Lange™ Skinfold calipers (or comparable brand of caliper).

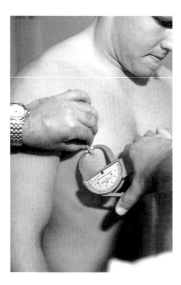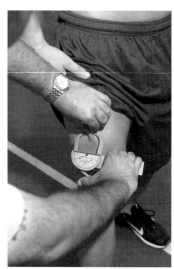

A good reliable pair of skinfold calipers will cost about $250 but if properly protected and maintained will last for several years. Although many people believe that the skinfold technique is a highly accurate method of measuring body fat, the fact is that results can vary considerably from tester to tester. This is why you must have the same person doing all of your tests, and the more experienced that person is at taking skinfold measurements, the better the results for comparison. The real value in assessing body fat by this technique is what is called the *test, retest reliability,* which simply means that any change in body fat percentage from test to test is a real change. If a player's percentage fat decreases then you can be confident that the change is real.

The protocol we recommend is the Jackson-Pollack Method that measures three skinfold sites on the right side of the body. This would include:

1) Mid-chest along the outside line of the pectoralis major (chest muscle) at the point between where the armpit starts and the nipple (This is a *diagonal fold*).

2) Abdominal one inch to the right of the naval (*vertical fold*).

3) Mid-thigh halfway between the hip joint and knee joint on the front of the thigh (vertical fold).

• Hold the calipers in your right hand and take the skin at the appropriate site in the fingertips of the left hand, with the left hand in a thumbs-down position. Pull the skin away from bone and muscle and place the caliper jaws below your fingers (this allows for an unobstructed view). Avoid placing the caliper too close to the fingers of the grasping hand because the compressing effect of pinching the skin will over-compress the skinfold (the calipers should be about half of an inch away from your fingers). Also avoid measuring too close to the non-fat tissue by not placing the calipers too deep (close to the muscle and bone). By pulling the skin as far away from muscle and bone as possible and placing the jaws of the caliper as close to the middle of the skin you will get the best measurements.

• Rotate through all three sites until you get three consistent measurements for each site and record as the skinfold score.

There are charts available for converting the skinfold total into a percent fat score (see Appendix), but for comparison purposes you can simple compare the pretest skinfold total to any subsequent test (assume that the same person conducts the skinfold test each time) and get a sense of whether the percentage body fat is changing. A local college or university may be a resource for training on the use of a skinfold caliper through their physical education or exercise science department.

or

• If skinfold calipers are not available, a simple test performed with a tape measure can be used to monitor changes in body composition. This test is the waist-to-hip ratio test.

Measure the player's waist at the naval while he is standing relaxed and not pulling in his stomach.

Measure around the hips, over the buttocks where girth is largest.

Divide the waist measurement by the hip measurement for a ratio.

Although not as accurate a way to monitor change in body composition, the waist-to-hip ratio test provides a way of monitoring progress in a player that is carrying too much body fat (which of courses means that this would be a high-priority target adaptation).

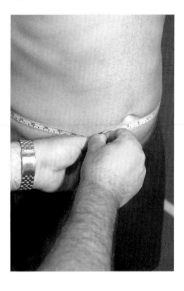 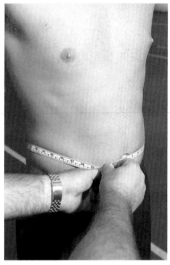 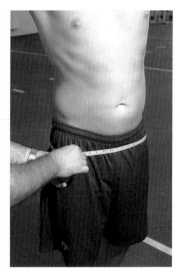

4) Sit and reach test—for testing low back and hamstring flexibility

Equipment needed—a sit and reach box (commercially available) or a yardstick.

• Have the player warm up his back and hamstring muscle by performing non-resistant movements and light jogging. Once he is sufficiently warmed up, stretch the hamstrings and low back muscle by holding a stretched position for at least six seconds.

• The player then removes his shoes and places his feet against a sit and reach box, or if one is not available, the player places his feet on a tape line, with a yardstick taped to the floor at a right angle to the tape line.

• The player must keep his knees locked at all times. He then places one hand directly on top of the other so that the middle fingers are aligned.

• He then exhales and leans as far forward as possible while either pushing the metal curser of the sit and reach box forward or moving his middle fingers along the yardstick taped to the floor. Do not allow the player to punch or stab the cursor because the momentum can cause an inaccurate score.

• The flexibility score can be read directly on the sit and reach box or in the case of the yardstick taped to the floor, the difference between the inch mark at the tapeline and the distance the middle fingers traveled on the yardstick.

• Perform three trials and record the highest of the three in which the legs stayed locked.

5) 1 RM bench press test—measures upper-body strength

Equipment needed—Olympic bar and weights, bench press bench.

• In order to make this a valid test for strength, the one repetition maximum must be achieved within five trials. It is important to allow several familiarization or practice trials so that players have some idea where to start, especially if they have little experience lifting free weights.

• Once players have warmed up and stretched using non-resistant movements and static stretches held for at least six seconds, they will be ready to start the test.

• Decide what form requirements you wish to establish on the lift (i.e., pausing the bar before pressing, hips must stay on the bench, no bouncing the bar off the chest, etc.) and be sure to enforce these standards on all subsequent tests.

• We know that the bench press is a popular way for players to gain bragging rights but consider the fact that you want to test in a safe, low injury risk protocol. Even if it means your team totals won't be as impressive as other teams where the risky form is allowed, it is not worth injuring a player (remember you won't get spotted extra touchdowns in a game because your team can bench press more weight than your opponent).

• Have a spotter hand off the weight to the player and stay attentive (for heavy weights use two spotters on the sides as well).

• The player must lower the bar and touch the chest, and fully lock the bar out at the top of the lift, following proper form considerations to count as a good lift.

• Use player feedback based on subjective information of how difficult the last attempt was to gauge each subsequent increase. Remember once you go beyond five trials the test becomes more of a muscular endurance/fatigue test than a strength test.

For inexperienced players we recommend a submaximal repetition test (using a lighter weight) in which a player performs a maximum number of repetitions that is then converted to a predicted 1 RM using a table included in the Appendix. This test poses a significantly lesser risk of injury with players who lack the experience or physical maturity to perform a 1 RM test.

6) 1 RM squat or leg press test—measures lower-body strength

Equipment needed—Olympic bar and weights, step rack or power rack, or leg press machine.

• Have the player warm up his back and hamstring muscle by performing non-resistant movements and light jogging. Once he is sufficiently warmed up, stretch the hamstrings and low back muscle by holding a stretched position for at least six seconds.

• As in the bench press, in order to make this a valid test for strength, the one repetition maximum must be achieved within five trials. It is important to allow several familiarization or practice trials so that players have some idea where to start, especially if they have little experience lifting free weights.

• Decide what form rules you wish to require on the lift (i.e., squatting depth, bar placement either high or low on the neck or upper back) and be sure to enforce these standards on all subsequent tests. A good way to give feedback to the lifter is by stretching a bungee cord across the back of the power rack at the appropriate depth so that the player can feel his buttocks touch the cord once he reaches that depth. We discourage the use of a bench or box, especially with inexperienced players because the spinal column can be compressed if the player loses control resulting in a high risk of injury.

• Spotters on either side of the lifter must communicate so that the bar does not become over balanced, causing potential risk of injury.

• The player must start in a controlled position at the beginning of the lift, lower slowly into the appropriate depth (most injuries in the squat are a result of rapid descent during the negative phase of the lift), and then return to a fully erect position.

• If a player has no experience with the squat, a leg press is a safe and valid way to measure lower body strength. Follow the same warmup and stretching procedures and establish criteria for the lift (i.e., feet width, depth of negative portion, etc.).

• As in the squat the leg press should be lowered slowly to an appropriate depth and legs fully extended on the lift.

7) Two-hand medicine ball throw—measures upper-body power

Equipment needed—bench, three-, five-, eight-, and 10-kilogram medicine ball, measuring tape.

Select a medicine ball weight appropriate for the size of the player. For test reliability use the same weight for all tests unless the player gains weight and moves to a higher category (weight categories should be broad—i.e., 140 lb. and under, 141-180 lb., 181-220 lb., 221-250 lb., 251 lb. and over).

• Have the player sit with his back against either a wall or a post (a post gives fuller range of motion) and throw the medicine ball as far as possible with a two-hand chest pass while maintaining back contact with the wall or post.

• Have a coach mark where the ball hits and measure from the bench to that mark.

• Following a brief rest period allow a total of three trials and record the highest of the three. For players who have never performed this test allow a familiarization trial on a separate day prior to the test.

8) 20-yard pro agility test—measures agility and quickness

Equipment needed—three cones, lines five yards apart (can be done on football field, artificial turf, or a basketball court), whistle, stopwatch.

• Following sufficient warmup and stretching arrange cones five yards apart on each line.

• The player starts by straddling the middle line in a three-point stance with his right hand on the line.

• On the whistle, the player sprints to the right line and touches the right line with his right hand. He then sprints across the middle line to the left line and touches the left line with his left hand. He immediately sprints back to his right and finishes at the middle line.

• The clock starts on the whistle and ends when the player crosses the middle line.

• Take the best of three trials with rest between trials. This is another drill that would require familiarization with inexperienced players on a separate day.

• The diagram below shows the proper running pattern for the pro agility test.

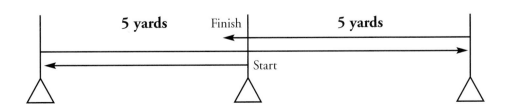

Basic Lifts for Developing Core Strength

As stated earlier, core strength and lean body mass development are the base of athleticism. With high school football players an increase in absolute strength alone will positively affect power, speed, and agility. Of course the aim of this book is to maximize athleticism, so specific exercises and drills for the development of power, speed, and agility will be addressed in the ensuing sections. The first grouping is designed to provide a menu of lifts organized in rank order starting with the very basic body weight exercises, progressing to weight lifting machines, and finally to free weights. Within the free weight groupings we will start with non-ballistic movements (less explosive, slower movements) and then move to ballistic movements that require explosive motions and require greater skill. There are a number of trade-offs in each of these categories. Body weight exercises pose the least risk of injury and require little in the way of equipment but are limited in terms of benefits once a player gains a certain level of strength. Weight lifting machines are convenient and safer than free weights but fail to develop stabilizer muscle groups during the lifts like free weights do. This is why we recommend that exercise machines should only be used as a transition to free weights or for certain lifts that cannot be done with free weights among high school football players. Non-ballistic movements are less risky than ballistic movements and allow for the player to handle heavier weights (remember the explosive strength deficit discussed in the last chapter) than in ballistic movements. Ballistic movements, on the other hand, allow for more speed specific training that has greater transfer specificity to performance on the playing field.

There are certain general guidelines to resistance training that must also be understood in designing an effective resistance workout. One of the most important is that the focus of a workout, which affects the lifts selected, training loads used, and order of those lifts, is dependent on a priority system. This could be based on the time of the season (which will be addressed in the next chapter) as well as the nature of the lifts you plan to have your players do in a given workout. In general we typically recommend that compound lifts, otherwise known as *multi-joint lifts* should be done before lifts that isolate muscles. In addition, among the multi-joint exercises, the ones using the largest muscle groups should be performed first, followed by lifts that use smaller muscle groups. A good rule of thumb is to determine which lifts involve the heaviest weights and perform those lifts before those that involve less heavy weights. The exception to this rule is when a lift is of a higher priority, based on such factors as the speed of movement, skill requirement of the lift, potential for transfer specificity of the lift, etc. So, for example, a lower-body strength workout might involve the back squat and the power clean in the same workout. Even though your player can handle a greater weight in the back squat, the power clean might be performed first based on the need for greater technical skill in performing the lift properly.

The following pages contain the core lifts and exercises for developing strength and increases in lean body mass. They are presented in groupings and listed progressively from basic to advanced.

Core Lifts for the Development of Absolute Strength and Lean Body Mass

The following groupings are menus of exercises for developing absolute strength and increasing lean body mass. Remember that this component is the base for our ultimate goal of maximizing performance on the field. The lifts are performed in a controlled manner and as a player approaches his 1 RM in a given lift, the speed of the lift will be slower due to the explosive strength deficit referred to in Chapter 2. Once we have described each exercise and/or lift in this chapter, we will see how to select and program these exercises in Chapter 5.

I. Squat Variations and Progressions

The muscles trained in these lifts are the major muscles of the hips and thighs. These include the gluteal (buttocks), quadriceps (front of the thigh), and hamstring (back of the thigh) muscle groups.

The figure below shows a good method of teaching proper squatting form to beginners. The player uses the uprights of the squat rack for a counter balance and keeps the feet flat, head and chest up, and a good arch in the lower back. The player also gets a feel for the proper squat depth.

Free-standing squat

This exercise allows inexperienced players to learn basic squatting technique without additional resistance.

The player should wear a flat sole shoe (avoid running shoes since these lack lateral stability and can increase a player's risk of injury) such as a basketball or tennis shoe, and keep the feet flat at all times.

Feet should be shoulder width apart or wider. Toes should be slightly pointed out and knees should stay over the toes during the descent so that knees remain pointed out.

The athlete's upper body should maintain a good posture with head up, shoulders back, and a big chest position during both the down and up phase of the movement. Holding the uprights of a power rack is a good preliminary exercise to get the feel of proper depth and posture.

The player should slowly descend to a point where the top of the thigh is parallel to the floor. This can be done in a squat rack with a bungee cord stretched across the rack at the bottom position.

The athlete can come out of the bottom position with an explosive upward motion, making sure that he leads with his chest as he comes up and that his hips follow his chest (as opposed to the hips coming up first).

As an athlete progresses in this exercise (with good form being the key), the coach can have the player hold a barbell plate tight against his chest to add resistance.

Have the players practice proper breathing during this and all lifts by inhaling on the downward, or negative, portion of the lift and exhaling during the positive phase.

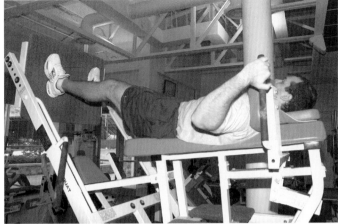

Leg press

A selectorized or plate loaded leg press machine is required for this lift.

The same body alignment factors for squatting should be addressed in the leg press form. This includes feet shoulder-width apart, toes pointed out, knees aligned with the toes (pointed out), and a stable upper body.

The weight should be lowered slowly to a point of 90 degrees of flexion at the knee joint and pressed up to a point just short of knee lockout. By keeping this slight flex in the knees at the top of the lift the player maintains constant tension on the thigh muscles.

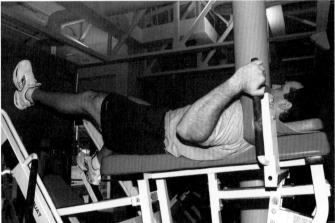

Single-leg leg press

This lift is performed on a leg press machine but is more difficult because greater balance and control is required.

The advantage to using this over a two-leg press is that each leg is trained separately so that the

chance of unbalanced development between legs is minimized.

Just as in the two-leg leg press a slow, controlled descent is required, and the toe is aligned with the knee throughout the lift.

Hack squat machine

The hack squat machine is similar to a squat machine except that the player pushes the weight at a slight angle backward.

The angle of the machine puts more resistance on the quadriceps muscles than a standard leg press and can be used to isolate this group.

The same body alignment factors for squatting should be addressed in the hack squat form. This includes feet shoulder-width apart, toes pointed out, knees aligned with the toes (pointed out), and a stable upper body.

Smith machine back squats

Feet are shoulder width apart or wider, toes pointed outward, knees aligned with the toes. The bar can be racked either across the base of the neck at the seventh cervical vertebrae (high bar position) or lower across the top of the shoulders. Research has found that this positioning has a greater effect on the emphasis of which quadriceps muscle were most active when performed during a parallel squat.

The advantage of the Smith machine is that stabilizer muscles are not activated as with a free weight back squat given the design of the Smith machine. This allows the player to concentrate on the prime mover muscles and not be as concerned with stabilization and balance. The trade-off is that the muscles, which provide stability and balance won't develop, so we recommend that this lift be used as a transition to free weight back squats.

Feet should stay flat on the floor, and a flat sole shoe is recommended over a running shoe. Elevating the heels is risky because it destabilizes the knee joint when the weight-bearing bone of the leg (tibia) is not in a fixed position. Usually the reason a player cannot descend and keep his feet flat is that he lacks balance and flexibility to do so. The best remedy is to gain flexibility.

It is important to emphasis good upper-body position and a slow descent during the negative phase of the lift to protect the lower back and knees respectively. This includes head up and a big chest posture with the bar positioned in alignment with the instep of both feet (over the hips).

The player should descend slowly, because research shows that most injuries in the back squat occur due to a rapid descent. The depth of descent is optional but because the research suggests that a deeper descent emphasizes the gluteal muscles more than a partial squat, we recommend a depth in which the top of the thigh is parallel to the floor.

Once the athlete reaches the end of the descent, he should extend explosively leading with his chest so that the hips follow the chest up. Avoid coming up hips first because this places undue stress on the lower back.

Bear machine squats

The Bear machine is a specialized machine that is useful in building strength and power while minimizing the risk of knee injuries with inexperienced lifters.

Foot placement allows minimization of *knee shear* (forces that can put undue stress on the knees) because the player stands with feet in an inclined position with his toes higher than his heels.

As with all squat variations the player executes the descent slowly to a position where the top of the thigh is parallel to the floor and then presses the weight upward.

Olympic-style squats

This lift is performed with free weights and is called Olympic style because the bar is racked higher on the back (seventh cervical spine, which is the most prominent spinal process at the base of the neck).

Some researchers believe that placing the bar in this position puts a greater emphasis on the quadriceps muscles (four muscles that make up the front of the thigh) and less on the hamstring muscle of the back of the thigh. Others believe that the difference is more related to which of the quadriceps muscles are emphasized, with the high bar rack stimulating the inner quads and low bar emphasizing the outer quads.

The form considerations are the same as in the Smith machine squat except that the feet are closer together and the toes point straight ahead. Good posture, big chest, and slow descents are critical coaching points.

Another variation to this lift is the speed squat. In the photo, this variation is done with 50 percent of a player's maximum usually for 5 repetitions. The athlete actually stops or pauses at the bottom of the descent phase and drives up as explosively as possible.

Power-style back squat

Again the power-style back squat is very similar to the Smith machine and Olympic squats except that the bar is placed lower on the shoulders. The ideal rack is when the top of the posterior deltoid muscles (rear shoulder muscles) forms the rack.

It often helps if the player cups his hands on the bar rather than grabbing the bar with thumbs wrapped around the bar and then pulls his elbows back. This allows the player to push the bar against his back rather than holding the bar up with his arms and to create a shelf for the bar.

The advantage to the low bar rack is that the player is better able to keep the bar over his hips and maintain a good upper body posture because the center of gravity of the bar is more in line with the lifter's center of gravity. Coach the players to hold the chest up and out and pull the shoulder blades toward each other, with a good arch in the lower back.

As mentioned earlier, the position of the bar appears to affect the emphasis of which thigh muscles are more active (quads vs. hamstrings; inner quads vs. outer quads) with the low rack emphasizing the hamstrings and/or outer quads.

The form considerations are the same as in the Smith machine squat. Good posture, toes out, big chest, slow descent. Keep the feet flat on the floor and a big chest throughout the lift with the first movement emphasizing hips back and weight on the heels. Do not bounce at the bottom of the lift. The upward motion should emphasize a motion in which the chest leads the hips, and the hips follow the chest.

Box squats

These are similar to the Olympic-style and power-style squats except that a box is placed behind the lifter to sit upon at the bottom of the lift. This removes all momentum and requires the player to generate strength from a dead stop.

Although this lift develops greater strength, it does carry a higher risk, especially if the player descends too rapidly or out of control. The spinal column can become compressed leading to injury to the intervertebral discs. However, box squats using very light resistance may be a good method for teaching beginning squatters to descend to a proper squat depth.

Front squats

This is another variation on the squat in which the bar is racked in front of the neck rather than on the back. The bar is held in the hands at shoulder level with the shoulders providing support and the elbow in a high position.

This is an advanced lift requiring good balance and technique. The front squat places more emphasis on the quadriceps of the thigh.

Place hands evenly on the bar with a grip that is slightly wider than shoulder width. Raise the elbows and rotate the hands around the bar.

Place the bar on the front deltoid (shoulder) muscles keeping the elbows up and upper arms parallel to the floor.

Align the hips under the bar with feet about hip width

Lift the chest up and out, and tilt the head up. Toes are pointed slightly outward. Coach the player to sit on his heels so that he remains flat footed.

Use the same slow downward movement as in the back squat, keeping the body erect and avoiding the bounce at the bottom. The emphasis is to avoid the tendency to lean forward, so stay flat footed with good posture by emphasizing that the athlete keeps his elbows high and chest up at the bottom of the lift.

This is a good developmental lift for the clean push press and push jerk because of the barbell rack position (hand and arm position).

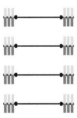

Snatch squat or extended squat

This variation of the squat requires the athlete to hold the barbell overhead in a snatch position with the arms wide and fully extended. This lift helps develop flexibility in the hips and ankles and develops shoulder stability.

The bar should be positioned slightly behind the head in the full arm extended position with elbows locked.

The squatting motion is then performed in a manner similar to the front squat. Remember to coach your athletes to keep the body erect and avoid the bounce at the bottom of the lift.

Even an experienced lifter should start with a light weight on this lift in order to practice maintaining a good arch in the lower back with the weight on the heels throughout the lift.

Box stepups

Chose a box height that creates a 90 degree angle at the knee when the foot is on the box (at least three different size boxes will be necessary to accommodate most players). This lift develops the quadriceps and gluteal muscles.

Position a barbell on the shoulders in a low rack position (see previous description) and start in front of the box at a distance of one to one and a half feet from the front side.

Maintaining an erect body position throughout the lift, step with one leg (the lead leg) onto the top of the box, placing the entire foot on the box.

The toes of the lead foot should point straight ahead or slightly inward.

Do not lean forward. Shift the body weight to the lead leg and push with the lead leg to move the body to a standing position on the box. It is important to coach the player to avoid pushing off with the trail leg.

At the top of the lift the hips and knees should be fully extended with feet together and weight evenly distributed.

On the downward movement, shift the body weight to the same lead leg used in the upward motion and, using the trail leg, step off the box onto the floor.

When the trail leg makes full contact with the floor, shift the body weight to the trail leg, and step off the box with the lead leg.

Once the lead leg is on the floor and the player has re-established his balance, repeat the movement with the other leg as the lead leg.

This isolateral lift, along with the lunge, is mechanically specific to sprinting and will help with speed development.

Lunges—stationary & walking

The basic bar position and mechanics of the lift will be the same for both variations of the lunge. We recommend taking the bar off a power rack, just as in the Olympic and back squats. The lift emphasizes development of the quadriceps, hamstrings, and gluteal muscles.

Start with the barbell across the shoulders in the low rack position. Posture of the upper body should be the same as in the back squat with chest up and out, shoulder blades back, and elbows up to create a shelf for the bar.

Lift the barbell out of the power rack and take at least three steps backward.

For the stationary lunge take one exaggerated step forward with one leg (the lead leg) keeping the foot and knee aligned and toes pointed straight ahead or slightly inward.

Plant the lead foot squarely on the floor and flex the lead leg so that the knee of the trailing leg is about one to two inches off the floor. Lower the body slowly in this movement and keep the upper body erect throughout the lift.

During this downward phase it is important to keep the knee of the lead foot directly over the lead foot (do not extend beyond the lead foot). Keep the lead foot flat on the floor and do not bounce at the bottom.

At the bottom of the lift, forcefully push off with the lead leg and bring the lead foot back into position beside the trail foot as the player stands to a fully erect position.

Pause and alternate lead legs as in the box step-ups. Once the player completes the set he steps forward and re-racks the weight.

In the walking lunge the lift is performed along a relatively long walkway that should be clear of normal weight room traffic and of an appropriate non-slip surface. The distance needed to perform this lift is typically 10 to 20 yards.

The player begins the lift in the same way as in the stationary lunge by stepping forward with the lead foot. However, at the bottom of the lift the player extends the lead leg while stepping forward with the trail leg so that the trail leg comes forward. The trail foot then joins the lead foot to allow the player to stand in a fully erect position.

Lateral squats or side lunges

This variation on the lunge is a good way to isolate the inner thigh muscles known as *adductors*, which provide stability to the hip and knee joints.

The bar position across the shoulders is the same as in the standing and walking lunges. Good upper body position is essential in minimizing injury.

Once the player removes the barbell from the rack and steps back three paces, he begins the lift by establishing a balanced stance with feet shoulder width apart.

He lifts the knee of the lead leg high, opens the hip by pointing the knee outward, and steps to the side (away from the midline of the body) with an exaggerated step rather than forward as in the standard lunge.

He then flexes the lead leg until the lead knee is at 90 degrees or thigh parallel to the floor. At the bottom of the lift he then pushes with the lead leg to bring the lead foot back toward the midline of the body and back into the original stance.

As in the standing lunge the player alternates legs until the set is complete and re-racks the weight.

All of these lunge variations can be performed with the player holding a dumbbell in each hand rather than a barbell across the shoulders. The player simply holds the dumbbells at his side while performing the lift.

Leg curls

The leg curl, performed on either a standing or prone (laying face down) leg curl machine is an important lift to include for good muscle balance. Research suggests that most hamstring injuries during sprinting occur because of over-developed quadriceps on the front of the thigh pull against under-developed hamstrings on the opposite side of the thigh.

The ideal ratio of quadriceps to hamstring strength is for the hamstrings to be at least two-thirds as strong as the quadriceps. This can be tested on standard leg curl and leg extension machines in the weight room.

The key to a proper leg curl is to keep the hips stabilized during the lift and use resistance that mirrors the training cycle. Thus, if you are in a high-intensity phase (heavy weights, low volume) use a heavy weight with low number of reps and sets for the leg curl. Also make sure the player moves though the full range of motion of leg flexion during the lift.

The lift may also be performed using only one leg at a time to ensure even development of the hamstrings in both legs.

II. Deadlift Variations and Progressions

The muscles trained in these lifts are the major muscles of the hips and thighs. These include the gluteal (buttocks), quadriceps (front of the thigh), and hamstring (back of the thigh) muscle groups. These also train the muscles of the low back (spinal erectors), upper back, and shoulder girdle.

Olympic deadlift to the knee

This lift can be done with dumbbells or a barbell. The stance is shoulder width, with the knees inside the arm. Hips are low, and the head is high.

Use a starting position with back arched, head up, shoulders over the bar, and knees flexed, similar to the starting position used in a standard Olympic-style lift. Grasp the bar with an overhand grip (pronated grip) with a hand spacing of a little wider than shoulder width.

Drive with the legs to lift the bar off the floor to a height just below the knees. This lift is an excellent way to teach the initial phase of the power clean to inexperienced athletes. The key coaching point is to instruct the player to lift with the legs rather than the lower back.

At the top position of the lift the player then lowers the bar back to the floor under control. The athlete should be sure to reset his position (back arched, head up, etc.) before attempting the next repetition.

Coach players not to jerk the weight off the floor but to slowly lift the weight under control.

Straight leg deadlift

This lift can be done with dumbbells, barbell, or a trap bar.

The player can start at the top of the lift by taking the bar off of a power rack or can start at the bottom of the lift by lifting the bar off the floor. The player should maintain a good arch in the lower back and keep his head up during the movement.

From the floor with the legs almost completely straight (slight bend in the knees), the player lifts the weight using hip and lower back muscles to a fully erect position.

The player then lowers the weight, bending at the waist, back to the floor while maintaining just a slight flex in the knees.

Given the relatively high risk of lower back injury, the coach must make sure that the player's lower back is well warmed up and stretched. The amount of weight used in this lift should also be relatively low considering the potential risk of injury.

Using a trap bar, rather than a barbell, lessens the risk of lower back injury, especially in inexperienced lifters.

Romanian deadlift (RDL)

This lift starts out in a similar position as the straight leg deadlift with a good arch in the lower back and head-up posture. The knees will be flexed to a slightly greater degree than in the straight leg deadlift, but knees will not bend.

The player assumes a shoulder-width stance with his knees inside the arms, similar to the Olympic-style deadlift, and keeps his feet flat on the floor at the start.

Maintaining a good lower back arch with arms fully extended, the player slowly stands up straight keeping the bar close to the body, thrusting the hips forward, and continues to pull until the knees are under the bar.

In the full body erect position maintaining a bend in the knees, the player flexes the hips, slowly and under control as if he were taking a bow. He lowers the bar to a point between the knees and ankles and then rocks back on his heels (it will vary how low a lifter can bring the bar due to hamstring flexibility).

The player will try to bring the toes up to the top of the shoes and move the hips back at the bottom of the lift. From the lowest point of the lift, the player slowly stands up straight and repeats the upward motion.

If performed properly, this lift targets the hamstrings and hip muscles very effectively. This is especially important for sprinting and speed development.

Sumo deadlifts

The starting position of the sumo-style deadlift is quite different that the other deadlifting styles described in this section. Rather than a conventional stance in which the feet are a shoulder width apart and arms are outside the thighs, the sumo uses an exaggerated wide stance with the arms inside the thighs.

The player steps up so the bar touches the inside of the shins with feet as wide as possible and toes pointed slightly outward. Keeping his elbows close to the body with arms straight, the player reaches straight down with an opposing grip (one hand palm up, one hand palm down) and grips the bar.

It is an important coaching point to instruct the player to keep his back straight, head up, and chest out to maintain proper posture and protect the lower back. He should also sit back in the lift by keeping his heels flat on the floor and using the weight as a counter-balance.

The initial drive should be from the legs with the upper body leading the hips, and the top of the lift occurs when the player is standing fully erect with shoulders back.

The weight is then lowered steadily back to the floor by flexing the legs. Avoid bending at the waist during the negative phase and make sure the athlete sets himself in the proper starting position before he starts the next repetition.

Conventional deadlift

The conventional deadlift is similar to the sumo-style deadlift except that the feet are closer together (in the range of shoulder width) and the arms are outside the thighs.

The player steps up so the bar touches the front of the shins with toes pointed forward or slightly outward. Keeping his elbows on the outside of the thighs with arms straight, the player reaches straight down with an opposing grip (one hand palm up, one hand palm down) and grips the bar.

It is an important coaching point to instruct the player to keep his back straight, head up, and chest out and up to maintain proper posture and protect the lower back. He should also sit back in the lift by keeping his heels flat on the floor and using the weight as a counter-balance.

The initial drive should be from the legs with the chest leading the hips, and the top of the lift occurs when the player is standing fully erect with shoulders back. Coach the athlete to push his feet through the floor.

The weight is then lowered under control back to the floor by flexing the legs. Avoid bending at the waist during the negative phase and make sure the athlete sets himself in the proper starting position before he starts the next repetition.

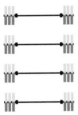

Conventional deadlift on blocks

The form considerations are exactly the same as in the conventional deadlift from the floor except that the player is standing on either wooden blocks or weight plates from two to four inches high.

The added starting height places a greater stress on the lower back so be sure the player is properly warmed up and stretched prior to attempting this lift. The benefit of the increased height is greater development of the hip and lower back muscles.

It is critical that the player avoids initiating the lift by straightening the legs forcing the lower back and hip muscles into an awkward position. The coaching cue is to have the player sit back in the lift and lead with his chest.

This is an advanced lift and more difficult than conventional deadlifts due to the extended range of motion involved. Strict form is critical in this lift to avoid injury.

III. Press Variations and Progressions

These lifts and exercises primarily focus on the muscles of the upper body, which includes the pectoral (chest), deltoid (shoulders), and tricep (back of the arm) muscles.

Push-up variations—modified, military, feet-elevated, and grip-width variation

The push-up is the most basic of upper body exercises, which can be done anywhere requiring little in the way of equipment. It is especially recommended as a prerequisite for the bench press.

In all varieties of push-up the same form considerations should be maintained: the head, shoulders, and hips should move together during the upward and downward phases, with the arms fully locked at the top of the lift and the chest touching the floor at the bottom of the exercise.

For players with low upper-body strength and/or a high body weight the modified push-up is recommended. Unfortunately this style of push-up is often referred to as a girl push-up, but the coach must dispel this misconception (to the whole team) and emphasize that the modified push-up is a progression phase that is important toward developing the bench press.

The modified push-up is done with the player starting on his knees and the body in an extended position supported by straight arms. The head, shoul-

ders, and hips should form a straight line, avoiding the tendency to elevate the hips.

The player lowers himself until his chest (not the stomach) touches the ground and then presses to a full arm locked position. The head, shoulders, and hips should move together.

The military-style push-up is performed in the same way except that the feet form the fulcrum of the exercise and are on the ground rather than the knees. Again, the head, shoulders, and hips should move together.

Feet-elevated push-ups are performed with the feet up on a bench in a style similar to military push-ups. Elevating the feet requires the player to press a greater percentage of his body weight to add a greater intensity to the exercise than standard military push-ups.

By variation of the width of the hands (grip width), the coach can emphasize different muscle groups. The general rule of thumb is that a wider grip puts more emphasis on the chest and front of the shoulders, while a narrower grip emphasizes the triceps.

As with all lifts the player should exhale on the positive motion (extension) and inhale on the negative motion (flexion).

Clapping push-ups

This is a plyometric form of the push-up that is more speed specific for power and is more advanced than the standard military push-ups. It would require a more advanced level of strength to perform.

The exercise starts out like the standard military push-ups with a slow downward motion to the low position, but the upward motion involves the athlete explosively pressing upward so that his hands actually leave the floor, and his feet momentarily support him. In this airborne state, the player claps his hands together and then catches himself in the original push-up position as his body moves downward.

The key coaching point is to instruct the player to accelerate through the upward motion.

Although this is listed as a strength exercise, it would also be a good power/plyometric exercise.

Medicine ball push-ups

The player places both hands on top of a medicine ball with fingers pointed forward. This requires the player to balance himself and may take a bit of practice.

The player then pushes off from the ball and extends his arms to the side at about a shoulder width. The player then catches himself in a push-up position and flexes the arms to allow the body to descend.

At the lowest point of the downward phase the player again pushes upward with an explosive motion so that the hands leave the floor and catches himself on the medicine ball in the original starting position.

Although this is listed as a strength exercise, it would also be a good power/plyometric exercise.

Cinder block push-ups—regular or feet elevated

The basic position is the same as the standard military push-up except that each hands is placed on one cinder block, with the player holding the sides of the block. A towel placed over the block will minimize the chance of hand injury due to the rough surface of the block.

He then lowers his body until his chest touches the block, explosively pushes off to elevate his body. In this position the palms will be facing each other.

By elevating the feet, the intensity is increased. The higher the feet are elevated, the greater the percentage of the player's body weight lifted.

Advanced athletes can add resistance by having a coach balance a plate on the upper back while the athlete performs the exercise.

Push-ups with chains

A length of heavy chain provides what is known as variable resistance to the standard push-up. The chain is suspended in a power rack and the athlete assumes the standard military push-up position with the end of the chain touching his back while he is in the down position.

As the athlete presses upward, a greater amount of chain is added to his back, thus increasing the resistance gradually as the player approaches the top position.

When the player moves downward, more of the chain is suspended so the resistance actually lessens.

Machine bench press—flat, inclined and declined

Once a player has advanced though the progression of push-ups, the next phase is to use any one of a variety of bench press machines. These lessen the risk of injury and are ideal for the beginning lifter because the machine will develop the prime mover muscles of the chest, shoulders, and triceps. The only trade-off is that the machines fail to stimulate the stabilizer muscles associated with the free weight version of the lift.

As mentioned in the push-up section, the width of the grip position affects the emphasis of which muscle groups work harder. The wider the hands are apart, the more emphasis is placed on the chest and front shoulders; as the hands move in toward the midline of the body, the more emphasis is on the triceps.

The level of incline or decline will affect the way the pectoral or chest muscle is developed. Many peo-ple think that the pecs are one united muscle, when in actuality the muscle consists of two distinct heads. The upper pectorals are isolated when an athlete performs an inclined bench press, where the upper body is higher than the hips. The lower head of the pectorals are isolated when the hips are higher than the upper body as in the decline bench press. The flat bench works both upper and lower pectorals.

With all machine lifts it is important to emphasize control of the weight, especially in the negative or downward motion. Weights should be lowered under control (no plates crashing).

Some machines are isolateral, allowing one arm to be exercised at a time.

Machine-seated shoulder press

Like the machine bench press variations, the machine-seated shoulder press is less risky and requires less balance and coordination than the free weight version of the lift.

Unlike the bench press, the seated shoulder press does not affect the chest muscles as much as it emphasizes the shoulders and triceps. Because a smaller muscle mass is involved in the shoulder press, a lower amount of weight will typically be used.

Most machines start the player in the down position with the bar starting at the shoulders, grasping the bar with a slightly wider than shoulder-width hand spacing and an overhand grip. This can be done in front of the neck or behind the neck with the variation placing more emphasis on the front shoulders with the former and the back shoulders and trapezius muscles with the latter.

In either case, the player presses the weight upward to a full lockout position above the head, and then slowly lowers the weight under control to the original position.

Some machines are isolateral, allowing one arm to be exercised at a time.

Free weight bench press variations—flat, inclined, and declined

The free weight bench press will be the next progression from the machine version of the lift because very important stabilizer muscles are used to balance the weight and maintain the groove which describes the normal pathway of the bar during the lift.

The player lies flat on the bench and takes an evenly spaced, pronated grip on the barbell. The width of the hands on the bar will emphasis either triceps (close grip) or chest and shoulders (wide grip). Offensive linemen will benefit most from a narrow grip. Some lifters like to use a false grip in which the bar rests on the palms of the hands and the thumbs are not wrapped around the bar (thumb and fingers all on the same side). For safety sake we recommend against this grip and suggest wrapping the thumb and fingers around the barbell.

Feet should be out to the sides of the bench and remain flat throughout the lift. The lower-body stability is very important because much of the mechanics of proper benching depends on it.

The chin should be tucked into the chest, and the lower back should have a slight arch. Hips and shoulder blades should remain on the bench during the lift, and excess arching of the back should be discouraged.

The barbell is removed from the rack and held above the chest in a full extension of the elbows. The lowering of the bar should be done under control until the bar touches the chest, followed by the immediate raising of the bar until the elbows are fully extended.

The upper arm should remain at a 45 degree angle to the torso throughout the lift. During the descent of the bar inhale; during the ascent exhale.

As with the machine bench press varying the angle of the bench places greater emphasis on the two different heads of the pectorals: Incline bench hits the upper pec; decline bench hits the lower pectorals.

Free weight bench press with chains

Form considerations are the same for this variation of the bench press as with the techniques discussed in the standard bench press. The exception is that heavy chains, weighing 25 to 30 pounds and approximately four feet long (this may require several length of chain depending on the thickness) are attached to each end of the barbell so that the chains just touch the floor when the weight is held in the up position of the lift.

As the player lowers the weight, the chains pile up on the floor below thereby reducing the amount of weight on the bar. As the player presses the weight and more of the chain length is raised off the floor, the barbell becomes heavier.

This lift allows for variable resistance to emphasize improved triceps strength and negate the effect of momentum as the weight moves upward. (Thus increasing the amount of force required to keep the weight moving upward.)

Bench press rack lockouts

Another way to work the bench press through its weakest range of motion is through the rack lockout. This is set up in a power rack by setting the spotting bars at a specific point in the lift, which represents that player's sticking point (anywhere from one inch off the chest to one inch short of the lockout).

Once the spotting bars are set, place a barbell on the power rack and position the player on the bench as you would for a regular flat bench press.

Choose an appropriate grip width (depending on which muscles need the most work) and press the weight from the rack to a fully extended position. Once lockout is achieved, lower the bar back to the rack and repeat.

The further the barbell is from the chest, the more weight the lifter can usually handle. This lift is designed to work on a player's sticking point in the bench by isolating that particular range of motion.

Stop and stab close grip bench press

This lift can be performed with dumbbells or a barbell. The form considerations are the same as with a standard bench except that the elbows are slightly closer to the body (a 30 degree angle as opposed to a 45 degree angle of the upper arm to the body).

The bar is slowly lowered to the chest and paused for a count of one-one-thousand and then raised to a full elbow extension with a short stabbing motion. The speed of the upward motion is emphasized in this lift.

This lift is ideal for offensive and defensive linemen because it mimics the arm action of pass blocking (elbows in close to the body) and defensive hand techniques.

Seated shoulder press and behind-the-neck press with free weights

The player sits in a seated press bench or on a flat bench and grasps the barbell with a pronated grip of about shoulder width.

The barbell is removed from the rack and extended overhead with elbows locked. The bar is lowered under control to the upper chest and then pressed to a full elbow extension.

The behind the neck version of this lift is performed in the same manner except that the bar is lowered behind the head until it touches the base of the neck. The bar is then pressed in the same manner as the standard lift.

The lift can also be performed with dumbbells by either lifting both dumbbell simultaneously or in an alternating fashion where one dumbbell is up while the other is down. In either case hold the dumbbells so that the palm of each hand is facing the opposite hand.

The overhead presses can also be performed in the standing position. An important coaching point is to minimize the amount of backward bending or back arch with players attempting this lift. Emphasize that the player keep his back straight as he presses the weight. Also the player should not use his legs to cheat on the lift (this is why many coaches stick to the seated version of the lift) or use excessive body movement, which could increase risk of injury.

Weight Lifting Exercises for Developing Explosive Power

Olympic Lift Variations and Plyometric Exercises

The following section represents a menu of lifts and plyometric exercises for developing power, which is the second tier of our model for developing athleticism outlined in Chapter 2. As in the preceding section we will describe each lift or exercise individually and later show you how to incorporate them into the training cycles. With these lifts and exercises velocity becomes a critical factor. The lifts are performed with lighter than maximum weights to preserve the velocity specific nature of the lift. The research suggests that most athletes can handle about 30 to 35 percent of their 1 RM weight at maximum velocity. Any weight heavier than that will result in a slower lift. Because this is a percent of the 1 RM, you should begin to see why gaining strength (increasing the 1 RM) has an effect on the ability to gain power because 30 percent of a high number is larger than 30 percent of a low number.

I. Clean Variations and Teaching Progressions

Muscles trained include the hip extensors (gluteals, lower back, and hamstrings) as well as muscles of the legs (quadriceps) and upper body pulling muscles (trapezius, shoulders, upper back, and biceps)

Machine shrugs

Some machine manufacturers like Hammer Strength® and Nautilus® have special machines designed to replicate this movement. If your facility does not have these specialized machines, you may use any machine that allows the player to hold a bar at a level just below waist height (i.e., universal bench press station, low pulley, etc.).

The player then uses an explosive motion of shrugging the shoulders while holding the bar. The shoulders should be raised as high as possible with the player attempting to touch his ears with the tops of his shoulders. At the top the player should hold the shrug position for a short pause and then lower his shoulders to the original starting position.

Remember that velocity is the target adaptation, so do not use a weight that is too heavy. If the athlete can't move his shoulders through a full range of motion (as measured by a non-weighted shrug) or

with the proper explosive motion, then lower the resistance.

This shoulder movement is closely related to the motion used in the power clean.

Barbell or dumbbell shrugs

The free weight version of the machine shrug. The player takes the barbell off of a power rack using opposing grip and holds the weight below the beltline at a full arm extension lowering the shoulders as much as possible while continuing to maintain good posture and a stable upper body.

The player shrugs the shoulders upward as high as possible, attempting the touch the top of the shoulders to the ears. As in the machine version, the shrug is paused at the top of the movement and the bar is lowered to the down position under control.

The shoulders should move straight up and down rather than in a circular motion (as if the player was

non-verbally saying "I don't know" by shrugging the shoulders).

This lift can be adapted to a power shrug by instructing the player to lower the bar in the hang position to the mid-thigh by flexing the knees and bending slightly at the waist. The player then uses an explosive hip and knee extension, immediately followed by the shoulder shrug to pull the bar up. The Kazmeyer shrug is a variation in which the player successively performs 10 reps with a wide grip, 10 reps with a normal grip, and 10 reps with a narrow grip for a total of 30 reps/set.

Barbell or dumbbell jump shrug

This lift can be performed from the floor or from the hang position in which the bar is held at arm's length just below the waist (can be taken from a power rack).

The lift teaches some of the elementary movements of the power clean, especially the initial drive phase of that lift.

From the floor the player assumes the same initial position as in the Olympic-style deadlift. Legs flexed, head is up, chest out, with a good arch in the lower back and hips are low. The shoulders should be over the bar when using a barbell.

The player drives with his legs, making sure that the chest leads with an explosive motion. He continues until he is standing erect and continues in a jumping motion so that the ankles are extended and he is up on his toes. The shoulder, hip, knee, and ankle joints should be in one line at full extension. The player also shrugs the shoulders explosively at the top of the lift keeping the head in a neutral position. It is important for the player to avoid putting his chin down, which may cause the body to lean forward.

This lift can also be performed with dumbbells or a trap bar.

Upright rows

The player holds the barbell in front of the body in an extended hang position with the hands close together (approximately six inches apart) on the center of the bar in an overhand grip.

While keeping the body stabilized, the player pulls the weight upward until the elbows are higher than the shoulders. Forward and backward motion of the hips and body should be minimized so that the shoulders and arms perform the work, and the bar should be kept as close to the body as possible.

The bar is held at the top of the lift just under the chin and then lowered under control.

Hang clean high pulls

This lift is similar to the upright row except that the form is not as strict relative to forward and backward body motion, and the hands are spaced shoulder width apart. In fact the hips are used in an explosive motion to elevate the bar from the initial hang position.

The player slightly flexes the knees at the start and drives the hips forward to initiate the upward motion. He continues to pull upward keeping the bar close to the body and pulls the bar as high as possible, extending the legs and shrugging the shoulders at the top of the lift.

At the top of the lift the bar is immediately lowered under control to the starting position with the legs slightly flexed to act as shock absorbers. The initial position is reestablished, and the next repetition can be done.

This lift can also be performed starting at the mid-thigh position, like a hang clean except that the player doesn't catch the bar, or from the floor like a combination of the Olympic deadlift and hang clean (again, without the catch).

Hang clean

Once the player progresses through the shrug and power pull variations described above, he will be ready for a more advanced level of the clean called a hang clean.

This exercise can be performed from blocks or with the barbell taken from a power rack, and can even be done with dumbbells.

The player grasps the bar with an overhand (pronated grip) and stands with the back arched and chest up. It is critical to maintain this posture and to avoid rounding the back during the lift.

Keeping the back tight the player flexes the knees and slides the bar down the thighs, bending forward at the waist, until the bar is just above the knees. The shoulders should be over or slightly in front of the bar at the lowest point.

From this position, the player explosively drives the hips forward and extends the legs, keeping the bar close to the body. As his hips rotate through the bar, he also rises up on the balls of the feet as if he were jumping.

Once the body is fully extended, the player bends the elbows and pulls the bar up as high as possible, keeping the bar close to the chest. All of this upward motion is continuous, but it is important to emphasize that the action of the hips and legs should occur before the arm pull. A typical mistake is for the player to begin the arm pull too early and lose the power of the hip extension and rotation.

When the bar reaches the highest point, under the chin, the player is ready for the catch phase of the lift where he jumps under the bar by quickly lowering his hips. Either the split, where one foot moves forward and one foot moves back very quickly; or the straddle, where the feet are quickly moved to the side into a wide stance, achieves this. Both of these will have the effect of quickly lowering the hips so that the player can jump under the bar and catch it in the front rack position.

A good coaching cue for completing the catch phase is to tell the player to imagine that he is breaking a stick with his hands. This action will rotate the elbows quickly allowing the rack position to occur, and help the player keep his elbows high. The bar should rest on the front shoulders and clavicle rather than being solely supported by the arms, with the hands holding the bar loosely.

The bar is then returned to the hang position under control in preparation for the next repetition. Hang cleans can be performed with dumbbells as well.

Power clean

The mechanics of the power clean is really a combination of the Olympic-style deadlift and the hang clean. This is why teaching the progression is so important, because the power clean is such a technically difficult lift to teach.

The lift can be broken down into three distinct phases: the drive phase or first pull, the scoop phase or second pull, and the catch phase.

The initial drive phase position is similar to the Olympic-style deadlift because the player takes a hip-width stance with feet flat and toes pointed slightly outward. He bends at the knees, head up with hips low and grasps the bar with a slightly wider than shoulder width, overhand grip. The back should be arched and rigid with the head facing forward, chest high, and shoulder blades back.

The arms remain straight, with elbows rotated slightly outward, as the player begins the initial motion of driving the legs to a full extension in an explosive manner. The angle of the back remains constant, and the player avoids flexing the arms during this phase.

The bar should move straight up (not around the knees), and shoulders should remain slightly in front of the bar. As the legs extend, the knees move back under the bar in preparation for the scoop phase.

The scoop phase or second pull occurs when the knees re-bend (also known as the *double knee bend*) once the bar passes the knees. This enables the lifter to flex the hips in preparation for the explosive hip extension similar to a jumping motion as the hips move forward. The coach should tell the player to move his hips through the bar.

The bar should brush off of the thighs with the arms still extended (again be careful that the athlete doesn't bend the arms too soon), followed by the player shrugging his shoulders and rising up on the balls of his feet, fully extending his body.

Once the body is fully extended, the player finally bends the arms and pulls the bar high in preparation for the catch phase. The catch phase requires the player to lower his hips quickly and catch the bar in the front rack position as described in the hang clean.

The player can use either the split or straddle method for the catch as previously described.

II. Snatch Variation

The snatch is similar to the clean except that the grip width is exaggerated in a much wider grip, and the arms remain straight (with one exception in the high pull) while the bar is lifted. The snatch variations will use the same muscle groups as the cleans.

Snatch grip shrug

Similar to the standard shrug except that the grip is wider.

The bar is taken from the power rack and held at full arm extension just below the waist.

Keeping the rest of the body stable the player shrugs the shoulder straight up as high as possible, with a slight pause at the top.

The power version of this is to perform the lift by flexing the knees and bending slightly forward at the waist at the start of the lift. The player then uses an explosive hip and knee extension, immediately followed by the shoulder shrug to pull the bar up.

Note the player finishes the lift by coming up on his toes similar to a jumping motion.

Snatch-grip Olympic-style deadlift

This is similar to the standard Olympic-style deadlift, except for the wider grip.

The player grips the bar in an overhand grip with his feet hip-width apart, chest high and hips low.

Using the legs the player extends at the knee to lift the barbell to a point just below the knees. He should avoid using his lower back as the prime mover muscle during this lift and lift with a good leg drive.

Hang snatch high pulls

This is like the standard power pulls except for the wide grip.

The bar is taken from the power rack and held at full arm extension just below the waist.

The player performs the lift by flexing the knees and bending slightly forward at the waist at the start of the lift until the bar is at mid-thigh. From this position, he explosively extends the hips and knees, shrugs the shoulders, and pulls the bar high by bending the elbows. The wide grip will not allow as high of a pull as in the standard version of this lift where the hands are close together.

It is important for the lifter to keep his elbows rotated outward and keep the bar close to the body during the upward phase. The head must stay in the neutral (avoid putting the head down) position, and the arms stay straight until the body reaches full extension.

Hang snatch

This is the snatch version of the hang clean and starts with the wide grip and full arm extension used in the hang snatch power pull.

The player will tend to lean forward more in this lift than in the hang clean due to the wide grip when he flexes the legs to lower the bar on the thighs just above the knees.

At the bottom of the lift the player extends the hips and knees and shrugs the shoulders in an explosive manner. The bar will brush the thighs and is lifted overhead in one motion if the lifter continues to keep his arms straight and relaxed as long as possible.

The bar is caught overhead with the elbows locked (there should be no pressing) and rotated outward, while the player simultaneously lowers his hips using either the split or straddle method described in the clean.

The arms should be behind the ears in the overhead lockout position, with the body leaning slightly forward. If you cannot catch in the proper position, your grip has to be wider.

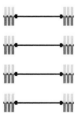

Power snatch

This lift is similar to the hang snatch except that the barbell starts on the floor or a lifting platform rather than the hang position.

The starting position is similar to the power clean except for the wider hand spacing. This is critical because the bar is lifted from the floor to the overhead position in one motion.

Extend the body and explode upward, shrugging the shoulders and driving with the legs as described in the power clean. The bar will brush a little higher on the thighs (and possibly on the hips) in the power snatch when compared to the power clean. The key coaching point is to emphasize the leg drive rather than using the lower back to lift the weight.

Keep his arms straight and relaxed as long as possible.

The bar is caught overhead with the elbows locked (there should be no pressing) and rotated outward, while the player simultaneously lowers his hips using either the split or straddle method described in the clean.

The arms should be behind the ears in the overhead lockout position, with the body leaning slightly forward. If you cannot catch in the proper position, your grip has to be wider.

The bar is guided back to the platform under control once the overhead position is established if bumper plates are used. If a conventional barbell is used, the player may lower the bar to the clean position and then down to the floor.

III. Push Press and Push Jerk Variations

The main muscle groups trained in this group of lifts are the hip extensors (gluteal, lower back, and hamstring) with the added involvement of the muscle groups that are used in pressing a weight overhead (trapezius, shoulders, and tricep).

Standard push press and behind the neck push press

This can be performed with the player power cleaning the weight to the initial position or taking the weight from a power rack with a shoulder-width grip.

The weight is held on the top of the chest, at the shoulder level, with the feet shoulder width apart and the lifter looking straight ahead.

The player slightly flexes his knees and hips as if preparing to jump and explosively extends the legs and hips, thrusting the bar up and off the chest and upward until the elbows lock out in full arm extension overhead.

The head should be placed in front of the bar (move forward) when the weight is locked out. The bar is then lowered under control to the top of the chest.

The lift can also be performed starting with the weight behind the neck. The bar is held at the base of the neck and, using the same leg and hip motion as the standard push press and thrust upward off of the neck to an overhead lockout position.

The bar is returned under control to the original behind the neck position. This variation will place more emphasis on the posterior shoulder muscles.

Push jerk

The lift is similar to the push press because the starting position is the same. The bar is held at the top of the chest at shoulder level and is thrust upward using the hips and legs to drive the weight upward.

As the bar progresses upward, the player re-bends his knees so that he drops under the weight and then locks his elbows out (unlike the push press where there is no re-bending of the knees).

The lift is complete when the lifter stands erect with the weight locked out overhead. The head should be placed in front of the bar (move forward) when the weight is locked out. The bar is then lowered under control to the top of the chest.

A variation to re-bending the knees in the push jerk would be to have the player perform a split or straddle motion to drop under the bar. This would be especially useful with advanced lifters who are lifting relatively heavy weights.

The lift can also be performed using dumbbells rather than a barbell.

Assistance Lifts

These lifts are used to specifically target smaller muscle groups involved in some of the compound weight training exercises, which use many muscle groups together. A *compound lift* is one that involves several joints, as oppose to an *isolation lift*, which includes only one or two. An example of a compound lift would be the power squat in which the ankle, knee, and hip joint are in motion. In comparison, a leg curl involves only the knee joint in motion and would be classified as an isolation lift. The assistance lifts are also variations on the major lifts outlined in the previous section, in which the lift is performed at different angles or by lifting with one arm at a time.

Gluteal/hamstring raises and hyperextensions for the low back

The gluteal/hamstring raises exercise, shown above, targets the lower back muscles that are used in the squats, deadlifts, and most Olympic-style lifts. Often the smaller muscle groups represent the weak link in the chain of the combined muscle groups used in a compound lift and can be isolated.

The feet are secured at the ankles, and the hips are stabilized so that the edge of the hip pad is at the beltline of the player. Hands are clasped behind the neck.

The player extends the lower back muscles under control until the lower back is in a hyperextended position with the knees flexed. It is important to pause in this up position before returning to the starting position.

The player then returns to the starting position under control and prepares for the next repetition.

A less advanced version of this exercise can also be performed on an angled hyperextension machine.

Reverse hyperextension

This exercise requires a specially designed apparatus that stabilizes the upper body while the movement occurs in the lower body. This essentially targets the lower back muscle as in the standard hyperextension exercise except that the lower body moves rather than the upper body.

The player stabilizes his upper body by grasping the handles and pulling his chest tight to the table.

His legs are restrained at the ankles by the strap attached to the action arm of the apparatus.

The player lifts his legs as high as possible by flexing the muscle of the lower back and gluteals.

Once the legs are elevated as high as possible, the player lowers the weight under control and prepares for the next repetition. This is an outstanding device for developing body core strength.

Incline bench press

This lift is performed on a bench that has a 33 to 45 degree angle of incline. The closer the incline is to 45 degrees, the more the front of the shoulders (anterior deltoids) is emphasized in the lift.

The purpose of including inclined bench presses in the workout is to isolate the upper chest muscles (upper pectorals). For certain positions, such as offensive linemen in a pass-blocking stance, this muscle group is used.

The player takes the bar from the rack and holds it in a position above the eyes. He then lowers the bar under control to a position at the top of the chest just below the collarbone.

He then presses the weight up to the original starting position. This lift can also be done with dumbbells—hands using a neutral grip.

Bar dips

This exercise is performed on parallel bars and can be augmented by adding weights to the player or can be done using the player's body weight alone.

The movement of bar dips emphasizes the lower chest muscles (lower pectorals) as well as the triceps of the arm.

The player starts in the up position with the arms locked in full extension. The downward motion must be under control or else the player will risk injury to the shoulders (especially rotator cuff).

The down position is achieved when the shoulders are lower than the elbows. If the player goes straight down and straight up while keeping his head down, there will be a greater emphasis on the triceps. If the player keeps his head up and chest out, while leaning forward on the downward motion, more emphasis will be on the lower chest muscles.

Weights can be added by using a weight belt with a chain.

Bench dips (weighted and unweighted)

The player places two benches in a parallel position as shown.

He places his feet on one bench and his hands on the other with his arms locked, with his body weight supported by the hands and feet.

Under control the player lowers his body until his elbows are in a position higher than his shoulders.

From this bottom position the player extends the arms back to the original starting position.

This can be performed without weight for the beginner as well as with a plate balanced on the legs for increased resistance.

This exercise develops the triceps, lats, and shoulders.

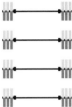

Dumbbell bench presses and alternate dumbbell presses

These lifts can be performed on a flat bench, an inclined bench, or a Swiss ball.

The Swiss ball will add a body balance component because the player must balance himself on the ball while performing the lift. This variation is more advanced so it should only be used among experienced lifters.

The dumbbells can be lifted together or can be lifted in an alternating fashion. The grip is a thumbs up position in which the wrist is held in a natural position.

The advantage to performing this lift is that it develops both sides of the body equally. This is especially useful in the case of a player who has an imbalance in his bench press where one arm lags behind during the pressing motion.

Dumbbell shoulder press

This is another variation on the overhead press that can also be performed in either an alternating fashion or with the arms lifting together.

The grip is a thumbs-up position in which the wrist is neutral. The dumbbell variation allows for even development of the shoulders and is a good way to correct an imbalance.

It is performed on an upright bench with good posture (head up, arch in the lower back) and feet flat on the floor.

In the alternating version the dumbbell in the down position counterbalances the dumbbell in the upward movement.

Rotator cuff dumbbell exercises

This is a great injury prevention lift, which strengthens the muscles that stabilize the shoulder. It is especially important for players who perform heavy bench presses.

The player lies on his side on a bench as shown, holding a dumbbell with an overhand grip.

While keeping his elbow close to his body, the player lifts the dumbbell until his forearm is parallel to the floor, pauses with the weight in this upward position, and then slowly lowers the weight to the starting position.

The form used in this exercise is very important, so a player should not use a weight that is so heavy that the proper form is compromised.

Dumbbell pullovers

The player assumes a position perpendicular to the bench with his shoulders supported by the bench and his feet flat on the floor.

A partner hands the player a dumbbell, which is held in his extended arms in a position above the forehead as shown.

The player lowers the weight as far down as possible with arms slightly bent, stretching the torso.

At the bottom the player lifts the weight to the upward position using chest and lat muscles.

Seated plate lift

This exercise targets the front shoulder muscles (anterior deltoids).

The player sits at the edge of a bench and holds a plate as shown in the figure above.

The exercise is performed with straight arms as the player lifts the plate to an overhead position and then lowers the weight under control to the starting position.

Dumbbell 21s

This lift isolates the three heads of the shoulders (front, middle, and rear).

The player performs seven repetitions of each variation, starting with lateral raises in which the dumbbells are lifted to the side until the arms are parallel with the floor. The player then performs front raises and then bends forward slightly to perform back raises.

In each variation the dumbbell is lifted to shoulder level with elbows higher than the shoulders.

One-arm dumbbell rows

This lift isolates the rear deltoid muscles as well as the lats.

The player kneels on a bench holding a dumbbell and uses his free hand to stabilize his body.

The weight is lifted straight up, with the arm flexed and the emphasis on squeezing the shoulder blades.

On the downward motion the player must control the descent and stretch the arm to its full range of extension, without moving the torso.

Abdominal Exercises

No core exercise manual would be complete without discussing abdominal muscles as a key core element. The abdominal muscles are the link between transmitting power from the lower body to the upper body. They are also critical in maintaining posture in many of the core lifts in which a weight is lifted in a standing position. The following are a variety of exercises that target the abdominal muscles. There are more than 20 different exercises listed, so boredom should not be a problem.

Crunches

This is probably the most familiar exercise for the abdominals, yet are often performed with incorrect form, which can place undue stress on the lower back and neck.

The proper form for crunches requires that the hip flexor muscles (the ones that lift the thigh in a standing position as in a high knee position) must be neutralized so that the abdominal muscles are used.

Placing the legs upon a bench neutralizes the hip flexors, so that the legs and hips are at a 90 degree angle. In addition, the player elevates the body off the floor until the shoulder blades barely clear the ground. Elevating the body any further results in greater hip flexor activity.

The player places his hands either on his ears or crosses his arms and places his hands on his shoulders. The player should not clasp his hands behind his neck because there is an increased risk of neck injury.

The player then concentrates on contracting his abdominal muscles until his shoulder blades clear the ground. At the top of the crunch he should pause momentarily and then return to the starting position. This is more effective than a fast ballistic movement toward targeting the abdominals. For added resistance the player can hold a medicine ball as shown above.

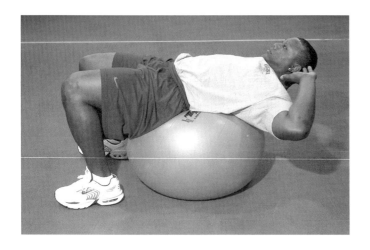

Swiss ball sit-ups

As with crunches, the Swiss ball sit-up is designed to reduce the hip flexor activity and target the abdominal muscles. In addition, the Swiss ball requires a certain amount of balance on the part of the player, which helps develop stabilizer muscles of the trunk.

The player balances himself on the Swiss ball with his feet on the floor and hands on his ears.

He then curls up flexing the abdominal muscles in a crunch style sit-up. Because the abdominals are used only in the first 30 percent of the sit-up, the player need only elevate the shoulder blades to complete the sit-up.

Swiss ball jackknives

The player lies on his back on the floor with a Swiss ball between his feet as shown in the figure above. His arms are extended overhead.

He grasps the Swiss ball with his feet and elevates it off the floor and lifts his upper body off the floor so that the shoulder blades clear the ground, holding for a six count. He then returns the ball and his upper body to the floor under control.

The player should use his arms as a counter-balance to elevate his upper body by reaching for the ball between his feet.

Reverse crunches

This variation of the crunch is performed with the player lying on a bench as shown, with his legs extended. Holding the bench with the hands overhead stabilizes the upper body.

The legs are drawn in toward the body by flexing the hips and knees. The player should exaggerate a

crunching motion at the end of the exercise by flexing the abdominal muscles.

The legs are then extended in preparation for the next repetition.

Hanging reverse crunch

A variation of the supine version previously described.

The legs are drawn in toward the body by flexing the hips and knees. The player should exaggerate a crunching motion at the end of the exercise by flexing the abdominal muscles.

The legs are then extended in preparation for the next repetition.

This exercise should always be performed with the knees bent rather than a straight leg lift to minimize hip flexor activity.

Other Abdominal Exercises

Regular sit-ups

The player lies on his back, knees bent at a 90 degree angle, and feet flat on the floor and shoulder width apart.

He places his fingertips at the side of his head (do not lock hands behind the neck because of excess stress on the vertebrae).

Sit up until the elbows touch the thighs (the abdominals are used only during the first 30 percent of the motion upward), then lower to the beginning position, making sure that the shoulder blades touch the floor.

The player should not relax the abdominal muscle at the bottom of this exercise, but instead keep constant tension on the abdominal muscles.

Keep your feet flat on the floor at all times.

"Rocky" sit-ups

Starting position is exactly the same as in regular sit-ups.

As the player sits up, he twists his body so that his right elbow touches his left thigh, and then quickly twists his body so that the right elbow touches the right thigh (The twists are very rapid and performed as quickly as possible).

The player returns to the beginning position and repeats.

Quick crunches

These have the same starting position and technique as described in regular crunches but are performed in a set amount of time (i.e., 30 seconds) and done as quickly as possible.

Side crunches

The player lays on the floor in the regular sit-up position keeping both shoulders on the floor.

He then places both knees together and shifts them to the right.

While maintaining this position with hands at the side of the head, the player lifts his shoulder blades off the floor.

This exercise isolates the oblique muscle of the abdominals if done correctly.

Once a prescribed number of repetitions has been performed on the right side, the knees are switched to the left side and the exercise is repeated.

Stack crunches

Using a bench, the player drapes his calves over the top and tucks his hips under the bench, keeping his back on the floor.

The player places his fingertips at the side of his head and sits up as far as possible so that the elbows go past the outside of his knees.

He then pauses and lowers himself to the starting position.

This can be done with a twisting motion by having the player lead his shoulder toward the opposite knee, so that the elbow reaches outside the opposite knee (i.e., right elbow to left knee). Alternate both right and left side crunches.

A medicine ball can also be added to this exercise to provide resistance.

TEACHING THE LIFTS AND DRILLS FROM BEGINNER TO ADVANCED

Stack crunch combo

There are 4 different positions for this exercise. If the prescription calls for 10 reps, the player will perform 10 reps in each position.

Position 1: The player performs the standard stack crunch, straight up the middle.

Position 2: The player performs a set of twisting stack crunches to one side only.

Position 3: Twisting stack crunches to the other side are now performed.

Position 4: This is a combo of the previous three techniques. The player crunches to the right side using a twisting stack crunch, then up the middle using the standard stack crunch, and then performs the stack crunch to the left (all of this constitutes one repetition).

Bicycle abs

The player lies on his back with his thighs perpendicular to the torso (elevated) keeping the calves parallel to the floor.

Fingertips are placed at the side of the head.

The athlete brings his right shoulder and left knee together while extending the right leg (keeping it off the floor).

He releases the right shoulder and left knee and performs a similar movement by bringing the left shoulder and right knee together, while extending the left leg.

The player keeps this motion continuous, as if he were riding a bike. He must be sure to maintain control and twist his entire torso each time.

Hokie leg raises

The player lies on his back with his hands at his sides (palms down) and legs extended straight out.

He then raises his feet six inches off the ground and brings his knees to his chest by bending them.

Once the legs are flexed the player then extends them to the original extended position and pauses for two seconds prior to the next repetition.

These can also be performed using a stretch cord attached to the ankles for added resistance.

Big 40s

The player lies on his back on a bench with his hips at the end of the bench (but not hanging off).

He holds on to the bench behind his head and assumes the beginning position with his knees tucked up to his chest.

The player then extends his legs out and downward in a scooping motion as if he were scooping sand with his toes.

The movement ends with the knees returning to the knee tuck position

Once the player performs 10 scoops, he straightens the legs to the extended position and swings them around in a circle.

Without taking a rest he performs 10 circles in a clockwise motion and 10 circles in a counterclockwise motion.

Figure eights

The player lies on the bench as if he were performing the Big 40s described above.

He extends his legs to the straight out position and moves them in a vertical figure eight pattern.

For the prescribed number of repetitions the player performs half the reps in one direction and then the rest in the opposite direction.

Dying cockroach

The player lies on his back on the floor.

He extends his arms and legs straight up so that they are parallel with each other.

He then elevates his shoulder blades so that they clear the floor and slightly raises his hips.

The position is held for a prescribed amount of time (i.e., 30 seconds) during which the shoulder blades must remain off the floor.

Three-man ab-assault

This is a very intense exercise, which will require two partners for each player.

The player performing the exercise will lie on a bench with his hips at the end but not off the bench.

His arms hold onto the bench overhead and legs extend straight out.

The first partner will be responsible for throwing the legs down in a plyometric fashion, with the player performing the exercise slightly resisting as the partner pushes the legs down. Each time the legs are thrown down, the player raises them up again.

While these leg throws are occurring, the second partner holds a medicine ball 12 to 14 inches above the player's abdominals, and drops and retrieves the ball during each leg throw.

ABC sit-ups

The player lays on his back with his legs straight up in the air so that they are perpendicular to his torso.

His arms are extended straight up so that they are parallel to the legs.

The player contracts his abdominal muscles by elevating the shoulders off of the floor and reaching with his arms so that the arms are to the outside of the right leg. The player resumes the original start position and immediately extends the arms to a position between the legs, and then upon returning to the start position extends the arms past the left leg and back down (this constitutes one repetition).

The player will complete the cycle for a prescribed number of reps, making sure to keep the arms and legs straight and keep his shoulder blades off of the floor.

Flutterkicks

The player assumes a position on his back with legs extended and arms at his side (palms down).

Keeping the legs straight, he lifts the legs approximately 6 to 12 inches off of the floor and performs a flutterkick similar to freestyle swimming.

The kicks should continue in a rapid style for the prescribed period of time.

Be sure the player's ankles stay off the floor and that his kicks are not too wide.

Figure four double crunches

The player assumes a position on his back with both legs extended. He bends his right leg and places his right foot on the opposite side of his left knee with his right knee in an upright position.

Fingertips are placed at the side of the head.

The player performs a crunch by elevating his shoulder blades so that his elbows touch the knee that is up.

Plyometric leg throws

This exercise is performed with a partner.

The player lies on his back on the floor with his legs extended. His partner stands facing the player's feet with the player's head positioned between the partner's feet.

The player raises his legs (feet together) as high as possible and back toward the partner. The partner catches the player's feet and throws his feet to the right, with the player providing slight resistance.

The player elevates his feet again and his partner throws the player's legs to the left, again with the player providing slight resistance.

The movement is then repeated with the partner throwing the player's legs straight up.

Plyometric Exercises

Plyometrics are a method of training borrowed from the Eastern European and Soviet training regimens that use the inherent stretch-recoil characteristics of human muscle to develop explosive power. This includes the natural elasticity of the connective tissue surrounding the muscle as well as the *stretch reflex,* which is a protective response to sudden changes in muscle length such as a rapid stretching of a muscle. With this last point, when a person stretches a muscle rapidly, a *reflex response* is for that muscle to contract to prevent potentially damaging elongation of the muscle that could result in a muscle tear. The plyometric exercises use these characteristics to develop explosive power.

Just as with weight training, there are different levels of intensity and difficulty with each of these plyometric exercises. We have classified three levels of difficulty: beginner, which are suitable for most players; intermediate, which are suitable once a player gains a basic level of strength; and advance, which are designed for advanced players who qualify based on performance tests. With this last point, an example of a qualifying level of strength would be if a player were able to squat 150 percent of his body weight, he would be ready to perform depth jumps.

First Level Plyometric Exercises

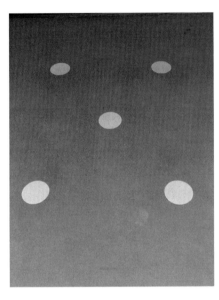  

Dot drills

This drill is best performed on a gym floor or a cement sidewalk. A grid of dots at least three inches in diameter are laid out in an X pattern in a square that measures two feet (width) by three feet (length).

The jumping patterns can vary: apart, together, apart, figure eight, zig-zag patterns, etc., and can be performed with both feet together or hopping on one foot at a time.

The coach can be creative and invent new patterns, but some of the most common drills are:

Figure eight—begin on the bottom right dot facing forward; jump to the center dot; jump to the top, right dot; jump to the top left dot; jump back to the center dot; jump back to the bottom left dot; and finish by jumping to the bottom right dot. This can be performed in reverse by starting on the bottom left dot.

Apart, together, apart—begin with each foot on the bottom dots as far left and right as possible, while facing forward; jump to the center dot with both feet together; then jump to the farthest top two dots with feet apart. The two variations on this drill are that the player can hop backward in reverse order (top to center to bottom) or can spin at the top position and return to the bottom position in a forward-facing stance.

Zig-zag—Start with both feet on the bottom right dot; jump with both feet together to the bottom left dot…jump with both feet to the center dot… jump to the top right dot…and finish at the top left dot with both feet. He can then reverse the order by jumping backward in a similar Z pattern. This drill can also be performed with the player starting on the left dot.

The key coaching point is to require players to move through a full range of motion on each drill (hitting every dot used in that particular drill) as quickly as possible. This drill not only develops foot speed but also develops balance.

Jump rope

The player should select a rope that is of a proper length. When standing on the rope with both feet together, the ends of the rope handles should come up to the player's arm pits.

The most elementary method of jumping rope is to keep the feet together with the weight balanced on the balls of the feet. The knees should be slightly flexed and with each jump the feet should just barely clear the floor. This action helps develop an explosive push-off from the ankle joint.

A more advanced method of skipping rope involves the player using only one leg at a time. He may jump a certain number on one side and then switch to the other leg or may alternate legs on each successive jump.

Another more advanced variation would be to have the player run in place as he skips the rope, hop from side to side, run forward down a court as he skips the rope, or hop with both feet down the court.

Speed ladder

The speed ladder is a rope or chain ladder with rungs that are 16 inches apart. The speed ladder is laid flat on the floor (if a speed ladder is not available, the coach can create a ladder by placing strips of tape on the floor at 16-inch intervals).

The drills can vary depending on the training goal. The player will try to get one or both feet in the space between rungs of the ladder.

The players can run through every rung (foot hits in each square) for foot speed. He can run through every other rung in order to increase stride length.

The player can step in each rung with the right and left foot each time or can take three steps per rung (right, left, right) to improve foot quickness.

Another variation would be to have players slide laterally through the speed latter hitting every rung backward, and using a carioca step.

Tuck jumps

These can be done in a knees-to-the-chest position or with a heels-up tuck.

In the knees-to-the-chest position, the player starts with a shoulder-width stance, keeping the body upright (don't bend at the waist).

The player then jumps up with an explosive motion and brings the knees to the chest, grasping the knees with his hands. He then lands in the ready position and repeats the next jump immediately.

The heel-up version starts with the same ready position. However, once the player jumps, he brings both heels up to the buttocks and swings the arms forward. In this version the knees are pointing downward rather than up.

Second Level Plyometric Exercises

Power skips

This is an exaggerated skip with the emphasis on the push-off phase of sprinting.

The player uses alternating arm action similar to sprinting and tries to achieve maximum hang time in the air between skips.

Bounding

This is an exaggerated run with the emphasis on the push-off phase of sprinting and with an immediate reaction off the ground upon foot contact.

After pushing off, the player drives the knee upward and forward with the heel tucked under the hip.

The ankle should be dorsiflexed (toe up toward the shin) to be ready for the next push-off.

The arms are swung in a running motion or can be used in a double arm motion.

The player must drive the rear leg forcefully by attaining full extension at the hip, knee, and ankle joints and gain as much height and distance as possible on each bound.

Single leg hops

This exercise requires the player to hop on one foot in a variety of drills.

The simplest would be the one-foot ankle hop in which the player uses only the ankle for momentum and hops continuously in one place. The player should extend the ankle as much as possible on each hop.

Another variation is to hop from side to side, alternating feet. The player hops laterally from one foot to the other.

Yet another variation of the side-to-side hop is to perform a lateral hop on one leg from side to side using the same leg for repetitions. Once a certain number of repetitions have been completed with one leg, the player switches to the other leg.

Third level plyometric exercises

Box Jumps

Single series

The player stands facing a box (12 to 42 inches tall) with his feet shoulder width apart.

He jumps with both feet onto the box, steps back down, and repeats. A more advanced version of this is to hop down from the box and immediately hop up again for repetitions.

Weighted

The same form considerations as the single series except that the player holds a relatively light weight during the jump. This could be a barbell plate held tightly against the chest, a pair of light dumbbells, or a weighted vest, which might be preferred from a safety standpoint.

Lateral

This can be performed with a single box or a row of boxes.

The player stands to the side of the box (12 to 42 inches) and jumps laterally onto the box and back to the ground on the other side of the box. With multiple boxes he would then jump onto the next box and so on until he reached the end of the row. The player would then reverse the order and jump laterally in the opposite direction until he reached the original starting point.

Endurance

This would involve either a single box or multiple boxes of the same height.

The player would jump up on the box and back down to the floor a certain number of times. With multiple boxes he would jump from the floor to the opposite side of the box so that he would be in position to jump up onto the next box.

This is a high-volume exercise for developing endurance and can be timed.

Multidirectional

The player stands in the center with boxes of the same height in front, behind and to each side, surrounding him.

He then jumps either forward, backward, or to either side and then back to the floor.

This can be a programmed drill in which a set order of jumping directions is set up, or it can be a reaction drill in which the coach gives visual or verbal signals to the player relative to the direction of movement.

Stadium step hops

This drill is performed on stadium steps or bleachers.

The player stands in a partial squat at the bottom of the steps and hops up the steps with both feet for 10 to 12 consecutive steps without pauses.

The player should jump from step to step as quickly as possible.

Depth jumps

The depth jump is one of the most advanced forms of plyometric exercise and should only be used if a player has a sufficient training history of strength training. The general rule of thumb is that a player should be able to squat 150 percent of his body weight to qualify for this exercise.

In this drill the player starts on the top of a box (start with 12 inches), jumps down to the ground, and

immediately jumps up onto another box of the same height. The key to a proper depth jump is to minimize the transition time from the downward to the upward motion. The coach should emphasize to the player to almost anticipate the landing and to jump up off the floor as quickly as possible.

Speed Drills for Acceleration and Maximum Velocity

I. Sprint Technique

A breakdown proper sprinting technique is a good place to start when a coach is teaching a player to be faster. In Chapter 2, we suggested that the secret to developing speed was to apply power to good running mechanics, hence the knowledge of sprinting technique is critical. Consider also that maximum velocity may not be the ultimate goal of speed training. It has been determined by track experts that sprinters do not achieve top speed or maximum velocity until they reach 30 to 35 meters. In a sport like football, which requires short bursts of sprinting, maximum velocity may not be as important as acceleration. However, training for maximum velocity improves overall speed by allowing an athlete to move his limbs at a high rate of movement and express power through these movements to propel the body at a high velocity. Thus, the training for maximum velocity is the basic foundation of speed development in which power, coordination, and dynamic flexibility all play an important role.

Posture

The player should keep his eyes on a horizontal plane. Because the head weighs more than most body parts, where the eyes go, the head goes, and where the head goes, the body follows.

The abdominal muscles should be tight and the player's hips aligned with the torso. The abdominal muscles stabilize the pelvis in an optimal position so that the hamstrings and gluteal muscles can apply maximum leg force against the ground, while allowing the hip flexor of the opposite leg the ability to recover that leg in preparation for the next stride.

Proper sprinting form dictates that shoulders should be slightly ahead of the hips with the shoulders down not hunched.

The athlete should maintain a tall posture with the pelvis projected forward and upward. The head should be level and the face and shoulder should remain relaxed.

Arm action

The arms play a considerable role in counterbalancing the motion of sprinting. Incorrect arm action is a common mistake among many players.

The arms should move forward and backward, rather than across the body, while maintaining a 90-degree bend at the elbows.

Remind the player that what he does with the right arm affects the left leg, and what he does with the left arm affects the right leg. This is why the arm action must be powerful to counteract the hip rotation occurring as a result of the leg movement. The player should drive the arms back as if they were hammering a nail by rotating the shoulders. The arms should swing through eye-level to hip-level range of motion.

Arms recover elastically through the stretch of the shoulder, and as soon as the recovery hand is back to shoulder level, the athlete should swing it backward again.

The hands are held in a relaxed and natural position (unless they are holding a football!).

Leg movement

The leg action should occur under the body rather than as an emphasis to achieve a greater stride length. In fact, the foot should be planted as close to under the hip as possible or else a breaking force will slow the runner due to over-striding.

As the player's leg recovers after the push off, his ankle should be dorsiflexed (toes up toward the shin) with his heel as close to his buttocks as possible. This shortens the leg level and reduces the residual time of the leg behind the body resulting in a faster leg turnover.

As the recovery leg comes forward, the thigh will reach a point where it is parallel to the ground (thigh block position) at which point the leg unfolds at the knee and extension begins at the hip. This extension is due to transfer of momentum rather than reaching characterized by quadriceps contraction. The latter action could result in over-striding, which actually has the effect of slowing the player down.

The recovery leg then makes ground contact and explosively strikes the ground under the hip with the extension of the ankle in a springboard action. Elastic force production is essential. The shorter the ground contact time, the more efficient the force application.

The key coaching points are 1) knees high with simultaneous thigh lift through full range of motion; 2) heel close to the butt on the recovery leg; 3) foot plants under the hips; 4) active plant involving the lower leg and ankle joint and downward, backward "claw" with thigh and lower leg; and 5) acceleration of the thigh on the downward movement of the leg with the ankle dorsiflexed (negative foot speed).

Drills for Speed Development

Fast arms drill

This can be done in both standing and seated position.

The player stands erect with his arms at his side. He swings his arms from the shoulders while keeping the arms straight (long/slow pendulum).

He then gradually bends his elbows until they reach 90 degrees and goes through a normal sprinting action.

The seated version of this drill requires the player to sit on the ground with his legs out in front, keeping his knees straight. If executed properly, the player's hips should bounce off the ground due to the movement of the arms.

Ankling

This drill is designed to develop the springboard action at the ankle joint in proper sprinting technique.

The athlete uses a forward quick shuffle of the feet with good running posture and steps over the opposite ankle as quickly as he can.

The player should pick up his toes as soon as the ball of each foot strikes the ground. He should apply the force into the ground by using a springboard action from the ankle along with a good arm action.

A march

This drill isolates the recovery and the ground preparation mechanics in a marching action.

While maintaining a good sprint posture, have the player recover his heel to his buttocks with the ankle dorsiflexed. At the same time he will lift the thigh to the thigh block position (thigh parallel to the ground) while keeping the foot tight to the buttocks and ankle dorsiflexed.

He then returns the foot to the ground and repeats the action with the opposite leg in a marching action. Be sure that the players use good arm action during this drill.

A skip

The mechanics of this drill are the same as the A march (heel to the buttocks, ankle dorsiflexed, and the thigh block position) with the addition of a rhythmic skipping action.

This emphasizes recovery and ground preparation (heels up, knees up, and toes up), and the skip occurs when the recovery foot hits the ground.

The player should keep the skip low to the ground because the emphasis of this drill is to develop recovery leg mechanics and simply add a quick skip when the recovery foot hits the ground.

The player should coordinate proper arm action in this drill.

A run

This drill uses the same mechanics as the other A drills mentioned above except that in addition to developing recovery and ground preparation mechanics, stride rate (turnover) is emphasized.

When the recovery foot lands on the ground, the athlete pushes off with a full running stride. The athlete may start out slowly to preserve proper form but will eventually emphasize stride rate by turning the legs over as quickly as possible.

Butt kicks

This drill teaches the athlete the sensation of a good active heel recovery.

The player brings his heel to his buttocks, alternation legs in a rapid-fire motion with the ankle dorsiflexed.

The player should maintain a good sprint posture, and foot plants should be under the hips (center of gravity) with coordinated arm action.

It is important for the coach to not emphasize horizontal speed in this drill, but focus on getting the heel as close to the buttocks as possible (ideally kicking the buttocks).

This drill is a good warmup exercise and a good dynamic stretching exercise.

Fast leg drills

This is a more advanced drill that requires good coordination and timing. The player will apply some of the skills learned in the A series drill to a running action.

Although the ultimate goal of these fast leg drills is increasing the speed of leg action (turnover) the coach should start the players at a slower speed and gradually progress to a faster speed.

The drill can be performed emphasizing one leg at a time or in an alternating fashion using both legs together.

For the single leg version the player starts with a slow jog while maintaining good sprint posture.

In concert with proper arm action, one leg is quickly cycled through the recovery cycle with good thigh lift, heel snapped to the buttocks (ankle dorsi-flexed), and acceleration to the ground.

The player would perform this cycle once for every two jogging steps so that each leg is involved every other cycle.

Make sure the player brings his heels tight to the thighs until a full thigh lift is achieved.

With the alternating leg version of this drill, the leg actions are the same except that the fast leg action alternates from left to right in succession following every three jogging steps.

Downhill running

This is another advanced drill for developing quick turnover and leg speed.

Select a hill that has a gradual slope (avoid a downhill that is steep) of about a four-percent grade. The length of each run will be 40 yards, so a relatively long gentle slope is needed.

The player starts at the top of the hill and runs down emphasizing rapid leg turnover. It is important to avoid over-striding by keeping the feet under the hips.

This drill should not be performed when the players are tired or have recently performed high-intensity or high-volume leg exercises.

Acceleration

Sprinting can be broken down into several phases, with acceleration as the second phase following the first two steps of the initial speed start phase. In football acceleration mechanics are extremely important for most players because the sport requires repetitive short bursts (acceleration and re-acceleration) with and without resistance.

The characteristics of good starting acceleration are a powerful full range of action with the arms and legs as well as a low, driving posture. The emphasis is generally on the generation of horizontal forces to overcome the inertia of the body (remember a body at rest tends to stay at rest). Once this initial inertia has been overcome, the athlete must efficiently increase speed and allow for a smooth transition to the maximum velocity sprinting posture discussed earlier in this chapter. This series of transition is compatible with good football fundamentals such as a running back coming out of his stance, hitting the "hole" in a low position, and then making the transition to open field running once he is in the clear.

Here are some key points to good acceleration:

The forward lean of the player should not occur by bending at the waist. Instead the lean should occur with the body aligned so that a straight line extends from the drive leg to the head.

The hips should be over the driving leg or slightly ahead of the driving leg.

The angle of the shin should be positive which means that the knee stays in front of the ankle joint.

The feet should stay close to the ground during acceleration, and the ankle should remain dorsiflexed until the push-off phase of ground reaction.

Unlike other phases of sprinting, the acceleration phase involves forceful muscular contraction at the hip, knee, and ankle rather than an elastic response.

It is important to emphasize full extension of the drive leg during acceleration with an equally powerful arm drive in which the elbows are driven back forcefully.

A visual to help players learn the low drive position is to have them imagine that they are pushing a car out of mud or snow.

Once the player hits his sixth to eighth stride, he must get tall to assume the optimal sprinting posture discussed earlier.

Stride length and stride frequency increase as you increase speed, but be sure to coach players so that they don't over-stride.

Acceleration Drills

Stick drill (acceleration ladder)

You will need a tape measure to mark distance as well as sticks or some sort of ground marker as a visual cue to the players to dictate quick stride lengths.

Place the first two sticks 16 inches apart and increase the distance between consecutive sticks (after stick No. 2) by four inches. Thus you will have a 20-inch difference between stick No. 2 and No. 3, a 24-inch distance between stick No. 3 and No. 4, and so on until you have marked off six to eight steps.

The player puts his foot on the first stick and leans forward into what can best be described as a *falling start*. His weight should be on his front leg, and the knee should be over or slightly ahead of the foot.

The player then uses each successive stick as a pattern for foot placement to learn to get to top speed quickly. Once he learns to execute correct acceleration mechanics at full speed, the player learns the sensation of the movement of quick acceleration.

When the player can run this drill at full speed, increase the distance between sticks by one to two inches to further increase quick acceleration.

Resistance running

There are many ways to add resistance to running mechanics. Some require special equipment; others can be achieved using common materials.

The main goal of resistance running is to emphasize power in the leg drive phase of the running cycle as well as some of the mechanics discussed earlier such as posture and a high knee action.

Uphill running provides not only the effect of gravity in developing good leg power, but the added benefit of emphasizing a high knee action. A fairly steep grade works best (although too steep a grade is counterproductive because player cannot sprint up an extreme grade) with a 40-yard distance. Good acceleration form should be emphasized.

Another variation of uphill running is stadium step running. The athletes should sprint up the steps but run slowly down the steps in order to recover and avoid injury. The high knee action and increase in running power is similar to uphill running.

Partner running involves a teammate holding a large towel by the ends, which is wrapped across the chest of the runner. The runner drives forward while his partner pulls back to increase resistance.

Flexicord running involves a player wearing a chest harness attached to a heavy-duty elastic cord anchored to a stable structure. As the runner drives forward and stretches the cord, the resistance increases.

A weighted sled can also be attached to the chest harness with resistance added by adding weights to the sled. This system is ideal if a wide variety of players are being trained based on size strength and experience.

A small parachute can also be attached to the chest harness creating wind resistance as the player accelerates. Some of these devices are designed to allow the parachute to be released at the point of maximum resistance so that the player can experience the sensation of quick acceleration.

Agility and Quickness Drills

Now that some of the basic exercises for strength, power, and speed have been addressed, the final progression will focus on developing quickness and agility. The game of football often requires certain players to have the ability to react, change direction, accelerate, decelerate, and generally perform in an open skill sport in which the situation on the field is constantly changing. We can separate the agility drills into two distinct categories: programmable drills in which an athlete follows a fixed pattern of motion and reaction drills in which the player responds to a visual or auditory cue (i.e., whistle).

I. Change of Direction Drills

Because some positions require multidirectional movement, training for change of direction is important. Improving a player's quickness in different directions will make most players better.

Power cuts

When an athlete must change direction at top speed or at a greater angle, he must plant the outside foot and push off with that foot explosively and quickly. At the same time, the player must open the angle of the hip toward the direction he wishes to go by rotating the inside (recovery) leg and foot in that direction. As he is about to plant the recovery foot, he proceeds to drive step with the planted foot in order to re-accelerate in the new direction.

When the player plants the outside foot, the toes should be pointed perpendicular to the direction that he ultimately wants to go, and there should be only a slight bend in the knees.

The player's midsection should remain tight to keep the hips under the torso so that a solid power position can be maintained.

After the push-off, the athlete turns his hips so that the toe of the outside foot is pointing toward the new direction with the ankle dorsiflexed.

The player should perform the power cut without false stepping (stepping out away from the directional change) that would indicate a lack of posture, balance, functional leg strength, and stability.

Key points to this drill:

The player should lower his center of gravity and extend the outside leg and foot (plant foot) out as hard as possible to stop his momentum.

He must control his upper body and keep it directly above his hip.

The inside foot is rotated out toward the direction of the cut, and the knee is bent for a powerful drive (positive shin angle).

Outside leg and foot are the quick side and change the direction of the hip.

The outside leg force is short and explosive followed by a low heel recovery for a quick placement of the first step onto the ground.

The inside leg and foot are the power side, which allows for quick re-acceleration in the direction of the cut.

Speed cuts

These are used when the change in direction involves a smaller angle (less than 90 degrees) or with sprinting at full speed.

The body position and mechanics are the same as in power cuts except that the outside leg and foot are not planted.

Instead, the quick change in direction occurs by stepping over with the outside leg toward the direction of the cut and by driving off the inside leg.

Spinning

This movement involves quick deceleration and powerful quick planting of the inside foot followed by reverse pivot of the same leg.

The player should maintain the tight midsection to keep the hips under the torso for a solid power position.

The player decelerates his body by putting his feet in front and lowering his center of gravity. He then plants the inside foot for a reverse pivot and quickly pushes off with the outside leg to move his hip to the direction of the cut while maintaining a solid body position.

The player maintains a low heel recovery and places the outside foot in a position of a positive shin angle.

It is important to transfer one's body weight (center of gravity) over the outside leg to resume a good acceleration mechanics.

II. Agility Drills

20-yard shuttle (pro agility drill)

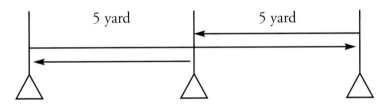

This drill uses power cuts.

Following sufficient warmup and stretching arrange cones five yards apart on each line.

The player starts by straddling the middle line in a three-point stance with his right hand on the line. On the whistle, the player sprints to the right line and touches the right line with his right hand. He then sprints across the middle line to the left line and touches the left line with his left hand. He immediately sprints back to his right and finishes at the middle line touching the middle line with his right hand.

Pattern run

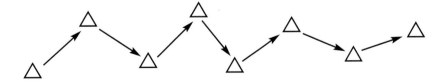

This drill can use either power cuts or speed cuts depending on the angle at each cone.

The cones are placed at random angles to expose the player to the types of cuts he might make during a game situation. The distance between cones can be varied, but five yards apart is standard.

The player starts at the cone on the left and runs in the direction indicated by the arrows in the diagram above.

This drill can also be performed using the spin movement with the player performing a reverse pivot at each cone.

Star drill

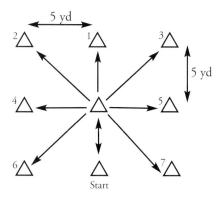

This drill can use power cuts, speed cuts, spins, and combinations of all three. It can also be performed as a programmed drill with a set pattern or as a reactive drill using either a visual or verbal signal.

The cones are placed five yards apart in three rows of three.

The above diagram shows the programmed version in which the player starts at the start cone by sprinting, side shuffling, or back pedaling to the middle cone. He then sprints to and breaks down at each numbered point to that cone and then jogs back to the starting point.

The reactive version of this drill has the player starting either at the start cone or the central cone from where he will quickly react to either a coach pointing to a cone or calling out a number.

T-drill or Texas drill

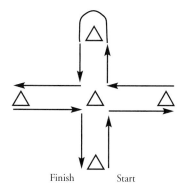

This drill can incorporate either power cuts, speed cuts, or a combination of the two. The distance between cones can be varied, but five yards from the center is standard.

The player sprints forward, makes a cut to the right at the middle cone, and sprints to the forward cone.

He then turns 180 degrees and sprints back to the middle cone, where he will turn right and run forward and around the far cone. He then runs back to the middle cone and cuts to the left, touches the left cone, turns 180 degrees, and sprints to the middle cone. After touching the middle cone, he sprints back to the starting cone and to the finish.

This drill can also be performed with the player maintaining a front facing position where he would sprint forward to the middle cone, slide laterally at the middle cone, and touch the forward cone.

He then slides to his right to touch the middle cone, sprints forward to the right cone, and then back-pedals out to the left cone.

90-degree power cut/spin drill

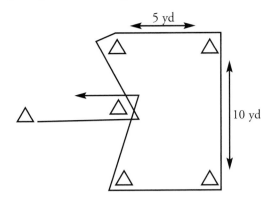

This is a drill that can be performed using either power cuts or spins.

Cones are five yards apart with the entire grid approximating a five-yard-by-10-yard pattern as shown in the diagram.

The player starts at the remote cone and sprints to the middle cone where he will cut to his left. He will then perform 90-degree cuts at the designated cones.

Hourglass

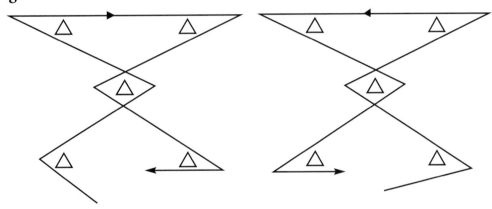

This drill can incorporate either power cuts, speed cuts, or a combination of the two. The distance between cones can be varied, but five yards from the center is standard.

The player starts by cutting to the left, keeping the middle cone to his left on each round trip.

The drill should also be reversed with the player cutting to his right, keeping the middle cone to his right on each round trip.

Four corner drill

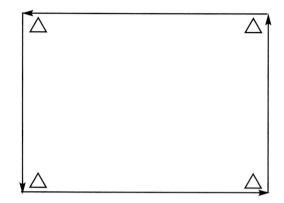 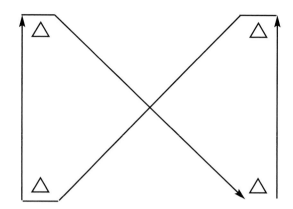

This drill uses a combination of all three cuts and can be performed as a square pattern or a crossing pattern as show above. The distance between cones can be varied, but five yards between cones is standard.

The coach can combine different movements such as sprinting forward, lateral and backward slide, carioca, diagonal run, and back-pedal.

The cuts can vary but reverse pivot at each corner increases the difficulty of the drill.

Carolina drill

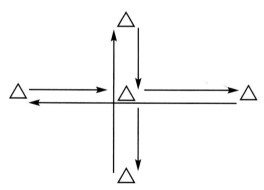 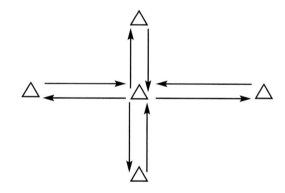

This drill uses a combination of all three cuts. The distance between cones can be varied, but five yards from the center is standard.

The player always faces forward in this drill.

He sprints forward from cone No. 1 to cone No. 2, back-pedals from cone No. 2 to the middle cone,

and then lateral slides between cones No. 3 and No. 4, following the arrows in the diagram above.

He finishes with a back-pedal from the middle cone to cone No. 1.

Hurdle hop to sprint, slide (multidirectional)

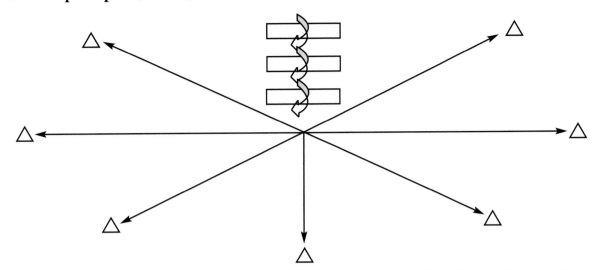

The player hops over three hurdles at the start of this drill. The height of the hurdle can vary, but about a knee high level will work for most players.

The player then sprints or slides to each cone, returning to the middle each time. The distance between cones can be varied, but five yards from the center is standard.

This drill can be used as a reaction drill by having a coach verbally or visually signal the player toward a specific cone.

Five-cone butterflies and 360-degree drill

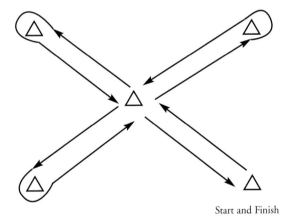

Start and Finish

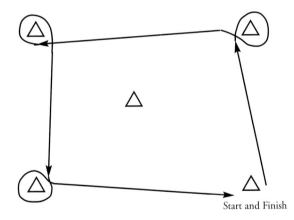

Start and Finish

The five-cone butterflies drill requires that the player starts on the lower right cone and sprints to the middle cone. He then sprints or back-pedals to the cone on his right, makes a tight turn around that cone, and heads back to the middle; he then sprints or back-pedals to the next cone on his right, makes a tight turn around that cone, and comes back to the middle; he repeats the same for the cone at the lower left.

He concludes by taking a sharp right turn at the middle cone and sprints for the start and finish line.

The 360-degree drill requires that the player sprints and makes tight turns or spins at each cone as shown in the second figure above.

This drill can also be performed using a combination of sprints, side shuffles, and back-pedals between cones with an appropriate turn at each cone.

Reaction Drills

Tennis ball drills

The player either faces or is at a right angle to a partner who is five yards away in a ready position with his knees flexed and weight distributed on the balls of the feet.

The player's partner stands with his arms extended out to the sides holding a tennis ball in each hand (shoulder level).

The partner drops one of the ball and the player must sprint to catch it before it bounces twice.

In the advanced form of this drill, the player stands with his back to his partner. The partner shouts go and drops a ball. On the go signal the player turns and responds by trying to catch the ball after the first bounce.

This drill develops reaction time, agility, and acceleration.

Crazy ball drills

This is similar to the tennis ball drill in terms of setup and general procedure.

The difference, however, is that the coach uses a crazy ball, which is an odd-shaped ball that takes unpredictable bounces due to its shape.

Wave drills

The player faces the coach in a ready position or position-specific stance. The player then responds to visual signals and moves in the appropriate position by back-pedaling, lateral sliding, or forward sprinting. A football can be used to allow players to respond to a ball in the air.

Competitive Games

Shark in a Tank

- Select an area approximately 30 by 30 yards square.
- Have 10 to 12 athletes inside the square.
- The game lasts for 10 to 12 seconds.
- At the start of each game, quickly call out the names of one or two "sharks."
- The designated "sharks" tag as many "fish" as possible during the 10- to 12-second period.

Capture the Flag

- Select an area approximately 30 by 30 yards square.
- Place one to two cones at two opposite ends of the square.
- Place towels or rags on top of the cones to act as flags.
- Divide a group of 10 to 16 athletes into two teams.
- Each team has a designated goalie to guard his team's flag.
- If the goalie tags an opposing player as he attempts to capture the flag, that player is out of the game.
- If a regular player tags an opposing player within a five-yard area around the flag, the tagged player must return to his team's side.
- The game is over when one team successfully captures the other team's flag.

Conditioning for Football

The conditioning program for football is designed to provide your athletes with the physical stamina to play at their best level of performance throughout the duration of a game. This component can also be manipulated to help the player reach and maintain his optimal level of lean body mass and minimum level of fat. For some players this may mean reducing body fat, for others, the issue may be to preserve lean body mass while improving physical stamina.

In Chapter 2, we describe the incorporation of running and other physical conditioning programs into a strength program. This is not as easy as simply adding extra running at the end of the workout. The coach must target specific goals, depending upon the needs of each athlete (given differences in body composition, maturity, experience, and demands of that player's particular position on the team), and he must adjust them to the time of the season. In Chapter 3, we broke down the training phases into three distinct periods: the off season, the preseason, and the in-season phases. Conditioning for each of these will be different, given the differences in priorities of each. You must recognize some unavoidable truths about conditioning:

A player cannot maintain peak conditioning year in and year out. A *peak* is just that—a high point that can be achieved only once or twice per year. The *timing* of the peak should occur when top conditioning is most important.

Not all physical conditioning carries over to the game. Some forms of conditioning will have a bigger impact on how well a player plays throughout the game than other forms of physical conditioning. The wrong type of physical conditioning can actually have a negative effect on gains in strength, power and speed. For example, excessive aerobic conditioning during the in-season phase does not carry over to the performance on the field since slow jogging is not part of the game performance, yet it will impede strength gains.

Rest is an important component of the physical conditioning process. It may be the most overlooked cause of players appearing to be out of condition during a game.

The in season is not the time to try to improve a player's level of conditioning. If a player is not in shape by the time the season starts, it is time to re-evaluate your preseason conditioning program.

With these major concepts in mind, let us look at the role of physical conditioning in the football player's program.

Body Composition

The off season is the ideal time to design workouts that target body composition as a training priority. This is the time for players who are overweight to shed some fat and for players who lack body mass to gain good quality lean body mass. The training groups should be based on where a player falls along this continuum. For example, you may have a lineman who carries excess fat, which impairs his speed and agility more so than lack of strength and muscle mass, as indicated by high preseason strength-testing scores. The training priority here will be geared toward fat reduction. At the other end of the spectrum, you might have a player who is underweight, regardless of how much he tries to put on weight. Although this player will still need a basic conditioning program, his highest priority will be in gaining muscle size.

Programs for Reducing Body Fat

The only way a human can reduce body fat (outside of surgical techniques such as liposuction) is to use up the calories stored in that fat (McArdle et al., 2001). We cannot sweat it away (fat actually contains much less water than muscle with muscle at about 75percent water and fat at 20 percent). There are no pills or special food combinations that makes fat disappear. The only way to use the stored fat in our bodies is to burn the potential energy stored in fat as fuel, because fat is nature's way of storing the most calories in the least space. A gram of fat contains about nine calories of energy, while a gram of carbohydrate or protein contains about four calories (McArdle et al., 2001). We store better than twice the energy in the same amount of mass by storing it as fat.

Our ancestors were hunters and gatherers and greatly depended on this system of storing calories in their feast to famine existence. Modern-day man has inherited this characteristic, which is why our bodies hang on to fat as an emergency source of calories for survival in time of low calorie intake. In order to avoid this natural tendency, we need to give our body the incentive to tap into those stored calories. One approach, too often used, is to severely restrict caloric intake by having a player go on a low-calorie diet. This is a big mistake for two reasons.

First, as we lower our caloric intake, our body slows down basal metabolism, the calories our body needs every minute of every day just to maintain basic life functions (Burgess, 1991; Fricker et al., 1991). In this mode of calorie conservation, the player actually burns fewer calories at rest. If they increase their caloric intake, they increase this tendency for the body to store the calories as fat (Elliot et al., 1989). Therefore, the low calorie diet will lead to the body's gaining fat.

Second, by reducing caloric intake, you are compromising the nutrients needed to build muscle. Again, let's look at this like building a house. You hire the best carpenter in town to build your house; but if you provide him with scraps of wood, rather than quality lumber, the carpenter cannot build the best house. The average football player needs not only the right amount of protein to build muscle, but a sufficient number of calories to provide energy to train and build muscle. In fact, if the caloric intake is not sufficient, the body begins tearing down muscle tissue to use as fuel. This is obviously counterproductive in the muscle-building process. Keep in mind the fact that, especially at the high school level, players are often still in a stage of growth and physical development. Restricting calories could unintentionally limit important nutrients vital to normal growth and development.

If restricting calories is not the best approach to reducing body fat in the football player, what is? We must expend extra calories through more physical activity while improving the quality of the athlete's diet. Ideally this increased caloric expenditure should be in the form of aerobic-type activity. Earlier we defined aerobic as with oxygen, meaning that the intensity of the activity should be low enough to provide a sufficient level of oxygen at the cellular level. The classic aerobic activities are walking, jogging, cycling and swimming. All of these involve large muscle groups, in rhythmic, low-intensity, long-duration (longer than 15 minutes of continuous activity) exercise. For players who are obese, these classic aerobic activities would be ideal since the highest priority for them is getting body fat levels lower. In fact, for many of these players, we recommend non-weight bearing activities such as riding a stationary bike to avoid potential injuries from excess weight putting stress on joints and ligaments as in activities such as jogging or running. Once a player loses weight, he can graduate to low-impact activities such as walking, and eventually, to jogging and running.

For most players, the transfer specificity of low-intensity aerobic activities (how well the exercises meet the performance goals) is very low. In the game, low-intensity activity is rarely a critical component on the field. The good news is that there is a way to stimulate the aerobic pathway of energy metabolism, while still involving a higher intensity work. It is achieved through interval training.

Interval training is a method of developing aerobic capacity while keeping the intensity of the activity at a level that mirrors the demands of a sport such as football. It consists of high-intensity activity such as running, followed by rest intervals of a predetermined length. The coach can select a work-to-rest ratio to keep the level of overall intensity at a level that fits into the priorities of that workout phase. For example, if the training phase calls for a low-volume workout, the work interval can be short (i.e., 30 seconds) with a relatively long rest interval (i.e., two minutes). This 1:4 work-to-rest ratio provides high-intensity work with a long recovery and, if coupled with a low number of repetitions, translates into a low-volume workout.

In contrast a 1:1 work-to-rest ratio, is one in which the coach has the players sprint for 30 seconds and then rest for 30 seconds. With a high number of repetitions it becomes a high-volume conditioning workout, which may be appropriate in a certain phase of the training cycle. Even though the work itself is high intensity, it is not aerobic work. The resting phase, in which the body recovers and restores stored energy in the muscle, places an aerobic stress on the aerobic metabolism system, which uses fat as an energy source and mirrors the types of physical stress the player encounters in a football game.

Finally, there is good research that supports gaining lean body mass because it increases the number of calories a player burns at rest (Hunter et al., 1998). Since muscle is metabolically capable as a calorie user, it makes sense that increasing lean body mass results in more calories expended to maintain that muscle at rest. Although the aerobic conditioning uses excess fat, strength training and anaerobic conitioning can be used to keep excess fat off throughout the season.

Programs for Preserving Lean Body Mass

Since the majority of football players are not obese, the largest number of players on a given team will rely on the conditioning program to prepare them to go the distance in a game. The temptation here is to simply tack on lots of running to the resistance workout and hope to cover all possibilities that the players will be in shape come season opener. But there are liabilities to such an approach. Overtraining is a very real possibility in this situation. The research is fairly consistent in demonstrating that too much aerobic work can impede an athlete's progress toward gaining muscle mass (Dudley & Fleck, 1987; Hennessy & Watson, 1995). This is due to the stress hormone cortisol, which has a muscle breakdown effect on skeletal muscle. Small amounts of cortisol are beneficial in the muscle remodeling process, since we must break down the muscle proteins in order to rebuild them back in greater number, but too much cortisol has a negative effect on gaining muscle. The amount of conditioning should be based on what is needed during a particular training cycle, and the cycles are designed to coincide with how close your team is to the actual competition.

The secret of avoiding overtraining and maintaining specificity is through the proper interval training work-to-rest ratio and through exercises that mirror the activities of the game. Running, of course, is the most specific activity (we have all heard the statement "… if you can't run, you can't play football."). But we can also incorporate types of activity that are more agility-oriented in the form of drills, that involve running and other physical performance associated with the game such as lateral and backward movement, and ground work such as grass drills, up-downs, monkey rolls, etc. These movements are especially valuable in season as a way of maintaining conditioning, while honing skills that are position specific. For linemen, the ground drills would be good, and for defensive backs, backward and lateral movements are best.

In terms of programming the conditioning, the most important concept that the football coach must understand is that it is very difficult to improve a player's conditioning level in season without running the risk of overtraining. *Improvements in a player's conditioning level should ideally occur in the off season and preseason, with the in season serving as a maintenance period*. The in-season practice should place a higher priority on skill development and refinement, as well as play development. In addition, the player must have time to rest and recover so that his physical capabilities are at their peak level. Far too often players will enter a game leg dead from the hard conditioning of the week preceding the game, affecting performance negatively, especially in the last quarter of the game, the worst time for players to be fatigued.

Training Phases for Conditioning

Off-Season Programming and Goals

In this original model, set up in Chapter 2, the main goal of the off season is to develop strength and lean body mass. To this end, the conditioning should not be of such a high volume (based on duration of the activity as well as work-to-rest interval) that it interferes with the muscle-building process, with a few exceptions. One exception is the previously mentioned case of the obese athlete who has a need to lose body fat. In his case the trade-off of retarding muscle growth to lose body fat via high-volume aerobic training is in line with what will make that particular player better in the long run. Maximizing fat loss would take a higher priority over maximizing muscle gains. Another exception is the multi-sport athlete, who really doesn't have an off season. The good news here is that we can assume that most sports are of a high enough level of physical rigor that the conditioning process will occur. The challenge will be to get these multi-sport athletes into the weight room during the season as addressed in Chapter 3.

With players who are not among these exceptions or are recovering from injuries, the off season conditioning program should start out with a three days per week format of agility-related interval work, such as the Virginia Tech Metabolic Speed Pac (outlined in the Appendix of this book). It is probably best to do the conditioning after the weight training, since the weight training holds a higher priority, and the ideal situation is to get a maximal effort out of the athletes in the weight room. It is also better to have days of complete rest rather than scheduling something every day. If the players lift weights three or four days per week, they should have three or four days of complete rest to fully maximize the recovery period. Eventually the frequency can be increased to four days per week but should not exceed five days per week. This higher frequency training is most appropriate for the player who must lose body fat. This should be offset by a lower intensity and often non-weight bearing activity.

The volume of each training session should start out low with a relatively high rest-to-work ratio and the total session lasting 20 to 30 minutes: 4:1 consisting of 110-yard, 220-yard, and 440-yard sprints. If the 110-yard sprints take 15 seconds, the rest would be one minute between reps. If the 220-yard sprint takes 30 seconds, then a two-minute rest would be used, and so on. By varying the distance of each workout you can keep workouts fresh and avoid accommodation. You can eventually increase the progression of the workouts by adding repetitions or keeping the same repetitions but reducing the rest interval so that the work-to-rest ratio is 1:3 or even 1:2 as you approach the end of this phase. The Metabolic Speed Pac for position-specific conditioning could also be used as athletes gain in fitness level and a conditioning base is achieved. This requires running drills that are position-related such as receivers running routes, linebackers doing pass drops, and so on. A complete outline of the Metabolic Speed Pac is included at the end of this section. Remember, the goal is to build a base of conditioning rather than getting the players into in-season shape. An overly ambitious off season conditioning program will sabotage the long-range goals.

Preseason Programming and Goals

In the preseason, we want to get more sport-specific with training goals. The resistance training shifts to a more speed and power priority while still maintaining the strength gained in the off season. The conditioning imitates this and places more emphasis on getting the players in game shape. The running intervals can be shortened and interspersed with agility drill-type activities including multidirectional movements and ground drills. The agility drills described in Chapter 4 are ideal for this type of interval. They can be adapted to ground drills by having the player in a four-point stance and reacting to visual and verbal cues from a coach. The work-to-rest ratio can be shortened in a progressive way so that by the end of this training phase the ratios may be 1:2 or even 1:1. The training must be economical because skill acquisition and other game-related learning must also take place during this phase. But with a good training base, the time commitment to the preseason training will be lower given the high-quality nature of these workouts.

In-Season Programming and Goals

It won't hurt to say it again: The in-season is not the ideal time to improve conditioning. Time constraints and the likelihood of overtraining make the in-season phase a bad time to push players with extensive work beyond the stress of preparing for each game. The exception to this might be a bye week where no game is scheduled, but even then the risk is high. Having said this, we must recognize that all of the hard work of the off season and preseason will be lost if a program of strength and conditioning maintenance is not included in the in-season cycles. The lifts and other resistance exercises must be performed regularly at a maintenance level. This is true for the conditioning. When conditioning, the intensity must remain high so the work-to-rest ratio is such that the rest intervals are short (1:3 or 1:1), but the number of repetitions and the frequency will be fewer during this phase. As mentioned earlier, these conditioning sessions should incorporate sport-specific, or probably even position-specific, activities and should be done three days per week with at least 24 hours rest prior to the game. Remember, we don't want to leave our team's best performance out on the practice field!

The Virginia Tech Metabolic Speed Pac

If we follow the specificity of training concept, it is logical that the best way to get in shape for football is to play the game. Although this may not be practical as a year-round training regimen, we can approximate the same game conditions through the Metabolic Speed Pac program. The Metabolic Speed Pac is designed to simulate the actual movements that are made on the football field with short intervals of recovery. The player performs ten consecutive movements with a walk back recovery (i.e., 15 seconds). These movements are specific to your position requirements on the football field. All are multidirectional, high-intensity runs that simulate receiver patterns, lineman techniques, running back plays, and so on. Ten consecutive movements make up a set. After each set the player should rest for two minutes prior to the start of the next set. This continues until the athlete completes the prescribed number of sets. It is important that each set is executed with game-like intensity. A Metabolic Speed Pac model with diagrams is presented in the Appendix of this book.

Precautions

In both the high school- and college-age population, there are a number of factors a coach must consider in implementing a conditioning program. Keeping the players safe and injury free is a high priority. Every year we hear of the tragic injuries and deaths that occur during participation in high school and collegiate athletics. Although some of these instances are unavoidable, we must do all we can to prevent them from occurring.

Pre-Existing Medical Conditions

Medical conditions ranging from asthma to musculoskeletal disorders such as Osgood-Slaughters (a disease that causes calcified growths on the knees of adolescents) afflict some of our young high school athletes. Although most states require a physical exam prior to participation, many coaches do not follow up on knowing about some of these pre-existing conditions. A short medical evaluation form should be administered to every player at the beginning of each year and kept on file. In addition to knowing about pre-existing conditions, it should ask about symptoms such as shortness of breath or dizziness during physical activity in order to detect some potential undiagnosed condition. It should ask about prescription medications, skeletal problems both diagnosed and undiagnosed, whom to contact in an emergency, and allergies (i.e., bee stings, medications, etc.). It is also important to know if your player is taking an over-the-counter medication or some type of performance-enhancing supplement. These often interact with prescription drugs and can set up a potentially dangerous condition during heavy exertion. Once collected, this information should be reviewed by the coaching staff and players so that potential medical problems can be identified. File these questionnaires alphabetically in an easily accessed form (computerized or in a filing system) so that the information can be quickly retrieved.

Once this information is known, the coach should take precautions. Adjust workouts for a player or groups of players to accommodate their precondition. It might be as simple as having players with asthma avoid the effect of grass pollen by conducting drills indoors. Make sure all players with asthma have their fast-acting inhalers with them before practice. Encourage your players to seek your advice on performance-enhancing supplements (which we will discuss in Chapter 7) before they take them. Some of these supplements are useless yet place athletes at a higher risk for certain medical problems.

For players with musculoskeletal problems, teach them how to work around the injured area by varying the lifts. It may be a matter of changing the angle of the lift (i.e., going from a flat bench to a declined bench) or switching from a barbell to dumbbells so that the arms are free to find a comfortable position. In addition, you may help prevent injuries by engaging in *prehab* which is similar to rehabilitating an injury except for the fact that the body part is exercised *before* the injury occurs rather than afterward. If your star quarterback is prone to shoulder problems, performing exercises designed to rehab a rotator cuff tear may prevent the injury from occurring at all by pre-strengthening the injury-prone area.

Staying Hydrated

Water is the most important nutrient a human being can consume. We can last far longer without solid food than we can without water. Athletes especially need plenty of water because so much is lost as sweat and must be replaced, and water is essential in allowing our kidneys to function at an optimal level for removing the waste products from our bodies. When a player engages in resistance training, the amount of waste generated in the muscle breakdown and building process is much higher than that found in a non-athlete. This is why football players must stay in a state of positive hydration, especially in a warm environment.

Many coaches and athletes believe that their thirst response is adequate in keeping us informed about our state of hydration. They erroneously believe that a person only has to drink when he is thirsty and that once the thirst is quenched that the body is in a state of full hydration. The fact is that the human thirst response is woefully inadequate. You can run a mule around in hot weather, causing it to lose a couple liters of fluid through sweat, and the mule will drink back every ounce of water lost at the drinking trough. A human, however, could lose a liter of water via sweating in a hot environment and quench his thirst by consuming only half a liter of water. That deficit of one-half of a liter of water may not have an immediate effect on athletic performance, but if you put several days of water loss with inadequate rehydration together (like what we see in a week of football practice) the cumulative effect of this water loss can significantly impair a player's performance. The research shows that muscular strength, muscular endurance and cardiovascular function are all negatively affected with as little as three percent of body weight lost through dehydration. In a 150-pound player that is about three liters of water. The effects of dehydration can also lead to injury and death if coupled with exercise in the heat, since the body's ability to regulate body temperature is compromised.

To prevent dehydration we recommend several precautions:

Monitor body weight—ideally every morning, after urinating and before practice (the athlete checks this on his own). If the player loses more than one to two percent of his body weight from the day before, suspect dehydration.

Suggest that players keep a gallon of water in their refrigerator and try to finish it by the end of each day.

This may mean drinking a large glass in the morning as well as drinking throughout the day and after practice. Drinking beverages other than water is not ideal, especially if they contain diuretics (caffeine, alcohol, etc.) or are carbonated (the carbonation makes the stomach feel full, thus less fluid is consumed) but a recent study shows that they are better than no consumption of fluids.

Give frequent water breaks during practice and training sessions, and encourage players to drink water.

Modify practice if extreme heat and humidity is in the weather forecast. This might include practicing at cooler times of the day (early morning or later in the day), practicing is shorts and t-shirts rather than full pads, etc.

Avoiding Heat-Related Illnesses

High heat and humidity represent a bad combination for heavy training in an outdoor environment. This is because the combined effect of excessive heat and high humidity impair the human body's system of regulating internal temperature. This system heavily depends upon sweat evaporation (also known as *evaporative heat loss*) as a way of giving up heat to the environment rather than storing it in the body core. Evaporative heat loss depends on sweat evaporating on the skin, which lowers skin temperature. Since blood flow to the skin increases when our core temperature rises, the cooler skin subsequently lowers our blood temperature. As this cooler blood circulates back to the body core, it picks up heat generated by working muscle, thereby cooling the body core. Even in hot climates, a low humidity allows this system of heat loss to work quite well.

Unfortunately, as the humidity rises to and above 65 percent the efficiency of sweat evaporation becomes less, and under extreme humidity, the sweat does not evaporate at all. These conditions place your players at a high risk of heat illness as the body core continues to rise unabated. These heat illnesses can range from muscle cramps to a life-threatening illness such as heat stroke.

The following is a synopsis of the three most common forms of heat illness. Included are the symptoms, mechanisms and treatments for each.

Heat Cramp—Characterized by muscle cramps and spasms, often in leg muscles such as calves and hamstrings. These are typically caused by electrolyte imbalance (sodium and potassium are out of balance relative to their concentration levels inside and outside the muscle and nerve cells, causing spontaneous activation of the nerve and muscle tissues.). It was once thought that the best treatment was to give electrolyte replacement fluids to an athlete suffering heat cramp, but today there is evidence that replacing the water is more important. Some sports drinks may actually slow down the water leaving the gut, thereby impeding the replacement of fluids. Have the athlete drink water first and stretch the cramping muscle for fastest relief.

Heat Exhaustion—Characterized by profuse sweating, nausea, dizziness, and a weak and thready pulse. These symptoms may not seem related but actually are due to the fact that the profuse sweating causes a rapid reduction of the plasma volume of the blood (the plasma being the clear liquid part of blood that provides the raw material for sweat). The reduced plasma volume reduces the total amount of blood volume, causing the heart to be a less efficient pump due to reduced return blood flow back to the heart (the heart can only pump out the amount of blood that comes in, hence the weak pulse). This reduces blood flow to the brain and causes the dizziness and nausea. The best treatment is to get the athlete to a cool environment and place ice on the pulse points of the body (anywhere you can feel a pulse, such as the wrist, neck, temples, etc.). Fluid replacement is also critical to replace the lost plasma. Again, studies show that cold water is the ideal fluid replacement in this instance.

Heat Stroke—is a much more severe form of heat exhaustion in which the athlete actually stops sweating (skin is hot and dry) and suffers from loss of motor control and mental confusion. This is due to the mechanism of heat response (an area in the brain called the *hypothallamus*) actually shutting down. It can lead to permanent damage to the hypothallamus and death. The athlete must be cooled down as soon as possible, and medical attention is warranted. At the hospital the patient is typically packed in ice and intravenous fluid replacement is administered.

Obviously, preventing these heat-related illnesses is the best approach, given their devastating effect on health and physical performance. Getting the athlete in top-level physical condition and keeping him fully hydrated is critical. One of the ways the human body adapts to aerobic-type activity (such as interval training) is by expanding the amount of blood plasma. This represents a reserve of plasma so that the sweat lost during a bout of hard physical exertion has less of an impact on total plasma volume changes, as would a state of full hydration. With regard to a game played in the heat, it is important that each player be fully loaded from a hydration standpoint by having a good aerobic base and paying attention to his hydration level in the week preceding the game.

With reference to practicing and training in the heat, good common sense would dictate that you adjust to the environmental conditions of high heat and humidity. Have players dress in clothing that allows heat dissipation and the evaporation of sweat. Natural fibers such as 100 percent cotton are better than synthetics so keep this in mind if you live in an area of the country where high heat and humidity are common. As mentioned earlier, shorts and t-shirt practices as well as altering the practice times to hit cooler times of the day should also be considered.

Avoiding Injuries

Injuries are a very real part of a sport like football, and some are inevitable. Often a team's success during a season is directly linked to how well they stay injury-free, especially if lack of depth is a problem. There are some precautions that a coach can take to minimize the chance of injuries in both the training sessions and ultimately in the game.

Proper weight room supervision

Many injuries occur as a result of improper technique, players lifting more weight than they can properly handle, and general horseplay in the weight room. All of these potential sources of injury can be prevented by having the proper amount of instruction and supervision in the weight training facility.

Many coaches complain that they are understaffed and simply cannot provide enough supervision during weight training. One strategy for overcoming this is to get other coaches from other sports to participate in an alliance of coaches who all help each other. It is a win-win situation since non-football athletes get good weight training instruction (remember, these may be multi-sport athletes of the future that may help your program) and you get help and supervision for your athletes. If you can get *every* coach of *every* sport offered in your school to buy into this arrangement, you can have a well supervised weight room that can be opened at a variety of times and accommodate all of the athletes in your school. This may also be important when you need leverage for funding the development and improvement of your training facility if all the coaches are included because all of the athletes in the school are served.

Proper warmup prior to heavy exercise

Think of muscle tissue as being like a rubber band. If you put a rubber band in the freezer overnight and try to stretch it what will happen? The rubber band will snap. On the other hand, if you allow that rubber band to warm up, it will become very elastic and stretch easily. It is the same way with muscle tissue. Muscle tissue that is cold will be more likely to tear than muscle tissue that is warmed up. As we expend energy in a muscle, most of the energy expended is lost as heat. Non-resistant movements generate enough heat to elevate the core temperature of the muscle (internal temperature) thereby making it more elastic. This type of movement also gets what is known as *synovial fluid* a natural joint lubricant, flowing in the joints. This helps to reduce the friction of tendons sliding over bone, which can help prevent tendonitis. More details on proper warmup are covered in Chapter 6.

Miscellaneous tips on preventing injury

Always use trained spotters on heavy lifts. The training of spotters should take place during all weight training instruction so that players learn both lifting and spotting techniques.

Only allow maximum lifts during testing times.

Wear lifting belts during heavy lifts. The abdominal muscles tighten against the belt, which increases intrathoracic pressure, thereby stabilizing the spinal column.

Establish proper decorum in the weight training facility. Enforce rules with consistently so that players and other non-football athletes know that the weight room is for serious training.

References

Burgess, N.S. "Effect of a very-low-calorie diet on body composition and resting metabolic rate in obese men and women" *J. Am. Diet. Assoc.* 91(4): pg. 430-434, Apr 1991.

Dudley, G.A., & S.J. Fleck. "Strength and endurance training: are they mutually exclusive?" *Sports Med.* Vol. 4: pg. 79 – 85, 1987.

Elliot, D.L., L. Goldberg, K.S. Kuehl, & W.M. Bennett. "Sustained depression of the resting metabolic rate after massive weight loss." *Am. J. Clin. Nutr.* 49(1): pg. 93 – 96, Jan., 1989.

Fricker, J., R. Rozen, J.C. Melchior, & M. Apfelbaum. "Energy-metabolism adaptation in obese adults on a very-low-calorie diet." *Am. J. Clin. Nutr.* 53(4): pg. 826 – 830, Apr., 1991.

Hennessy, L.C., & A.W.S. Watson. "The interference effects of trining for strength and endurance simultaneously" *Jour. Strength Cond. Res.* Vol. 8, no. 1, pg. 12-19, 1994.

Hunter, G.R., R.L. Weinsier, M.M. Bamman, & D.E. Larson. "A role for high intensity exercise on energy balance and weight control" *Int. J. Obes. Relat. Metab. Disord.* 22(6): pg. 489-493, Jun. 1998.

McArdle, W.D., F.I. Katch, & V.L. Katch. *Exercise Physiology: Energy, Nutrition, and Human Performance* 5th ed. Lippincott, Williams and Wilkins, Baltimore, MD pg.752-867, 2001.

Flexibility Training

The Physiology of Flexibility

Flexibility is the most overlooked athletic performance enhancer by young athletes and coaches alike. Maybe it is because the training adaptations in the body aren't as obvious as they are in other strength and conditioning parameters, like changes in muscularity or a reduction in percent of body fat. When we observe an accomplished athlete perform at a high level of agility and athleticism, we know that athlete has put a lot of time and effort into developing and maintaining flexibility. The development of good flexibility, the ability to move easily through a full range of joint motion, is an excellent way to prevent injuries to soft tissues of the body such as muscles and tendons. In this chapter we will look at what limits flexibility and how you can develop a program to increase range of motion.

Muscles and tendons are held together by connective tissues. This is the covering of tissue that both surrounds and runs through the muscle, and then tapers into the tendon that connects the muscle to the bone (McMinn & Hutchings, 1988). It is a relatively tough tissue, adding structural strength to the entire musculoskeletal system, and it has some degree of elasticity due to a component called *elastin*. When we're young this connective tissue is elastic and can stretch to extreme ranges of joint motion. Children can assume body positions that few adults can manage and stay in those positions quite comfortably. As we get older, those connective tissues become thicker and stronger

and lose some elasticity. Research suggests that resistance training over time will also cause these connective tissues, especially the tendons, to become thicker and stronger, and therefore less elastic. The net result of this potential loss of elasticity is that it may leave the athlete with less than a full range of motion. Equally important, a strong or explosive muscle contraction pulling against a tight antagonistic muscle (muscle on the opposite side of a joint) can cause a tear or muscle pull. The loss of full range of motion not only limits performance, such as speed and agility, it may also be a ticking time bomb for muscle and tendon injuries in a young athlete.

The best way to avoid loss of flexibility, especially in football players engaging in heavy resistance training, is to regularly stretch these connective tissues and move them through their full range of motion (Allerheiligan, 1994). The best way to achieve this is through three specific approaches:

Warmup

Some coaches and players believe that warmup and stretching are the same thing. They are not. The warmup is actually an important prerequisite to stretching because a warm muscle or tendon is more elastic than a cold one (Shellock 1986). The goal of the warmup is to literally elevate the *core temperature* of the muscle (internal temperature) by performing non-resistive movements (motions that do not use weights). The heat released in the muscle is then transferred into the connective tissues that surround and run through both muscle and tendons. Warmed up connective tissues are much more likely to be stretched without tearing; they can be taken to extreme ranges of motion much more safely than when they are cold. You might want to schedule flexibility training after the resistance training workout to ensure players are thoroughly warmed up prior to an extensive stretching program, especially for some of the more advanced stretching methods outlined in this chapter.

Make sure that players lift through a full range of motion in their weightlifting techniques.

Often players limit their range of motion by not bringing the bar down all the way to the chest on a bench press or all the way down to the collarbone on an overhead press. By limiting range of motion, they miss an opportunity to stretch the connective tissue and develop flexibility at the same time they are developing strength. Remember to make sure the player is sufficiently warmed up to prevent injury.

Stretching

Stretching can be static, which is holding a stretched position for a minimum of 10 seconds or a maximum of 30 seconds, or dynamic in which the stretched position is coupled with movement, such as in the walking toe touch. Ultimately, the goal is to move to some extreme range of motion to a point of mild discomfort. If the player experiences any sharp pain or extreme discomfort, the stretch position is too extreme and should be reduced. Stretches can be performed individually or with a partner to achieve greater range of motion. With the assisted stretches, it is very important for partners to communicate well when the stretch is too much or not enough.

Warmup and Dynamic Flexibility

Never try to stretch a cold muscle. At best you will achieve no more than you would stretching a warm muscle. At worst, you can tear or irritate connective tissue in tendon or muscle, often resulting in a nagging soft tissue injury. Non-resistive motions (using no weights or other resistance), using the same muscle groups that are about to be stretched, must be performed to elevate core temperature. This occurs because adenosinetriphosphate (ATP), which is the immediate source of usable energy stored in the muscle, is not 100 percent efficient in transferring its energy to the muscle work. About 75 percent of the energy released from ATP breakdown is lost as heat. This is why we shiver when we are cold. Our body is trying to generate heat by rapidly contracting muscle tissue and generating this heat (this is why our teeth chatter). The non-resistive movements involve enough work to get this ATP breakdown to occur without placing too much stress on cold muscles.

A particularly important benefit of nonresistive movements prior to heavy exercise is what is commonly referred to as *joint readiness*. Our joints are designed so that the tendons, which cross the joint, glide over bones with as little friction as possible. To facilitate this, we generate a type of lubricant called synovial fluid, which acts much like oil in machinery to reduce friction. Without this fluid, dry tendons moving over hard surfaces would quickly generate heat, resulting in inflammation as the heat buildup caused tendons to swell. Over time this could lead to chronic inflammation known as tendonitis. The warmup routine is critical in preparing the joints and the connective tissues for heavy exercise.

We mentioned earlier that the warmup should be muscle group specific, using a variety of movements and angle variation of the same movements. For example, if a player was preparing for a leg workout involving squats and deadlifts as the major lifts, lowerbody warmup exercises as well as some shoulder and trapezius exercises would be warranted.

This might include a light jog around the gymnasium, followed by some freestanding squats, lower back warmups (standing twists, alternating toe touch, etc.) and some shoulder circles. A good rule of thumb for whether or not a player has warmed up sufficiently is to require that a player break a sweat before being allowed to start stretching.

Dynamic flexibility is attained through movement. This involves preparing the athlete for more rigorous activity, such as weight training, by having them move in a variety of body positions. Have the players perform walking toe touches in which they kick their leg up as high as possible and touch the toe of the extended leg on every step. This can be followed by knee hugs in which the player brings the knee of the lead foot high and hugs it to his chest on each step, alternating knees. Both of these activities can be adapted to skipping toe touches and skipping knee hugs by having the player use a skip step rather than a normal walking gait. A more advanced dynamic flexibility drill has players skipping backward. To perform this drill, the player throws his knees outward while pushing off with a skip step (flight phase).

If space concerns are an issue, you can offer dynamic flexibility through what are commonly known as *rack stretches*. The rack stretch is performed by setting up an unloaded barbell on a power rack at a height that is about chest high. The side pins are placed so that one is at about waist height and the other is about knee height. The player is instructed to move around the rack either by bending his knees to move under the bar, or stepping over the pins. The players can vary their movement by approaching each obstacle from different sides and by moving forward laterally and backward. If several power racks are available, each rack can be set up with a variety of bar and pin heights, allowing the players to perform the drill as a circuit. This drill adds to the warmup by

requiring players to put their bodies in positions of extreme range of motion while moving. It not only develops dynamic flexibility but also develops balance and coordination. If a power rack is not available, the coach can improvise, using objects that players can step over or move under. You can use adjustable hurdles set at various heights to perform this drill.

You can develop dynamic flexibility through drills in which a player is required to move in a position-specific posture. For example, a key to good offensive line play is for linemen to play low, meaning that their center of gravity should be lower than that of the opponent. This can be used as a variation to any of the agility drills outlined in Chapter 4. The drills can be programmed (having a set sequence of movements) or reactive (responding to a verbal or visual cue from a coach) and/or can be multidirectional. The coach then requires the players to move through the drill in a low stance. Specific drills for dynamic flexibility are the low, slow shuffle in which the place maintains a low center of gravity by bending at the knee and shuffles forward, backward, and laterally. For skill position players, a low carioca step drill is effective because it develops speed and balance in the low position.

Static Flexibility

Static stretching, in which a player assumes a position that puts a specific body part in an extreme range of motion and then holds that position, is an easy and effective way to gain flexibility. The American College of Sports Medicine (ACSM) in its 1998 position statement on exercise prescription recommended that each stretch place the muscle being stretched in a position of mild discomfort and that each stretch be held for a minimum of 10 seconds and a maximum of 30 seconds. This mild discomfort is needed to trigger the muscle's protective system, known as the muscle spindle, which attempts to protect the muscle from overstretching by causing it to contract. This muscle spindle is the same sensory structure that plays a role in plyometric training by eliciting the stretch reflex (see plyometric section in Chapter 4). In the static stretch, the player resists this

muscle contraction and holds the stretched position for the minimum of 10 seconds.

An optional variation to this type of stretch is a two-man stretch, in which a partner assists the player in attaining and holding the stretched position. This requires good communication between the partners to avoid injury. Once the point of mild discomfort is achieved, the player tells his partner to stop and the partner holds the position without using excess force. The partner must establish a strong, balanced position to be effective, especially when stretching large muscle groups in the hips and legs.

The training effect of static stretching is to elongate and render more pliable the elastic tissues of the muscle and tendon. Stretches should be performed at every workout in some form.

PNF Stretching

PNF stretching (which stands for proprioceptive neuromuscular facilitation) is a technique used by

physical therapists to improve flexibility by actually overriding the stretch reflex mentioned in the previous section. The stretch reflex is initiated when the muscle spindles sense that the muscle is in danger of stretching too far, resulting in a reflex contraction (involuntary contraction) to shorten and thereby protect the muscle. The PNF method actually incorporates voluntary isometric muscle contractions (contractions in which the muscle doesn't shorten but becomes tense) to satisfy the muscle spindle. This causes the muscle spindle to temporarily shut down allowing for a greater elongation of the muscle being stretched. Keep in mind that the player is overriding a safety mechanism in the muscle, so great care must be taken in using this flexibility technique.

PNF stretching uses alternating six-second bouts of static stretching immediately followed by six-second isometric contractions. It is best performed using a partner who is strong enough to provide resistance against which the player pushes during the isometric contractions. The player assumes a normal stretching position and has his partner assist him in attaining a range of motion to a point that elicits mild discomfort (good communication between partners is essential). The player holds that position for a six count and then immediately performs an isometric contraction of the muscle that is being stretched. The partner must position himself in a strong and balanced position to ensure that the muscle being stretched does not shorten. This isometric contraction is maintained for six seconds and then the player relaxes the muscle and allows his partner to push him a little further into the stretch. This is where the partner must be careful not to push too hard or to an excessive range of motion. Once the mild discomfort sets in, the player tells the partner to stop and holds the stretch for another six-second period and the cycle is repeated. Typically, the cycle is repeated three times for each stretch. Since this is such a high-risk stretch, it should only be used under the strict supervision of coaches and only when the players are well warmed up.

Active Isolation Stretching

This form of flexibility stretching is used by many college programs because it incorporates the advantages of two-man stretching but does not require a partner. Instead, the player uses a long nylon strap with a loop on the end to provide the counterforce of the muscle-tightening effect of the stretch reflex. The player places his foot in the loop while holding the opposite end of the nylon strap, pulling his leg into a stretched position. Once the point of mild discomfort is achieved, the player can pull the strap to gain a slightly greater extreme range of motion and hold it for two seconds. This two-second hold is short enough to avoid the full effect of the muscle spindle-induced stretch reflex from occurring, but long enough to help facilitate an increased range of motion. Usually these stretches work best for hamstring and other leg muscles. On a more advanced level, the active isolation stretch can incorporate the PNF technique by having the player alternate static stretches with isometric contractions. In this case, a partner will not be used, so the player can directly control the extent of the stretch.

We recommend the active isolation stretching over PNF or two-man stretching simply because it is effective and can be performed when a player is alone. There is less risk of miscommunication, which could lead to injury if the partner accidentally places too much pressure on the player during a stretch.

Examples of Stretches for Each Category

To be as helpful as we can, we want to provide some sampling of the many stretches possible in each category. Coaches and players can apply our stretching concepts to stretches that they are already using.

Dynamic Flexibility

Walking toe touch

The players line up along a yard line with adequate spacing so they don't kick the player in front of them, facing the coach.

Each player steps forward with the right foot and the left arm extended in front of his body, so that the hand is at about shoulder height.

He then brings the left foot off of the ground and attempts to kick his left hand with a straight leg kick, and immediately returns the left foot to the ground.

On the next step he extends his right arm in front of his body and using the right foot to kick the hand, which is also at shoulder height.

The player continues this alternating sequence down the field.

This exercise is designed to warm up and stretch the low back and hamstrings. The player should try to keep his leg as straight as possible.

Low shuffle

Players line up single file along a line facing the coach in a low wide stance.

Keeping the feet close to the ground, the players side shuffle their feet as quickly as possible, moving along the ground as quickly as possible.

The player continues this side shuffle down the field staying in a low position. The player's head and shoulders must stay at the same level all the way down the field and should not bob up and down.

This exercise is use to warm up the groin as well as hip flexors and extensors.

This drill is a good balance and technique drill for offensive linemen to learn to play low.

Knee hugs

The players line up along a yard line with adequate spacing in front of them facing the coach.

Each player steps forward with the right foot and brings the left knee up as high and close to his chest as possible.

He immediately grasps the leg with both arms and holds it tight to his chest for a one-one-thousand count then returns the left foot to the ground in an advanced position.

He then repeats the sequence with his right knee up as high and close to his chest as possible.

The player continues this alternating sequence down the field.

This exercise is designed to warm up and stretch the low back and hamstrings.

Backward skip

The players line up along a yard line with adequate spacing behind them, facing away from the coach.

The players skip backward by pushing off with their left foot, bringing the left knee up and outward as high as possible.

When the left foot hits the ground, they repeat the motion by pushing off with their right foot and bringing the right knee up and out.

The sequence is repeated in a rhythmic, skipping motion down the field.

This exercise is designed to warm up and stretch the hip and groin muscles.

Static stretches

Wide stance head-to-knee stretch

The player takes a stance that is as wide as possible.

Keeping a slight bend in the knee, the player brings his forehead as close as possible (to a point of mild discomfort) to his right knee and holds it for 10 seconds.

The player then moves to the left leg and attempts to bring his forehead as close as possible to his left knee, holding for a 10-second count.

As the player gains flexibility, he should eventually be able to perform the exercise with the legs straight.

This exercise is designed to stretch the lower back, groin, and hamstrings.

Two-man hamstring stretch

This exercise is performed with a partner and targets the hamstring muscle of the thigh.

It is very important that the partner is in a good balanced position when applying pressure to stretch the leg, and that the two partners must communicate well so the stretched muscle is not pushed to a point of injury.

The player who is stretching assumes a position on his back with the right leg extended along the ground and his heel of his left leg resting on his partner's shoulder.

The partner slowly pushes the left leg back until the player stretching tells him to stop.

The leg being stretched should remain straight, and the opposite leg should remain on the ground. Once in this position, the stretch is held for a 10-second count.

The stretch is then repeated with the opposite leg.

POW stretch

This upper-body stretch also uses a partner and is designed to target the chest, shoulders, and arms.

The player who is stretching kneels on the ground, keeping his body as straight as possible, and places his hands on top of his head (like a prisoner of war, which is where the POW comes from).

The player's partner stands directly behind him and places his arms over the player's arms near the player's elbows. The partner then locks his hands behind the player's back.

The partner then exerts a gentle stretch by pulling his elbows backward, which in turn causes the player's elbows to be pulled back. This continues to a point of mild discomfort and is held for the 10-second count.

Leg over stretch

The player lies on the ground face up, with both legs fully extended. This stretch can be performed solo or with a partner to assist.

The player raises his left leg and extends it across the right leg until the left foot is close to touching the ground. It is important that the player remain flat on his back during this part of the stretch.

A partner can assist the player by pushing the opposite shoulder to the ground while bracing the leg being stretched.

Once the player feels mild discomfort, the stretch is held for 10 seconds.

The player returns to the starting position, and the exercise is repeated with the right leg.

If done properly, with the back flat on the ground, this exercise stretches the lower back and outside hip muscles.

Knee hug stretch

The player lies flat on his back and pulls the knee of one leg as close to his chest as possible.

The opposite leg should remain extended and on the ground throughout the stretch.

The stretch is held for 10 seconds for each leg. This stretch targets the lower back and gluteal muscles.

Overhead arm stretch

This stretch can be performed solo or with a partner.

The player stretching will stand or kneel on the ground (when using a partner) with one arm extended overhead but bent at the elbow.

With the player or a partner holding the elbow of the extended arm, the elbow is slowly pulled across the midline of the body to a point of mild discomfort.

The stretch is held for a 10-second count. This stretch is ideal for targeting the lat muscles of the back (lats) and the triceps of the back of the arm.

PNF Stretches

Any two-man stretch can be converted into a PNF stretch by simply adding isometric muscle contractions by tightening the muscle against an immovable object or partner. It is critical that the muscle flexes but there is no movement. A PNF stretch overrides the stretch reflex described earlier to allow the muscle to stretch beyond normal resting lengths. Since the muscle spindle is designed to cause the muscle to contract as an involuntary reflex, the voluntary contraction of the same muscle causes the muscle spindle to shut down briefly. This actually relaxes the muscle and allows the athlete to override the mechanism that would normally limit range of motion. Keep in mind that you are overriding a protective mechanism in the muscle so some precautions are important.

This type of stretching should be done only with experienced players and even then under strict supervision of a qualified coach.

The players must be warmed up properly prior to PNF stretching using nonresistant movements or dynamic flexibility exercises. A good way to know if players are warmed up sufficiently is to be sure they break a sweat before engaging in these stretches.

Partners must communicate well throughout the stretch so that the muscles are not overstretched. The partner who is providing the resistance (for the isometric contraction) must be in a strong and balanced position.

PNF stretching should not be performed with players who have a pre-existing injury or players who are prone to muscle pulls. These players should stick to static stretching.

The PNF stretch is performed in the following manner:

The player who is stretching assumes the stretched position, with the partner assisting him to a point of mild discomfort.

The stretch is held for a six-second count.

Without moving, the player then performs an isometric muscle contraction against resistance supplied by his partner. Tell the player to contract the muscle that is being stretched (i.e., hamstring) and have the player's partner counteract the muscle contraction with enough opposing resistance to prevent movement.

The isometric contraction is held for a six count, and then the muscle is immediately relaxed. The partner should tell the player when to relax.

Upon relaxation of the muscle, the partner gently pushes the limb being stretched into a deeper stretch until the player tells him to stop. This position is held for a six-count static stretch.

This sequence of stretch-flex-relax is repeated for two to three cycles.

IV. Active isolation stretches

One-leg hamstring stretch

This stretching series requires a nylon strap with a loop at the end.

The player places the foot of the leg being stretched into the loop and wraps the other end of the strap around his hand.

The player keeps the leg straight with the knee locked slowly pulls the leg toward him until he feels mild discomfort.

The stretch is held for 10 seconds and then released.

This stretch isolates the hamstring muscles. It also may be used as a one-man PNF stretch by alternating static stretches with six-second isometric contractions.

Leg over stretch

The player places the foot of the leg being stretched into the loop and wraps the other end of the strap around his hand in a similar fashion to the hamstring stretch (see figure above).

Keeping the leg that is being stretched straight, the player brings the leg across the opposite leg, attempting to touch the ground with his foot while keeping his shoulders flat on the ground.

The stretch is held for 10 seconds and then released.

This stretch isolates the muscles of the outside of the hip and the lower back.

Quadriceps stretch

This stretch is one of the few stretches that isolates the quadriceps (front of the thigh) muscle group.

The player lies on his side and places the foot of the leg being stretched (the high leg, not the leg he is lying on) into the loop.

The player wraps the other end of the strap around his hand in a similar fashion to the hamstring stretch and pulls the nylon strap over his shoulder.

This position allows the player to pull the heel of his foot as close to his buttocks as possible (to a point of mild discomfort), thereby stretching the quads.

This stretch can also be done using the PNF principle.

References

Allerheiligen, W.B. "Stretching and warm-up" In: *Essentials of Strength and Conditioning* T.R. Baechle, ed. Human Kinetics; Champaign Ill. Pg. 289-313, 1994.

McMinn, R.M.H., & R.T. Hutchings. *Color Atlas of Human Anatomy 2nd ed.*, Year Book Medical Publ. 1988.

Shellock F.G. "Physiological, psychological, and injury prevention aspects of warm-up" *NSCA Jour.* Vol. 8, no.5 1986.

The Role of Proper Nutrition

So far we have focused on the physical exercises and programming variables involved in the design of a strength and conditioning program for football players. This book would be incomplete, however, if we didn't address an important factor that affects the athlete's performance in the training process—nutrition.

Before we get into specific nutritional advice, it should be noted that athletic nutrition encompasses a very broad spectrum of topics ranging from a basic healthy diet to performance-specific eating plans, including the use of supplements. It would be a daunting task to attempt to cover all aspects of proper nutrition, so our approach is to develop an easy-to-follow program that is useful to the coach and player. This may lead to simplification of some topics and extensive details in others, but our aim is to provide enough scientific background to help the reader understand why this program is effective for providing proper nutrition for the athletic population.

We will start with some general information on how the body digests, absorbs and metabolizes the food we eat and offer some practical advice that can be applied to any athlete based on individual needs. The same principle that helps the overweight player can be modified to serve the player who is trying to gain lean body mass by understanding the underlying mechanisms of how the body acquires nutrients.

Basic Nutrition

Generally, the food we eat serves three major functions: 1) providing an energy source or fuel; 2) providing raw material for tissue maintenance, growth and development; and 3) providing chemical components that regulate all functions in the body such as muscle contraction, nerve conduction, etc. In all of the research focused in this area, we find that each of these functions can be conducted simultaneously, and at maximum levels, when there are sufficient and well-balanced nutrients consumed regularly by a young athlete. The reality, however, is that very few young men pay close attention to what they consume every day. They typically develop bad eating habits at very early ages, and often these bad habits affect performance without their being aware of it. Such practices as skipping breakfast in the morning, skipping meals, eating junk food, avoiding entire food groups such as fruits and vegetables, not drinking enough water, or eating too many sweets are some of the most common bad habits among young athletes. What many of them don't understand is that they are going through an important stage of growth and development that requires essential raw materials in order for optimum results to occur. If you add to this the fact that the football player in a year-round training program also has increased energy requirements, it is clear that good eating habits are a critical component of the overall training program.

So what happens if a football player has less than ideal eating habits and denies his body the nutrients he needs? The body will attempt to respond by signaling the brain that more and/or different food is needed. If that doesn't work, the body will try to adjust in an effort to survive by maintaining components of the body through the sacrifice of what it considers to be non-essential. Many scientists believe that this response originated when humans were hunters and gatherers, surviving on a catch-as-can basis in the wilds. Anthropologists believe that this type of existence characterized most of prehistoric man's existence. In the hunter-gatherer model there were two undeniable facts.

First, the food supply was not consistent, almost a feast or famine situation where food would be abundant during one time period, but scarce over another time period. This required the ability to store extra calories during the feast so that living off stored calories insured survival during the famine. Those among our ancestors who acquired this ability to store calories, usually in the form of fat, survived, while those who could not perished. This is why our bodies tend to hold on to fat, even if body fat levels get excessively high, as a way to insure survival. If an overweight athlete tries to shed excess pounds, he must counteract this natural tendency to store excess fat.

The second fact is that the food our ancestors ate probably underwent very little in the way of processing. Outside of occasionally cooking the food, very little was done to change the food prehistoric man consumed. Physiologically, humans adapted to digesting and metabolizing nutrients from food found in their unadulterated, unprocessed form. This may not seem important today except for strong evidence that overly processed food can fool the body into thinking that more calories must be consumed by stimulating appetite.

Modern-day humans hold on to the same physiological responses of our ancient ancestors, but the food we eat has drastically changed, as have our eating habits. Today, much of the food we eat is over-processed, which can have an effect on how that food is digested and absorbed. Many of the nutrients found in the unprocessed form of the food are missing once that food is processed. Now you might ask, if processing or overprocessing food is so bad, why do the companies who sell prepared food do this? The answer is economics—getting people to buy your product because it looks and tastes good is the bottom line in today's competitive food industry. The nutritional value of the food that is sold is usually not as high a priority as selling the food. It is important for the coach to provide guidance to players as to good eating habits, to maximize performance and keep these young men healthy.

Carbohydrate and Glycemic Index

Carbohydrates represent a relatively quick and easily digested source of fuel for various functions in the body. It is the exclusively preferred source of energy for the brain and central nervous system. Foods high in carbohydrates are broken down into the simplest form of sugar known as glucose. This glucose is then absorbed into the blood stream in the digestive tract at varying rates (the rate of absorption is known as glycemic index, a term we will discuss later). This glucose in the blood stream is referred to as the blood-glucose level (sometimes call the blood-sugar level) and is maintained at a fairly consistent level. Once the glucose is in our blood stream, it is delivered to various tissues (i.e., muscle, brain, and liver) where it is taken up by the tissues to be used as fuel or stored for later use.

An important hormone critical in the tissue uptake is **insulin**. Think of insulin as the door keeper of the liver and muscle cells, because when the pancreas secretes it, it opens receptors (openings in the cell wall) to allow glucose to enter either the liver or muscle cells. As long as the insulin is present, the door stays opened. Once the glucose is inside the cell, it is used for all forms of work, including both anaerobic (sprints, weight lifting, and all short term, high intensity exercise) and aerobic (long-duration, low-intensity exercise) activity. In fact, it is a preferred fuel because it is easy for the body to metabolize and convert to energy, particularly when compared to fat.

If there is no demand for energy in a given cell, such as resting muscle or a liver cell, the glucose taken up can be stored for later use. It can be stored in the muscle and liver as glycogen, but this is limited to the available area inside the cell, or can be converted in the liver to fat. Ironically, once converted to fat, carbohydrate cannot be converted back to glucose, which means that once glycogen stores are spent, they can only be replenished by eating more carbohydrate rich foods.

The muscle glycogen is eventually used within the muscle cell in which it is stored, while the liver glycogen is available once the levels of blood-glucose drop, to bring the blood-glucose levels back to normal. If the liver glycogen stores are used up, the drop in blood glucose has the effect of stimulating the appetite to compel a person to eat some carbohydrates and restore normal levels. Regardless of whether an athlete depletes his stored carbohydrates by using it as fuel, or fails to replace it following a workout, the result will be a drop in overall physical performance.

Based on this information, it seems simple to advise a player on carbohydrates—eat lots of carbohydrates. But not all carbohydrates are the same. Some carbohydrates, either by nature or due to processing, are absorbed into the blood stream more quickly than others (this is the glycemic index issue). In addition, certain foods, especially processed foods, contain concentrated amounts of carbohydrates. We refer to the latter as having a high caloric density, since a lot of calories are packed into a relatively small amount of food. In fact, sometimes the worst combination is when a food has a high glycemic index coupled with a high caloric density, something coaches need to understand better.

Glycemic index rates the rapidity of glucose movement from the digestive system into the blood. In a food that has a low glycemic index, the carbohydrate would be digested and absorbed, in the form of glucose, into the blood stream slowly. This would keep the blood-glucose level much more even and minimize the amount of insulin secreted by the pancreas, especially if that food had a low caloric density, less carbohydrates being introduced into the blood stream slowly. If a food has a high caloric density but a relatively low glycemic index, the glucose would be abundant, but because it is introduced into the system slowly it causes only moderate levels of insulin to be secreted. This would keep the blood glucose level in the ideal range rather than allowing wild swings that can negatively affect the way a player feels and performs during exercise. A food with a low caloric density but a high glycemic index pushes the glucose into the blood system quickly, but the absolute amount of glucose must be low enough to keep the insulin response to a moderate level.

All three of these combinations would probably have a minimal effect on physical performance and appetite in an individual. The worst case scenario occurs when a person consumes a high glycemic index, high caloric density food immediately prior to a workout or a game. This causes a large level of insulin to be secreted in response to the high amount of glucose that is pushed very rapidly into the system. If you recall, the role of insulin is to open the door of the cell receptors to allow glucose into the cell. Initially, the large presence of insulin is a good thing when large amounts of glucose are elevating blood-glucose levels to dangerously high point. Glucose levels that are too high or too low can cause shock to the central nervous system resulting in coma or death. If insulin stays around too long, it causes blood-glucose levels to actually get too low as the door stays open too long, almost like a pendulum that swings too far one way causing it to swing too far back the opposite way. Remember, our ancestors didn't eat refined food, so our insulin hasn't adapted to the relatively recent abundance of refined carbohydrates available today. These include refined sugar, refined flours such as white flour, corn syrup, and other ingredients found in the foods we all tend to have in our homes today (just look at the ingredients on package labels of cereals, breads and other processed foods).

Why is a low blood glucose level bad? It depends on what the individual is trying to accomplish. For a person trying to lose excess body fat, this sugar roller coaster of high glucose causing a large influx of insulin, which in turn causes a big drop in blood-glucose, causes excessive stimulation of the appetite. An overweight player craves more carbohydrates when he is in the low blood-glucose state, and more than likely will end up eating too many excess empty calories. Even the player who didn't have to be concerned about excess body fat would suffer performance variation (both mental and physical) while in the low blood-glucose condition, also known as **reactive hypoglycemia**. Most of the time, with one exception, high glycemic index foods should be avoided by players. The exception is immediately following a high intensity or long duration workout. The high glycemic index foods may actually be beneficial in restoring the glycogen to the working muscles because this time window immediately following a hard workout is when the working muscle cells are more sensitive to taking up glucose. Restoring muscle glycogen is an important part of the recovery process.

The Importance of Breakfast

Breakfast is, by far, the most important meal of the day as long as the right type of food is eaten. The reason for this is that breakfast has the potential for setting a player up on an even and steady blood-glucose level that is easily maintained throughout the remainder of the day. Skipping breakfast can cause a rapid drop in the blood-glucose level since the liver glycogen stores are usually depleted following eight-hours of sleep. Thus, you are simply getting on the sugar roller coaster at a different point (the low blood-glucose level rather than the high blood-glucose level experienced with high glycemic index foods). The net result is still the same—the player craves carbohydrates, eats the wrong, high glycemic index foods that satisfy the cravings, but eventually experiences a rapid drop in blood glucose, leading to new cravings, and poor performance.

Some young players may think a soft drink and a donut qualify as breakfast. Others may eat some sugary cereal or breakfast pastry, thinking that it represents a nutritious breakfast. But remember, refined sugar and flour that makes up the bulk of the calories will eventually cause the insulin reaction causing the blood-glucose to plummet. A much more effective approach is to eat foods that are of a low glycemic index for breakfast (identified under the Gold category in the Virginia Tech eating plan). This would include certain fruits and whole grain cereals, yogurts, eggs, and other such breakfast fare that are easy to prepare and just as quick as the junk food breakfasts. A player can hard boil a couple eggs the night before,

and eat that with some whole grain toast, and a piece of fruit, just as easily as eating a donut and a cola. It is a matter of getting a player into a good habit; getting him out of bed 15 minutes earlier than normal; and letting him experience how well it prepares him to meet the challenges of the day.

Consuming six or seven small meals per day rather than three large meals is a recommendation that can also benefit a player to help maintain an even blood glucose level. The composition of the meals will affect blood-glucose, but if properly planned, this eating regimen will help the athlete build and maintain lean body mass and muscle. One reason for this is that when the central nervous system is denied its required glucose for normal energy metabolism (remember the brain and central nervous system functions best on glucose) it will seek other sources of glucose by breaking down muscle tissue. As stated earlier, fat cannot be converted to glucose even when it was created from excess glucose in the liver. Muscle, on the other hand, can be catabolized (broken down) and its protein converted to glucose in the liver. Since muscle is only about 20 percent protein and 75 percent water, it takes five pounds of muscle to yield one pound of protein. This muscle wasting is obviously counterproductive to the muscle-building process, and can easily be avoided if the blood glucose levels are properly maintained. Eating six to seven meals per day may not be practical for the typical high school athlete, so meal replacement drinks might be used between meals to provide sufficient nutrients for this population.

Fats in the Diet

Fat is nature's most economical way of storing calories. A gram of fat is more than twice as calorically dense as a gram of unrefined carbohydrate or a gram of protein; this allows more calories of energy to be stored in the same amount of space. For this reason, when we consume fat, we are consuming more calories, gram for gram, than any other energy source. Those who are trying to lose weight will often minimize fat consumption and eat more food in the form of carbohydrates and protein. But fat in the diet is not necessarily a bad choice, as long as the right types of fats and moderate amounts of fat are consumed. In fact, many scientists believe that an athlete requires a

certain amount of fat to produce anabolic (muscle-building) hormones such as testosterone, which use fat as a basic building block in its molecular structure.

A moderate amount of fat in the diet is as important to a football player as any rich source of energy. For the player who is trying to maintain lean body mass, fat represents a concentrated form of calories to meet the requirements of a high level of activity coupled with a naturally fast metabolism. It would be difficult for this type of athlete to consume enough calories by eating just carbohydrates and protein. Even the overweight athlete can benefit from some fat in the diet, since fat takes longer to digest in the gastrointestinal tract, it provides satiety giving him a full feeling, helping him control his appetite. This goes hand in hand with low glycemic index food consumption, which keeps the overweight athlete from overeating.

Fats come in two basic forms: saturated fats that typically come from animal sources, and unsaturated fats that typically are derived from plant sources. There are a couple of exceptions to this. Fish, although being classified as an animal source, often contain essential oils that are unsaturated forms of fat. Certain plant fats are processed into what are called *trans fatty acids,* which are hydrogenated so that they can exist as solid fats (i.e., margarines, peanut butter,

etc.) rather than their natural state as oil. From a health standpoint, it is better to consume unsaturated fats than saturated fats since the saturated fats are linked to an increased risk of heart disease, and you can never start too early protecting arteries from this. Our recommendation is that football players consume about 30 percent of their total calories in a day from fats, preferably from the unsaturated form of fat. Get the players in a habit of reading labels on food packages and taking note of the percentage breakdown of the calories they consume. Perhaps you can have some team meetings where they bring in packages and compare labels.

Protein and Misinformation

Protein is often the most misunderstood nutrient and the source of much misinformation regarding athletic nutrition. Classic research studies suggest that the typical athlete needs no more than the Recommended Dietary Allowance (RDA) of .8 grams of protein per kilogram of body weight. Their nitrogen balance studies found that any amount beyond this level was simply eliminated from the body and not taken up by the cells to stimulate increased muscle growth. The weakness of many of these studies is that the athletes tested were not specifically defined as a particular type of athlete, namely the strength-power athlete typical of football players. Recent studies, with more specific populations typical of football players found strong evidence that about twice the RDA, or 1.6 grams of protein per kilogram of body weight had an effect on strength gains when compared to the accepted RDA of .8 grams.

Protein serves a dual role as both a source of energy and a building block for tissues such as muscle. The

role of protein as a fuel is one that only occurs when the body is in a less than ideal state of metabolism such as the low blood glucose levels discussed earlier in this chapter. In this case, muscle is broken down and converted to glucose in the liver to provide fuel for the nervous system as the body tries to maintain a high-priority system at the expense of the muscle. This is counterproductive to strength gains. Ideally, with sufficient protein and carbohydrates (of the right type) the stage is set for maximum recovery from workouts and optimum protein synthesis in the muscle.

It is best to get one's daily protein requirement from good balanced meals, but the reality with football players is that eating balanced meals evenly distributed throughout the day may be easier said than done. This is where protein supplement drinks may be useful in insuring that adequate protein is consumed each day.

Vitamins and Minerals

Vitamins and minerals are important nutrients even though they are not used as fuel. Instead, vitamins and minerals are involved as regulators of chemical reactions that allow the body to build and maintain tissues, contract muscles, and generally conduct the proper chemical reactions that are critical to life itself. As with protein, the ideal diet should be varied and balanced to provide sufficient vitamins and minerals for the high school player. This would require the consumption of mostly fruits and vegetables of vari-

ous types each and every day. Because some players won't eat several servings of fruits and vegetables a day due to limited variety in their diet, a vitamin supplement is highly recommended. This does not need to be some megavitamin sold at health food stores. This can be a standard generic vitamin sold at grocery stores for a very reasonable price that meets the RDA for each vitamin. It is not necessary for athletes to consume more than the RDA since the standards set far exceed the needs of 98 percent of the population.

Hydration and the Need for Water

We typically do not think of water as a nutrient, but it is probably the most important nutrient we consume. We can last several weeks without food, but only a few days without water. Water is an important component of muscle tissue (75 percent of our muscle is made up of water) and it provides the medium in which many of the vitamins and minerals are dissolved and distributed in the body. If a person is suffering some sort of electrolyte imbalance, it is not due to lack of minerals such as potassium, but actually due to lack of water throwing off relative concentrations of these electrolytes. Players should drink plenty of water and drink often, especially with hard training in hot environments. Players should carry water bottles everywhere they go throughout the day and drink often, before they are actually thirsty. Remember from the section on heat illness, that dehydration is usually the result of long-term or chronic dehydration rather than a result of a single event.

The Virginia Tech Bronze, Silver, and Gold System

The Virginia Tech eating plan was designed to apply the principles outlined in the earlier sections of this chapter to enhance the physical development and, ultimately, the performance of their players. It takes into account not only what to eat, but also when to eat based on the player's level of activity for that particular day. Each of the major energy source foods (carbohydrates, fats and protein) are categorized based on the quality of each. The Gold category includes the highest quality foods based on fat content, quality of protein and glycemic index factors. The Silver category describes those foods that are still wholesome but perhaps contain more fats, fewer complete proteins, and higher glycemic index foods. The Bronze foods are the least nutritious by comparison but, under certain circumstances, are okay to eat occasionally. Remember, we don't want our athletes to feel deprived because they can't eat ice cream occasionally. The following are the major energy source foods broken down by category.

Protein

Proteins are a potential source of energy, but actually are best used as the building block of muscle tissue.

First Choice, Gold Medal Proteins are foods that contain less than 12 grams of fat per serving (consider a serving as being the size of a standard deck of cards or approximately the size of a persons hand minus the fingers). These foods also contain high-quality protein meaning that the body assimilates and uses the protein effectively. If a player is trying to lose body fat, these protein sources are best.

Examples of Gold Medal proteins are:
Roast turkey (especially white meat)
Baked chicken (white meat, no skin)
Lean roast beef (removing all visible fat)
Baked fish
Skim milk (one percent or less)
Egg whites (boiled or fried with no fat)
Lean baked ham
Canned tuna packed in water

Low fat or non-fat yogurt
Dried beans and peas

Silver Medal Proteins are good quality protein sources that contain 13 to 25 grams of fat per serving, which are considered a moderate level of fat.

Examples of Silver Medal proteins are:
85 percent lean ground beef (usually ground chuck or ground round)
85 percent lean ham
Trimmed choice steak (removing all visible fat)
Trimmed pork chops (removing all visible fat)
Baked breaded chicken strips
Two percent milk
Regular yogurt
Dark chicken meat (no skin)
Peanut butter

Bronze Medal Proteins are somewhat lower in high-quality protein and/or high in fat with more than 25 grams per serving.

Examples of Bronze Medal proteins are:
  Bacon
  Hot dogs
  Chicken with skin (especially dark meat)
  Fried chicken
  Fried fish
  Whole eggs (especially fried in fat)
  Whole milk
  Ham on bone
  Processed meats (lunchmeat, bologna, etc.)

Carbohydrates

Carbohydrates provide easily accessible fuel for working muscles and central nervous system function. In fact, the higher the intensity of work (i.e., heavy weight, high-speed running) the more one depends on carbohydrates for a fuel source.

As outlined previously, not all carbohydrates are the same. Some release glucose (the simplest form of sugar) into the blood more quickly than others. These quick-release carbohydrates are termed high glycemic index foods.

When blood sugar levels rise rapidly, the body responds by producing large amounts of insulin, which overcompensates and causes a big drop in blood sugar. This promotes fat storage and stimulates appetite, which can lead to overeating.

A low blood sugar level causes a player to feel tired and reduces the capacity to train or compete at the highest level of his ability.

First choice Gold Medal carbohydrates are foods that have a low glycemic index. They are best for supplying the muscle with a consistent, long lasting supply of energy. Generally, Gold Medal carbohydrates can be eaten any time, especially on low activity days.

Examples of Gold Medal carbohydrates are:

Dried beans and peas	Pears
Squash	Plums
Cucumbers	Onions
Green beans	Eggplant
Broccoli	Lentils
Spinach	Peanuts
Mushrooms	Kidney beans
Nectarines	Oranges
Apples	

Silver Medal carbohydrates are foods with a moderate glycemic index. These should be eaten on active days.

Silver Medal carbohydrate foods are helpful in restoring muscle fuels if consumed within one hour of training or competition, since the muscle cell is more sensitive to taking up glucose immediately following physical activity.

Examples of Silver Medal carbohydrates are:
  Unsweetened cereal (oatmeal, Grapenuts, and other whole grain cereals)
  Whole-wheat pasta
  Whole-grain breads
  Wild or brown rice
  Cornbread
  Tortillas
  Whole-wheat pita
  Potatoes with skin
  Grapes and bananas
  Corn and carrots

Bronze Medal carbohydrate foods produce the highest glycemic response and may have a high fat content as well. These are okay for occasional consumption on highly active days.

If a player is trying to lose body fat, these carbohydrates should be avoided. Decreasing Bronze Medal carbohydrate foods reduces calorie intake, decreases fat storage, and most importantly keeps you from overeating by allowing a stable and consistent blood sugar level.

Examples of Bronze Medal carbohydrate foods are:
  Candy
  Pretzels
  Cookies and cakes
  Sweetened cereal
  Doughnuts and pastries
  White bread (i.e., French bread, bagels, etc.)
  French fries and hashbrowns
  White rice
  Mashed potatoes
  Sweetened and soft drinks

The Bottom Line

On active days you want about half of the food on your plate to be Gold Medal and Silver Medal carbohydrates.

On inactive days (rest), reduce your total intake of carbohydrates and avoid Bronze Medal carbohydrates.

Gold Medal carbohydrates are best for those trying to lose fat and provide long-lasting energy.

Silver and Bronze Medal carbohydrates are best eaten within one hour after playing or training.

For gaining weight, eat Gold Medal and Silver Medal carbohydrates and consume six or seven smaller meals rather than three big meals. Meal replacement drinks and/or quality protein or weight gain supplements can be used as one or two of these meals.

For losing body fat, stay with Gold Medal choices for both carbohydrates and proteins. Drink plenty of water throughout the day, and avoid fast foods that are loaded with fat. Do not skip meals, especially breakfast. Eat snacks between meals but limit Silver Medal and avoid Bronze Medal choices.

The Role of Supplements and Meal Replacement Drinks

The nutritional supplement trade in the United States is a multibillion dollar industry that is, in the opinion of many, under-regulated by the Food and Drug Administration (FDA). Because of this, many of the nutritional supplements sold on the market today are not effective in producing what is commonly termed an *ergogenic effect*, a performance enhancement that is usually physical in nature (although certain psychological practices like mental imaging, meditation, etc., have been considered as potential sources of enhanced physical performance). With so many products claiming to enhance physical performance, it is difficult to determine which of these products are safe and effective. Even the scientific research on some of the most common supplements presents conflicting results and further clouds the effectiveness of these preparations. However, making the most of the current research, and our own real world experiences, we have identified those supplements that appear to have the best ergogenic effects. But let us say here, and in the strongest possible way, coaches and players should never assume or expect supplementation to take the place of proper training, good nutrition, and high quality rest.

Before we present some of the supplements that appear to be safe and effective, we would like to mention supplements that should definitely be avoided. Any supplement that is designed to affect hormonal levels should be avoided. This includes oral and injectible steroids as well as what are known as *prohormones,* which are oral preparations such as androstiene and DHEA that are precursors to testosterone. The side effects of these drugs are well known and range from premature closure of the epiphyseal plates in developing bone structure to liver toxicity (Yesalis, 1993). In addition, these are banned substances, and using them is nothing less than cheating. We should not lose sight of the purpose of athletics in building character. We must convince the young men in our charge that eventually they can get stronger without resorting to the use of illegal drugs.

There are anecdotal reports of athletes using preparations that contain ephedrine and/or Mah Huong extracts, which can be legally obtained in health food stores. These products are potentially dangerous because they have caused sudden heartbeat irregularities in some young athletes, which could lead to sudden death on the practice field. It is obvious that discouraging the use of these preparations is important. Make sure your players consult with you before using any supplement and be sure to search through the ingredients of any preparation that your athlete is considering to using.

The following are our choices for supplements that may benefit the football player:

Water—Water is the most important supplement out there. Studies have shown that as little as three percent of body weight lost through dehydration can result in a 20 percent drop in muscle endurance (Caterisano, 1988). Other research has shown this same level of water loss to negatively affect strength and cardiovascular function as well.

Lack of proper hydration affects your body's ability to use fats by forcing your liver to take over the blood filtration duties normally performed by the kidneys. Since the liver normally is heavily involved in fat metabolism, it cannot function at full capacity when given this extra burden.

Lack of proper hydration is often the cause of electrolyte imbalances that can lead to muscle cramping. The balance of electrolytes is dependent on the relative concentrations of electrolytes such as sodium and potassium. Although many players think an electrolyte imbalance is caused by lack of these minerals, it may be more due to lack of the fluid in which these are dissolved causing higher concentrations in the blood.

Muscle is 75 percent water. Think of water as being one of the major components of muscle tissue.

The best way to monitor hydration level is to weigh yourself every morning, as well as before and after every training session or game. If body weight drops one to two percent (for a 200-pound player this is two to four pounds) from one morning to the next, suspect dehydration and drink extra water throughout the day.

Prehydrate by drinking 12 to 20 ounces of water several hours prior to practice. Drink regularly throughout practice or training sessions. Don't wait until you are thirsty—by then it is too late.

Rehydrate following all practice sessions and games. Drink 24 ounces of water for every pound lost due to sweating.

Vitamin and minerals supplements—The ideal way to get all of the vitamins and minerals needed in a day is through a well-balanced diet that contains a variety of fruits and vegetables. The reality is that most high school athletes don't consume enough nor a great variety of fruits and vegetables in their diet. For this reason we recommend taking vitamin supplements.

Mega-doses of vitamins (defined as 10 times the recommended dietary allowance or RDA) are not any more effective than normal, over-the-counter vitamins that meet the RDA.

Vitamins are classified as either fat soluable or water soluable, which describes how they are stored in the body. The *fat-soluable vitamins* are stored in our body fat and stored for a relatively long period of time. The *water-soluable vitamins* are stored in the body fluids and are stored for less time.

Consuming more than the RDA cause the body to store excess fat-soluable vitamins that can actually reach a toxic level if taken to extremes. The water-soluable vitamins are simply eliminated in the urine if taken to excess.

Meal replacement drinks—As mentioned previously, a player should consume five to six meals per day to maintain an even blood-glucose level and assimilate sufficient calories to meet the demands of heavy activity. This may not be convenient given the normal school schedule of most athletes. Here is where powdered forms of meal replacements that mix with water may be of practical use.

Have players carry dry meal replacement powder in a water bottle with them to school. At mid-morning they can add water from any drinking fountain when moving between classes and consume their liquid nutrients.

Choose a meal replacement drink that is low in sugar but has a good balance of carbohydrates and protein (read labels). This should contain 20 to 30 grams of high-quality protein such as whey protein and an equal amount of complex carbohydrate such as a glucose polymer. It should also be low in fat.

Remember that the word supplement means to add. The meal replacement drinks should only be part of a well-balanced eating plan and never take the place of a well-balanced diet.

Creatine Monohydrate—This supplement is probably one of the most well known and highly touted ergogenic aids on the market. It provides one of the basic sources of immediately available fuel to the muscle cell and can be loaded to a point of *supercompensation*, a term that describes levels far beyond normal amount in the cell. For all the hype and claims associated with this supplement, there are some things a player should know about creatine.

Much research has focused on creatine with conflicting results reported. Much of this has to do with differences in methods of testing the supplement, individual variation among subjects tested (some people cannot take up high levels of creatine), as well as differences in dosages, consumption regimens and loading cycles.

Studies that do report ergogenic effects involve improvements in strength-power activities of high intensity (weight training, sprinting, etc.). Most involve a loading phase of 20 grams of creatine monohydrate taken for five days, followed by five grams of creatine monohydrate a day as a maintenance dose. These dosages are depended upon the body weight of the athlete, with less needed for smaller players and more needed for larger players.

Very little empirical research has been done on short-term side effects of taking creatine. Some anecdotal reports of muscle cramping and gastrointestinal distress have been reported. This may be a hydration issue since the creatine is reported to draw fluids into the muscle cells, and throw off the delicate balance of fluids and electrolytes inside and outside the cell. The granular crystals of creatine may also draw fluids into the gut, which can cause cramps and diarrhea in some who report these effects.

There have been no long-term effects studied or reported regarding prolonged use of creatine, so the risks are unknown. This is especially true regarding young populations such as high school aged players, who are often still in the developmental phases of growth. *For this reason the high school coach should be cautious in recommending the use of this supplement.* Only players who are physically mature and have a long history of weight training experience should probably use it.

Post-Exercise Recovery Drinks

As mentioned earlier, the hour immediately following a high-volume or high-intensity workout represents a window of opportunity for the muscle cells to take up nutrients. For this reason, a post-exercise recovery drink that is high in carbohydrates to replace the stored carbohydrate in the muscle and/or a high protein drink is recommended.

Whey protein that is commercially available (usually powder form that mixes with water) is a good source of quality protein that is low in fat. This is especially recommended for athletes trying to gain lean body mass.

Meal replacements that have a balance of protein and carbohydrate are also good post-exercise drinks.

For muscle carbohydrate stores, a post-exercise carbohydrate loading drink is effective. The player may also use a high glycemic index drink for this purpose since the rapidity of glucose uptake and subsequent insulin response enhances the cell's stores.

A Game Plan for Good Nutrition

Variety—a balanced diet will ensure that an athlete is being supplied all of the major nutrients: water, carbohydrates, protein, fat, vitamins, and minerals.

Moderation—you do not need to give up junk food completely, just eat it sparingly and balance it out with nutrient-wise choices at your next meal. Never replace a balanced meal with refined sugars.

Wholesome is best—choose foods that are in their most natural state or at most lightly processed are more nutritious than overly processed foods. Generally try to eat foods as close to their original form as possible.

Try to avoid fast foods because they are loaded with saturated fats and refined carbohydrates. You can still make eating right convenient by planning ahead and packing a wholesome meal rather than relying on the fast foods

Break the fast—for an athlete, breakfast is the most important meal of the day. Your body needs the fuel to perform both mentally and physically, plus you allow your body to rebuild muscle tissue better if it is not deprived of calories. You should eat breakfast whether you are trying to lose weight or gain weight.

Eat four to six meals each day—eating at regular intervals helps prepare the body for training and competition and aids in the recovery process.

To gain lean body mass:
- Increase caloric intake by 200 to 500 calories per day with wholesome foods.
- Eat four to six meals per day and add healthy, nutrient rich snacks between meals.
- Increase your consumption of lean meats (beef, chicken, and turkey), fish, and low-fat dairy products.
- Increase complex carbohydrate consumption (whole grain breads and cereals, pasta and beans) especially after training.
- Incorporate strength training, working large muscle groups, or several muscle groups together, into your program.

To lose body fat:
- Select lean cuts of meat, skinless poultry, and fish for protein sources.

- Limit high-calorie, low-nutrient foods such as sweets, junk food, fried foods, etc.
- Increase your water intake.
- Limit sweetened beverages (sweet tea, Kool-aid, soda, and sports drinks).
- Select low-fat dairy products such as skimmed milk (one percent) over full fat or two percent milk.
- Do not skip meals—eat three meals per day (especially breakfast) as well as one to three healthy snacks (fruits, vegetables, low-fat yogurt) each day.

- Stay active—in addition to your regular training walk as much as possible (i.e., take stairs instead of elevators, park in a parking space further away than usual when shopping, walk short distances rather than ride). Aerobic work burns fat.

See you doctor before beginning any body fat reduction program.

References

Caterisano, A., D.N. Camaione, R.T. Murphy, & J.V. Gonino. "The effect of differential training on isokinetic muscular endurance during acute thermally induced hypohydration." *American Jour. Of Sports Medicine*, May-June, 1988.

Yesalis, C.E. *Anabolic Steroids in Sport and Exercise*, Human Kinetics Publ., Champaign, Ill., 1993.

Training Motivation

Ask professional strength and conditioning coaches to name their primary objective, and most will tell you motivation. Getting players to give 100 percent effort and believe in a less-than-perfect training regimen is more effective than having the perfect training program that athletes won't believe in and are not willing to do. Ideally you want the perfect training regimen, and to get the athletes giving you 100 percent. This chapter is designed to provide insight into the process of promoting intrinsic motivation within each player. The goal is to get the players to believe in your program and put in the honest effort necessary for achieving maximum gains. A significant part of this process depends on how the players relate to the coach.

From the coach's perspective, motivation should come from educating the athlete on the underlying purpose of the training routine, and recognizing and rewarding the players for hard work and effort. For the player, motivation comes from within as a quest to achieve personal goals. Personal goals could be training-related, such as achieving certain performance objectives like increasing one-repetition maximums in lifts, or reducing times in sprinting and agility tests. The goals may also be football related, such as moving up the depth charts in their position or gaining All-Conference or All-American honors. Setting goals will lead to a greater chance of individual motivation and, eventually, team success on the playing field.

Young athletes are strongly motivated by peer recognition and acceptance. The effective coach designs motivational strategies to provide recognizable rewards that fill this need. Such things as t-shirts for attaining strength goals, posting individual records by position in a conspicuous place in the weight room, and visual awards (such as the lunch pail at Virginia Tech that symbolizes the hard-work ethic) are great incentives for rewarding players.

Evaluation and Goal Setting

One of the purposes of testing athletes periodically is to make them aware of their progress and the fact that their progress is being monitored. Athletes by nature are competitive, so we need to provide objective feedback about their advancement in pursuit of their goals. We recommend that players be tested at the end of each training phase (off season, preseason and in season), keeping in mind that the end of one phase is typically the beginning of the next. Just knowing that they will be tested often is enough of a motivating factor to keep an athlete compliant with your program. This is especially true during the summer months when an advanced player might be working out in a facility off campus.

Have players set goals at the beginning of each phase of training to help motivate and direct their

tion problems involving family, girlfriends, and teammates.

Goals should be measurable and realistic. Since all players progress at different rates, a conservative and achievable goal is preferred to an overly ambitious goal that will most likely end in failure. *Remember, the goal is not as important as achieving the goal.* Have the player write his goal down so that both you and he have a copy of it. The player might even write his goal on a sign and post it on his bedroom wall so that he can see it every day.

Evaluation is also an important component of developing strength and conditioning awards. This could include performance standards that place players in elite clubs based on attaining certain benchmarks on lifts, sprints, and timed agility tests. Virginia Tech uses a system of progressive performance standards to award players. These are grouped by playing position (i.e., linemen, skill players, etc.) and all have minimum standards in strength speed and agility. Meeting the minimum standard allows an athlete membership in the Maroon Strength Award club, followed by Orange Strength Award, Iron Hokie Strength Award, Super Iron Hokie Strength Award, and finally the highest Excalibur Strength Award. Minimum standards for each can be determined by past performance standards of players who have already been through the program. The minimum award level should be attainable by most of the athletes with consistent training. Awarding t-shirts to players who accomplish a certain performance level is a good way to emphasize the importance of reaching goals. Incorporating the school colors and school mascot serves to emphasize team identity and unity among players.

efforts. Sit down with each player for five or 10 minutes and help him set realistic goals based on past progress. In addition to setting goals, this short meeting will provide an opportunity for personal interaction between the player and the coach that may involve issues outside of strength and conditioning. Counseling the players about off-field problems is often important for their overall well being as young men. This could include issues related to their progress in the classroom as well as interpersonal rela-

Variety as a Motivating Factor

So far we have presented external factors that help motivate football players to work hard. There are, however, variables related to the workouts that help keep the athletes from getting stale, simply going through the motions. One simple but effective approach is to create a positive environment in the weight room using signs with inspiring words (i.e., "Pain is temporary, pride is forever"; "respect every opponent, fear none"). Be aware, however, that putting up too much signage risks sensory overload. It might be more effective to pick one theme and change

it every week, and then the coaches can direct the players' focus on that week's theme. Often players will be excited to see what the new theme is for the upcoming week. Many of these themes come from quotations taken from books like *The Art of War* by Sun Tzu (some of these quotations are included in the sample programs in Chapter 9). The key is to keep the environment fresh and interesting.

Variety in the workout itself is very important for keeping the players from getting psychologically and physically stale. Periodizing the training loads and changing the lifts and exercises regularly helps to prevent boredom. The core lifts can be periodized (varying sets, reps and the amount of resistance) while changing the assistance lifts regularly and frequently. The coach could post on a blackboard the workout for the day or week with inspirational quotations above them. Many of the exercises and lifts outlined in this book can be traded off for other exercises and lifts, as long as they work the same muscle groups and are of the same skill level. Many of the lifts are progressive. A player or group of players, after mastering a basic lift, can be advanced to the next level of that lift. For example, a group of players who have trained using the upright row, Olympic deadlift, and shoulder shrug in their routine could progress to the jump shrug, power pull, and hang clean. Eventually as they

EXCALIBUR AWARD CRITERIA

master those lifts, they could eventually perform the full power clean and some of the snatch grip variations of the Olympic lifts.

Assigning Athletes into Training Groups

A recurring theme in this book is that the football athletes exhibit a wide range of maturity levels and abilities. For this reason, separating athletes into training groups according to maturity, ability, and level of experience is a critical motivating factor. By allowing players to lift with other players of equal ability, you spark healthy competition within the group and avoid the likelihood that players will attempt to lift weights too heavy for proper lifting technique. Objective test results and information based on individual player/coach conferences help the coach determine the appropriate training group assignment for each player. Ultimately, the coach's judgment will determine the right chemistry and composition for each grouping. Some groups may require more supervision than others based on experience and capabilities. This is usually less true for experienced college-level athletes, but may be a factor to consider.

Awards and Incentives

The most important motivation component for a good strength and conditioning program is the head football coach's involvement. He sends the message that the training program is important at a level that goes beyond lip service. One way to achieve this is through awards and incentives that come directly from the head coach. This could include helmet awards for training achievements, depth chart and special teams opportunities for individuals who work hard and achieve training goals; t-shirts; and certificate awards. Individual and group achievements could be recognized by the head coach specifically at team banquets and picnics.

Awards can also come in the form of a board posted in the gym or weight room with team and individual records. We recommend that coaches establish a hall of fame with pictures in the training facilities. Players can be recognized in newsletters to parents and boosters for attaining training goals. The awards could also recognize perfect attendance among players who never miss a workout. All of these provide the opportunity for peer recognition and motivation from within the players in your program.

Traditions and Expectations

Nothing breeds success like success! If players *expect* to do well, they are much more likely to do well. The expectation to win is a major part of any successful football program. That expectation must be taken into the strength and conditioning program by insisting on and maintaining a good work ethic among your athletes.

Everyone who enters the training facility in your school must take an active role in creating a tradition of positive effort. This good work ethic is critical. No program gains much without it.

It starts with good leadership from the strength and conditioning coach. He must lay the foundation of a positive training environment by setting rules and expectations, and he must enforce those rules in an even-handed and fair manner. It must be clear to every athlete who enters your facility that this is a place where serious athletes work hard to get better. It is not a place to socialize or engage in horseplay. Everyone from the All-American to the last player on the depth charts must be expected to conduct themselves in the same serious and positive manner, or be expelled. Players are expected to put away equipment after they use it and keep the facility clean (no eating or drinking beverages other than water or sports drinks). Every player and every coach should be positive and encouraging during the training and testing sessions.

Once the coach has established those expectations, it is important to get the veteran players to lead by example and reinforce the positive work ethic. This can be established initially by meeting with the older, more experienced players and convincing them of the importance of their role in a positive workout environment. Involving them in establishing some of the rules in the training facility, gives them a sense of importance in bringing on the younger players. They could help decide what types of music to play in the weight room during training sessions, what types of penalties should be enacted for players who violate rules, and so on. Point out that they will be helping to maintain a tradition that will help the overall football program that will carry on long after they have moved on. Once set in motion, the younger athletes will follow the lead of the veteran players and be leaders for the new players coming in.

One potential tool for establishing tradition and providing the opportunity for intra-squad competition is the Ironman or Strongman concept. This could be an annual affair held at the end of the school year during the off season training phase in which the athletes compete both as an individuals and as teams in various feats of strength, speed, power, and agility. The coach should select some football-related and diverse events that test players' athletic strength and ability. Most programs are modeled after the World's Strongest Man competition as seen on some of the cable sports networks today. Modified versions of this competition could be developed that are appropriate for the high school and college athlete, especially if you develop two or three divisions that are age- and maturity level-oriented. You may have a junior-senior division and a freshman-sophomore division, or break it down by class if you have a large number of players in your program. Within the division you can break the team up into groups of four or five based on keeping the teams even and competitive (use testing results to ensure that the teams are equally distributed with both high- and low-level performers, and equal-sized athletes).

Once teams are established, you can develop a point system for individual performance on the various events and keep a team score. The team concept encourages players to support each other and develops a sense of teamwork. Some of the events used in the Virginia Tech Ironman Competition include a Farmer's Walk, which is a timed event in which a player carries heavy dumbbells a certain distance (usually 50 to 100 yards), a tug-o-war, a timed tire flip using a tractor tire, a race to the top of the stadium using a weighted vest, a truck or car push in a parking lot, and so on. These can be modified to be appropriate for high school players and provides a fun aspect to the training regimen. This type of training also develops what the Eastern Europeans refer to as *special strength* defined as a whole body-type strength that has a big carryover to sport performance. Since football is a sport that requires the use of many muscle groups working together, training for special strength development has a high degree of carryover to performance on the field. Ironman competition is a great way of motivating players to work at developing special strength.

The ironman competition can be a five- or six-week period in the off season training phase with one event per week being contested during one conditioning session. Most events are timed and provide a good objective measure of physical prowess. An award can be given (certificate, trophy, t-shirts, etc) to the top individual athletes in each division, and a team trophy can be given for the best team point total in each. Points can be given for participation (give one point for every player who competes to encourage and reward perfect attendance) as well as achievement (i.e., five points for first place, four points for second, etc., in each event).

Dos and Don'ts of Motivating Athletes

Don't

Don't constantly yell and raise your voice to try to motivate players. They become desensitized to this and when you do need to get their attention, raising your voice becomes less effective.

Don't criticize a player in front of his teammates. Pull the player aside and talk to him to correct the problem. Remember to focus the criticism on the behavior and not on the player.

Don't group players into training groups simply based on their playing position. Group them by maturity and performance capability so that players don't feel inadequate or are tempted to lift weights that are beyond their ability.

Don't compare a player to anyone else in a negative way. Use positive incentives to get players to set goals and work toward those goals. Inspire the player to try to improve based on his own personal records and past accomplishments.

Don't show favoritism toward any player or group of players at the expense of less accomplished players. Remember that, especially in the high school-aged population, physical maturity can occur at any time, so that this year's weakest player may be next year's strongman.

Do

Be a good role model by staying fit—leading by example is always the best way to inspire your athletes.

Stay up on current literature so that you can answer your athletes' questions with the best possible information.

Make every athlete who enters your training facility feel important—there is an old saying, "the players don't care what you know, they just want to know that you care." Also, remember that even the smallest and weakest athlete could mature into the biggest and strongest athlete in the weight room. Invest in all of your athletes, because each one of them has a potential to excel if trained properly.

Use positive reinforcement whenever a player does something well or shows great improvement. Praise the athlete in front of his teammates.

Get the upperclassmen involved in leading by example to establish and maintain a good work ethic among the younger players. This becomes a self-perpetuating process that will serve your program for years to come.

Use the conditioning program to build team pride and unity.

Sample Programs

The following pages list samples programs designed using the principles related in this book. The programs are divided into beginner, intermediate and advanced workouts, which are further divided into off season, preseason, and in-season programs. Using the concepts outlined in the preceding chapters, the strength coach can easily adapt the sample programs to fit the particular situation, based on equipment availability, schedule restraints, and other facility-related factors.

The sample programs are presented week by week with the lift or exercise (i.e., plyometric, speed drill, agility drill, etc.) followed by the training volume (sets and repetitions). In some cases, especially with the early phases of the beginning program, the intensity (resistance or weight used, speed of the movement) have been purposely left out allowing the coach to use his own judgment based on the number of repetitions required that day. So if an exercise calls for 12 repetitions, the coach should start with a weight that the athlete can lift 12 times quite easily. Once all reps in all sets can be achieved, the player can increase the resistance for the next workout. The advantage to this is that the player can concentrate on proper form by lifting lighter weights and will not quickly plateau, but instead, progress from workout to workout. This progress can continue until the athlete fails to complete all reps in all sets, at which time the athlete must use the same resistance that was used in the prior workout until all reps are achieved. In other cases, especially with more advanced phases, the intensity of

the lift is designated as a percentage of the one repetition maximum (1 RM). A chart that calculates percentages of the 1 RM is provided in the Appendix of this book.

A description of most of the lifts in the sample programs can be found in Chapter 4 along with key coaching points for each lift or exercise. The exception to this would be in any lifts such as calf raises, curls, and triceps extensions, which are generic lifts that can be performed with a wide degree of variation depending on your facilities, equipment, and individual preferences.

In developing the beginner off season program, we will summarize the programming guidelines outlined in the preceding chapters:

We selected lifts that are compound lifts (using more than one joint) designed to ingrain specific movement patterns. It is also critical in these initial phases to train all muscle groups and work opposing muscle groups to develop muscle balance.

Because the target adaptation is to improve muscle hypertrophy, the training load starts out with a relatively high volume (i.e., 12 reps per set) and a relatively low intensity necessary to achieve such a high number of repetitions per set.

As we move from phase I to phase II you will notice the training volume is decreased from 12 reps/set to six to 10 reps/set. This would facilitate the increased intensity (more weight) needed to shift the target adaptation from increased muscle hypertrophy to increased absolute strength. The lifts are also changed to more advanced versions as the athlete gains sensitivity to the lifting movement patterns and is able to perform more complicated lifts.

By phase III the training loads again change to higher intensity and lower volume, sometimes prescribing multiple sets of three reps/set.

We also made sure to build in active rest periods in order to enhance recovery and avoid overtraining.

Periodic testing is also programmed, with the beginner off season program testing players during the sixth week. This allows players to learn proper lifting technique and prepare physically for maximum. testing, thereby reducing the risk of soreness and injury that can potentially occur with maximum efforts.

In developing the intermediate program, many of the programming guidelines are the same as the beginner program (i.e., relatively high-volume, low-intensity training loads, incorporation of compound lifts that are preliminary exercises designed to develop movement patterns for more complicated lifts, etc.). There are some distinct differences, as follows:

We use a higher frequency of training sessions per week (four days/week as opposed to three days/week) since we will assume that the intermediate group will have a more extensive training history than the beginners.

Despite the fact that muscle hypertrophy and absolute strength are the target adaptations, we introduce some basic power-oriented lifts earlier with this group.

Just as in the beginner program, the training phases progress from high-volume, low-intensity to lower-volume and higher-intensity training loads (including higher velocity lifts), and the lifts progress to more complicated Olympic-style lifts.

With respect to increased velocity of lifts, coaches should remember that the amount of weight used must be reduced due to the force-time relationship presented in Chapter 2. This theory suggests that heavy weights cannot be lifted with high velocity, because it takes too long to develop maximum force in a muscle. The general rule of thumb is that maximum velocities require about one-third of the 1 RM for optimum speed.

The advanced off season program will incorporate similar training load progressions as the beginner and intermediate programs, but will be designed under the assumption that the players are well versed in proper lifting techniques. The progression is much faster to more complicated Olympic lifts, and the program is divided into distinct programs for skill position players, and linemen/linebackers. This distinction mainly involves the types of lifts and training loads selected based on maximizing the so-called transfer specificity of each.

Beginner: Off-Season/Preseason Program

BEGINNER OFF SEASON　　SPEED AGILITY QUICKNESS CONDITIONING SCHEDULE　　WEEK 1 PHASE 1

MONDAY	TUESDAY	WEDNESDAY	THURSDAY	FRIDAY
Pre-Strength Workout	**Dynamic Warmup**	**Pre-Strength Workout**	**Dynamic Warmup**	**Pre-Strength Workout**
Jump Rope 1. Both Feet—1 set: 15 seconds 2. Right Foot 1 set: 15 seconds 3. Left Foot—1 set: 15 seconds 4. Alternate Feet 1 set: 15 seconds 5. 2 on Right, 2 on Left 1 set: 15 seconds 6. Speed Jump 1 set: 15 seconds **Post-Strength Workout** **Static Stretch Routine** OFF after STRETCH	1. Walking Toe Touches 1 set: 20 yards 2. Walking Knee Hugs 1 set: 20 yards 3. Low Shuffle 2 sets: 20 yards **Static Stretch Routine** **Competitive Games** Basketball Volleyball Dodgeball variations Tag Football, etc.	**Jump Rope**—with movement 1. Running—1 set: 20 yards 2. Double Leg Hops—forward 1 set: 20 yards 3. Right Leg Hops 1 set: 20 yards 4. Left Leg Hops 1 set: 20 yards 5. Running—1 set: 20 yards **Post-Strength Workout** **Static Stretch Routine** OFF after STRETCH	1. Walking/Skipping Knee Hugs 1 set: 10 yards each 2. Walking/Skipping Toe Touches—1 set: 10 yards 3. Low Carioca 2 sets: 20 yards 4. Starts—Football Stance 4-6 reps **Static Stretch Routine** **Competitive Games** Basketball Volleyball Dodgeball variations Tag Football, etc.	OFF ACTIVE REST
Stretch Lower Back, Hamstrings	Stretch Lower Back, Hamstrings	Strtech Lower Back, Hamstrings	Stretch Lower Back, Hamstrings	Stretch Lower Back, Hamstrings

General Adaptation and Hypertrophy

BEGINNER OFF SEASON
Phase 1

WEEK 1

MONDAY	WEDNESDAY	FRIDAY
Dot Drills—4-5 sets – 10-15 seconds	**Jump Rope**—4-5 sets – 15-20 seconds	**Dot Drills**—3-4 sets – 10-15 seconds
Abs Big 40s—1 set Slow Crunches—10-15	**Abs** Hokie Leg Raises—1 set: 15-20 reps Twisting Sit-Ups—1 set: 10-20 reps	**Abs** Figure 8s—1 set: 10 reps Slow Crunches—1 set: 10-15 reps
Legs Leg Press—3 sets: 12 reps	**Legs** Back Squats—3 sets: 12 reps	**Legs** Leg Press—3 sets: 12 reps
Chest Bench Press—3 sets: 12 reps	**Chest** Incline Bench Press—3 sets: 12 reps	**Chest** Close Grip Bench Press—3 sets: 12 reps
Back Lat Pulldowns (front, underhand)—3 sets: 12 reps	**Back** Dumbbell Shrugs—2 sets: 12 reps	**Back** Lat Pulldowns (front, underhand)—3 sets: 12 reps
Shoulder Seated Dumbbell Shoulder Press—2 sets: 12 reps	**Shoulder** Upright Rows—2 sets: 12 reps	**Shoulder** Seated Barbell or Dumbbell Overhead Shoulder Press—2 sets: 12 reps
Bicep Barbell Curls—2 sets: 10 reps or Cable Curls—2 sets: 12 reps	**Bicep** Dumbbell Standing Alternate Curls 2 sets: 12 reps	**Bicep** Barbell or Cable Curls—2 sets: 12 reps
Tricep Tricep Pushdowns—2 sets: 12-15 reps	**Tricep** Close Grip Push-Ups—2 sets: 12-15 reps	**Tricep** Tricep Pushdowns—2 sets: 12-15 reps
Hamstrings Seated or Prone Leg Curls—2 sets: 12 reps	**Hamstrings** Back Extensions—2 sets: 8-12 reps	**Hamstrings** Seated or Prone Leg Curls—2 sets: 12 reps
Calf Standing Calf Raise Machine—2 sets: 15 reps	**Calf** Seated Calf Raises—2 sets: 15 reps	**Calf** Standing Calf Raise Machine—2 sets: 15 reps
Static Stretch Routine	**Static Stretch Routine**	**Static Stretch Routine**

BEGINNER OFF SEASON SPEED AGILITY QUICKNESS CONDITIONING SCHEDULE WEEK 2 PHASE 1

MONDAY	TUESDAY	WEDNESDAY	THURSDAY	FRIDAY
Pre-Strength Workout	**Dynamic Warmup**	**Pre-Strength Workout**	**Dynamic Warmup**	**Pre-Strength Workout**

Dot Drills
  15 seconds each
1. In and Out—both feet
2. Figure 8—both feet right side
3. Figure 8—both feet left side
4. In and Out—turns
	1. Walking Knee Hugs
	   1 set: 20 yards
	2. Skipping Knee Hugs
	   1 set: 20 yards
	3. Walking Toe Touches
	   1 set: 20 yards
	4. Skipping Toe Touches
	   1 set: 20 yards
	5. Backward Skips
	   1 set: 20 yards
		Jump Rope
		1. Both Feet—15 seconds
		2. Right Foot—15 seconds
		3. Left Foot—15 seconds
		4. 2 on Right, 2 on Left 15 seconds
			1. Walking Toe Touches
			   1 set: 20 yards
			2. Skipping Toe Touches
			   1 set: 20 yards
			3. High Knee Crossovers
			   1 set—20 yards
			4. Backward Skips
			   1 set: 20 yards
				Dot Drills
				  15 seconds intervals
				1. In and Out—both feet
				2. Figure 8—both feet right side
				3. Figure 8—both feet left side
				4. Create your own pattern

Post-Strength Workout	**Static Stretch Routine**	**Post-Strength Workout**	**Static Stretch Routine**	**Post-Strength Workout**
Static Stretch Routine	**Competitive Games**	Static Stretch Routine	**Competitive Games**	Static Stretch Routine

Speed Development
1. Heel-to-Butt Kicks
   2 sets: 20 yards
2. A Marches
   2 sets: 20 yards
3. A Skips
   2 sets: 20 yards
	Basketball
	Volleyball
	Tag Football, etc.
		Speed Development
		1. A Marches
		   2 sets: 20 yards
		2. A Skips—2 sets: 20 yards
		3. A Runs— 2 sets: 20 yards
			Volleyball
			Ultimate Frisbee
			Team Handball
			Basketball, etc.
				Competitive Drills
				1. Shark in a Tank
				   5-7 sets: 10 seconds each

Programmable Agility
1. 20-yard Shuttle—4 sets
		Reactive Agility
		1. Four-Cone Reaction Drill
		   visual cues—4-5 sets:
		   10-15 seconds each		

Stretch Lower Back, Hamstrings	Stretch Lower Back, Hamstrings	Stretch Lower Back, Hamstrings	Stretch Lower Back, Hamstrings	Stretch Lower Back, Hamstrings

General Adaptation
and Hypertrophy

BEGINNER OFF SEASON
Phase 1

WEEK 2

MONDAY	WEDNESDAY	FRIDAY
Dot Drills—3-4 sets – 10-15 seconds	**Jump Rope**—4-5 sets – 15-20 seconds	**Dot Drills**—3-4 sets – 10-15 seconds
Abs Big 40s—1 set Slow Crunches—10-15	**Abs** Hokie Leg Raises—1 set: 15-20 reps Twisting Sit-Ups—1 set: 10-20 reps	**Abs** Figure 8s—1 set: 10 reps Slow Crunches—1 set: 10-15 reps
Legs Leg Press—3 sets: 12 reps	**Legs** Back Squats—3 sets: 12 reps	**Legs** Leg Press—3 sets: 12 reps
Chest Bench Press—3 sets: 12 reps	**Chest** Incline Bench Press—3 sets: 12 reps	**Chest** Close Grip Bench Press—3 sets: 12 reps
Back Lat Pulldowns (front, underhand)—3 sets: 12 reps	**Back** Dumbbell Shrugs—2 sets: 12 reps	**Back** Lat Pulldowns (front, underhand)—3 sets: 12 reps
Shoulder Seated Dumbbell Shoulder Press—2 sets: 12 reps	**Shoulder** Upright Rows—2 sets: 12 reps	**Shoulder** Seated Barbell or Dumbbell Overhead Shoulder Press—2 sets: 12 reps
Bicep Barbell or Cable Curls—2 sets: 12 reps	**Bicep** Dumbbell Standing Alternate Curls 2 sets: 12 reps	**Bicep** Barbell or Cable Curls—2 sets: 12 reps
Tricep Tricep Pushdowns—2 sets: 12-15 reps	**Tricep** Close Grip Push-Ups—2 sets: 12-15 reps	**Tricep** Tricep Pushdowns—2 sets: 12 reps
Hamstrings Seated or Prone Leg Curls—2 sets: 12 reps	**Hamstrings** Back Extensions—2 sets: 8-12 reps	**Hamstrings** Seated or Prone Leg Curls—2 sets: 12 reps
Calf Standing Calf Raise Machine—2 sets: 15-20 reps	**Calf** Seated Calf Raises—2 sets: 15 reps	**Calf** Standing Calf Raise Machine—2 sets: 15 reps
Static Stretch Routine	**Static Stretch Routine**	**Static Stretch Routine**

BEGINNER OFF SEASON   SPEED AGILITY QUICKNESS CONDITIONING SCHEDULE   WEEK 3 PHASE 1

MONDAY	TUESDAY	WEDNESDAY	THURSDAY	FRIDAY
Pre-Strength Workout	**Dynamic Warmup**	**Pre-Strength Workout**	**Dynamic Warmup**	**Pre-Strength Workout**
Dot Drills 10 seconds each 1. In and Out—both feet 2. Figure 8—both feet right side 3. Figure 8—both feet left side 4. In and Out—turns	1. Walking Toe Touches 1 set: 20 yards 2. Skipping Knee Hugs 1 set: 20 yards 3. High Knee Crossovers 1 set: 20 yards 4. Backward High Knees 1 set: 20 yards	**Jump Rope** 1. Both Feet—15 seconds 2. Right Foot—10 seconds 3. Left Foot—10 seconds 4. Alternate Feet—10 seconds 5. Speed Jump—20 seconds	1. Walking Knee Hugs 1 set: 20 yards 2. Skipping Toe Touches 1 set: 20 yards 3. Low Shuffle 2 sets: 20 yards	**Dot Drills** 10 seconds 1. In and Out—both feet 2. Figure 8—both feet right side 3. Figure 8—both feet left side 4. Create your own pattern
Post-Strength Workout	**Static Stretch Routine**	**Post-Strength Workout**	**Static Stretch Routine**	**Post-Strength Workout**
Static Stretch Routine	**Competitive Games** Volleyball Basketball Tag Football, etc.	**Static Stretch Routine**	**Competitive Games** Basketball Volleyball Ultimate Frisbee, etc.	**Static Stretch Routine**
Speed Development 1. Fast Arms Drill 2 sets: 15 seconds 2. A Marches 2 sets: 20 yards 3. A Skips 2 sets: 20 yards 4. A Runs 2 sets: 20 yards		**Speed Development** 1. Heel-to-Butt Kick 2 sets: 20 yards 2. A Marches 2 sets: 20 yards 3. A Skips 2 sets: 20 yards 4. A Runs 2 sets: 20 yards		**Competitive Drills** 1. Get Up and Sprint 4-5 sets: 20 yards
Programmable Agility 1. 20-yard Shuttle—4 sets		**Reactive Agility** 1. Four-Cone Reaction Drill verbal cues—4-5 sets 10-15 seconds each		
Stretch Lower Back, Hamstrings	Stretch Lower Back, Hamstrings	Stretch Lower Back, Hamstrings	Stretch Lower Back, Hamstrings	Stretch Lower Back, Hamstrings

WEEK 3

BEGINNER OFF SEASON
Phase 1

General Adaptation and Hypertrophy

MONDAY	WEDNESDAY	FRIDAY
Dot Drills—3-4 sets – 10 seconds	Jump Rope—4-5 sets – 15-20 seconds	Dot Drills—4-5 sets – 10 seconds

MONDAY — Dot Drills—3-4 sets – 10 seconds

Abs
Big 40s—1 set
Slow Crunches—10-15

Legs
Leg Press—3 sets: 10 reps

Chest
Bench Press—3 sets: 10 reps

Back
Lat Pulldowns (front, underhand)—3 sets: 10 reps

Shoulder
Seated Dumbbell Shoulder Press—2 sets: 10 reps

Bicep
Barbell or Cable Curls—3 sets: 10 reps

Tricep
Tricep Pushdowns—3 sets: 10-12 reps

Hamstrings
Seated or Prone Leg Curls—2 sets: 12 reps

Calf
Standing Calf Raise Machine—3 sets: 12-15 reps

Static Stretch Routine

WEDNESDAY — Jump Rope—4-5 sets – 15-20 seconds

Abs
Hokie Leg Raises—1 set: 15-20 reps
Twisting Sit-Ups—1 set: 10-20 reps

Legs
Back Squats—3 sets: 10 reps

Chest
Incline Bench Press—3 sets: 10 reps

Back
Dumbbell Shrugs—3 sets: 10 reps

Shoulder
Upright Rows—2 sets: 12 reps

Bicep
Dumbbell Standing Alternate Curls 3 sets: 10 reps

Tricep
Close Grip Push-Ups—3 sets: 15 reps

Hamstrings
Back Extensions—2 sets: 8-12 reps

Calf
Seated Calf Raises—2 sets: 12-15 reps

Static Stretch Routine

FRIDAY — Dot Drills—4-5 sets – 10 seconds

Abs
Figure 8s—1 set: 10 reps
Slow Crunches—1 set: 10-15 reps

Legs
Leg Press—3 sets: 10 reps

Chest
Close Grip Bench Press—3 sets: 10 reps

Back
Lat Pulldowns (front, underhand)—3 sets: 10 reps

Shoulder
Seated Barbell or Dumbbell Overhead Shoulder Press—3 sets: 10 reps

Bicep
Barbell or Cable Curls—3 sets: 10 reps

Tricep
Tricep Pushdowns—3 sets: 10 reps

Hamstrings
Seated or Prone Leg Curls—2 sets: 10-12 reps

Calf
Standing Calf Raise Machine—3 sets: 15 reps

Static Stretch Routine

BEGINNER OFF SEASON   SPEED AGILITY QUICKNESS CONDITIONING SCHEDULE   WEEK 4 PHASE 1

MONDAY	TUESDAY	WEDNESDAY	THURSDAY	FRIDAY
Pre-Strength Workout	**Dynamic Warmup**	**Pre-Strength Workout**	**Dynamic Warmup**	**Pre-Strength Workout**

Dot Drills
15 seconds
1. In and Out—both feet
2. Figure 8—right foot only
  right side
3. Figure 8—left foot only
  left side
4. In and Out—turns
  both feet
 	
Post-Strength Workout
 	
Static Stretch Routine
 	
Speed Development
1. A Marches
  2 sets: 20 seconds
2. A Skips
  2 sets: 20 yards
3. A Runs
  2 sets: 20 yards
 	
Programmable Agility
1. Texas Drill—3-4 sets
	1. High Knee Crossovers
	  2 sets: 20 yards
	2. Backward Skips
	  2 sets: 20 yards
	3. Low Shuffle
	  2 sets: 20 yards
	
	Static Stretch Routine
	
	Competitive Games
	
	Basketball
	Softball
	Volleyball
	Tag Football, etc.
		Jump Rope
		1. Both Feet—10 seconds
		2. Alternate Feet—10
		  seconds
		3. 2 on the Right, 2 on the
		  Left—10 seconds
		4. Double Over—10
		  seconds
		5. Speed Jump—20 seconds
		
		Post-Strength Workout
		
		Static Stretch Routine
		
		Speed Development
		1. Acceleration Ladders
		  6 sets: 30 yards
		
		Reactive Agility
		1. Two-Point Wave Drill
		  4 sets: 10-15 seconds
		  (include shuffles, jumps,
		  Hit It, etc.)
			1. Walking Toe Touches
			  2 sets: 20 yards
			2. Skipping Knee Hugs
			  2 sets: 20 yards
			3. Carioca
			  2 sets: 20 yards
			
			Static Stretch Routine
			
			Competitive Games
			
			Volleyball
			Dodgeball variations
			Basketball, etc.
				Dot Drills
				10 seconds
				1. In and Out—both feet
				2. Figure 8—both feet
				  right side
				3. Figure 8—both feet
				  left side
				4. Create your own pattern
				
				Post-Strength Workout
				
				Static Stretch Routine
				
				Competitive Drills
				1. Capture the Flag

Stretch Lower Back, Hamstrings	Stretch Lower Back, Hamstrings	Stretch Lower Back, Hamstrings	Stretch Lower Back, Hamstrings	Stretch Lower Back, Hamstrings

General Adaptation
and Hypertrophy

BEGINNER OFF SEASON
Phase 1

WEEK 4

MONDAY

Dot Drills—4-5 sets – 15 seconds

Abs
Big 40s—1 set
Slow Crunches—10-15

Legs
Leg Press—3 sets: 10 reps

Chest
Bench Press—3 sets: 10 reps

Back
Lat Pulldowns (front, underhand)—3 sets: 10 reps

Shoulder
Seated Dumbbell Shoulder Press—3 sets: 10 reps

Bicep
Barbell or Cable Curls—3 sets: 10 reps

Tricep
Tricep Pushdowns—3 sets: 10 reps

Hamstrings
Seated or Prone Leg Curls—3 sets: 10 reps

Calf
Standing Calf Raise Machine—3 sets: 15 reps

Static Stretch Routine

WEDNESDAY

Jump Rope—4-5 sets – 15 seconds

Abs
Hokie Leg Raises—1 set: 15-20 reps
Twisting Sit-Ups—1 set: 10-20 reps

Legs
Back Squats—3 sets: 10 reps

Chest
Incline Bench Press—3 sets: 10 reps

Back
Dumbbell Shrugs—3 sets: 10 reps

Shoulder
Upright Rows—3 sets: 10 reps

Bicep
Dumbbell Standing Alternate Curls 3 sets: 10 reps

Tricep
Close Grip Push-Ups—3 sets: 10-15 reps

Hamstrings
Back Extensions—3 sets: 8-12 reps

Calf
Seated Calf Raises—3 sets: 15-20 reps

Static Stretch Routine

FRIDAY

Dot Drills—4-5 sets – 15 seconds

Abs
Figure 8s—1 set: 10 reps
Slow Crunches—1 set: 10-15 reps

Legs
Leg Press—3 sets: 10 reps

Chest
Close Grip Bench Press—3 sets: 10 reps

Back
Lat Pulldowns (front, underhand)—3 sets: 10 reps

Shoulder
Seated Barbell or Dumbbell Overhead Shoulder Press—3 sets: 10 reps

Bicep
Barbell or Cable Curls—3 sets: 10 reps

Tricep
Tricep Pushdowns—3 sets: 10 reps

Hamstrings
Seated or Prone Leg Curls—3 sets: 10 reps

Calf
Standing Calf Raise Machine—3 sets: 15 reps

Static Stretch Routine

173

BEGINNER OFF SEASON   SPEED AGILITY QUICKNESS CONDITIONING SCHEDULE   WEEK 5 PHASE 1

MONDAY	TUESDAY	WEDNESDAY	THURSDAY	FRIDAY
Pre-Strength Workout	**Dynamic Warmup**	**Pre-Strength Workout**	**Dynamic Warmup**	**Pre-Strength Workout**
Dot Drills 10- 15 seconds 1. In and Out—both feet 2. Figure 8—both feet right side 3. Figure 8—both feet left side 4. In and Out—turns **Post-Strength Workout** **Speed Development** 1. Heel-to-Butt Kicks 2 sets: 20 seconds 2. A Marches 2 sets: 20 seconds 3. A Skips 2 sets: 20 seconds 4. A Runs 2 sets: 20 seconds **Programmable Agility** 1. Carolina Drill—3-4 sets	1. Walking/Skipping Toe Touches 1 set: 10 yards each 2. Walking/Skipping Knee Hugs 1 set: 10 yards each 3. Low Shuffle 2 sets: 20 yards **Static Stretch Routine** **Competitive Games** Basketball Volleyball Tag Football, etc.	**Jump Rope** 1. Both Feet—10 seconds 2. Right Foot—10 seconds 3. Left Foot—10 seconds 4. Alternate Feet—10 seconds 5. 2 on the Right, 2 on the Left 10 seconds 6. Speed Jump—10 seconds **Post-Strength Workout** **Speed Development** 1. Acceleration Ladders 6 sets: 30 yards **Reactive Agility** 1. Tennis Ball Drills 6-8 sets	1. Walking/Skipping Knee Hugs 1 set: 10 yards each 2. Walking/Skipping Toe Touches 1 set: 10 yards each 3. Low Shuffle 2 sets: 20 yards 4. Carioca 2 sets: 20 yards **Static Stretch Routine** **Competitive Games** Dodgeball variations Basketball Volleyball, etc	**Dot Drills** 10-15 seconds 1. In and Out—both feet 15 seconds 2. Figure 8—right foot only right side—10 seconds 3. Figure 8—left foot only left side—10 seconds 4. Create your own pattern 15 seconds **Post-Strength Workout** **Static Stretch Routine** **Competitive Drills** 1. Get Up and Sprint 4-6 sets: 30 yards
Stretch Lower Back, Hamstrings	Stretch Lower Back, Hamstrings	Stretch Lower Back, Hamstrings	Stretch Lower Back, Hamstrings	Stretch Lower Back, Hamstrings

WEEK 5   BEGINNER OFF SEASON
Phase 1

MONDAY	WEDNESDAY	FRIDAY
Dot Drills—4-5 sets – 15 seconds	Jump Rope – 4-5 sets – 15-20 seconds	Dot Drills—3-5 sets – 10-15 seconds

MONDAY

Abs
Big 40s—1 set
Slow Crunches—10-15

Legs
Leg Press—3 sets: 10 reps

Chest
Bench Press—3 sets: 10 reps

Back
Lat Pulldowns (front, underhand)—3 sets: 10 reps

Shoulder
Seated Dumbbell Shoulder Press—3 sets: 10 reps

Bicep
Barbell or Cable Curls—3 sets: 10 reps

Tricep
Tricep Pushdowns—3 sets: 10-12 reps

Hamstrings
Seated or Prone Leg Curls—3 sets: 10 reps

Calf
Standing Calf Raise Machine—3 sets: 15-20 reps

Static Stretch Routine

WEDNESDAY

Abs
Hokie Leg Raises—1 set: 15-20 reps
Twisting Sit-Ups—1 set: 10-20 reps

Legs
Back Squats—4 sets: 8 reps

Chest
Incline Bench Press—4 sets: 8 reps

Back
Dumbbell Shrugs—3 sets: 10 reps

Shoulder
Upright Rows—3 sets: 10 reps

Bicep
Dumbbell Standing Alternate Curls 3 sets: 10 reps

Tricep
Close Grip Push-Ups—3 sets: 15-20 reps

Hamstrings
Back Extensions—3 sets: 8-12 reps

Calf
Seated Calf Raises—3 sets: 15-20 reps

Static Stretch Routine

FRIDAY

Abs
Figure 8s—1 set: 10 reps
Slow Crunches—1 set: 10-15 reps

Legs
Leg Press—4 sets: 8 reps

Chest
Close Grip Bench Press—4 sets: 8 reps

Back
Lat Pulldowns (front, underhand)—3 sets: 10 reps

Shoulder
Seated Barbell or Dumbbell Overhead Shoulder Press—3 sets: 10 reps

Bicep
Barbell or Cable Curls—3 sets: 10 reps

Tricep
Tricep Pushdowns—3 sets: 10 reps

Hamstrings
Seated or Prone Leg Curls—3 sets: 10 reps

Calf
Standing Calf Raise Machine—3 sets: 15 reps

Static Stretch Routine

BEGINNER OFF SEASON — SPEED AGILITY QUICKNESS CONDITIONING SCHEDULE — WEEK 6 PHASE 1

MONDAY	TUESDAY	WEDNESDAY	THURSDAY	FRIDAY
Pre-Strength Workout	**Dynamic Warmup**	**Pre-Strength Workout**	**Dynamic Warmup**	**Pre-Strength Workout**
Dot Drills 10-15 seconds 1. In and Out—both feet 2. Figure 8—both feet right side 3. Figure 8—both feet left side 4. In and Out—turns both feet **Post-Testing** **Static Stretch Routine** **Speed Development** 1. Heel-to-Butt Kicks 2 sets: 20 seconds 2. A Marches 2 sets: 20 seconds 3. A Skips 2 sets: 20 seconds 4. A Runs 2 sets: 20 seconds **Programmable Agility** 1. 20-yard Shuttle Drill 3-4 sets	1. Walking/Skipping Toe Touches 1 set: 10 yards each 2. Walking/Skipping Knee Hugs 1 set: 10 yards each 3. Low Shuffle 1 set: 20 yards 4. Starts—2 each **Static Stretch Routine** **Competitive Games** Basketball Volleyball Tag Football, etc.	**Jump Rope** 1. Both Feet—15 seconds 2. Right Foot—10 seconds 3. Left Foot—10 seconds 4. Alternate Feet—15 seconds 5. 2 on the Right, 2 on the Left—15 seconds **Post-Testing** **Static Stretch Routine** **Speed Development** 1. A March—1 set: 20 yards 2. A Skip—1 set: 20 yards 3. A Runs—2 sets: 20 yards **Reactive Agility** 1. Two-Point Wave Drill 4 sets: 10-15 seconds (include shuffles, jumps, Hit It, etc. Also have a player on command get out in front for the group to mirror)	1. High Knee Crossovers 2 sets: 20 yards 2. Backward Skips 2 sets: 20 yards 3. Carioca 2 sets: 20 yards 4. Starts—Football Stance 2-4 sets **Static Stretch Routine** **Competitive Games** Volleyball Basketball Team Handball, etc.	**No Weights or Organized Training** **PLAYERS OFF**
Stretch Lower Back, Hamstrings	Stretch Lower Back, Hamstrings	Stretch Lower Back, Hamstrings	Stretch Lower Back, Hamstrings	Stretch Lower Back, Hamstrings

WEEK 6 TESTING WEEK

BEGINNER OFF SEASON
Phase 1

General Adaptation and Hypertrophy

MONDAY	WEDNESDAY	FRIDAY
Dot Drills—3-4 sets – 10-15 seconds	Jump Rope—4-5 sets – 15-20 seconds	OFF
Abs Big 40s—1 set Slow Crunches—1 set: 15 reps	**Abs** Hokie Leg Raises—1 set: 15-20 reps Twisting Sit-Ups—1 set: 10-20 reps	**Active Rest** Play basketball, racquetball, tennis, etc.
TEST—Vertical Jump (using Vertic machine)	**TEST**—10-yard sprint (electronically timed)	
TEST—Back Squats Rep Test (up to 10 reps) convert to 1 RM	**TEST**—20-yard shuttle best of three trials	
TEST—Pullups (overhand grip) Max reps	**TEST**—Bench Press Rep Test (up to 10 RM)—convert to 1 RM	
Get Body Weight	**TEST**—Dips Max reps	
	TEST—Sit and Reach Hamstring Lower Back Flexibility	
Static Stretch Routine	Static Stretch Routine	

BEGINNER OFF SEASON SPEED AGILITY QUICKNESS CONDITIONING SCHEDULE WEEK 7 PHASE 2

MONDAY	TUESDAY	WEDNESDAY	THURSDAY	FRIDAY
Pre-Strength Workout	**Dynamic Warmup**	**Pre-Strength Workout**	**Dynamic Warmup**	**Pre-Strength Workout**
<u>Jump Rope</u>—with movement 1. Running—1 set: 20 yards 2. Double Leg Hops Forward—1 set: 20 yards 3. Right Leg Hops—Forward 1 set: 20 yards 4. Left Leg Hops—Forward 1 set: 20 yards 5. Running—1 set: 20 yards	1. Walking Toe Touches 1 set: 20 yards 2. Walking Knee Hugs 1 set: 20 yards 3. Skipping Toe Touches 1 set: 20 yards 4. Skipping Knee Hugs 1 set: 20 yards	<u>Dot Drills</u> 10 seconds each 1. In and Out—both feet 2. Figure 8—both feet right side 3. Figure 8—both feet left side 4. In and Out—turns	1. High Knee Crossovers 2 sets: 20 yards 2. Low Shuffle 2 sets: 20 yards 3. Backward High Knees 2 sets: 20 yards 4. Starts—Football Stance 2-4 sets	<u>Jump Rope</u> 1. Both Feet—15 seconds 2. Right Foot—15 seconds 3. Left Foot—15 seconds 4. Alternate Feet—15 seconds 5. Speed Jump—15 seconds
Post-Strength Workout	**Static Stretch Routine**	**Post-Strength Workout**	**Static Stretch Routine**	**Post-Strength Workout**
Static Stretch Routine	**Competitive Games**	**Static Stretch Routine**	**Competitive Games**	**Static Stretch Routine**
<u>Speed Development</u> 1. Fast Arm Drill 2 sets: 20 yards 2. Heel-to-Butt Kick 2 sets: 20 seconds 3. A Skips 2 sets: 20 seconds 4. A Runs 2 sets: 20 seconds	Tag Football Basketball Volleyball Dodgeball variations	<u>Speed Development</u> (Acceleration) 1. Sled Pulls 4-6 sets: 20-30 yards (up to 50 pounds resistance)	Volleyball Basketball	**Competitive Games** Capture the Flag
<u>Programmable Agility</u> 1. Pattern Runs (speed cuts, power cuts) 2 sets: 20 yards each		<u>Reactive Agility</u> 1. Eight-Cone Reaction Drill visual cues 3-5 sets: 10 seconds		
Stretch Lower Back, Hamstrings	Stretch Lower Back, Hamstrings	Stretch Lower Back, Hamstrings	Stretch Lower Back, Hamstrings	Stretch Lower Back, Hamstrings

Hypertrophy and Absolute Strength

BEGINNER OFF SEASON
Phase 2

WEEK 7

MONDAY	WEDNESDAY	FRIDAY
Dot Drills—4-5 sets – 10-15 seconds	Jump Rope—4-5 sets – 15-20 seconds	Dot Drills—3-4 sets – 10-15 seconds
Abs Big 40s—1 set Twisting Stack Crunches—1 set: 15-20 reps	**Abs** Hokie Leg Raises 1 set: 15-20 reps Medicine Ball Stack Crunches—1 set: 10-15 reps	**Abs** Figure 8s—1 set: 10-12 reps Twisting Stack Crunches (unload) 1 set: 15-20 reps
Legs Back Squats (warmup—8 reps) 50%—4 sets: 8 reps 55%—4 sets: 8 reps 61%—4 sets: 8 reps 64%—4 sets: 8 reps	**Legs** Leg Press—3 sets: 10 reps	**Legs** Back Squats (80% of Monday's weight) 4 sets: 8 reps
Chest Bench Press (warmup—8 reps) 50%—4 sets: 8 reps 55%—4 sets: 8 reps 64%—4 sets: 8 reps 67%—4 sets: 8 reps	**Chest** Incline Dumbbell Bench Press—3 sets: 8 reps	**Chest** Close Grip Bench Press (stop and stab) 4 sets: 8 reps
Back Barbell Shrugs—3 sets: 10 reps Lat Pulldowns (front, underhand) 3 sets: 10 reps	**Back** Seated Cable Rows—3 sets: 8 reps	**Back** Dumbbell Shrugs—3 sets: 12 reps Lat Pulldowns (front, underhand) 3 sets—8 reps
Shoulder Upright Rows—3 sets: 10 reps	**Shoulder** Rotator Cuff Dumbbell Exercises 1 set each exercise: 20 reps	**Shoulder** Upright Rows—3 sets: 8 reps
Lower Back/Hamstrings Back Extensions—3 sets: 10 reps	**Lower Back/Hamstrings** Seated or Prone Leg Curls—3 sets: 10 reps	**Lower Back/Hamstrings** Back Extensions 3 sets: 10 reps
Bicep Barbell or Cable Curls—3 sets: 10 reps	**Bicep** Seated Dumbbell Alternate Curls—3 sets: 8 reps	**Bicep** Barbell or Cable Curls—3 sets: 8 reps
Tricep Dips or Bench Dips—3 sets: 10 reps	**Tricep** Tricep Pushdowns—3 sets: 10 reps	**Tricep** Dips or Bench Dips—3 sets: 10 reps
Calf Standing Calf Raises—3 sets: 15 reps	**Calf** Seated Calf Raises—3 sets: 15 reps	**Calf** Standing Calf Raises—3 sets: 15 reps
Static Stretch Routine	Static Stretch Routine	Static Stretch Routine

BEGINNER OFF SEASON   SPEED AGILITY QUICKNESS CONDITIONING SCHEDULE   WEEK 8 PHASE 2

MONDAY	TUESDAY	WEDNESDAY	THURSDAY	FRIDAY
Pre-Strength Workout	**Dynamic Warmup**	**Pre-Strength Workout**	**Dynamic Warmup**	**Pre-Strength Workout**

<u>Jump Rope</u>—with movement
1. Running—1 set: 20 yards
2. Right Leg Hops
   1 set: 20 yards
3. Left Leg Hops
   1 set: 20 yards
4. Double Leg Lateral Hops right—1 set: 20 yards
5. Double Leg Lateral Hops left—1 set: 20 yards
6. Running—1 set: 20 yards
 	
Post-Strength Workout
 	
Static Stretch Routine
 	
<u>Speed Development</u>
1. Heel-to-Butt Kicks
   2 sets: 20 yards
2. A March
   2 sets: 20 yards
3. A Skips
   2 sets: 20 yards
4. A Runs
   2 sets: 20 yards
 	
<u>Programmable Agility</u>
1. 20-yard Shuttle
   4-5 sets
	1. Walking/Skipping Toe Touches
	   1 set: 10 yards each
	2. Walking/Skipping Knee Hugs
	   1 set: 10 yards each
	3. Duck Walks
	   2 sets: 10 yards
	
	Static Stretch Routine
	
	Competitive Games
	Basketball
	Volleyball
	Ultimate Frisbee, etc.
		<u>Dot Drills</u>
		   10-15 seconds
		1. In and Out—both feet
		2. Figure 8—both feet right side
		3. Figure 8—both feet left side
		4. Make up your own pattern
		
		Post-Strength Workout
		
		Static Stretch Routine
		
		<u>Speed Development</u>
		(Acceleration)
		1. Acceleration Ladder
		   6 sets: 30 yards
		or
		2. Walk Runs
		   3 sets: 15 seconds
		
		<u>Reactive Agility</u>
		1. Four-Cone Reaction Drill visual cues
		   4-5 sets: 10 seconds
			1. High Knee Crossovers
			   1 set: 20 yards
			2. Backward High Knees
			   1 set: 20 yards
			3. Low Shuffle
			   2 sets: 20 yards
			
			Static Stretch Routine
			
			Competitive Games
			Basketball
			Volleyball
			Tag Football
			Softball, etc.
				<u>Jump Rope</u>
				1. Both Feet—15 seconds
				2. Alternate Feet—15 seconds
				3. 2 on Right, 2 on Left 15 seconds
				4. Speed Jump—15 seconds
				
				Post-Strength Workout
				
				Static Stretch Routine
				
				Competitive Games
				Shark in a Tank
				   4-5 sets: 10 seconds each

Stretch Lower Back, Hamstrings	Stretch Lower Back, Hamstrings	Stretch Lower Back, Hamstrings	Stretch Lower Back, Hamstrings	Stretch Lower Back, Hamstrings

Hypertrophy and Absolute Strength

BEGINNER OFF SEASON
Phase 2

WEEK 8

MONDAY	WEDNESDAY	FRIDAY
Jump Rope—4-5 sets – 15 seconds	Dot Drills—3-5 sets – 15 seconds	Jump Rope—4-5 sets – 15 seconds

MONDAY

Jump Rope—4-5 sets – 15 seconds

Abs
Big 40s—1 set
Twisting Stack Crunches—1 set: 15-20 reps

Legs
Back Squats (warmup—8 reps)
50%—4 sets: 8 reps
61%—4 sets: 8 reps
64%—4 sets: 8 reps
67%—4 sets: 8 reps

Chest
Bench Press (warmup—8 reps)
55%—4 sets: 8 reps
61%—4 sets: 8 reps
67%—4 sets: 8 reps
70%—4 sets: 8 reps

Back
Barbell Shrugs—3 sets: 10 reps
Lat Pulldowns (front, underhand)
3 sets: 8-10 reps

Shoulder
Upright Rows—3 sets: 8 reps

Lower Back/Hamstrings
Back Extensions—3 sets: 10 reps

Bicep
Barbell or Cable Curls—3 sets: 8-10 reps

Tricep
Dips or Bench Dips—3 sets: 8-10 reps

Calf
Standing Calf Raises—3 sets: 15 reps

Static Stretch Routine

WEDNESDAY

Dot Drills—3-5 sets – 15 seconds

Abs
Hokie Leg Raises—1 set: 15-20 reps
Medicine Ball Stack Crunches—1 set: 10-15 reps

Legs
Leg Press—3 sets: 10 reps

Chest
Incline Dumbbell Bench Press—4 sets: 8 reps

Back
Seated Cable Rows—3 sets: 8 reps

Shoulder
Rotator Cuff Dumbbell Exercises
1 set each exercise—20 reps

Lower Back/Hamstrings
Seated or Prone Leg Curls—3 sets: 8 reps

Bicep
Seated Dumbbell Alternate Curls—3 sets: 8 reps

Tricep
Tricep Pushdowns—3 sets: 10 reps

Calf
Seated Calf Raises—3 sets: 15 reps

Static Stretch Routine

FRIDAY

Jump Rope—4-5 sets – 15 seconds

Abs
Figure 8s—1 set: 10-12 reps
Twisting Stack Crunches (unload)
1 set: 15-20 reps

Legs
Back Squats (80% of Monday's weight)
4 sets: 8 reps

Chest
Close Grip Bench Press (stop and stab)
4 sets: 8 reps

Back
Dumbbell Shrugs—3 sets: 12 reps
Lat Pulldowns (front, underhand)—3 sets: 10 reps

Shoulder
Upright Rows—3 sets: 8 reps

Lower Back/Hamstrings
Back Extensions—2 sets: 12 reps

Bicep
Barbell or Cable Curls—3 sets: 8 reps

Tricep
Dips
or
Bench Dips—3 sets: 10 reps

Calf
Standing Calf Raises—3 sets: 15 reps

Static Stretch Routine

BEGINNER OFF SEASON   SPEED AGILITY QUICKNESS CONDITIONING SCHEDULE   WEEK 9 PHASE 2

MONDAY	TUESDAY	WEDNESDAY	THURSDAY	FRIDAY
Pre-Strength Workout	**Dynamic Warmup**	**Pre-Strength Workout**	**Dynamic Warmup**	**Pre-Strength Workout**
Jump Rope—with movement 1. Running—1 set: 20 yards 2. Double Leg Hops Forward—1 set: 20 yards 3. Right Leg Hops—Forward 1 set: 20 yards 4. Left Leg Hops—Forward 1 set: 20 yards 5. Running—1 set: 20 yards **Post-Strength Workout** **Static Stretch Routine** **Speed Development** 1. Fast Arms Drill 2 set: 15 seconds 2. A Marches 2 sets: 20 yards 3. A Skips 2 sets: 20 yards 4. A Runs 2 sets: 20 yards **Programmable Agility** 1. Pattern Runs 2-3 sets each—20 yards (speed cuts, power cuts, and spins)	1. Walking Knee Hugs 1 set: 20 yards 2. Skipping Toe Touches 1 set: 20 yards 3. Low Shuffle 2 sets: 20 yards 4. Starts—Football Stance 2-4 sets **Static Stretch Routine** **Competitive Games** Basketball Volleyball Softball Tag Football, etc.	**Dot Drills** 10-15 seconds 1. In and Out—both feet 2. Figure 8—both feet right side 3. Figure 8—both feet left side 4. In and Out—turns **Post-Strength Workout** **Static Stretch Routine** **Speed Development** (Acceleration) 1. Uphill Runs 20-30 yards—6-8 reps sprint up, walk back or 2. Sled Pulls 20-30 yards (50 pounds max weight on sled) **Reactive Agility** 1. Eight-Cone Reaction Drill visual cues 4-5 sets: 10 seconds	1.High Knee Crossovers 1 set: 20 yards 2.Backward Skips 1 set: 20 yards 3.Carioca 2 sets: 20 yards **Static Stretch Routine** **Competitive Games** Basketball Volleyball Tag Football Team Handball, etc.	**Jump Rope** 1. Both Feet—10-15 seconds 2. Right Foot—10-15 seconds 3. Left Foot—10-15 seconds 4. Alternate Feet 10-15 seconds 5. 2 on Right, 2 on Left 10-15 seconds 6. Speed jump—10-15 seconds **Post-Strength Workout** **Static Stretch Routine** **Competitive Games** Get Up and Sprint Variations 4-6 sets: 20-30 yards
Stretch Lower Back, Hamstrings	Strretch Lower Back, Hamstrings	Stretch Lower Back, Hamstrings	Stretch Lower Back, Hamstrings	Stretch Lower Back, Hamstrings

WEEK 9

BEGINNER OFF SEASON
Phase 2

Hypertrophy and Absolute Strength

MONDAY	WEDNESDAY	FRIDAY
Jump Rope—4-5 sets – 20 seconds	Dot Drills—4-5 sets – 15 seconds	Jump Rope—4-5 sets – 20 seconds
Abs Big 40s—1 set Twisting Stack Crunches—1 set: 15-20 reps	**Abs** Hokie Leg Raises—1 set: 15-20 reps Medicine Ball Stack Crunches—1 set: 10-15 reps	**Abs** Figure 8s—1 set:10-12 reps Twisting Stack Crunches (unload) 1 set: 15-20 reps
Legs Back Squats (warmup—6 reps) 55%—4 sets: 6 reps 61%—4 sets: 6 reps 67%—4 sets: 6 reps 70%—4 sets: 6 reps	**Legs** Leg Press—4 sets: 8 reps	**Legs** Back Squats (80% of Monday's weight) 4 sets: 8 reps
Chest Bench Press (warmup—6 reps) 55%—4 sets: 6 reps 64%—4 sets: 6 reps 70%—4 sets: 6 reps 73%—4 sets: 6 reps	**Chest** Incline Dumbbell Bench Press—3 sets: 8 reps	**Chest** Close Grip Bench Press (stop and stab) 4 sets: 8 reps
Back Barbell Shrugs—3 sets: 8 reps Lat Pulldowns (front, underhand) 3 sets: 8 reps	**Back** Seated Cable Rows—3 sets: 8 reps	**Back** Dumbbell Shrugs—3 sets: 10 reps Lat Pulldowns (front, underhand)—3 sets: 8 reps
Shoulder Upright Rows—3 sets: 8 reps	**Shoulder** Rotator Cuff Dumbbell Exercises 1 set each exercise: 20 reps	**Shoulder** Upright Rows—3 sets: 8 reps
Lower Back/Hamstrings Back Extensions—3 sets: 8-10 reps	**Lower Back/Hamstrings** Seated or Prone Leg Curls—3 sets: 10 reps	**Lower Back/Hamstrings** Back Extensions—2 sets: 10-12 reps
Bicep Barbell or Cable Curls—3 sets: 8 reps	**Bicep** Seated Dumbbell Alternate Curls—3 sets: 8 reps	**Bicep** Barbell or Cable Curls—3 sets: 8 reps
Tricep Weighted Dips or Bench Dips—3 sets: 8 reps	**Tricep** Tricep Pushdowns—3 sets: 10 reps	**Tricep** Dips or Bench Dips—3 sets: 10 reps
Calf Standing Calf Raises—3 sets: 15-20 reps	**Calf** Seated Calf Raises—3 sets: 15 reps	**Calf** Standing Calf Raises—3 sets: 15 reps
Static Stretch Routine	**Static Stretch Routine**	**Static Stretch Routine**

BEGINNER OFF SEASON SPEED AGILITY QUICKNESS CONDITIONING SCHEDULE WEEK 10 PHASE 2

MONDAY	TUESDAY	WEDNESDAY	THURSDAY	FRIDAY
Pre-Strength Workout	**Dynamic Warmup**	**Pre-Strength Workout**	**Dynamic Warmup**	**Pre-Strength Workout**

<u>Jump Rope</u>—with movement
1. Running—1 set: 20 yards
2. Double Leg Forward
   1 set: 20 yards
3. Double Leg Lateral
   Right—1 set: 20 yards
4. Double Leg Lateral
   Left—1 set: 20 yards
5. Running—1 set: 20 yards
	1. Walking/Skipping Knee
	   Hugs—1 set: 10 yards
	2. Walking/Skipping Toe
	   Touches
	   1 set: 10 yards each
	3. Low Shuffle
	   2 sets: 20 yards
	4. Starts—Football Stance
	   2-4 sets
		<u>Dot Drills</u>
		   10-15 seconds
		1. In and Out—both feet
		2. Figure 8—right foot only
		   right side
		3. Figure 8—left foot only
		   left side
		4. Make up your own
		   pattern
			1. High Knee Crossovers
			   2 sets: 20 yards
			2. Lunge Walk (no weight)
			   1 set: 20 yards
			3. Backward Skips
			   1 set: 20 yards
			4. Starts—Football Stance
			   2-4 sets
				<u>Jump Rope</u>
				1. Both Feet—10-15
				   seconds
				2. Right Foot—10-15
				   seconds
				3. Left Foot—10-15 seconds
				4. 2 on Right, 2 on Left
				   10-15 seconds
				5. Speed Jump—10-15 sec
				   onds

Post-Strength Workout	**Static Stretch Routine**	**Post-Strength Workout**	**Static Stretch Routine**	**Post-Strength Workout**
Static Stretch Routine	**Competitive Games**	**Static Stretch Routine**	**Competitive Games**	**Static Stretch Routine**

Speed Development
1. Acceleration Ladder
   6 sets: 30 yards
	Dodgeball variations
	Basketball
	Volleyball
	Tag Football, etc.
		Speed Development
		1. Fast Arms Drill
		   2 sets: 15 seconds
		2. Heel-to-Butt Kicks
		   2 sets: 20 yards
		3. A Marches
		   1 set: 20 yards
		4. A Skips
		   1 set: 20 yards
		5. A Runs—2 sets: 20 yards
			Basketball
			Volleyball
			Team Handball, etc.
				Competitive Games
				Capture the Flag
				or
				Shark in a Tank

Programmable Agility
1. Texas-Drill—3 sets
2. Pattern Runs—2 sets each
   (speed cuts, power cuts,
   and spins)
		Reactive Agility
		1. Crazy Ball Drills
		   6-8 sets		

Stretch Lower Back, Hamstrings	Stretch Lower Back, Hamstrings	Stretch Lower Back, Hamstrings	Stretch Lower Back, Hamstrings	Stretch Lower Back, Hamstrings

Hypertrophy and
Absolute Strength

WEEK 10   BEGINNER OFF SEASON
Phase 2

MONDAY	WEDNESDAY	FRIDAY
Jump Rope—4-5 sets – 15-20 seconds	**Dot Drills**—4-5 sets – 15 seconds	**Jump Rope**—4-5 sets – 20 seconds
Abs Big 40s—1 set	**Abs** Hokie Leg Raises—1 set: 15-20 reps	**Abs** Figure 8s—1 set: 10-12 reps
Twisting Stack Crunches—1 set: 15-20 reps	Medicine Ball Stack Crunches—1 set: 10-15 reps	Twisting Stack Crunches (unload) 1 set: 15-20 reps
Legs Back Squats (warmup—6 reps) 55%—4 sets: 6 reps 64%—4 sets: 6 reps 70%—4 sets: 6 reps 73%—4 sets: 6 reps	**Legs** Leg Press—4 sets: 8 reps	**Legs** Back Squats (80% of Monday's weight) 4 sets: 8 reps
Chest Bench Press (warmup—6 reps) 61%—4 sets: 6 reps 67%—4 sets: 6 reps 73%—4 sets: 6 reps 79%—4 sets: 6 reps	**Chest** Incline Dumbbell Bench Press—3 sets: 8 reps	**Chest** Close Grip Bench Press (stop and stab) 4 sets: 8 reps
Back Barbell Shrugs—3 sets: 8 reps Lat Pulldowns (front, underhand)—3 sets: 8 reps	**Back** Seated Cable Rows—3 sets: 8 reps	**Back** Dumbbell Shrugs—3 sets: 8 reps Lat Pulldowns (front, underhand)—3 sets: 8 reps
Shoulder Upright Rows—3 sets: 8 reps	**Shoulder** Rotator Cuff Dumbbell Exercises 1 set each exercise: 20 reps	**Shoulder** Upright Rows—3 sets: 8 reps
Lower Back/Hamstrings Back Extensions—3 sets: 8-12 reps	**Lower Back/Hamstrings** Seated or Prone Leg Curls—3 sets: 8 reps	**Lower Back/Hamstrings** Back Extensions—3 sets: 8-12 reps
Bicep Barbell or Cable Curls—3 sets: 8 reps	**Bicep** Seated Dumbbell Alternate Curls—3 sets: 8 reps	**Bicep** Barbell or Cable Curls—3 sets: 8 reps
Tricep Weighted Dips or Weighted Bench Dips 3 sets: 8 reps	**Tricep** Tricep Pushdowns—3 sets: 10 reps	**Tricep** Dips or Bench Dips—3 sets: 8-10 reps
Calf Standing Calf Raises—3 sets: 15 reps	**Calf** Seated Calf Raises—3 sets: 15 reps	**Calf** Standing Calf Raises—3 sets: 15 reps
Static Stretch Routine	**Static Stretch Routine**	**Static Stretch Routine**

BEGINNER OFF SEASON   SPEED AGILITY QUICKNESS CONDITIONING SCHEDULE   WEEK 11 PHASE 2

MONDAY	TUESDAY	WEDNESDAY	THURSDAY	FRIDAY
Pre-Strength Workout	**Dynamic Warmup**	**Pre-Strength Workout**	**Dynamic Warmup**	**Pre-Strength Workout**

Jump Rope—with movement
1. Running—1 set: 20 yards
2. Right Leg Forward
  1 set: 20 yards
3. Left Leg Forward
  1 set: 20 yards
4. Double Leg Forward
  1 set: 20 yards
5. Running—1 set: 20 yards
	1. Walking/Skipping Knee
	  Hugs—1 set: 10 yards
	2. Walking/Skipping Toe
	  Touches
	  1 set: 10 yards each
	3. Low Shuffle
	  2 sets: 20 yards
	4. Starts—Football Stance
	  2-4 sets
		Dot Drills
		  10-15 seconds
		1. In and Out
		2. Figure 8—both feet
		  right side
		3. Figure 8—both feet
		  left side
		4. In and Out
		  Turn—both feet
			1. High Knee Crossovers
			  1 set: 20 yards
			2. Backward High Knees
			  1 set: 20 yards
			3. Carioca 2 sets: 20 yards
			4. Starts—Football Stance
			  2-4 sets
				Jump Rope
				1. Both Feet—10-15
				  seconds
				2. Right Foot—10-15
				  seconds
				3. Left Foot—10-15 seconds
				4. 2 on Right, 2 on Left
				  10-15 seconds
				5. Speed Jump—10-15
				  seconds

Post-Strength Workout	**Static Stretch Routine**	**Post-Strength Workout**	**Static Stretch Routine**	**Post-Strength Workout**
Static Stretch Routine	**Competitive Games**	**Static Stretch Routine**	**Competitive Games**	**Static Stretch Routine**

Speed Development
1. A Marches
  2 sets: 20 yards
2. A Skips
  2 sets: 20 yards
3. A Runs
  2 sets: 20 yards
	Basketball
	Volleyball
	Tag Football, etc.
		Speed Development
		(Acceleration)
		1. Uphill Runs
		  6-8 reps—30 yards
		  (sprint up, walk down)
		
		or
		
		2. Sled Pulls
		  6-8 reps—20-30 yards
		  (50 pounds max weight
		  on sled)
			Tag Football
			Ultimate Frisbee
			Basketball
			Volleyball, etc.
				Competitive Games
				Shark in a Tank
				  3-5 sets: 10 seconds
				
				or
				
				Get Up and Sprint
				  Variations
				  4-6 sets: 30 yards

Plyometrics
1. Power Skips
  2 sets: 20 yards
2. Bounding
  2 sets: 20 yards
3. Double Leg Long
  Jumps—5 (measure
  distance)
		Reactive Agility
		1. Two-Point Wave Drill
		  3-4 sets include shuffles,
		  jumps, Hit It, etc. Also
		  have a player on com-
		  mand get out in front for
		  the group to mirror.		

Stretch Lower Back, Hamstrings	Stretch Lower Back, Hamstrings	Stretch Lower Back, Hamstrings	Stretch Lower Back, Hamstrings	Stretch Lower Back, Hamstrings

Hypertrophy and
Absolute Strength

BEGINNER OFF SEASON
Phase 2

WEEK 11

MONDAY	WEDNESDAY	FRIDAY
Jump Rope—4-5 sets – 20 seconds	**Dot Drills—4-5 sets – 10-15 seconds**	**Jump Rope—4-5 sets – 20 seconds**

MONDAY

Jump Rope—4-5 sets – 20 seconds

Abs
Big 40s—1 set
Twisting Stack Crunches—1 set: 15-20 reps

Legs
Back Squats (warmup—6 reps)
55%—4 sets: 6 reps
64%—4 sets: 6 reps
70%—4 sets: 6 reps
76%—4 sets: 6 reps

Chest
Bench Press (warmup—6 reps)
64%—4 sets: 6 reps
70%—4 sets: 6 reps
76%—4 sets: 6 reps
82%—4 sets: 6 reps

Back
Barbell Shrugs—3 sets: 8 reps
Lat Pulldowns (front, underhand)—3 sets: 8 reps

Shoulder
Upright Rows—3 sets: 8 reps

Lower Back/Hamstrings
Back Extensions—3 sets: 8-12 reps

Bicep
Barbell or Cable Curls—3 sets: 8 reps

Tricep
Weighted Dips or Weighted Bench Dips
3 sets: 8-10 reps

Calf
Standing Calf Raises—3 sets: 15 reps

Static Stretch Routine

WEDNESDAY

Dot Drills—4-5 sets – 10-15 seconds

Abs
Hokie Leg Raises—1 set: 15-20 reps
Medicine Ball Stack Crunches—1 set: 10-15 reps

Legs
Leg Press—4 sets: 8 reps

Chest
Incline Dumbbell Bench Press—3 sets: 8 reps

Shoulder
Rotator Cuff Dumbbell Exercises
1 set each exercise: 20 reps

Lower Back/Hamstrings
Seated or Prone Leg Curls—3 sets: 8 reps

Bicep
Seated Dumbbell Alternate Curls—3 sets: 8 reps

Tricep
Tricep Pushdowns—3 sets: 10 reps

Calf
Seated Calf Raises—3 sets: 15 reps

Static Stretch Routine

FRIDAY

Jump Rope—4-5 sets – 20 seconds

Abs
Figure 8s—1 set: 12 reps
Twisting Stack Crunches (unload)
1 set: 15-20 reps

Legs
Back Squats (80% of Monday's weight)
4 sets: 8 reps

Chest
Close Grip Bench Press (stop and stab)
4 sets: 8 reps

Back
Lat Pulldowns (front, underhand)—3 sets: 8 reps

Shoulder
Upright Rows—3 sets: 8 reps

Lower Back/Hamstrings
Back Extensions—3 sets: 8-12 reps

Bicep
Barbell or Cable Curls—3 sets: 8 reps

Tricep
Dips or Bench Dips—3 sets: 8-10 reps

Calf
Standing Calf Raises—3 sets: 15 reps

Static Stretch Routine

BEGINNER OFF SEASON　　SPEED AGILITY QUICKNESS CONDITIONING SCHEDULE　　WEEK 12 PHASE 2

MONDAY	TUESDAY	WEDNESDAY	THURSDAY	FRIDAY
Pre-Strength Workout	**Dynamic Warmup**	**Pre-Strength Workout**	**Dynamic Warmup**	**Pre-Strength Workout**
Jump Rope—with movement 1. Running—1 set: 20 yards 2. Double Leg Hops 　Forward—1 set: 20 yards 3. Double Leg Lateral Hops 　2 sets: 20 yards 4. Running—1 set: 20 yards	1. High Knee Crossovers 　1 set: 20 yards 2. Backward High Knees 　1 set: 20 yards 3. Duck Walk 　1 set: 20 yards 4. Starts 　2-4 sets for 30 yards	**Dot Drills** 　10 seconds 1. In and Out 2. Figure 8—right foot 　right side 3. Figure 8—left foot 　left side 4. Make up your own 　pattern	1. Walking Knee Hugs 　1 set: 20 yards 2. Skipping Toe Touches 　1 set: 20 yards 3. Low Shuffle 　2 sets: 20 yards 4. Starts—Football Stance 　2-4 sets for 20 yards	REST PLAYERS OFF
Post-Strength Workout	**Static Stretch Routine**	**Static Stretch Routine**	**Static Stretch Routine**	
Static Stretch Routine	**Competitive Games**	**Speed Development**	**Competitive Games**	
Speed Development (Acceleration) 1. Acceleration Ladder 　6 sets: 30 yards	Basketball Volleyball Tag Football, etc.	1. Fast Arms 　1 set: 15 seconds 2. Heel-to-Butt Kicks 　1 set: 20 yards 3. A Marches 　1 set: 20 yards 4. A Skips 　1 set: 20 yards 5. A Runs—1 set: 20 yards	Team Handball Tag Football Basketball Volleyball, etc.	
Programmable Agility 1. 20-yard Shuttle—4 sets		**Programmable Agility** 1. Four-Cone Reaction Drill 　visual cues—3-4 sets: 10 　seconds		
Stretch Lower Back, Hamstrings	Stretch Lower Back, Hamstrings	Stretch Lower Back, Hamstrings	Stretch Lower Back, Hamstrings	Stretch Lower Back, Hamstrings

Hypertrophy and
Absolute Strength

BEGINNER OFF SEASON
Phase 2

WEEK 12
TESTING WEEK

MONDAY	WEDNESDAY	FRIDAY
Jump Rope—4-5 sets – 20 seconds	Dot Drills—4-5 sets – 10-15 seconds	OFF
Abs Big 40s—1 set Twisting Stack Crunches—1 set: 15-20 reps	**Abs** Hokie Leg Raises—1 set: 15-20 reps Medicine Ball Stack Crunches 1 set: 15-20 reps	**Active Rest** Play Basketball, Racquetball, Tennis, etc.
TEST—Vertical Jump (using Vertic machine)	**TEST**—10-yard Sprint (electronically timed)	
TEST—Back Squats Rep Test (up to 5 reps)—convert to 1 RM	**TEST**—20-yard Shuttle best of three trials	
TEST—Pullups (overhand grip) max reps	**TEST**—Bench Press Rep Test (up to 5 reps)—convert to 1 RM	
Get Body Weight	**TEST**—Dips max reps	
	TEST—Sit and Reach Hamstring Lower Back Flexibility	
Static Stretch Routine	**Static Stretch Routine**	

BEGINNER PRESEASON · SPEED AGILITY QUICKNESS CONDITIONING SCHEDULE · WEEK 1 PHASE 3

MONDAY	TUESDAY	WEDNESDAY	THURSDAY	FRIDAY
Pre-Strength Workout	**Dynamic Warmup**	**Pre-Strength Workout**	**Dynamic Warmup**	**Pre-Strength Workout**
Jump Rope	1. Walking/Skipping Knee Hugs	**Jump Rope** with movement	1. High Knee Crossovers	**Dot Drills**
1. Both Feet—1 set: 15 seconds	1 set: 10 yards each	1. Running—1 set: 20 yards	1 set: 20 yards	10-15 seconds
2. Right Foot	2. Walking/Skipping Toes Touches	2. Double Leg Hops Forward—1 set: 20 yards	2. Backward Skips	1. In and Out
1 set: 15 seconds	1 set: 10 yards each	3. Right Leg Hops	1 set: 20 yards	2. Figure 8—both feet right side
3. Left Foot—1 set: 15 seconds	3. Low Shuffle	1 set: 20 yards	3. Low Carioca	3. Figure 8—both feet left side
4. Alternate Feet	2 sets—20 yards	4. Left Leg Hops	2 sets: 20 yards	4. Make up your own pattern
1 set: 15 seconds	4. Starts—Football Stance	1 set: 20 yards	**Static Stretch Routine**	**Post-Strength Workout**
5. 2 on Right, 2 on Left	2-4 sets	5. Running—1 set: 20 yards	**Competitive Team or**	**PNF Partner Stretch**
1 set: 15 seconds	**PNF Partner Stretch**	**Post-Strength Workout**	**Individual Games**	**Conditioning**
6. Speed Jump	**Conditioning**	**Static Stretch Routine**	Basketball	4 Modified Suicides
1 set: 15 seconds	6 110s	**Reactive Agility**	Tag Football	10 yards and back
Post-Strength Workout	Linemen—20 seconds	1. Tennis Ball Reaction Drill Variations—4-8 sets	Racquetball	15 yards and back
Static Stretch Routine	TE, LB, QB, Spec, FB, DE 18 seconds	**Speed Development**	Tennis, etc.	20 yards and back
Speed Development	WR, TB, DB—16 seconds	1. Sled Pulls		Linemen—22 seconds
1. A Marches	Work-to-Rest Ratio—1:3	4-6 sets: 20 yards (50 pounds max weight on sled)		TE, LB, QB, Spec, FB, DE 20 seconds
1 set: 20 yards				WR, TB, DB—18 seconds
2. A Skips				
1 set: 20 yards				
3. A Runs				
1 set: 20 yards				
4. Power Skips				
1 set: 20 yards				
5. Bounding				
1 set: 20 yards				
Programmable Agility				
1. 20-yard Shuttle 3-4 sets				
Stretch Lower Back, Hamstrings	Stretch Lower Back, Hamstrings	Stretch Lower Back, Hamstrings	Stretch Lower Back, Hamstrings	Stretch Lower Back, Hamstrings

Absolute Strength and Peaking

BEGINNER PRESEASON
Phase 3

WEEK 1

MONDAY	WEDNESDAY	FRIDAY
Jump Rope	Speed Ladder	Dot Drills
Abs Bronco Partner Ab Program	**Abs** Big 40s—1 set Twisting Stack Crunches—1 set: 15-20 reps	**Abs** Hokie Leg Raises—1 set: 10 reps ABC Sit-Ups—1 set: 5-10 reps Dying Cockroach—30 seconds
Legs Back Squats (unload) (warmup—10 reps) 55%—5 reps 64%—5 reps 70%—5 reps 73%—5 reps	**Legs** Single-Leg Leg Press (each leg)—3 sets: 10 reps	**Legs** Speed Squats (50% of Monday's weight) 4 sets: 5 reps
Chest Bench Press (unlaod) (warmup—10 reps) 55%—5 reps 64%—5 reps 70%—5 reps 76%—5 reps	**Chest** Incline Bench Press—4 sets: 6 reps	**Chest** Close Grip Bench Press (stop and stab) 4 sets: 5 reps
Back Dumbbell Shrugs—3 sets: 10 reps Pullups or Lat Pulldowns (front, underhand) 2-3 sets: 5-10 reps	**Back** Upright Rows—3 sets: 10 reps Seated Cable Rows—3 sets: 8 reps	**Back** Barbell Shrugs—3 sets: 10 reps Pullups or Lat Pulldowns (front, underhand) 3 sets: 8 reps
Shoulder Seated Dumbbell Alternate Overhead Press (each arm)—3 sets: 6 reps	**Shoulders** Dumbbell 21s—2 sets (front raises, lat raises, bent overlaterals)—7 reps each	**Shoulder** Seated Overhead Barbell Press 3 sets: 10, 8, 6 reps
Bicep Barbell or Cable Curls—3 sets: 10 reps	**Bicep** Standing Alternate Dumbbell Curls 3 sets: 8 reps	**Bicep** Barbell or Cable Curls—3 sets: 10 reps
Tricep Dips—3 sets: 10 reps	**Tricep** Tricep Pushdowns—3 sets: 10 reps	**Tricep** Bench Dips—3 sets: 10 reps
Lower Back/Hamstrings Back Extensions—2 sets: 10 reps	**Lower Back/Hamstrings** Seated or Prone Leg—3 sets: 10 reps	**Lower Back/Hamstrings** Back Extensions—3 sets: 10 reps
Calf Standing Calf Raises—3 sets: 15 reps	**Calf** Seated Calf Raises—3 sets: 15 reps	**Calf** Standing Calf Raises—2 sets: 15 reps
Static Stretch Routine	Static Stretch Routine	Static Stretch Routine

BEGINNER PRESEASON   SPEED AGILITY QUICKNESS CONDITIONING SCHEDULE   WEEK 2 PHASE 3

MONDAY	TUESDAY	WEDNESDAY	THURSDAY	FRIDAY
Pre-Strength Workout	**Dynamic Warmup**	**Pre-Strength Workout**	**Dynamic Warmup**	**Pre-Strength Workout**
Jump Rope 1. Both Feet—1 set: 15 seconds 2. Right Foot 1 set: 15 seconds 3. Left Foot—1 set: 15 seconds 4. Alternate Feet 1 set: 15 seconds 5. 2 on Right, 2 on Left 1 set: 15 seconds 6. Speed Jump 1 set: 15 seconds	1. Walking Toe Touches 1 set: 20 yards 2. Skipping Toe Touches 1 set: 20 yards 3. Low Shuffle 2 sets: 20 yards 4. Starts—Football Stance 2-4 sets	**Jump Rope**—with movement 1. Running—1 set: 20 yards 2. Double Leg Hops forward—1 set: 20 yards 3. Right Leg Hops 1 set: 20 yards 4. Left Leg Hops 1 set: 20 yards 5. Running—1 set: 20 yards	1. High Knee Crossovers 1 set: 20 yards 2. Backward High Knees 1 set: 20 yards 3. Low Carioca 2 sets: 20 yards 4. Starts—Football Stance 2-4 sets	**Dot Drills** 10-15 seconds 1. In and Out 2. Figure 8 both feet—right side 3. Figure 8 both feet—left side 4. Make up your own pattern
Post-Strength Workout	**PNF Partner Stretch**	**Post-Strength Workout**	**Static Stretch Routine**	**Post-Strength Workout**
Static Stretch Routine	**Conditioning** 8 110s Linemen—20 seconds TE, LB, QB, Spec, FB, DE 18 seconds WR, TB, DB—16 seconds Work-to-Rest Ratio—1:3	**Static Stretch Routine**	**Competitive Team** or **Individual Games**	**PNF Partner Stretch**
Programmable Agility 1. Carolina Box Drill 4 sets		**Programmable Agility** 1. Texas-Drill—4 sets	Basketball Wrestling Volleyball Racquetball, etc.	**Conditioning** 4 Modified Suicides 10 yards and back 15 yards and back 20 yards and back Linemen—22 seconds TE, LB, QB, Spec, FB, DE 20 seconds WR, TB, DB—18 seconds Work-to-Rest Ratio—1:3
Speed Development 1. Fast Arms 1 set: 15 seconds 2. Heel-to-Butt Kicks 1 set: 20 yards 3. A Marches—1 set: 20 yards 4. A Skips—1 set: 20 yards 5. A Runs—1 set: 20 yards 6. Power Skips 1 set: 20 yards 7. Bounding—1 set: 20 yards		**Reactive Agility** 1. Two-Point Wave Drill 4 sets: (include jumps, shuffles, "Hit It", etc.)		
Stretch Lower Back, Hamstrings	Stretch Lower Back, Hamstrings	Stretch Lower Back, Hamstrings	Stretch Lower Back, Hamstrings	Stretch Lower Back, Hamstrings

Absolute Strength
and Peaking

WEEK 2

BEGINNER PRESEASON
Phase 3

MONDAY	WEDNESDAY	FRIDAY
Jump Rope	Speed Ladder	Dot Drills

MONDAY

Abs
Bronco Partner Ab Program

Legs
Back Squats (warmup—10 reps)
  55%—5 reps
  64%—5 reps
  70%—5 reps
  76%—5 reps

Chest
Bench Press (warmup—10 reps)
  55%—5 reps
  64%—5 reps
  70%—5 reps
  76%—5 reps
  79%—5 reps

Back
Dumbbell Shrugs—3 sets: 10 reps
Pullups—3 sets: 5-10 reps
or
Lat Pulldowns (front, underhand)
  3 sets: 8-10 reps

Shoulder
Seated Dumbbell Alternate Overhead Press
  (each arm)—3 sets: 6 reps

Bicep
Barbell or Cable Curls—3 sets: 8-10 reps

Tricep
Dips (use weight if possible)—3 sets: 8 reps

Lower Back/Hamstrings
Back Extensions—2 sets: 10-12 reps

Calf
Standing Calf Raises—3 sets: 15 reps

Static Stretch Routine

WEDNESDAY

Abs
Big 40s—1 set
Twisting Stack Crunches—1 set: 15-20 reps

Legs
Single-Leg Leg Press (each leg) 3 sets: 10 reps

Chest
Incline Bench Press 4 sets: 6 reps

Back
Upright Rows 3 sets: 8-10 reps
Seated Cable Rows 3 sets: 8 reps

Shoulders
Dumbbell 21s—2 sets (front raises, lat raises,
  bent over laterals)—7 reps each

Bicep
Standing Alternate Dumbbell Curls
  3 sets: 8-10 reps

Tricep
Tricep Pushdowns—3 sets: 10 reps

Lower Back/Hamstrings
Seated or Prone Leg—3 sets: 10 reps

Calf
Seated Calf Raises 3 sets: 15 reps

Static Stretch Routine

FRIDAY

Abs
Hokie Leg Raises—1 set: 10 reps
ABC Situps—1 set: 5-10 reps
Dying Cockroach—30 seconds

Legs
Speed Squats (50% of Mondays weight)
  4 sets: 5 reps

Chest
Close Grip Bench Press (stop and stab)
  4 sets: 5 reps

Back
Barbell Shrugs—3 sets: 10 reps
Pullups—3 sets: 5-10 reps
or
Lat Pulldowns (front, underhand)
  3 sets: 8-10 reps

Shoulder
Seated Overhead Barbell Press
  3 sets: 8, 6, 6 reps

Bicep
Barbell or Cable Curls—3 sets: 10 reps

Tricep
Bench Dips—3 sets: 10 reps

Lower Back/Hamstrings
Back Extensions—2 sets: 10 reps

Calf
Standing Calf Raises—3 sets: 15 reps

Static Stretch Routine

BEGINNER PRESEASON   SPEED AGILITY QUICKNESS CONDITIONING SCHEDULE   WEEK 3 PHASE 3

MONDAY	TUESDAY	WEDNESDAY	THURSDAY	FRIDAY
Pre-Strength Workout	**Dynamic Warmup**	**Pre-Strength Workout**	**Dynamic Warmup**	**Pre-Strength Workout**
Jump Rope	1. Walking/Skipping Knee Hugs	**Jump Rope**—with movement	1. High Knee Crossovers	**Dot Drills**
1. Both Feet—1 set: 15 seconds	1 set: 20 yards	1. Running—1 set: 20 yards	2 sets: 20 yards	10-15 seconds
2. Right Foot	2. Walking/Skipping Toe Touches	2. Double Leg Hops Forward—1 set: 20 yards	2. Backward Skips 2 sets: 20 yards	1. In and Out
1 set: 15 seconds	1 set: 20 yards	3. Right Leg Hops	3. Low Shuffle	2. Figure 8—both feet right side
3. Left Foot—1 set: 15 seconds	3. Low Shuffle 2 sets: 20 yards	1 set: 20 yards	2 sets: 20 yards	3. Figure 8—both feet left side
4. Alternate Feet	4. Starts—Football Stance	4. Left Leg Hops 1 set: 20 yards	4. Starts—Football Stance 4-6 reps	4. Make up your own pattern
1 set: 15 seconds	2-4 sets	5. Running—1 set: 20 yards	**Static Stretch Routine**	**Post-Strength Workout**
5. 2 on Right, 2 on Left 1 set: 15 seconds	**PNF Partner Stretch**	**Post-Strength Workout**	**Competitive Games**	**PNF Partner Stretch**
6. Speed Jump 1 set: 15 seconds	**Conditioning**	**Static Stretch Routine**	Basketball	**Conditioning**
Post-Strength Workout	8 110s	**Speed Development**	Ultimate Frisbee	4 Modified Suicides
Static Stretch Routine	Linemen—20 seconds TE, LB, QB, Spec, FB, DE 18 seconds	1. Acceleration Ladder 6 sets: 20 yards	Tag Football Racquetball, etc.	10 yards and back 15 yards and back 20 yards and back
Speed Development	WR, TB, DB—16 seconds Work-to-Rest Ratio—1:3	**Reactive Agility**		Linemen—22 seconds TE, LB, QB, Spec, FB, DE 20 seconds
1. A Marches—2 sets: 20 yards		1. Four-Cone Reaction Drill visual cues—4 sets 10 seconds		WR, TB, DB—18 seconds Work-to-Rest Ratio—1:3
2. A Skips—2 sets: 20 yards				
3. A Runs—2 sets: 20 yards				
4. Power Skips 1 set: 20 yards				
5. Bounding—1 set: 20 yards				
Programmable Agility				
1. 20-yard Shuttle—4 sets				
Stretch Lower Back, Hamstrings	Stretch Lower Back, Hamstrings	Stretch Lower Back, Hamstrings	Stretch Lower Back, Hamstrings	Stretch Lower Back, Hamstrings

Absolute Strength
and Peaking

WEEK 3   BEGINNER PRESEASON
Phase 3

MONDAY	WEDNESDAY	FRIDAY
Jump Rope	Speed Ladder	Dot Drills

MONDAY

Abs
Bronco Partner Ab Program

Legs
Back Squats (warmup—8 reps)
  55%—5 reps
  64%—5 reps
  70%—5 reps
  76%—5 reps
  79%—5 reps

Chest
Bench Press (warmup—8 reps)
  55%—5 reps
  64%—5 reps
  70%—5 reps
  76%—5 reps
  82%—5 reps

Back
Dumbbell Shrugs—3 sets: 10 reps
Pullups—3 sets: 5-10 reps
or
Lat Pulldowns (front, underhand)
3 sets: 8-10 reps

Shoulder
Seated Dumbbell Alternate Overhead Press
(each arm)—3 sets: 6 reps

Bicep
Barbell or Cable Curls—3 sets: 10 reps

Tricep
Dips (use weight if possible)—3 sets: 8 reps

Lower Back/Hamstrings
Back Extensions—2 sets: 10 reps

Calf
Standing Calf Raises—3 sets: 15 reps

Static Stretch Routine

WEDNESDAY

Abs
Big 40s—1 set
Twisting Stack Crunches—1 set: 15-20 reps

Legs
Single-Leg Leg Press (each leg)—3 sets: 10 reps

Chest
Incline Bench Press—4 sets: 5 reps

Back
Upright Rows—3 sets: 8-10 reps
Seated Cable Rows—3 sets: 8 reps

Shoulders
Dumbbell 21s—2 sets: (front raises, lat raises,
  bent over laterals)—7 reps each

Bicep
Standing Alternate Dumbbell Curls
3 sets: 8 reps

Tricep
Tricep Pushdowns—3 sets: 10 reps

Lower Back/Hamstrings
Seated or Prone Leg—3 sets: 10 reps

Calf
Seated Calf Raises—3 sets: 15 reps

Static Stretch Routine

FRIDAY

Abs
Hokie Leg Raises—1 set: 10 reps
ABC Situps—1 set: 5-10 reps
Dying Cockroach 30 seconds

Legs
Speed Squats (50% of Monday's weight)
4 sets: 5 reps

Chest
Close Grip Bench Press (stop and stab)
4 sets: 5 reps

Back
Barbell Shrugs—3 sets: 10 reps
Pullups—3 sets: 5-10 reps
or
Lat Pulldowns (front, underhand)
3 sets: 8-10 reps

Shoulder
Seated Overhead Barbell Press—3 sets: 6 reps

Bicep
Barbell or Cable Curls—3 sets: 10 reps

Tricep
Bench Dips—3 sets: 10 reps

Lower Back/Hamstrings
Back Extensions—2 sets: 10 reps

Calf
Standing Calf Raises—3 sets: 15 reps

Static Stretch Routine

BEGINNER PRESEASON   SPEED AGILITY QUICKNESS CONDITIONING SCHEDULE   WEEK 4 PHASE 3

MONDAY	TUESDAY	WEDNESDAY	THURSDAY	FRIDAY
Pre-Strength Workout	Dynamic Warmup	Pre-Strength Workout	Dynamic Warmup	Pre-Strength Workout
Jump Rope 1. Both Feet—1 set: 15 seconds 2. Right Foot 1 set: 15 seconds 3. Left Foot—1 set: 15 seconds 4. Alternate Feet 1 set: 15 seconds 5. 2 on Right, 2 on Left 1 set: 15 seconds 6. Speed Jump 1 set: 15 seconds **Post-Strength Workout** **Static Stretch Routine** **Speed Development** 1. Heel-to-Butt Kicks 2 sets: 20 yards 2. A Marches—2 sets: 20 yards 3. A Skips—2 sets: 20 yards 4. A Runs—2 sets: 20 yards **Programmable Agility** 1. Carolina Box Drill 4 sets	1. Walking Knee-Ups 1 set: 20 yards 2. Skipping Toe Touches 1 set: 20 yards 3. Low Carioca 2 sets: 20 yards 4. Starts—Football Stance 4-6 reps **PNF Partner Stretch** **Conditioning** 8 110s Linemen—19 seconds TE, LB, QB, Spec, FB, DE 17 seconds WR, TB, DB—15 seconds Work-to-Rest Ratio—1:3	**Jump Rope**—with movement 1. Running—1 set: 20 yards 2. Double Leg Hops Forward—1 set: 20 yards 3. Right Leg Hops 1 set: 20 yards 4. Left Leg Hops 1 set: 20 yards 5. Running—1 set: 20 yards **Post-Strength Workout** **Static Stretch Routine** **Reactive Agility** 1. Tennis Ball Drill Variations 6-8 sets **Speed Development** 2. Uphill Runs 6-8 sets: 30 yards (sprint up, walk down)	1. Walking Toe Touches 1 set: 20 yards 2. Skipping Knee Hugs 1 set: 20 yards 3. Low Shuffle 2 sets: 20 yards 4. Starts—Football Stance 6-8 reps **Static Stretch Routine** **Competitive Games** Basketball Volleyball Dodgeball variations, etc.	**Dot Drills** 10-15 seconds 1. In and Out 2. Figure 8—both feet right side 3. Figure 8—both feet left side 4. Make up your own pattern **Post-Strength Workout** **PNF Partner Stretch** **Conditioning** 4 Modified Suicides 10 yards and back 15 yards and back 20 yards and back Linemen—22 seconds TE, LB, QB, Spec, FB, DE 20 seconds WR, TB, DB—18 seconds
Stretch Lower Back, Hamstrings	Stretch Lower Back, Hamstrings	Stretch Lower Back, Hamstrings	Stretch Lower Back, Hamstrings	Stretch Lower Back, Hamstrings

Absolute Strength and Peaking

WEEK 4   BEGINNER PRESEASON
Phase 3

MONDAY	WEDNESDAY	FRIDAY
Jump Rope	Speed Ladder	Dot Drills
Abs Bronco Partner Ab Program **Legs** Back Squats (warmup—8 reps) 55%—5 reps 64%—5 reps 70%—5 reps 76%—5 reps 82%—5 reps **Chest** Bench Press (warmup—8 reps) 55%—5 reps 67%—5 reps 73%—5 reps 79%—5 reps 85%—5 reps **Back** Dumbbell Shrugs—3 sets: 10 reps Pullups—3 sets: 5-10 reps or Lat Pulldowns (front, underhand) 3 sets: 8-10 reps **Shoulder** Seated Dumbbell Alternate Overhead Press (each arm) 3 sets: 6 reps **Bicep** Barbell or Cable Curls—3 sets: 8-10 reps **Tricep** Dips (use weight if possible)—3 sets: 8 reps **Lower Back/Hamstrings** Back Extensions—3 sets: 10 reps **Calf** Standing Calf Raises—3 sets: 15 reps Static Stretch Routine	**Abs** Big 40s—1 set Twisting Stack Crunches—1 set: 15-20 reps **Legs** Single-Leg Leg Press (each leg)—3 sets: 10 reps **Chest** Incline Bench Press—4 sets: 5 reps **Back** Upright Rows—3 sets: 8 reps Seated Cable Rows—3 sets: 8 reps **Shoulders** Dumbbell 21s—2 sets: (front raises, lat. raises, bent over laterals)—7 reps each **Bicep** Standing Alternate Dumbbell Curls (each arm) 3 sets: 8 reps **Tricep** Tricep Pushdowns—3 sets: 10 reps **Lower Back/Hamstrings** Seated or Prone Leg—3 sets: 10 reps **Calf** Seated Calf Raises—3 sets: 15 reps Static Stretch Routine	**Abs** Hokie Leg Raises—1 set: 10 reps ABC Situps—1 set: 5-10 reps Dying Cockroach—30 seconds **Legs** Speed Squats (50% of Monday's weight) 4 sets: 5 reps **Chest** Close Grip Bench Press (stop and stab) 4 sets: 5 reps **Back** Barbell Shrugs—3 sets: 10 reps Pullups—3 sets: 5-10 reps or Lat Pulldowns (front, underhand) 3 sets: 8-10 reps **Shoulder** Seated Overhead Barbell Press—3 sets: 6 reps **Bicep** Barbell or Cable Curls—3 sets: 8-10 reps **Tricep** Bench Dips—3 sets: 10 reps **Lower Back/Hamstrings** Back Extensions—3 sets: 10 reps **Calf** Standing Calf Raises—3 sets: 15 reps Static Stretch Routine

BEGINNER PRESEASON SPEED AGILITY QUICKNESS CONDITIONING SCHEDULE WEEK 5 PHASE 3

MONDAY	TUESDAY	WEDNESDAY	THURSDAY	FRIDAY
Pre-Strength Workout	**Dynamic Warmup**	**Pre-Strength Workout**	**Dynamic Warmup**	**Pre-Strength Workout**
Jump Rope	1. High Knees	**Jump Rope**—with movement	1. Walking Toe Touches	**Dot Drills**
1. Both Feet—1 set: 15 seconds	2 sets: 20 yards	1. Running—1 set: 20 yards	1 set: 20 yards	10-15 seconds
2. Right Foot—1 set: 15 seconds	2. Backward Skips	2. Double Leg Hops	2. Skipping Knee Hugs	1. In and Out
3. Left Foot—1 set: 15 seconds	2 sets: 20 yards	Forward—1 set: 20 yards	1 set: 20 yards	2. Figure 8
4. Alternate Feet—1 set: 15 seconds	3. Low Shuffle	3. Right Leg Hops	3. Low Shuffle	both feet—right side
5. 2 on Right, 2 on Left	2 sets: 20 yards	1 set: 20 yards	2 sets: 20 yards	3. Figure 8
1 set: 15 seconds	4. Starts—Football Stance	4. Left Leg Hops	4. Starts—Football Stance	both feet—left side
6. Speed Jump—1 set: 15 seconds	4-6 reps	1 set: 20 yards	4-6 reps	4. Make up your own pattern
		5. Running—1 set: 20 yards		
Post-Strength Workout	**PNF Partner Stretch**		**Static Stretch Routine**	**Post-Strength Workout**
Static Stretch Routine	**Conditioning**	**Post-Strength Workout**	**Competitive Games**	**PNF Partner Stretch**
	8 110s	**Static Stretch Routine**	Tag Football	**Conditioning**
Speed Development	Linemen—19 seconds		Basketball	4 Modified Suicides
1. Acceleration Ladder	TE, LB, QB, Spec, FB, DE	**Speed Development**	Volleyball, etc.	10 yards and back
6 sets: 20 yards	17 seconds	1. Fast Arms Drill		15 yards and back
	WR, TB, DB—15 seconds	1 set: 20 yards		20 yards and back
Programmable Agility	Work-to-Rest Ratio—1:3	2. A Marches		Linemen—22 seconds
Texas-Drill—4 sets		2 sets: 20 yards		TE, LB, QB, Spec, FB, DE
		3. A Skips—2 sets: 20 yards		20 seconds
		4. A Runs—2 sets: 20 yards		WR, TB, DB—18 seconds
				Work-to-Rest Ratio—1:3
		Reactive Agility		
		1. Two-Point Wave Drill		
		4 sets: 10-15 seconds		
		(Also have a player on command get out in front for the group to mirror.)		
Stretch	Stretch	Stretch	Stretch	Stretch
Lower Back, Hamstrings	Lower Back, Hamstrings	Lower Back, Hamstrings	Lower Back, Hamstrings	Lower Back, Hamstrings

Absolute Strength
and Peaking

WEEK 5

BEGINNER PRESEASON
Phase 3

MONDAY	WEDNESDAY	FRIDAY
Jump Rope—4-5 sets – 15-20 seconds	Speed Ladder—4-5 sets	Dot Drills—3-4 sets – 10-15 seconds

MONDAY

Abs
Bronco Partner Ab Program

Legs
Back Squats (warmup—8 reps)
61%—3 reps
67%—3 reps
73%—3 reps
79%—3 reps
85%—3 reps

Chest
Bench Press (warmup—8 reps)
64%—3 reps
70%—3 reps
76%—3 reps
82%—3 reps
88%—3 reps

Back
Dumbbell Shrugs—3 sets: 10 reps
Pullups—3 sets: 5-10 reps
or
Lat Pulldowns—3 sets: 8-10 reps

Shoulder
Seated Dumbbell Alternate Overhead Press
3 sets: 6 reps

Bicep
Barbell or Cable Curls—3 sets: 8-10 reps

Tricep
Weighted Dips—3 sets: 6 reps

Lower Back/Hamstrings
Back Extensions—3 sets: 10 reps

Calf
Standing Calf Raises—3 sets: 15 reps

Static Stretch Routine

WEDNESDAY

Abs
Big 40s—1 set
Twisting Stack Crunches—2 sets: 20 reps

Legs
Single-Leg Leg Press (each leg)—3 sets: 10 reps

Chest
Incline Bench Press—4 sets: 5 reps

Back
Upright Rows—3 sets: 8 reps
Seated Cable Rows—3 sets: 8 reps

Shoulders
Dumbbell 21s—2 sets (front raises, lat raises, bent over laterals)—7 reps each

Bicep
Standing Alternate Dumbbell Curls
3 sets: 8 reps

Tricep
Tricep Pushdowns—3 sets: 10 reps

Lower Back/Hamstrings
Seated or Prone Leg—3 sets: 10 reps

Calf
Seated Calf Raises—3 sets: 15 reps

Static Stretch Routine

FRIDAY

Abs
Hokie Leg Raises—1 set: 10-15 reps
ABC Sit-Ups—1 set: 5-10 reps
Dying Cockroach—30 seconds

Legs
Speed Squats (50% of Monday's weight)
4 sets: 5 reps

Chest
Close Grip Bench Press (stop and stab)
4 sets: 5 reps

Back
Barbell Shrugs—3 sets: 10 reps
Pullups—3 sets: 5-10 reps
or
Lat Pulldowns—3 sets: 8-10 reps

Shoulder
Seated Overhead Barbell Press—3 sets: 6 reps

Bicep
Barbell or Cable Curls—3 sets: 8-10 reps

Tricep
Bench Dips—3 sets: 10 reps

Lower Back/Hamstrings
Back Extensions—3 sets: 10 reps

Calf
Standing Calf Raises—3 sets: 15 reps

Static Stretch Routine

BEGINNER PRESEASON   SPEED AGILITY QUICKNESS CONDITIONING SCHEDULE   WEEK 6 PHASE 3

MONDAY	TUESDAY	WEDNESDAY	THURSDAY	FRIDAY
Pre-Strength Workout	**Dynamic Warmup**	**Pre-Strength Workout**	**Dynamic Warmup**	**Pre-Strength Workout**
Jump Rope 1. Both Feet—1 set: 15 seconds 2. Right Foot 1 set: 15 seconds 3. Left Foot—1 set: 15 seconds 4. Alternate Feet 1 set: 15 seconds 5. 2 on Right, 2 on Left 1 set: 15 seconds 6. Speed Jump 1 set: 15 seconds **Post-Strength Workout** **Static Stretch Routine** **Speed Development** 1. Heel-to-Butt Kicks 2 sets: 20 yards 2. A Marches 2 sets: 20 yards 3. A Skips 2 sets: 20 yards 4. A Runs—2 sets: 20 yards **Programmable Agility** 1. 20-yard Shuttle 4 sets	1. Walking/Skipping Knee Hugs 1 set: 10 yards each 2. Walking/Skipping Toe Touches—1 set: 10 yards 3. Low Shuffle 2 sets: 20 yards 4. Starts—Football Stance 4-6 reps **PNF Partner Stretch** **Conditioning** 8 110s Linemen—19 seconds TE, LB, QB, Spec, FB, DE 17 seconds WR, TB, DB—15 seconds Work-to-Rest Ratio—1:3	**Jump Rope**—with movement 1. Running—1 set: 20 yards 2. Double Leg Hops Forward—1 set: 20 yards 3. Right Leg Hops 1 set: 20 yards 4. Left Leg Hops 1 set: 20 yards 5. Running—1 set: 20 yards **Post-Strength Workout** **Static Stretch Routine** **Reactive Agility** 1. Tennis Ball Drill Variations 8-10 sets **Speed Development** (Acceleration) 1. Sled Pulls 6 sets: 20 yards (50 pounds max on sled)	1. High Knee Crossovers 2 sets: 20 yards 2. Backward Skips 2 sets: 20 yards 3. Low Carioca 2 sets: 20 yards 4. Starts—Football Stance 4-6 reps **Static Stretch Routine** **Competitive Games** Basketball Volleyball Tag Football Racquetball, etc.	**Dot Drills** 10-15 seconds 1. In and Out 2. Figure 8—both feet right side 3. Figure 8—both feet left side 4. Make up your own pattern **Post-Strength Workout** **PNF Partner Stretch** **Conditioning** 4 Modified Suicides 10 yards and back 15 yards and back 20 yards and back Linemen—22 seconds TE, LB, QB, Spec, FB, DE 20 seconds WR, TB, DB—18 seconds
Stretch Lower Back, Hamstrings	Stretch Lower Back, Hamstrings	Stretch Lower Back, Hamstrings	Stretch Lower Back, Hamstrings	Stretch Lower Back, Hamstrings

Absolute Strength and Peaking

WEEK 6

BEGINNER PRESEASON
Phase 3

MONDAY	WEDNESDAY	FRIDAY
Jump Rope—4-5 sets – 15-20 seconds	Speed Ladder—4-5 sets	Dot Drills—4 sets – 10-15 seconds

MONDAY

Abs
Bronco Partner Ab Program

Legs
Back Squats (unlaod) (warmup—8 reps)
55%—3 reps
64%—3 reps
70%—3 reps
76%—3 reps
85%—1 rep

Chest
Bench Press (warmup—8 reps)
55%—3 reps
64%—3 reps
70%—3 reps
76%—3 reps
82%—3 reps
88%—1 rep

Back
Dumbbell Shrugs—3 sets: 10 reps
Pullups—3 sets: 5-10 reps
or
Lat Pulldowns—3 sets: 8 reps

Shoulder
Seated Dumbbell Alternate Overhead Press
3 sets: 6 reps

Bicep
Barbell or Cable Curls—3 sets: 8-10 reps

Tricep
Weighted Dips—3 sets: 6 reps

Lower Back/Hamstrings
Back Extensions—3 sets: 10 reps

Calf
Standing Calf Raises—3 sets: 15 reps

Static Stretch Routine

WEDNESDAY

Abs
Big 40s—1 set
Twisting Stack Crunches—2 sets: 20 reps

Legs
Single-Leg Leg Press (each leg)—3 sets: 10 reps

Chest
Incline Bench Press—4 sets: 5 reps

Back
Upright Rows—3 sets: 8 reps
Seated Cable Rows—3 sets: 8 reps

Shoulders
Dumbbell 21s—2 sets (front raises, lat raises, bent over laterals)—7 reps each

Bicep
Standing Alternate Dumbbell Curls
3 sets: 8 reps

Tricep
Tricep Pushdowns—3 sets: 10 reps

Lower Back/Hamstrings
Seated or Prone Leg—3 sets: 10 reps

Calf
Seated Calf Raises—3 sets: 15 reps

Static Stretch Routine

FRIDAY

Abs
Hokie Leg Raises—1 set: 10-15 reps
ABC Situps—1 set: 5-10 reps
Dying Cockroach—30 seconds

Legs
Speed Squats (50% of Monday's weight)
4 sets: 5 reps

Chest
Close Grip Bench Press (stop and stab)
4 sets: 5 reps

Back
Barbell Shrugs—3 sets: 10 reps
Pullups—3 sets: 5-10 reps
or
Lat Pulldowns—3 sets: 8-10 reps

Shoulder
Seated Overhead Barbell Press
3 sets: 6 reps

Bicep
Barbell or Cable Curls—3 sets: 8-10 reps

Tricep
Bench Dips—3 sets: 10 reps

Lower Back/Hamstrings
Back Extensions—3 sets: 10 reps

Calf
Standing Calf Raises—3 sets: 15 reps

Static Stretch Routine

BEGINNER PRESEASON   SPEED AGILITY QUICKNESS CONDITIONING SCHEDULE   WEEK 7 PHASE 3

MONDAY	TUESDAY	WEDNESDAY	THURSDAY	FRIDAY
Pre-Strength Workout	**Dynamic Warmup**	**Pre-Strength Workout**	**Dynamic Warmup**	**Pre-Strength Workout**
Jump Rope 1. Both Feet—1 set: 15 seconds 2. Right Foot 1 set: 15 seconds 3. Left Foot—1 set: 15 seconds 4. Alternate Feet 1 set: 15 seconds 5. 2 on Right, 2 on Left 1 set: 15 seconds 6. Speed Jump 1 set: 15 seconds	1. Walking Toe Touches 1 set: 20 yards 2. Walking Knee Hugs 1 set: 20 yards 3. Low Shuffle 2 sets: 20 yards **PNF Partner Stretch** **Conditioning** 8 110s Linemen—19 seconds TE, LB, QB, Spec, FB, DE 17 seconds WR, TB, DB—15 seconds Work-to-Rest Ratio—1:3	**Jump Rope**—with movement 1. Running—1 set: 20 yards 2. Double Leg Hops Forward—1 set: 20 yards 3. Right Leg Hops 1 set: 20 yards 4. Left Leg Hops 1 set: 20 yards 5. Running 1 set: 20 yards **Post-Strength Workout** **Static Stretch Routine**	1. Walking/Skipping Knee Hugs 1 set: 10 yards each 2. Walking/Skipping Toe Touches 1 set: 10 yards 3. Low Carioca 2 sets: 20 yards 4. Starts—Football Stance 4-6 reps **Static Stretch Routine** **Competitive Games** Basketball Volleyball Dodgeball variations Tag Football, etc.	OFF ACTIVE REST
Post-Strength Workout **Static Stretch Routine** OFF after STRETCH		OFF after STRETCH		
Stretch Lower Back, Hamstrings	Stretch Lower Back, Hamstrings	Stretch Lower Back, Hamstrings	Stretch Lower Back, Hamstrings	Stretch Lower Back, Hamstrings

Absolute Strength
and Peaking

BEGINNER PRESEASON
Phase 3

WEEK 7
TESTING WEEK

MONDAY	WEDNESDAY	FRIDAY
Jump Rope—4-5 sets – 15-20 seconds	Dot Drills—4-5 sets – 10-15 seconds	OFF
Abs Bronco Partner Abs Program	**Abs** Hokie Leg Raises—1 set: 15-20 reps Twisting Stack Crunches—2 sets: 20 reps	**Active Rest** Play basketball, racquetball, tennis, etc.
TEST—Vertical Jump (using Vertic machine)	**TEST**—10-yard Sprint (electronically timed)	
TEST—Back Squats Rep Test (up to 3 reps) convert to 1 RM	**TEST**—20-yard Shuttle best of three trials	
TEST—Pullups (overhand grip) max reps	**TEST**—Bench Press 3 rep max test, convert to 1 RM	
Get Body Weight	**TEST**—Body Weight Dips max reps	
	TEST—Sit and Reach Hamstring Lower Back Flexibility	
Static Stretch Routine	**Static Stretch Routine**	

Intermediate: Off-Season/Preseason Program

PHASE 1

	BENCH	SQUAT
Week 1	12-58%	12-55%
Week 2	10-61%	10-58%
Week 3	10-64%	10-61%
Week 4	8-67%	8-64%
Week 5	8-70%	8-67%
Week 6	Max reps up 10	Max reps up 10

PHASE 2

	BENCH	SQUAT	PUSH JERK
Week 7	8-70%	8-67%	5-50%
Week 8	8-73%	8-70%	5-55%
Week 9	6-76%	6-73%	5-61%
Week 10	5-79%	5-76%	5-64%
Week 11	5-82%	5-79%	5-67%
Week 12	Max 5 reps	Max 5 reps	Max 3 reps

PRESEASON PHASE 3

	BENCH	SQUAT	HANG CLEAN	PUSH JERK
Week 1	5-79%	5-76%	Max 3 reps	
Week 2	5-82%	5-79%	5-67%	5-67%
Week 3	5-85%	5-82%	5-70%	5-73%
Week 4	3-88%	3-85%	3-76%	3-76%
Week 5	3-91%	3-88%	3-79%	3-79%
Week 6	Unload 3 (82%)	Unload 3 (79%)	3-82%	3-82%
TEST	3 rep test	3 rep test	3 rep test	3 rep test

INTERMEDIATE OFF SEASON   SPEED AGILITY QUICKNESS CONDITIONING SCHEDULE   WEEK 1 PHASE 1

MONDAY	TUESDAY	WEDNESDAY	THURSDAY	FRIDAY
Pre-Strength Workout	Pre-Strength Workout	Active Rest	Pre-Strength Workout	Pre-Strength Workout
Dot Drills 10-15 seconds 1. In and Out 2. Figure 8—both feet right side 3. Figure 8—both feet left side 4. In and Out—turns **Post-Strength Workout** **Static Stretch Routine** **Programmable Agility** 1. Carolina Box Drill 3-4 sets **Reactive Agility** 1. Four-Cone Reaction Drill verbal cues 3-4 sets: 10-12 seconds	**Jump Rope** with movement 1. Running—1 set: 20 yards 2. Double Leg Hops Forward 1 set: 20 yards 3. Forward Right Leg Hops 1 set: 20 yards 4. Forward Left Leg Hops 1 set: 20 yards 5. Running—1 set: 20 yards **Post-Strength Workout** **Static Stretch Routine** **Speed Development** 1. Fast Arms Drill 2 sets: 15 seconds 2. Heel-to-Butt Kicks 2 sets: 20 yards 3. A Marches 2 sets: 20 yards 4. A Skips 2 sets: 20 yards 5. A Runs 2 sets: 20 yards	**Competitive Games** Basketball Volleyball Tag Football Racquetball, etc.	**Speed Ladder** 5-7 sets 1. Run Through High Knees 2. Lateral Shuffle 3. Hop Scotch 4. Slalom Jumps 5. Ickey Shuffle 6. Backward Ickey Shuffle **Post-Strength Workout** **Programmable Agility** 1. 20-yard Shuttle 3-4 sets: record best time **Reactive Agility** 1. Two-Point Wave Drill 3-4 sets: (include jumps, shuffle, "Hit It," etc.)	**Jump Rope** 5-6 sets: 10-15 seconds 1. Both Feet 2. Right Foot 3. Left Foot 4. Alternate Feet 5. 2 on Right, 2 on Left Foot 6. Speed Jump **Post-Strength Workout** **Static Stretch Routine** **Competitive Drills** 1. Get Up and Sprint 4-6 sets: 20 yards
Stretch Lower Back, Hamstrings	Stretch Lower Back, Hamstrings	Stretch Lower Back, Hamstrings	Stretch Lower Back, Hamstrings	Stretch Lower Back, Hamstrings

WEEK 1 INTERMEDIATE OFF SEASON Phase 1 Muscular Hypertrophy

MONDAY	TUESDAY	THURSDAY	FRIDAY
Dot Drills—3-5 sets – 10-15 reps	Jump Rope—3-5 sets – 15-20 seconds	Speed Ladder—5-7 sets	Jump Rope—3-5 sets - 15-20 seconds
Abs Hanging Leg Raises—1 set: 15-20 reps Twisting Stack Crunches 2 sets: 15-20 reps	**Abs** Flutterkicks—30 seconds Bicycle Abs—30 seconds Dying Cockroach—30 seconds	**Abs** Hanging Leg Raises—1 set: 15-20 reps Medicine Ball Stack Crunches 2 sets: 15-20 reps	**Abs** Hokie Leg Raises—1 set: 15-20 reps ABC Sit-Ups—1 set: 10 reps Side Crunches—1 set: 10 reps each side
Power Jump Shrugs (clean grip)—4 sets: 3 reps	**Power** Explosive Box Stepups (each leg) 3 sets: 5 reps Olympic Deadlifts to Knee 3 sets: 5 reps	**Power** Jump Shrugs (snatch grip) 2 sets: 3 reps Hang Snatch High Pulls 2 sets: 3 reps	**Power** Explosive Box Stepups 3 sets: 5 reps Olympic Deadlifts to Knee 3 sets: 5 reps
Chest Bench Press (warmup—12 reps) 50%—12 reps 55%—12 reps 58%—12 reps	**Legs** Back Squats (warmup—12 reps) 50%—12 reps 55%—12 reps (2 sets)	**Shoulder** Standing Behind Neck Press 3 sets: 12 reps	**Legs** Front Squats—3 sets: 12 reps
Shoulder Seated Alternate Dumbbell Press 3 sets: 12 reps Dumbbell Lateral Raises 2 sets: 12 reps	**Hamstrings** Seated or Prone Leg Curls 2 sets: 12 reps	**Chest** Dumbbell Bench Press 3 sets: 10 reps Upright Rows—2 sets: 12 reps	**Back** Barbell Shrugs—3 sets: 12 reps Pullups—3 sets: 10-12 reps
Tricep Lying Tricep Extensions (barbell or curl bar) 3 sets: 12 reps	**Back** Barbell Shrugs—3 sets: 12 reps Seated Cable Rows—3 sets: 12 reps	**Tricep** Dips—3 sets: 10-12 reps	**Lower Back** Back Extensions—2 sets
Bicep Barbell Curls—3 sets: 12 reps	**Lower Back** Reverse Hyperextensions 2 sets: 15 reps	**Bicep** Dumbbell Curls—2 sets: 10 reps	**Calf** Seated Calf Raises—3 sets Standing Calf Raises—3 sets
Wrist Forearm Wrist Rollers (up and down)—2 sets	**Calf** Seated Calf Raises—2 sets: 15 reps Standing Calf Raises—2 sets: 15 reps	**Wrist** Wrist Rollers (up and down)—2 sets	
Neck Neck Machine—1 sets: 10 reps		**Neck** Neck Machine—1 set: 10 reps	
Static Stretch Routine	Static Stretch Routine	Static Stretch Routine	Static Stretch Routine

INTERMEDIATE OFF SEASON — SPEED AGILITY QUICKNESS CONDITIONING SCHEDULE — WEEK 2 PHASE 1

MONDAY	TUESDAY	WEDNESDAY	THURSDAY	FRIDAY
Pre-Strength Workout	**Pre-Strength Workout**	**Active Rest**	**Pre-Strength Workout**	**Pre-Strength Workout**
Dot Drills 10-15 seconds 1. In and Out 2. Figure 8—both feet right side 3. Figure 8—both feet left side 4. In and Out—turns **Post-Strength Workout** **Static Stretch Routine** **Programmable Agility** 1. Pattern Runs 6-8 sets: 20 yards (incorporate speed cuts, power cuts, and spins) **Reactive Agility** 1. Tennis Ball Drills (all variations) 6-8 sets	**Jump Rope** with movement 1. Running —1 set: 20 yards 2. Double Leg Hops Forward 1 set: 20 yards 3. Forward Right Leg Hops 1 set: 20 yards 4. Forward Left Leg Hops 1 set: 20 yards 5. Running —1 set: 20 yards **Post-Strength Workout** **Static Stretch Routine** **Speed Development** 1. Fast Arms Drill 2 sets: 15 seconds 2. A Marches 2 sets: 20 yards 3. A Skips 2 sets: 20 yards 4. A Runs 2 sets: 20 yards 5. Acceleration Ladder 6 sets: 20 yards	**Competitive Games** Basketball Volleyball Tag Football Racquetball, etc.	**Speed Ladder** 5-7 sets 1. Run Through High Knees 2. Lateral Shuffle 3. Hop Scotch 4. Slalom Jumps 5. Ickey Shuffle 6. Backward Ickey Shuffle **Post-Strength Workout** **Static Stretch Routine** **Programmable Agility** 1. Texas-Drill—4 sets **Reactive Agility** 1. Two-Point Wave Drill 4-6 sets: (include jumps, shuffle, "Hit It," etc.)	**Jump Rope** 5-6 sets: 10-15 seconds 1. Both Feet 2. Right Foot 3. Left Foot 4. Alternate Feet 5. 2 on Right, 2 on Left Foot 6. Speed Jump **Post-Strength Workout** **Static Stretch Routine** **Competitive Drills** 1. Shark in the Tank 5-7 sets: 10 seconds
Stretch Lower Back, Hamstrings	Stretch Lower Back, Hamstrings	Stretch Lower Back, Hamstrings	Stretch Lower Back, Hamstrings	Stretch Lower Back, Hamstrings

WEEK 2

INTERMEDIATE OFF SEASON
Phase 1

Muscular Hypertrophy

MONDAY	TUESDAY	THURSDAY	FRIDAY
Dot Drills—3-5 sets – 10-15 reps	Jump Rope—3-5 sets – 15-20 seconds	Speed Ladder—5-7 sets	Jump Rope—3-5 sets - 15-20 seconds
Abs Hanging Leg Raises 1 set: 15-20 reps Twisting Stack Crunches 2 sets: 15-20 reps **Power** Jump Shrugs (clean grip) 4 sets: 3 reps **Chest** Bench Press (warmup—10 reps) 55%—10 reps 58%—10 reps 61%—10 reps **Shoulder** Seated Alternate Dumbbell Press 3 sets: 10 reps Dumbbell Lateral Raises 3 sets: 10 reps **Tricep** Lying Tricep Extensions (barbell or curl bar) 3 sets: 10 reps **Bicep** Barbell Curls—3 sets: 10 reps **Wrist Forearm** Wrist Rollers (up and down)—2 sets **Neck** Neck Machine—1 sets: 10 reps	**Abs** Flutterkicks—30 seconds Bicycle Abs—30 seconds Dying Cockroach—30 seconds **Power** Explosive Box Stepups (each leg) 3 sets: 5 reps Olympic Deadlifts to Knee 3 sets: 5 reps **Legs** Back Squats (warmup—10 reps) 50%—10 reps 55%—10 reps 58%—10 reps **Hamstrings** Seated or Prone Leg Curls 3 sets: 10 reps **Back** Barbell Shrugs—3-4 sets: 10 reps Seated Cable Rows—3 sets: 10 reps **Lower Back** Reverse Hyperextensions 2 sets: 15 reps **Calf** Seated Calf Raises—2 sets: 12 reps Standing Calf Raises—2 sets: 12 reps	**Abs** Hanging Leg Raises—1 set: 15-20 reps Medicine Ball Stack Crunches 2 sets: 15-20 reps **Power** Jump Shrugs (snatch grip) 3 sets: 3 reps Hang Snatch High Pulls 3 sets: 3 reps **Shoulder** Standing Behind Neck Press 3 sets: 10 reps **Chest** Dumbbell Bench Press 3 sets: 10 reps Upright Rows—2 sets: 10 reps **Tricep** Dips—3 sets: 8-10 reps **Bicep** Standing Dumbbell Curls 2 sets: 10 reps **Wrist** Wrist Rollers—2 sets **Neck** Neck Machine—1 set: 10 reps	**Abs** Hokie Leg Raises—1 set: 15-20 reps ABC Sit-Ups—1 set: 10 reps Side Crunches—1 set: 10 reps each side **Power** Explosive Box Stepups 3 sets: 5 reps Olympic Deadlifts to Knee 3 sets: 5 reps **Legs** Front Squats—4 sets: 6 reps **Back** Barbell Shrugs—3 sets: 10 reps Pullups—3 sets: 5-10 reps **Lower Back** Back Extensions—2 sets: 10 reps **Calf** Seated Calf Raises—2 sets: 15 reps Standing Calf Raises—2 sets: 15 reps
Static Stretch Routine	Static Stretch Routine	Static Stretch Routine	Static Stretch Routine

INTERMEDIATE OFF SEASON — SPEED AGILITY QUICKNESS CONDITIONING SCHEDULE — WEEK 3 PHASE 1

MONDAY	TUESDAY	WEDNESDAY	THURSDAY	FRIDAY
Pre-Strength Workout	**Pre-Strength Workout**	**Active Rest**	**Pre-Strength Workout**	**Pre-Strength Workout**
Dot Drills 10-15 seconds 1. In and Out 2. Figure 8—both feet right side 3. Figure 8—both feet left side 4. In and Out—turns **Post-Strength Workout** **Static Stretch Routine** **Programmable Agility** 1. Pattern Runs 6-8 sets: 20 yards (incorporate speed cuts, power cuts, and spins) **Reactive Agility** 1. Crazy Ball Drills (all variations)—6-8 sets	**Jump Rope** with movement 1. Running—1 set: 20 yards 2. Double Leg Hops Forward 1 set: 20 yards 3. Forward Right Leg Hops 1 set: 20 yards 4. Forward Left Leg Hops 1 set: 20 yards 5. Running—1 set: 20 yards **Post-Strength Workout** **PNF Partner Stretch** **Speed Development** 1. Heel-to-Butt Kicks 2 sets: 20 yards 2. A Marches 2 sets: 20 yards 3. A Skips 2 sets: 20 yards 4. A Runs 2 sets: 20 yards 5. Starts—Football Stance 4-6 reps	**Competitive Games** Basketball Volleyball Tag Football Racquetball, etc.	**Speed Ladder** 5-7 sets 1. Run Through High Knees 2. Lateral Shuffle 3. Hop Scotch 4. Slalom Jumps 5. Ickey Shuffle 6. Backward Ickey Shuffle **Post-Strength Workout** **Static Stretch Routine** **Programmable Agility** 1. 20-yard Shuttle 4-6 sets: record best time **Reactive Agility** 1. Four-Cone Reaction Drill visual cues	**Jump Rope** 5-6 sets: 10-15 seconds 1. Both Feet 2. Right Foot 3. Left Foot 4. Alternate Feet 5. 2 on Right, 2 on Left Foot 6. Speed Jump **Post-Strength Workout** **Static Stretch Routine** **Competitive Drills** 1. Get Up and Sprint 4-5 sets: 20 yards
Stretch Lower Back, Hamstrings	Stretch Lower Back, Hamstrings	Stretch Lower Back, Hamstrings	Stretch Lower Back, Hamstrings	Stretch Lower Back, Hamstrings

WEEK 3

INTERMEDIATE OFF SEASON — Phase 1

Muscular Hypertrophy

MONDAY	TUESDAY	THURSDAY	FRIDAY
Dot Drills—3-5 sets – 10-15 reps	Jump Rope—3-5 sets – 15-20 seconds	Speed Ladder—5-7 sets	Jump Rope—3-5 sets - 15-20 seconds
Abs Hanging Leg Raises 1 set: 15-20 reps Twisting Stack Crunches 2 sets: 15-20 reps	**Abs** Flutterkicks—30 seconds Bicycle Abs—30 seconds Dying Cockroach—30 seconds	**Abs** Hanging Leg Raises 1 set: 15-20 reps Medicine Ball Stack Crunches 2 sets: 15-20 reps	**Abs** Hokie Leg Raises—1 set: 15-20 reps ABC Sit-Ups—1 set: 10 reps Side Crunches—1 set: 10 reps each side
Power Jump Shrugs (clean grip) 3 sets: 3 reps	**Power** Explosive Box Stepups (each leg) 3 sets: 5 reps Olympic Deadlifts to Knee 3 sets: 5 reps	**Power** Jump Shrugs (snatch grip) 3 sets: 3 reps Hang Snatch High Pulls 3 sets: 3 reps	**Power** Explosive Box Stepups 3 sets: 5 reps Olympic Deadlifts to Knee 3 sets: 5 reps
Chest Bench Press (warmup—10 reps) 55%—10 reps 61%—10 reps 64%—10 reps	**Legs** Back Squats (warmup—10 reps) 50%—10 reps 55%—10 reps 61%—10 reps	**Shoulder** Standing Behind Neck Press 3 sets: 8 reps	**Legs** Front Squats—4 sets: 6 reps
Shoulder Seated Alternate Dumbbell Press 3 sets: 10 reps Dumbbell Lateral Raises 3 sets: 10 reps	**Hamstrings** Seated or Prone Leg Curls 3 sets: 10 reps	**Chest** Dumbbell Bench Press 3 sets: 10 reps Upright Rows—2 sets: 10 reps	**Back** Barbell Shrugs—3 sets: 10 reps Pullups—3 sets: 5-10 reps
Tricep Lying Tricep Extensions (barbell or curl bar) 3 sets: 10 reps	**Back** Barbell Shrugs—3 sets: 10 reps Seated Cable Rows—3 sets: 10 reps	**Tricep** Dips—3 sets: 8-10 reps	**Lower Back** Back Extensions—2 sets: 10 reps
Bicep Barbell Curls—3 sets: 10 reps	**Lower Back** Reverse Hyperextensions 2 sets: 15 reps	**Bicep** Standing Dumbbell Curls 3 sets: 10 reps	**Calf** Seated Calf Raises—2 sets: 15 reps Standing Calf Raises—2 sets: 15 reps
Wrist Forearm Wrist Rollers (up and down)—2 sets	**Calf** Seated Calf Raises—2 sets: 12 reps Standing Calf Raises—2 sets: 12 reps	**Wrist** Wrist Rollers—2 sets	
Neck Neck Machine—1 sets: 10 reps		**Neck** Neck Machine—1 set: 10 reps	
Static Stretch Routine	Static Stretch Routine	Static Stretch Routine	Static Stretch Routine

211

INTERMEDIATE OFF SEASON   SPEED AGILITY QUICKNESS CONDITIONING SCHEDULE   WEEK 4 PHASE 1

MONDAY	TUESDAY	WEDNESDAY	THURSDAY	FRIDAY
Pre-Strength Workout	**Pre-Strength Workout**	**Active Rest**	**Pre-Strength Workout**	**Pre-Strength Workout**
Dot Drills 10-15 seconds 1. In and Out 2. Figure 8—both feet right side 3. Figure 8—both feet left side 4. In and Out—turns **Post-Strength Workout** **Static Stretch Routine** **Programmable Agility** 1. 90 Spin Power Cut Drill 4 sets **Reactive Agility** 1. Two-Point Wave Drill 4-6 sets	**Jump Rope** with movement 1. Running—1 set: 20 yards 2. Double Leg Hops Forward 1 set: 20 yards 3. Forward Right Leg Hops 1 set: 20 yards 4. Forward Left Leg Hops 1 set: 20 yards 5. Running—1 set: 20 yards **Post-Strength Workout** **PNF Partner Stretch** **Speed Development** 1. Fast Arms Drill 2 sets: 15 seconds 2. A Marches 2 sets: 20 yards 3. A Skips 2 sets: 20 yards 4. A Runs 2 sets: 20 yards 5. Starts—Football Stance 4-6 reps	**Competitive Games** Basketball Volleyball Tag Football Racquetball, etc.	**Speed Ladder** 5-7 sets 1. Run Through High Knees 2. Lateral Shuffle 3. Hop Scotch 4. Slalom Jumps 5. Ickey Shuffle 6. Backward Ickey Shuffle **Post-Strength Workout** **Static Stretch Routine** **Programmable Agility** 1. Four-Corner Drill 4 sets: (include shuffle, back-pedal, carioca) **Reactive Agility** 1. Tennis Ball Drills (all variations)—6-8 sets	**Jump Rope** 5-6 sets: 10-15 seconds 1. Both Feet 2. Right Foot 3. Left Foot 4. Alternate Feet 5. 2 on Right, 2 on Left Foot 6. Speed Jump **Post-Strength Workout** **Static Stretch Routine** **Competitive Drills** 1. Capture the Flag
Stretch Lower Back, Hamstrings	Stretch Lower Back, Hamstrings	Stretch Lower Back, Hamstrings	Stretch Lower Back, Hamstrings	Stretch Lower Back, Hamstrings

Muscular Hypertrophy

INTERMEDIATE OFF SEASON
Phase 1

WEEK 4

MONDAY	TUESDAY	THURSDAY	FRIDAY
Dot Drills—3-5 sets – 10-15 reps	Jump Rope—3-5 sets – 15-20 seconds	Speed Ladder—5-7 sets	Jump Rope—3-5 sets - 15-20 seconds
Abs Hanging Leg Raises—1 set: 20 reps Twisting Stack Crunches 2 sets: 15-20 reps **Power** Jump Shrugs (clean grip) 3 sets: 3 reps **Chest** Bench Press (warmup—10 reps) 55%—8 reps 61%—8 reps 64%—8 reps 67%—8 reps **Shoulder** Seated Dumbbell Alternate Overhead Press—3 sets: 8 reps Dumbbell Lateral Raises 3 sets: 10 reps **Tricep** Lying Tricep Extensions (barbell or curl bar) 3 sets: 8 reps **Bicep** Barbell Curls—3 sets: 8 reps **Wrist Forearm** Wrist Rollers (up and down)—2 sets **Neck** Neck Machine—1 sets: 10 reps	**Abs** Flutterkicks—30 seconds Bicycle Abs—30 seconds Dying Cockroach—30 seconds **Power** Explosive Box Stepups (each leg) 3 sets: 4 reps Olympic Deadlifts to Knee 3 sets: 4 reps **Legs** Back Squats (warmup—10 reps) 55%—8 reps 61%—8 reps 64%—8 reps **Hamstrings** Seated or Prone Leg Curls 3 sets—10 reps **Back** Barbell Shrugs—3 sets: 10 reps Seated Cable Rows—3 sets: 8 reps **Lower Back** Reverse Hyperextensions 3 sets: 12 reps **Calf** Seated Calf Raises—2 sets: 15 reps Standing Calf Raises—2 sets: 15 reps	**Abs** Hanging Leg Raises—1 set: 20 reps Medicine Ball Stack Crunches 2 sets: 20 reps **Power** Jump Shrugs (snatch grip) 3 sets: 3 reps Hang Snatch High Pulls 3 sets: 3 reps **Shoulder** Standing Behind Neck Press 3 sets: 8 reps Upright Rows—2 sets: 10 reps **Chest** Dumbbell Bench Press 3 sets: 8 reps **Tricep** Weighted Dips—3 sets: 8 reps **Bicep** Standing Dumbbell Curls 3 sets: 8 reps **Wrist/Forearm** Wrist Rollers—2 sets **Neck** Neck Machine—1 set: 10 reps	**Abs** Hokie Leg Raises—1 set: 20 reps ABC Sit-Ups—1 set: 10 reps Side Crunches 1 set: 15 reps each side **Power** Explosive Box Stepups 3 sets: 4 reps Olympic Deadlifts to Knee 3 sets: 5 reps **Legs** Front Squats—4 sets: 6 reps **Back** Barbell Shrugs—3 sets: 10 reps Pullups—3 sets: 5-10 reps **Lower Back** Back Extensions—3 sets: 10 reps **Calf** Seated Calf Raises—2 sets: 15 reps Standing Calf Raises—2 sets: 15 reps
Static Stretch Routine	Static Stretch Routine	Static Stretch Routine	Static Stretch Routine

INTERMEDIATE OFF SEASON   SPEED AGILITY QUICKNESS CONDITIONING SCHEDULE   WEEK 5 PHASE 1

MONDAY	TUESDAY	WEDNESDAY	THURSDAY	FRIDAY
Pre-Strength Workout	**Pre-Strength Workout**	**Active Rest**	**Pre-Strength Workout**	**Pre-Strength Workout**
Dot Drills 10-15 seconds 1. In and Out 2. Figure 8—both feet right side 3. Figure 8—both feet left side 4. In and Out—turns **Post-Strength Workout** **Static Stretch Routine** **Programmable Agility** 1. Carolina Drill 4 sets **Reactive Agility** 1. Eight-Cone Reaction Drill visual cues 4 sets: 10-12 seconds	**Jump Rope** with movement 1. Running—1 set: 20 yards 2. Double Leg Hops Forward 1 set: 20 yards 3. Forward Right Leg Hops 1 set: 20 yards 4. Forward Left Leg Hops 1 set: 20 yards 5. Running—1 set: 20 yards **Post-Strength Workout** **PNF Partner Stretch** **Speed Development** 1. A Marches 2 sets: 20 yards 2. A Skips 2 sets: 20 yards 3. A Runs 2 sets: 20 yards 4. Acceleration Ladder 2 sets: 20 yards	**Competitive Games** Basketball Volleyball Tag Football Racquetball, etc.	**Speed Ladder** 5-7 sets 1. Run Through High Knees 2. Lateral Shuffle 3. Hop Scotch 4. Slalom Jumps 5. Ickey Shuffle 6. Backward Ickey Shuffle **Post-Strength Workout** **Static Stretch Routine** **Programmable Agility** 1. Hourglass Drill— 4 sets: (incorporate speed and power cuts) **Reactive Agility** 1. Two-Point Wave Drill 4 sets	**Jump Rope** 5-6 sets: 10-15 seconds 1. Both Feet 2. Right Foot 3. Left Foot 4. Alternate Feet 5. 2 on Right, 2 on Left Foot 6. Speed Jump **Post-Strength Workout** **Static Stretch Routine** **Competitive Drills** 1. Get Up and Sprint 4-6 sets: 30 yards
Strretch Lower Back, Hamstrings	Stretch Lower Back, Hamstrings	Stretch Lower Back, Hamstrings	Stretch Lower Back, Hamstrings	Stretch Lower Back, Hamstrings

Muscular Hypertrophy

INTERMEDIATE OFF SEASON
Phase 1

WEEK 5

MONDAY	TUESDAY	THURSDAY	FRIDAY
Dot Drills—3-5 sets – 10-15 reps	Jump Rope—3-5 sets – 15-20 seconds	Speed Ladder—5-7 sets	Jump Rope—3-5 sets - 15-20 seconds
Power Jump Shrugs (clean grip) 3 sets: 3 reps	**Power** Explosive Box Stepups (each leg) 3 sets: 4 reps Olympic Deadlifts to Knee 3 sets: 4 reps	**Power** Jump Shrugs (snatch grip) 3 sets: 3 reps Hang Snatch High Pulls 3 sets: 3 reps	**Power** Explosive Box Stepups 3 sets: 4 reps Olympic Deadlifts to Knee 3 sets: 5 reps
Chest Bench Press (warmup—8 reps) 55%—8 reps 61%—8 reps 67%—8 reps 70%—8 reps	**Legs** Back Squats (warmup—10 reps) 55%—8 reps 61%—8 reps 64%—8 reps 67%—8 reps	**Shoulder** Standing Behind Neck Press 3 sets: 8 reps Upright Rows—2 sets: 10 reps	**Legs** Front Squats—5 sets: 6 reps
Shoulder Seated Dumbbell Alternate Overhead Press—3 sets: 8 reps Dumbbell Lateral Raises 3 sets: 10 reps	**Hamstrings** Seated or Prone Leg Curls 3 sets—10 reps	**Chest** Dumbbell Bench Press 3 sets: 8 reps	**Back** Barbell Shrugs—3 sets: 10 reps Pullups—3 sets: 5-10 reps
Tricep Lying Tricep Extensions (barbell or curl bar)—3 sets: 8 reps	**Back** Barbell Shrugs—3 sets: 10 reps Seated Cable Rows—3 sets: 8 reps	**Tricep** Weighted Dips—3 sets: 8 reps	**Lower Back** Back Extensions—3 sets: 10 reps
Bicep Barbell Curls—3 sets: 8 reps	**Lower Back** Reverse Hyperextensions 3 sets: 12 reps	**Bicep** Standing Dumbbell Curls 3 sets: 8 reps	**Calf** Seated Calf Raises—2 sets: 15 reps Standing Calf Raises—2 sets: 15 reps
Wrist Forearm Wrist Rollers (up and down)—2 sets	**Calf** Seated Calf Raises—2 sets: 15 reps Standing Calf Raises—2 sets: 15 reps	**Wrist/Forearm** Wrist Rollers—2 sets	
Neck Neck Machine—1 sets: 10 reps		**Neck** Neck Machine—1 set: 10 reps	
Static Stretch Routine	Static Stretch Routine	Static Stretch Routine	Static Stretch Routine

INTERMEDIATE OFF SEASON   SPEED AGILITY QUICKNESS CONDITIONING SCHEDULE   TEST WEEK 6 PHASE 1

MONDAY	TUESDAY	WEDNESDAY	THURSDAY	FRIDAY
Pre-Testing	Active Rest	Pre-Testing	Active Rest	Active Rest

Dot Drills
10-15 seconds
1. In and Out
2. Figure 8—both feet right side
3. Figure 8—both feet left side
4. In and Out—turns
 	
Post-Testing Workout
 	
PNF Stretch
	Competitive Games
	Basketball
	Volleyball
	Tag Football
	Racquetball, etc.
		Dynamic Warmup
		1. Walking Knee Hugs
		   2 sets: 20 yards
		2. Walking Toe Touches
		   2 sets: 20 yards
		3. Skipping Knee Hugs
		   2 sets: 20 yards
		4. Skipping Toe Touches
		   2 sets: 20 yards
		
		Post-Testing Workout
			Competitive Games
			Basketball
			Volleyball
			Dodgeball variations
				Competitive Games
				Basketball
				Tag Football
				Volleyball, etc.

Stretch Lower Back, Hamstrings	Stretch Lower Back, Hamstrings	Stretch Lower Back, Hamstrings	Stretch Lower Back, Hamstrings	Stretch Lower Back, Hamstrings

WEEK 6 TESTING WEEK

INTERMEDIATE OFF SEASON Phase 1

Muscular Hypertrophy

MONDAY	TUESDAY	THURSDAY	FRIDAY
Dot Drills—3-5 sets – 10-15 reps	Jump Rope—3-5 sets – 15-20 seconds	Speed Ladder—5-7 sets	Jump Rope—3-5 sets - 15-20 seconds
Abs Hanging Leg Raises—2 sets: 20 reps Twisting Stack Crunches 2 sets: 20 reps	**Active Rest** Play basketball, tennis, volleyball, racquetball, etc.	**Abs** Hanging Leg Raises—1 set: 20 reps Medicine Ball Stack Crunches 2 sets: 15 reps	**Active Rest** Play basketball, tennis, volleyball, racquetball, etc.
Test—Vertical Jump		**Test**—10-yard Sprint (electronically timed)	
Test—Back Squats Rep Test—up to 10 reps convert to 1 rep max		**Test**—20-yard Shuttle	
Test—Max Pullups—max reps		**Test**—Bench Press 5 rep max Test convert to 1 RM	
		Test—Body Weight Dips max reps	
		Test—Hamstring/Lower Back Flexibility	
Static Stretch Routine **Get Body Weight**	**Static Stretch Routine**	**Static Stretch Routine**	**Static Stretch Routine**

INTERMEDIATE OFF SEASON SPEED AGILITY QUICKNESS CONDITIONING SCHEDULE WEEK 7 PHASE 2

MONDAY	TUESDAY	WEDNESDAY	THURSDAY	FRIDAY
Pre-Strength Workout	**Pre-Strength Workout**	**Active Rest**	**Pre-Strength Workout**	**Pre-Strength Workout**
Dot Drills 10-15 seconds 1. In and Out 2. Figure 8—both feet right side 3. Figure 8—both feet left side 4. In and Out—turns **Post-Strength Workout** **PNF Partner Stretch** **Programmable Agility** 1. 20-yard Shuttle 4 sets: record best time **Reactive Agility** 1. Four-Cone Reaction Drill visual cues 4 sets: 10-15 seconds	**Jump Rope** with movement 1. Running—1 set: 20 yards 2. Double Leg Hops Forward 1 set: 20 yards 3. Forward Right Leg Hops 1 set: 20 yards 4. Forward Left Leg Hops 1 set: 20 yards 5. Running—1 set: 20 yards **Post-Strength Workout** **Static Stretch Routine** **Speed Development** 1. A Marches 2 sets: 20 yards 2. A Skips 2 sets: 20 yards 3. A Runs 2 sets: 20 yards 4. Acceleration Ladder 6 sets: 20 yards	**Competitive Games** Basketball Volleyball Tag Football Racquetball, etc.	**Speed Ladder** 5-7 sets 1. Run Through High Knees 2. Lateral Shuffle 3. Hop Scotch 4. Slalom Jumps 5. Ickey Shuffle 6. Backward Ickey Shuffle **Post-Strength Workout** **PNF Partner Stretch** **Programmable Agility** 1. Pattern Runs 6-8 sets: 20 yards (incorporate speed cuts, power cuts, and spins) **Reactive Agility** 1. Crazy Ball Drills (all variations) 8-10 sets	**Jump Rope** 5-6 sets: 10-15 seconds 1. Both Feet 2. Right Foot 3. Left Foot 4. Alternate Feet 5. 2 on Right, 2 on Left Foot 6. Speed Jump **Post-Strength Workout** **Static Stretch Routine** **Competitive Drills** 1. Capture the Flag
Stretch Lower Back, Hamstrings	Stretch Lower Back, Hamstrings	Stretch Lower Back, Hamstrings	Stretch Lower Back, Hamstrings	Stretch Lower Back, Hamstrings

WEEK 7

INTERMEDIATE OFF SEASON
Phase 2

Power and Absolute Strength

MONDAY	TUESDAY	THURSDAY	FRIDAY
Jump Rope—4-5 sets – 15 seconds	Speed Ladder—5-7 sets	Dot Drills—4-5 sets - 10-15 reps	Jump Rope—4-5 sets - 15 seconds

MONDAY

Abs
Denver Bronco Partner Abs

Power
Olympic Deadlifts to Knee
2 sets; 5 reps
Hang Clean Combo
Jump Shrugs—3-4 sets: 1 rep
Hang Clean High Pulls
3-4 sets: 1 rep
Hang Cleans—3-4 sets: 1 rep

Legs
Back Squats (warmup—10 reps)
55%—8 reps
61%—8 reps
64%—8 reps
67%—8 reps

Back
One Arm Dumbbell Rows
3 sets: 8 reps
Lateral Pulldowns (front, underhand)
3 sets: 8-10 reps

Lower Back/Hamstrings
Romanian Deadlifts—3 sets: 6 reps

Calf
Standing Calf Raises—2 sets: 15 reps
Seated Calf Raises—2 sets: 15 reps

PNF Partner Stretch

TUESDAY

Abs
Partner-Assisted Timed Sit-Ups
30 seconds
Leg Throws—30 seconds

Power
Explosive Box Stepups (each leg)
with weighted vest if possible
3 sets: 3 reps

Chest
Bench Press (warmup—8 reps)
55%—8 reps
61%—8 reps
67%—8 reps
70%—8 reps
Dumbbell Incline Bench Press
3 sets: 8 reps

Bicep
Dumbbell Incline Curls
3 sets: 8-10 reps

Tricep
Weighted Dips—3 sets: 8 reps

Wrist/Forearm
Wrist Rollers—2 sets

Neck
Neck Machine—1 set: 10 reps
or
Neck Iso with partner
1 set: 6 reps

Static Stretch Routine

THURSDAY

Abs
Hanging Leg Raises—2 sets: 20 reps
Medicine Ball Stack Crunches
2 sets: 20 reps

Power
Hang Snatch Combo
Hang Snatch Jump Shrugs
3-4 sets: 1 rep
Hang Snatch High Pulls
3-4 sets: 1 rep
Hang Snatch—3-4 sets: 1 rep
Power Shrugs—3 sets: 6 reps

Legs
Front Squats—4 sets: 6 reps

Back
Seated Cable Rows
3 sets: 8 reps
Pullups—3 sets: 5-10 reps

Lower Back
Glute Ham Raises
2 sets: 10 reps

Calf
Standing Calf Raises—2 sets: 15 reps
Seated Calf Raises—2 sets: 15 reps

PNF Partner Stretch

FRIDAY

Abs
Figure Four Double Crunches
2 sets: 10 reps
Bicycle Abs—30 seconds

Power
Push Press—4 sets: 5 reps
Up to 55%

Chest
Close Grip Bench Press
(stop and stab)
4 sets: 6 reps

Bicep
Standing Curls (barbell or curl bar)
3 sets: 8-10 reps

Tricep
Dumbbell Lying Tricep Extensions
4 sets: 10 reps

Forearms
Grippers—2 round trips

Neck
Neck Machine—1 set: 10 reps
or
Neck Iso with partner
1 set: 6 reps

Static Stretch Routine

INTERMEDIATE OFF SEASON   SPEED AGILITY QUICKNESS CONDITIONING SCHEDULE   WEEK 8 PHASE 2

MONDAY	TUESDAY	WEDNESDAY	THURSDAY	FRIDAY
Pre-Strength Workout	**Pre-Strength Workout**	**Active Rest**	**Pre-Strength Workout**	**Pre-Strength Workout**
Dot Drills 10-15 seconds 1. In and Out 2. Figure 8—both feet right side 3. Figure 8—both feet left side 4. In and Out—turns **Post-Strength Workout** **PNF Partner Stretch** **Programmable Agility** 1. Hourglass Drill 4-6 sets: (incorporate speed and power cuts) **Reactive Agility** 1. Eight-Cone Reaction Drill visual cues 4 sets: 10-15 seconds	**Jump Rope** with movement 1. Running—1 set: 20 yards 2. Double Leg Hops Forward 1 set: 20 yards 3. Forward Right Leg Hops 1 set: 20 yards 4. Forward Left Leg Hops 1 set: 20 yards 5. Running—1 set: 20 yards **Post-Strength Workout** **Static Stretch Routine** **Speed Development** 1. Heel-to-Butt Kicks 2 sets: 20 yards 2. A Marches 2 sets: 20 yards 3. A Skips 2 sets: 20 yards 4. A Runs 2 sets: 20 yards 5. Sled Pulls (acceleration) 4-6 sets: 20 yards (50 pounds max resistance on sled)	**Competitive Games** Basketball Volleyball Tag Football Racquetball, etc.	**Speed Ladder** 5-7 sets 1. Run Through High Knees 2. Lateral Shuffle 3. Hop Scotch 4. Slalom Jumps 5. Ickey Shuffle 6. Backward Ickey Shuffle **Post-Strength Workout** **PNF Partner Stretch** **Programmable Agility** 1. 90 Spin Power Cut Drill 4-6 sets **Reactive Agility** 1. Four-Cone Reaction Drill verbal cues 4 sets: 10-15 seconds	**Jump Rope** 5-6 sets: 10-15 seconds 1. Both Feet 2. Right Foot 3. Left Foot 4. Alternate Feet 5. 2 on Right, 2 on Left Foot 6. Speed Jump **Post-Strength Workout** **Static Stretch Routine** **Competitive Drills** 1. Shark in a Tank 4-6 sets: 10 seconds each
Stretch Lower Back, Hamstrings	Stretch Lower Back, Hamstrings	Stretch Lower Back, Hamstrings	Stretch Lower Back, Hamstrings	Stretch Lower Back, Hamstrings

WEEK 8

INTERMEDIATE OFF SEASON
Phase 2

Power and
Absolute Strength

MONDAY	TUESDAY	THURSDAY	FRIDAY
Jump Rope—4 sets – 15 seconds	Speed Ladder—5-7 sets	Dot Drills—4-5 sets – 10-15 reps	Jump Rope—4-5 sets - 15 seconds
Abs	**Abs**	**Abs**	**Abs**
Denver Bronco Partner Abs	Partner-Assisted Timed Sit-Ups 30 seconds	Hanging Leg Raises—2 sets: 20 reps	Figure Four Double Crunches 2 sets: 10 reps
Power	Leg Throws—30 seconds	Medicine Ball Stack Crunches 2 sets: 20 reps	Bicycle Abs—30 seconds
Olympic Deadlifts to Knee 2 sets: 5 reps	**Power**	**Power**	**Power**
Hang Clean Combo	Explosive Box Stepups (each leg) with weighted vest if possible	Hang Snatch Combo Hang Snatch Jump Shrugs	Push Press—4 sets: 5 reps
Jump Shrugs—3-4 sets: 1 rep	3 sets: 3 reps	3-4 sets: 1 rep	**Chest**
Hang Clean High Pulls 3-4 sets: 1 rep	**Chest**	Hang Snatch High Pulls 3-4 sets: 1 rep	Close Grip Bench Press (stop and stab)
Hang Cleans—3-4 sets: 1 rep	Bench Press (warmup—8 reps)	Hang Snatch—3-4 sets: 1 rep	4 sets: 6 reps
Legs	55%—8 reps	Power Shrugs—3 sets: 6 reps	**Bicep**
Back Squats (warmup—8 reps)	61%—8 reps	**Legs**	Standing Curls (barbell or curl bar)
55%—8 reps	67%—8 reps	Front Squats—4 sets: 6 reps	3 sets: 8 reps
64%—8 reps	73%—8 reps	**Back**	**Tricep**
70%—8 reps	Dumbbell Incline Bench Press	Seated Cable Rows	Dumbbell Lying Tricep Extensions
Back	3 sets: 8 reps	3 sets: 8 reps	4 sets: 10 reps
One Arm Dumbbell Rows	**Bicep**	Pullups—3 sets: 5-10 reps	**Forearm**
3 sets: 8 reps	Dumbbell Incline Curls	**Lower Back**	Grippers—2 round trips
Lat Pulldowns (front, underhand)	3 sets: 8 reps	Glute Ham Raises	**Neck**
3 sets: 8 reps	**Tricep**	2 sets: 10 reps	Neck Machine—1 set: 10 reps
Lower Back/Hamstrings	Weighted Dips—3 sets: 8 reps	**Calf**	
Romanian Deadlifts—3 sets: 6 reps	**Wrist/Forearm**	Standing Calf Raises—2 sets: 15 reps	
Calf	Wrist Rollers—2 sets	Seated Calf Raises—2 sets: 15 reps	
Standing Calf Raises—2 sets: 15 reps	**Neck**		
Seated Calf Raises—2 sets: 15 reps	Neck Machine—1 set: 10 reps		
PNF Partner Stretch	Static Stretch Routine	PNF Partner Stretch	Static Stretch Routine

INTERMEDIATE OFF SEASON   SPEED AGILITY QUICKNESS CONDITIONING SCHEDULE   WEEK 9 PHASE 2

MONDAY	TUESDAY	WEDNESDAY	THURSDAY	FRIDAY
Pre-Strength Workout	**Pre-Strength Workout**	**Active Rest**	**Pre-Strength Workout**	**Pre-Strength Workout**

Dot Drills
10-15 seconds
1. In and Out
2. Figure 8—both feet right side
3. Figure 8—both feet left side
4. In and Out—turns
 	
Post-Strength Workout
 	
PNF Partner Stretch
 	
Programmable Agility
1. Four-Corner Drill
  4-6 sets: (include back-pedal, shuffle and carioca)
 	
Reactive Agility
1. Two-Point Wave Drill
  4-5 sets:
  (use one player as a leader for others to mirror)
	Jump Rope with movement
	1. Running—1 set 20 yards
	2. Double Leg Hops Forward
	  1 set: 20 yards
	3. Forward Right Leg Hops
	  1 set: 20 yards
	4. Forward Left Leg Hops
	  1 set: 20 yards
	5. Running—1 set: 20 yards
	
	Post-Strength Workout
	
	Static Stretch Routine
	
	Speed Development
	1. A Marches
	  2 sets: 20 yards
	2. A Skips
	  2 sets: 20 yards
	3. A Runs
	  2 sets: 20 yards
	4. Acceleration Ladder
	  6 sets: 20 yards
		Competitive Games
		Basketball
		Volleyball
		Tag Football
		Racquetball, etc.
			Speed Ladder
			5-7 sets
			1. Run Through High Knees
			2. Lateral Shuffle
			3. Hop Scotch
			4. Slalom Jumps
			5. Ickey Shuffle
			6. Backward Ickey Shuffle
			
			Post-Strength Workout
			
			PNF Partner Stretch
			
			Programmable Agility
			1. 20-yard Shuttle
			  4 sets: record best time
			
			Reactive Agility
			1. Tennis Ball Drills
			  (all variations) 8-10 sets
				Jump Rope
				5-6 sets: 10-15 seconds
				1. Both Feet
				2. Right Foot
				3. Left Foot
				4. Alternate Feet
				5. 2 on Right, 2 on Left Foot
				6. Speed Jump
				
				Post-Strength Workout
				
				Static Stretch Routine
				
				Competitive Drills
				1. Get Up and Sprint Variations
				  4-6 sets: 30 yards

Stretch Lower Back, Hamstrings	Stretch Lower Back, Hamstrings	Stretch Lower Back, Hamstrings	Stretch Lower Back, Hamstrings	Stretch Lower Back, Hamstrings

WEEK 9

INTERMEDIATE OFF SEASON
Phase 2

Power and Absolute Strength

MONDAY	TUESDAY	THURSDAY	FRIDAY
Jump Rope—4 sets – 15 seconds	Speed Ladder—5-7 sets	Dot Drills—4-5 sets – 15 reps	Jump Rope—4-5 sets – 15 seconds

MONDAY

Abs
Denver Bronco Partner Abs

Power
Olympic Deadlifts to Knee
2 sets: 5 reps
Hang Clean Combo
Jump Shrugs—3-4 sets: 1 rep
Hang Clean High Pulls
3-4 sets: 1 rep
Hang Cleans—3-4 sets: 1 rep

Legs
Back Squats (warmup—8 reps)
55%—6 reps
61%—6 reps
67%—6 reps
73%—6 reps

Back
One Arm Dumbbell Rows
3 sets: 8 reps
Lat Pulldowns (front, underhand)
3 sets: 8 reps

Lower Back/Hamstrings
Romanian Deadlifts—3 sets: 6 reps

Calf
Standing Calf Raises—2 sets: 15 reps
Seated Calf Raises—2 sets: 15 reps

PNF Partner Stretch

TUESDAY

Abs
Partner-Assisted Timed Sit-Ups
30 seconds
Leg Throws—30 seconds

Power
Explosive Box Stepups (each leg)
with weighted vest if possible
3 sets: 3 reps

Chest
Bench Press (warmup—8 reps)
55%—6 reps
64%—6 reps
70%—6 reps
76%—6 reps
Dumbbell Incline Bench Press
3 sets: 8 reps

Bicep
Dumbbell Incline Curls
3 sets: 8 reps

Tricep
Weighted Dips—3 sets: 8 reps

Wrist/Forearm
Wrist Rollers—2 sets

Neck
Neck Machine—1 set: 10 reps

Static Stretch Routine

THURSDAY

Abs
Hanging Leg Raises—2 sets: 20 reps
Medicine Ball Stack Crunches
2 sets: 20 reps

Power
Hang Snatch Combo
Hang Snatch Jump Shrugs
3-4 sets: 1 rep
Hang Snatch High Pulls
3-4 sets: 1 rep
Hang Snatch—3-4 sets: 1 rep
Power Shrugs—3 sets: 6 reps

Legs
Front Squats—4 sets: 6 reps

Back
Seated Cable Rows
3 sets: 8 reps
Pullups—3 sets: 5-10 reps

Lower Back
Glute Ham Raises
3 sets: 10 reps

Calf
Standing Calf Raises—2 sets: 15 reps
Seated Calf Raises—2 sets: 15 reps

PNF Partner Stretch

FRIDAY

Abs
Figure Four Double Crunches
2 sets: 10 reps
Bicycle Abs—30 seconds

Power
Push Press—4 sets: 5 reps

Chest
Close Grip Bench Press
(stop and stab)
4 sets: 6 reps

Bicep
Standing Curls (barbell or curl bar)
3 sets: 8 reps

Tricep
Dumbbell Lying Tricep Extensions
4 sets: 8 reps

Forearm
Grippers—2 round trips

Neck
Neck Machine—1 set: 10 reps

Static Stretch Routine

223

INTERMEDIATE OFF SEASON   SPEED AGILITY QUICKNESS CONDITIONING SCHEDULE   WEEK 10 PHASE 2

MONDAY	TUESDAY	WEDNESDAY	THURSDAY	FRIDAY
Pre-Strength Workout	**Pre-Strength Workout**	**Active Rest**	**Pre-Strength Workout**	**Pre-Strength Workout**

Dot Drills
10-15 seconds
1. In and Out
2. Figure 8—both feet right side
3. Figure 8—both feet left side
4. In and Out—turns
	Jump Rope with movement
	1. Running—1 set: 20 yards
	2. Double Leg Hops Forward
	  1 set: 20 yards
	3. Forward Right Leg Hops
	  1 set: 20 yards
	4. Forward Left Leg Hops
	  1 set: 20 yards
	5. Running—1 set: 20 yards
		Competitive Games
		Basketball
		Volleyball
		Tag Football
		Racquetball, etc.
			Speed Ladder
			5-7 sets
			1. Run Through High Knees
			2. Lateral Shuffle
			3. Hop Scotch
			4. Slalom Jumps
			5. Ickey Shuffle
			6. Backward Ickey Shuffle
				Jump Rope
				5-6 sets: 10-15 seconds
				1. Both Feet
				2. Right Foot
				3. Left Foot
				4. Alternate Feet
				5. 2 on Right, 2 on Left Foot
				6. Speed Jump

Post-Strength Workout	**Post-Strength Workout**		**Post-Strength Workout**	**Post-Strength Workout**
PNF Partner Stretch	**Static Stretch Routine**		**PNF Partner Stretch**	**Static Stretch Routine**

Programmable Agility
1. Star Drill—3 sets
  (incorporate speed cuts, power cuts, and spins)
	Speed Development
	1. A Marches
	  1 set: 20 yards
	2. A Skips
	  1 set: 20 yards
	3. A Runs
	  1 set: 20 yards
	4. Starts—Football Stance
	  4-6 reps
			Programmable Agility
			1. Texas-Drill—4 sets
				Competitive Drills
				1. Shark in a Tank
				  6-10 sets: 10 seconds

Reactive Agility 1. Four-Cone Reaction Drill verbal cues 4 sets: 10-15 seconds			**Reactive Agility** 1. Tennis Ball Drills (all variations) 8-10 sets	
Stretch Lower Back, Hamstrings	Stretch Lower Back, Hamstrings	Strretch Lower Back, Hamstrings	Stretch Lower Back, Hamstrings	Stretch Lower Back, Hamstrings

WEEK 10

INTERMEDIATE OFF SEASON
Phase 2

Power and Absolute Strength

MONDAY	TUESDAY	THURSDAY	FRIDAY
Jump Rope—4 sets – 15 seconds	Speed Ladder—5-7 sets	Dot Drills—4-5 sets – 15 reps	Jump Rope—4-5 sets – 15 seconds
Abs Denver Bronco Partner Abs	**Abs** Partner-Assisted Timed Sit-Ups 30 seconds Leg Throws—30 seconds	**Abs** Hanging Leg Raises—2 sets: 20 reps Medicine Ball Stack Crunches 2 sets: 20 reps	**Abs** Figure Four Double Crunches 2 sets: 10 reps Bicycle Abs—30 seconds
Power Olympic Deadlifts to Knee 2 sets: 5 reps Hang Clean Combo Jump Shrugs—3-4 sets: 1 rep Hang Clean High Pulls 3-4 sets: 1 rep Hang Cleans—3-4 sets: 1 rep	**Power** Explosive Box Stepups (each leg) with weighted vest if possible 3 sets: 3 reps	**Power** Hang Snatch Combo Hang Snatch Jump Shrugs 3-4 sets: 1 rep Hang Snatch High Pulls 3-4 sets: 1 rep Hang Snatch—3-4 sets: 1 rep Power Shrugs—3 sets: 6 reps	**Power** Push Press—4 sets: 3 reps
Legs Back Squats (warmup—8 reps) 55%—5 reps 64%—5 reps 70%—5 reps 76%—5 reps	**Chest** Bench Press (warmup—8 reps) 61%—5 reps 67%—5 reps 73%—5 reps 79%—5 reps Dumbbell Incline Bench Press 3 sets: 6 reps	**Legs** Front Squats—4 sets: 5 reps	**Chest** Close Grip Bench Press (stop and stab) 4 sets: 5 reps
Back One Arm Dumbbell Rows 3 sets: 8 reps Lat Pulldowns (front, underhand) 3 sets: 8 reps	**Bicep** Dumbbell Incline Curls 3 sets: 8 reps	**Back** Seated Cable Rows 3 sets: 8 reps Pullups—3 sets: 5-10 reps	**Bicep** Standing Curls (barbell or curl bar) 3 sets: 8 reps
Lower Back/Hamstrings Romanian Deadlifts—3 sets: 6 reps	**Tricep** Weighted Dips—3 sets: 8 reps	**Lower Back** Glute Ham Raises 3 sets: 10 reps	**Tricep** Dumbbell Lying Tricep Extensions 4 sets: 8 reps
Calf Standing Calf Raises—2 sets: 15 reps Seated Calf Raises—2 sets: 15 reps	**Wrist/Forearm** Wrist Rollers—2 sets	**Calf** Standing Calf Raises—2 sets: 15 reps Seated Calf Raises—2 sets: 15 reps	**Forearm** Grippers—2 round trips
	Neck Neck Machine—1 set: 10 reps		**Neck** Neck Machine—1 set: 10 reps
PNF Partner Stretch	Static Stretch Routine	PNF Partner Stretch	Static Stretch Routine

INTERMEDIATE OFF SEASON   SPEED AGILITY QUICKNESS CONDITIONING SCHEDULE   WEEK 11 PHASE 2

MONDAY	TUESDAY	WEDNESDAY	THURSDAY	FRIDAY
Pre-Strength Workout	**Pre-Strength Workout**	**Active Rest**	**Pre-Strength Workout**	**Pre-Strength Workout**

Dot Drills
10-15 seconds
1. In and Out
2. Figure 8—both feet right side
3. Figure 8—both feet left side
4. In and Out—turns
 	
Post-Strength Workout
 	
PNF Partner Stretch
 	
Speed Development
1. Heel-to-Butt Kicks
  2 sets: 20 yards
2. A Marches
  2 sets: 20 yards
3. A Skips
  2 sets: 20 yards
4. A Runs
  2 sets: 20 yards
	Jump Rope with movement
	1. Running—1 set: 20 yards
	2. Double Leg Hops Forward
	  1 set: 20 yards
	3. Forward Right Leg Hops
	  1 set: 20 yards
	4. Forward Left Leg Hops
	  1 set: 20 yards
	5. Running—1 set: 20 yards
	
	Post-Strength Workout
	
	Static Stretch Routine
	
	Conditioning
	6 110s
	Linemen—20 seconds
	TE, LB, QB, Spec, FB, DE 18 seconds
	WR, TB, DB—16 seconds
	Work-to-Rest Ratio—1:3
		Competitive Games
		Basketball
		Volleyball
		Tag Football
		Racquetball, etc.
			Speed Ladder
			5-7 sets
			1. Run Through High Knees
			2. Lateral 2 feet in, 2 feet out
			3. Slalom Jumps
			4. Backward Slalom Jumps
			5. Ickey Shuffle
			6. Make up your own pattern
			
			Post-Strength Workout
			
			PNF Partner Stretch
			
			Programmable Agility
			1. Four-Corner Drill
			
			Reactive Agility
			1. Tennis Ball Drills (all variations)
				Jump Rope
				5-6 sets: 10-15 seconds
				1. Both Feet
				2. Right Foot
				3. Left Foot
				4. Alternate Feet
				5. 2 on Right, 2 on Left Foot
				6. Speed Jump
				
				Post-Strength Workout
				
				Static Stretch Routine
				
				Conditioning
				4 Modified Suicides
				  10 yards and back
				  15 yards and back
				  20 yards and back
				Linemen—22 seconds
				TE, LB, QB, Spec, FB, DE 20 seconds
				WR, TB, DB—18 seconds
				Work-to-Rest Ratio—1:3
				
				Competitive Drill
				1. Shark in a Tank
				  6-10 sets: 10 seconds

Stretch Lower Back, Hamstrings	Stretch Lower Back, Hamstrings	Stretch Lower Back, Hamstrings	Stretch Lower Back, Hamstrings	Stretch Lower Back, Hamstrings

Power and Absolute Strength

WEEK 11 — INTERMEDIATE OFF SEASON — Phase 2

MONDAY	TUESDAY	THURSDAY	FRIDAY
Jump Rope—4-5 sets - 15 seconds	Speed Ladder—5-7 sets	Dot Drills—4-5 sets – 15 reps	Jump Rope—4-5 sets – 15 seconds
Abs Denver Bronco Partner Abs	**Abs** Partner-Assisted Timed Sit-Ups 30 seconds Leg Throws—30 seconds	**Abs** Hanging Leg Raises—2 sets: 20 reps Medicine Ball Stack Crunches 2 sets: 20 reps	**Abs** Figure Four Double Crunches 2 sets: 10 reps Bicycle Abs—30 seconds
Power Olympic Deadlifts to Knee 3 sets: 3 reps Hang Clean Combo Jump Shrugs—4 sets: 1 rep Hang Clean High Pulls 4 sets: 1 rep Hang Cleans—4 sets: 1 rep	**Power** Explosive Box Stepups (each leg) with weighted vest if possible 3 sets: 3 reps	**Power** Hang Snatch Combo Hang Snatch Jump Shrugs 4 sets: 1 rep Hang Snatch High Pulls 4 sets: 1 rep Hang Snatch—4 sets: 1 rep Power Shrugs—3 sets: 6 reps	**Power** Push Press—4 sets: 3 reps
Legs Back Squats (warmup—8 reps) 55%—5 reps 61%—5 reps 67%—5 reps 73%—5 reps 79%—5 reps	**Chest** Bench Press (warmup—8 reps) 61%—5 reps 67%—5 reps 73%—5 reps 76%—5 reps 82%—5 reps Dumbbell Incline Bench Press 3 sets: 6 reps	**Legs** Front Squats—4 sets: 5 reps	**Chest** Close Grip Bench Press (stop and stab) 4 sets: 5 reps
Back One Arm Dumbbell Rows 3 sets: 8 reps Lat Pulldowns (front, underhand) 3 sets: 8 reps	**Bicep** Dumbbell Incline Curls 3 sets: 8 reps	**Back** Seated Cable Rows 3 sets: 8 reps Pullups—3 sets: 5-10 reps	**Bicep** Standing Curls (barbell or curl bar) 3 sets: 8 reps
Lower Back/Hamstrings Romanian Deadlifts—3 sets: 6 reps	**Tricep** Weighted Dips—3 sets: 8 reps	**Lower Back** Glute Ham Raises 3 sets: 10 reps	**Tricep** Dumbbell Lying Tricep Extensions 4 sets: 8 reps
Calf Standing Calf Raises—2 sets: 15 reps Seated Calf Raises—2 sets: 15 reps	**Wrist/Forearm** Wrist Rollers—2 sets	**Calf** Standing Calf Raises—2 sets: 15 reps Seated Calf Raises—2 sets: 15 reps	**Forearm** Grippers—2 round trips
	Neck Neck Machine—1 set: 10 reps		**Neck** Neck Machine—1 set: 10 reps
PNF Partner Stretch	Static Stretch Routine	PNF Partner Stretch	Static Stretch Routine

INTERMEDIATE OFF SEASON   SPEED AGILITY QUICKNESS CONDITIONING SCHEDULE   WEEK 12 PHASE 2

MONDAY	TUESDAY	WEDNESDAY	THURSDAY	FRIDAY
Pre-Strength Workout	**Pre-Strength Workout**	**Active Rest**	**Pre-Strength Workout**	**Pre-Strength Workout**

Dot Drills
10–15 seconds
1. In and Out
2. Figure 8—both feet right side
3. Figure 8—both feet left side
4. In and Out—turns
 	
Post-Strength Workout
 	
PNF Partner Stretch
 	
Speed Development
1. A Marches
  2 sets: 20 yards
2. A Skips
  2 sets: 20 yards
3. A Runs
  2 sets: 20 yards
4. Power Skips
  2 sets: 20 yards
5. Bounding
  2 sets: 20 yards
6. Sled Pulls (acceleration)
  4–6 sets: 20 yards (50 pounds max resistance on sled)
	Jump Rope with movement
	1. Running—1 set: 20 yards
	2. Double Leg Hops Forward
	  1 set: 20 yards
	3. Forward Right Leg Hops
	  1 set: 20 yards
	4. Forward Left Leg Hops
	  1 set: 20 yards
	5. Running—1 set: 20 yards
	
	Post-Strength Workout
	
	Static Stretch Routine
	
	Conditioning
	6 110s
	Linemen—20 seconds
	TE, LB, QB, Spec, FB, DE 18 seconds
	WR, TB, DB—16 seconds
	Work-to-Rest Ratio—1:3
		Competitive Games
		Basketball
		Volleyball
		Tag Football
		Racquetball, etc.
			Speed Ladder
			5–7 sets
			1. Run Through High Knees
			2. Lateral Shuffle
			3. Hop Scotch
			4. Slalom Jumps
			5. Ickey Shuffle
			6. Backward Ickey Shuffle
			
			Post-Strength Workout
			
			PNF Partner Stretch
			
			Programmable Agility
			1. 20-yard Shuttle
			  4 sets: record best time
			
			Reactive Agility
			1. Four-Cone Reaction Drill visual cues
			  4 sets: 10–15 seconds
				Jump Rope
				5–6 sets—10–15 seconds
				1. Both Feet
				2. Right Foot
				3. Left Foot
				4. Alternate Feet
				5. 2 on Right, 2 on Left Foot
				6. Speed Jump
				
				Post-Strength Workout
				
				Static Stretch Routine
				
				Conditioning
				4 Modified Suicides
				  10 yards and back
				  15 yards and back
				  20 yards and back
				Linemen - 22 seconds
				TE, LB, QB, Spec, FB, DE 20 seconds
				WR, TB, DB—18 seconds
				Work-to-Rest Ratio—1:3
				
				Competitive Drill
				1. Shark in a Tank
				  6–10 sets: 10 seconds

Stretch Lower Back, Hamstrings	Stretch Lower Back, Hamstrings	Stretch Lower Back, Hamstrings	Stretch Lower Back, Hamstrings	Stretch Lower Back, Hamstrings

INTERMEDIATE OFF SEASON
Phase 2

Power and Absolute Strength

WEEK 12

MONDAY	TUESDAY	THURSDAY	FRIDAY
Jump Rope—4-5 sets – 15 seconds	Speed Ladder—5-7 sets	Dot Drills—4-5 sets – 15 reps	Jump Rope—4-5 sets – 15 seconds
Abs Denver Bronco Partner Abs	**Abs** Partner-Assisted Timed Sit-Ups 30 seconds Leg Throws—30 seconds	**Abs** Hanging Leg Raises—2 sets: 20 reps Medicine Ball Stack Crunches 2 sets: 20 reps	**Abs** Figure Four Double Crunches 2 sets: 10 reps Bicycle Abs—30 seconds
Power Olympic Deadlifts to Knee 3 sets: 3 reps Hang Cleans (warmup—3 reps) 61%—3 reps 73%—1 rep 79%—1 rep Final 3 rep max, convert to 1 RM	**Power** Explosive Box Stepups (each leg) with weighted vest if possible 3 sets: 3 reps	**Power** Hang Snatch Combo Hang Snatch Jump Shrugs 4 sets: 1 rep Hang Snatch High Pulls 4 sets: 1 rep Hang Snatch—4 sets: 1 rep Power Shrugs—3 sets: 6 reps	**Power** Push Press—(warmup—3 reps) 4 sets: 3 reps (work up to a 3 rep max, convert to a 1 RM)
Legs Back Squats (warmup—8 reps) 64%—5 reps 70%—5 reps 76%—5 reps Final 3 rep max, convert to 1 RM	**Chest** Bench Press (warmup—8 reps) 61%—3 reps 67%—3 reps 73%—3 reps 79%—3 reps Final 5 rep max, convert to 1 RM Dumbbell Incline Bench Press 3 sets: 6 reps	**Legs** Front Squats—4 sets: 5 reps	**Chest** Close Grip Bench Press (stop and stab) 4 sets: 5 reps
Back One Arm Dumbbell Rows 3 sets: 8 reps Lat Pulldowns (front, underhand) 3 sets: 8 reps	**Bicep** Dumbbell Incline Curls 3 sets: 8 reps	**Back** Seated Cable Rows 3 sets: 8 reps Pullups—3 sets: 5-10 reps	**Bicep** Standing Curls (barbell or curl bar) 3 sets: 8 reps
Lower Back/Hamstrings Romanian Deadlifts—3 sets: 6 reps	**Tricep** Weighted Dips—3 sets: 8 reps	**Lower Back** Glute Ham Raises 3 sets: 10 reps	**Tricep** Dumbbell Lying Tricep Extensions 4 sets: 8 reps
Calf Standing Calf Raises—2 sets: 15 reps Seated Calf Raises—2 sets: 15 reps	**Wrist/Forearm** Wrist Rollers—2 sets	**Calf** Standing Calf Raises—2 sets: 15 reps Seated Calf Raises—2 sets: 15 reps	**Forearm** Grippers—2 round trips
	Neck Neck Machine—1 set: 10 reps		**Neck** Neck Machine—1 set: 10 reps
PNF Partner Stretch	Static Stretch Routine	PNF Partner Stretch	Static Stretch Routine

INTERMEDIATE PRESEASON SPEED AGILITY QUICKNESS CONDITIONING SCHEDULE WEEK 1 PHASE 3

MONDAY	TUESDAY	WEDNESDAY	THURSDAY	FRIDAY
Pre-Strength Workout	Pre-Strength Workout	Active Rest	Pre-Strength Workout	Pre-Strength Workout

Dot Drills
10-15 seconds
1. In and Out
2. Figure 8—both feet right side
3. Figure 8—both feet left side
4. In and Out—turns
 	
Post-Strength Workout
 	
PNF Partner Stretch
 	
Speed Development
1. A Marches
   1 set: 20 yards
2. A Skips
   1 set: 20 yards
3. A Runs
   1 set: 20 yards
4. Power Skips
   1 set: 20 yards
5. Bounding
   1 set: 20 yards
6. Starts—4-6 sets: 20 yards
7. Acceleration Ladder
   4-6 sets: 20 yards
	Jump Rope with movement
	1. Running—1 set: 20 yards
	2. Double Leg Hops
	   Forward
	   1 set: 20 yards
	3. Forward Right Leg Hops
	   1 set: 20 yards
	4. Forward Left Leg Hops
	   1 set: 20 yards
	5. Running—1 set: 20 yards
	
	Post-Strength Workout
	
	Static Stretch Routine
	
	Conditioning
	6 110s
	Linemen—20 seconds
	TE, LB, QB, Spec, FB, DE
	   18 seconds
	WR, TB, DB—16 seconds
	Work-to-Rest Ratio—1:3
		Competitive Games
		Basketball
		Volleyball
		Tag Football
		Racquetball, etc.
			Speed Ladder
			5-7 sets
			1. Run Through High Knees
			2. Lateral Shuffle
			3. Hop Scotch
			4. Slalom Jumps
			5. Ickey Shuffle
			6. Backward Ickey Shuffle
			
			Post-Strength Workout
			
			PNF Partner Stretch
			
			Programmable Agility
			1. Pattern Runs
			   6-8 sets: 20 yards
			   (speed cuts, power cuts, and spins)
			
			Reactive Agility
			1. Tennis Ball Drills
			   (all variations) 8-10 sets
				Jump Rope
				5-6 sets: 10-15 seconds
				1. Both Feet
				2. Right Foot
				3. Left Foot
				4. Alternate Feet
				5. 2 on Right, 2 on Left Foot
				6. Speed Jump
				
				Post-Strength Workout
				
				Static Stretch Routine
				
				Conditioning
				4 Modified Suicides
				   10 yards and back
				   15 yards and back
				   20 yards and back
				Linemen—22 seconds
				TE, LB, QB, Spec, FB, DE
				   20 seconds
				WR, TB, DB—18 seconds
				Work-to-Rest Ratio—1:3
				
				Competitive Drill
				1. Capture the Flag
				   6-8 times

Stretch Lower Back, Hamstrings	Stretch Lower Back, Hamstrings	Strretch Lower Back, Hamstrings	Stretch Lower Back, Hamstrings	Stretch Lower Back, Hamstrings

INTERMEDIATE PRESEASON
Phase 3

WEEK 1

MONDAY	TUESDAY	THURSDAY	FRIDAY
Speed Ladder—5-7 sets	Jump Rope—4-5 sets – 15 seconds	Dot Drills—4-5 sets – 15 reps	Jump Rope—4-5 sets – 15 seconds

MONDAY

Abs
Hanging Leg Raises—2 sets: 20 reps
Twisting Stack Crunches
2 sets: 20 reps

Power
Hang Cleans (warmup—5 reps)
61%—5 reps
64%—5 reps
67%—5 reps

Legs
Back Squats (warmup—8 reps)
61%—5 reps
67%—5 reps
70%—5 reps
76%—5 reps

Back
Seated Cable Rows
8-8-6-6 reps
Pullups—3 sets: 5-10 reps

Lower Back/Hamstrings
Reverse Hyperextensions
2 sets: 15 reps

Calf
Standing Calf Raises—3 sets: 15 reps

Flexibility—Grip
Bar Hang—45 seconds

PNF Partner Stretch

TUESDAY

Abs
Flutterkicks—30 seconds
Bicycle Abs—30 seconds
Dying Cockroach—30 seconds

Power
Olympic Deadlifts to Knee
3 sets: 3 reps
Clean Pulls from Floor—3 sets: 3 reps

Chest
Bench Press (warmup—8 reps)
55%—5 reps
61%—5 reps
67%—5 reps
73%—5 reps
79%—5 reps
Dumbbell Alternate Bench Press
3 sets: 5 reps (each arm)

Shoulder
Dumbbell 21s—1-2 sets: 7 reps each
(front raise, lateral raise, bent over lateral)

Bicep
Barbell Curls or Cable Curls
3 sets: 8 reps

Tricep
Lying Tricep Extensions
3 sets: 10 reps

Wrist/Forearm
Wrist Rollers—2 sets

Neck
Neck Machine—1 set: 10 reps

Static Stretch Routine

THURSDAY

Abs
Hanging Leg Raises—2 sets: 20 reps
Medicine Ball Stack Crunches
2 sets: 20 reps

Power
Hang Snatch (Speed!)
4 sets: 3 reps

Legs
Speed Squats (50 percent of max)
4 sets: 5 reps

Back
Pullups (vary grip)
3 sets: 5-10 reps
Lying Dumbbell Pullovers
2 sets: 12 reps

Lower Back/Hamstrings
Back Extensions or Glute Ham Raises
3 sets: 10 reps

Calf
Standing Calf Raises—2 sets: 15 reps
Seated Calf Raises—2 sets: 15 reps

PNF Partner Stretch

FRIDAY

Abs
Hokie Leg Raises—1 set: 20 reps
Figure Four Double Crunches
(each side)—2 sets: 10 reps

Power
Push Jerks (warmup—5 reps)
53%—5 reps
61%—5 reps
64%—5 reps
67%—5 reps

Chest
Dumbbell Bench Press
(stop and stab)
3 sets: 6 reps

Shoulder
Seated Plate Raises—2 sets: 20 reps

Bicep
Standing Alternate Dumbbell Curls
3 sets: 8 reps

Tricep
Weighted Dips or Bench Dips
3 sets: 8 reps

Forearm
Grippers—2 round trips

Neck
Neck Machine—1 set: 10 reps

Static Stretch Routine

INTERMEDIATE PRESEASON   SPEED AGILITY QUICKNESS CONDITIONING SCHEDULE   WEEK 2 PHASE 3

MONDAY	TUESDAY	WEDNESDAY	THURSDAY	FRIDAY
Pre-Strength Workout	Pre-Strength Workout	Active Rest	Pre-Strength Workout	Pre-Strength Workout
Dot Drills 10-15 seconds 1. In and Out 2. Figure 8—both feet right side 3. Figure 8—both feet left side 4. In and Out—turns Post-Strength Workout PNF Partner Stretch **Speed Development** 1. A Marches 1 set: 20 yards 2. A Skips—1 set: 20 yards 3. A Runs—1 set: 20 yards 4. Power Skips 1 set: 20 yards 5. Bounding—1 set: 20 yards 6. Speed Hops—(right and left leg) 1 set: 20 yards **Acceleration** 1. Starts—Football Stance 4-6 reps 2. Sled Pulls—4-6 sets: 20 yards (50 pounds max weight on sled) or 3. Uphill Runs 6 sets: 20-30 yards	**Jump Rope** with movement 1. Running—1 set: 20 yards 2. Double Leg Hops Forward 1 set: 20 yards 3. Forward Right Leg Hops 1 set: 20 yards 4. Forward Left Leg Hops 1 set: 20 yards 5. Running—1 set: 20 yards Post-Strength Workout Static Stretch Routine **Conditioning** 8 110s Linemen—20 seconds TE, LB, QB, Spec, FB, DE 18 seconds WR, TB, DB—16 seconds Work-to-Rest Ratio—1:3	**Competitive Games** Basketball Volleyball Tag Football Racquetball, etc.	**Speed Ladder** 5-7 sets 1. Run Through High Knees 2. Lateral Shuffle 3. Hop Scotch 4. Slalom Jumps 5. Ickey Shuffle 6. Backward Ickey Shuffle Post-Strength Workout PNF Partner Stretch **Programmable Agility** 1. 90 Spin Power Cut Drill 4-6 sets **Reactive Agility** 1. Eight-Cone Reaction Drill visual cues 4 sets: 10-15 second	**Jump Rope** 5-6 sets: 10-15 seconds 1. Both Feet 2. Right Foot 3. Left Foot 4. Alternate Feet 5. 2 on Right, 2 on Left Foot 6. Speed Jump Post-Strength Workout Static Stretch Routine **Conditioning** 4 Modified Suicides 10 yards and back 15 yards and back 20 yards and back Linemen—22 seconds TE, LB, QB, Spec, FB, DE 20 seconds WR, TB, DB—18 seconds Work-to-Rest Ratio—1:3 **Competitive Drill** 1. Get Up and Sprint (variations) 4-6 sets
Stretch Lower Back, Hamstrings	Stretch Lower Back, Hamstrings	Strretch Lower Back, Hamstrings	Stretch Lower Back, Hamstrings	Stretch Lower Back, Hamstrings

INTERMEDIATE PRESEASON
Phase 3

WEEK 2

MONDAY	TUESDAY	THURSDAY	FRIDAY
Speed Ladder—5-7 sets	Jump Rope—4-5 sets – 15 seconds	Dot Drills—4-5 sets – 15 reps	Jump Rope—4-5 sets – 15 seconds

MONDAY

Abs
Hanging Leg Raises—2 sets: 20 reps
Twisting Stack Crunches
2 sets: 20 reps

Power
Hang Cleans (warmup—5 reps)
55%—5 reps
61%—5 reps
64%—5 reps
70%—5 reps

Legs
Back Squats (warmup—8 reps)
55%—5 reps
61%—5 reps
67%—5 reps
73%—5 reps
79%—5 reps

Back
Seated Cable Rows
8-8-6-6 reps
Pullups—3 sets: 5-10 reps

Lower Back/Hamstrings
Reverse Hyperextensions
2 sets: 15 reps

Calf
Standing Calf Raises—3 sets: 15 reps

Flexibility—Grip
Bar Hang—60 seconds

PNF Partner Stretch

TUESDAY

Abs
Flutterkicks—30 seconds
Bicycle Abs—30 seconds
Dying Cockroach—30 seconds

Power
Olympic Deadlifts to Knee
3 sets: 3 reps
Clean Pulls from Floor
3 sets: 3 reps

Chest
Bench Press (warmup—8 reps)
55%—5 reps
64%—5 reps
70%—5 reps
76%—5 reps
82%—5 reps
Dumbbell Alternate Bench Press
3 sets: 5 reps

Shoulder
Dumbbell 21s—1-2 sets: 7 reps each
(front raise, lateral raise, bent over lateral)

Bicep
Barbell Curls or Cable Curls
3 sets: 8 reps

Tricep
Straight Bars or Curl Bars
3 sets: 8 reps
Lying Tricep Extensions
3 sets: 8 reps

Wrist/Forearm
Wrist Rollers—2 sets

Neck
Neck Machine—1 set: 10 reps

Static Stretch Routine

THURSDAY

Abs
Hanging Leg Raises—2 sets: 20 reps
Medicine Ball Stack Crunches
2 sets: 20 reps

Power
Hang Snatch (Speed!)
4 sets: 3 reps

Legs
Speed Squats (50 percent of max)
4 sets: 5 reps

Back
Pullups (vary grip)
3 sets: 5-10 reps
Lying Dumbbell Pullovers
2 sets: 12 reps

Lower Back/Hamstrings
Back Extensions or Glute Ham Raises
3 sets: 10 reps

Calf
Standing Calf Raises—2 sets: 15 reps
Seated Calf Raises—2 sets: 15 reps

PNF Partner Stretch

FRIDAY

Abs
Hokie Leg Raises—1 set: 20 reps
Figure Four Double Crunches
(each side)—2 sets: 10 reps

Power
Push Jerks (warmup—3 reps)
55%—3 reps
61%—3 reps
67%—3 reps
73%—3 reps

Chest
Dumbbell Bench Press
(stop and stab)
3 sets: 6 reps

Shoulder
Seated Plate Raises—2 sets: 20 reps

Bicep
Standing Alternate Dumbbell Curls
3 sets: 8 reps

Tricep
Weighted Dips or Bench Dips
3 sets: 8 reps

Forearm
Grippers—2 round trips

Neck
Neck Machine—1 set: 10 reps

Static Stretch Routine

INTERMEDIATE PRESEASON   SPEED AGILITY QUICKNESS CONDITIONING SCHEDULE   WEEK 3 PHASE 3

MONDAY	TUESDAY	WEDNESDAY	THURSDAY	FRIDAY
Pre-Strength Workout	Pre-Strength Workout	Active Rest	Pre-Strength Workout	Pre-Strength Workout
Dot Drills 10-15 seconds 1. In and Out 2. Figure 8—both feet right side 3. Figure 8—both feet left side 4. In and Out—turns **Post-Strength Workout** **PNF Partner Stretch** **Speed Development** (Acceleration) 1. Acceleration Ladder 6 sets: 20 yards 2. Sled Pulls 6 sets: 20 yards (50 pounds max weight on sled)	**Jump Rope** with movement 1. Running—1 set: 20 yards 2. Double Leg Hops Forward 1 set: 20 yards 3. Forward Right Leg Hops 1 set: 20 yards 4. Forward Left Leg Hops 1 set: 20 yards 5. Running—1 set: 20 yards **Post-Strength Workout** **Static Stretch Routine** **Conditioning** 8 110s Linemen—20 seconds TE, LB, QB, Spec, FB, DE 18 seconds WR, TB, DB—16 seconds Work-to-Rest Ratio—1:3	**Competitive Games** Basketball Volleyball Tag Football Racquetball, etc.	**Speed Ladder** 5-7 sets 1. Run Through High Knees 2. Lateral Shuffle 3. Hop Scotch 4. Slalom Jumps 5. Ickey Shuffle 6. Backward Ickey Shuffle **Post-Strength Workout** **PNF Partner Stretch** **Programmable Agility** 1. 20-yard Shuttle 4 sets: record best time **Reactive Agility** 1. Two-Point Wave Drill 4 sets	**Jump Rope** 5-6 sets: 10-15 seconds 1. Both Feet 2. Right Foot 3. Left Foot 4. Alternate Feet 5. 2 on Right, 2 on Left Foot 6. Speed Jump **Post-Strength Workout** **Static Stretch Routine** **Conditioning** 4 Modified Suicides 10 yards and back 15 yards and back 20 yards and back Linemen—22 seconds TE, LB, QB, Spec, FB, DE 20 seconds WR, TB, DB—18 seconds Work-to-Rest Ratio—1:3 **Competitive Drill** 1. Shark in a Tank 5-7 sets
Stretch Lower Back, Hamstrings	Stretch Lower Back, Hamstrings	Stretch Lower Back, Hamstrings	Stretch Lower Back, Hamstrings	Stretch Lower Back, Hamstrings

WEEK 3

INTERMEDIATE PRESEASON
Phase 3

MONDAY	TUESDAY	THURSDAY	FRIDAY
Dot Drills—3-5 sets – 10-15 reps	Jump Rope—3-5 sets – 15-20 seconds	Speed Ladder—5-7 sets	Jump Rope—3-5 sets – 15-20 seconds
Abs Hanging Leg Raises—2 sets: 20 reps Twisting Stack Crunches 2 sets: 20 reps	**Abs** Flutterkicks—30 seconds Bicycle Abs—30 seconds Dying Cockroach—30 seconds	**Abs** Hanging Leg Raises—2 sets: 20 reps Medicine Ball Stack Crunches 2 sets: 20 reps	**Abs** Hokie Leg Raises—1 set: 20 reps Figure Four Double Crunches (each side) 2 sets: 10 reps
Power Hang Cleans (warmup—3 reps) 55%—3 reps 64%—3 reps 70%—3 reps 76%—3 reps	**Power** Olympic Deadlifts to Knee 3 sets: 3 reps Clean Pulls from Floor 3 sets: 3 reps	**Power** Hang Snatch (Speed!) 4 sets: 3 reps	**Power** Push Jerks (warmup—3 reps) 55%—3 reps 64%—3 reps 70%—3 reps 76%—3 reps
Legs Back Squats (warmup—8 reps) 55%—5 reps 64%—5 reps 70%—5 reps 76%—5 reps 82%—5 reps	**Chest** Bench Press (warmup—8 reps) 61%—5 reps 67%—5 reps 73%—5 reps 79%—5 reps 85%—5 reps Dumbbell Alternate Bench Press 3 sets: 6 reps	**Legs** Speed Squats (50 percnet of max) 4 sets: 5 reps	**Chest** Dumbbell Bench Press (stop and stab) 3 sets: 6 reps
Back Seated Cable Rows 8-6-6-6 reps Pullups—3 sets: 5-10 reps	**Shoulder** Dumbbell 21s—1-2 sets: 7 reps each (front raise, lateral raise, bent over lateral)	**Back** Pullups (vary grip) 3 sets: 5-10 reps Lying Dumbbell Pullovers 2 sets: 12 reps	**Shoulder** Seated Plate Raises—2 sets: 20 reps
Lower Back/Hamstrings Reverse Hyperextensions 2 sets: 15 reps	**Bicep** Barbell Curls or Cable Curls 3 sets: 8 reps	**Lower Back/Hamstrings** Back Extensions or Glute Ham Raises 3 sets: 10 reps	**Bicep** Standing Alternate Dumbbell Curls 3 sets: 8 reps
Calf Standing Calf Raises—3 sets: 15 reps	**Tricep** Straight Bars or Curl Bars 3 sets: 8 reps Lying Tricep Extensions 3 sets: 8 reps	**Calf** Standing Calf Raises—2 sets: 15 reps Seated Calf Raises—2 sets: 15 reps	**Tricep** Weighted Dips or Bench Dips 3 sets: 8 reps
Flexibility—Grip Bar Hang—60 seconds	**Wrist/Forearm** Wrist Rollers—2 sets		**Forearm** Grippers—2 round trips
	Neck Neck Machine—1 set: 10 reps		**Neck** Neck Machine—1 set: 10 reps
PNF Partner Stretch	Static Stretch Routine	PNF Partner Stretch	Static Stretch Routine

INTERMEDIATE PRESEASON SPEED AGILITY QUICKNESS CONDITIONING SCHEDULE WEEK 4 PHASE 3

MONDAY	TUESDAY	WEDNESDAY	THURSDAY	FRIDAY
Pre-Strength Workout	**Pre-Strength Workout**	**Active Rest**	**Pre-Strength Workout**	**Pre-Strength Workout**

Dot Drills
 10-15 seconds
 1. In and Out
 2. Figure 8—both feet right side
 3. Figure 8—both feet left side
 4. In and Out—turns
 5. Make up your own pattern
	Jump Rope with movement
	 1. Running—1 set: 20 yards
	 2. Double Leg Hops Forward
	    1 set: 20 yards
	 3. Forward Right Leg Hops
	    1 set: 20 yards
	 4. Forward Left Leg Hops
	    1 set: 20 yards
	 5. Running—1 set: 20 yards
		Competitive Games
		 Basketball
		 Volleyball
		 Tag Football
		 Racquetball, etc.
			Speed Ladder
			 5-7 sets
			 1. Run Through High Knees
			 2. Lateral 2 feet in, 2 feet out
			 3. Slalom Jumps
			 4. Backward Slalom Jumps
			 5. Ickey Shuffle
			 6. Make up your own pattern
				Dynamic Warmup
				 2 sets: 20 yards
				 1. Walking/Skipping Knee Ups
				 2. Walking/Skipping Toe Touches
				 3. Low Shuffle
				 4. Starts—Football Stance
				    4-6 sets

Post-Strength Workout	**Post-Strength Workout**		**Post-Strength Workout**	**Post-Strength Workout**
PNF Partner Stretch	**Static Stretch Routine**		**PNF Partner Stretch**	**Static Stretch Routine**

Speed Development
 1. A Marches
    1 set: 20 yards
 2. A Skips—1 set: 20 yards
 3. A Runs—1 set: 20 yards
	Conditioning
	 8 110s
	 Linemen—19 seconds
	 TE, LB, QB, Spec, FB, DE
	    17 seconds
	 WR, TB, DB—15 seconds
	 Work-to-Rest Ratio—1:3
			Programmable Agility
			 1. Carolina Drill—4 sets
				Conditioning
				 4-5 Modified Suicides
				    10 yards and back
				    15 yards and back
				    20 yards and back
				 Linemen—22 seconds
				 TE, LB, QB, Spec, FB, DE
				    20 seconds
				 WR, TB, DB - 18 seconds
				 Work-to-Rest Ratio—1:3

Acceleration 1. Sled Pulls—4-6 sets: 20 yards (50 pound max weight on sled)			**Reactive Agility** 1. Crazy Ball Drills (all variations) 8-10 sets	
Stretch Lower Back, Hamstrings	Stretch Lower Back, Hamstrings	Stretch Lower Back, Hamstrings	Stretch Lower Back, Hamstrings	Stretch Lower Back, Hamstrings

WEEK 4

INTERMEDIATE PRESEASON
Phase 3

MONDAY	TUESDAY	THURSDAY	FRIDAY
Speed Ladder—5-7 sets	Jump Rope—4-5 sets – 15 seconds	Dot Drills—4-5 sets – 15 reps	Jump Rope—4-5 sets – 15 seconds

MONDAY

Abs
Hanging Leg Raises—2 sets: 20 reps
Twisting Stack Crunches
2 sets: 20 reps

Power
Hang Cleans (warmup—3 reps)
55%—3 reps
61%—3 reps
67%—3 reps
73%—3 reps
79%—3 reps

Legs
Back Squats (warmup—8 reps)
55%—3 reps
64%—3 reps
70%—3 reps
76%—3 reps
85%—3 reps

Back
Seated Cable Rows
8-6-6-6 reps
Pullups—3 sets: 5-10 reps

Lower Back/Hamstrings
Reverse Hyperextensions
2 sets: 15 reps

Calf
Standing Calf Raises—3 sets: 15 reps

Flexibility—Grip
Bar Hang—60 seconds

PNF Partner Stretch

TUESDAY

Abs
Flutterkicks—30 seconds
Bicycle Abs—30 seconds
Dying Cockroach—30 seconds

Power
Olympic Deadlifts to Knee
3 sets: 3 reps
Clean Pulls from Floor
3 sets: 3 reps

Chest
Bench Press (warmup—8 reps)
64%—3 reps
70%—3 reps
76%—3 reps
82%—3 reps
88%—3 reps
Dumbbell Alternate Bench Press
3 sets: 5 reps

Shoulder
Dumbbell 21s—1-2 sets: 7 reps each
(front raise, lat raise,
bent over lateral)

Bicep
Barbell Curls or Cable Curls
3 sets: 8 reps

Tricep
Straight Bars or Curl Bars
3 sets: 8-10 reps
Lying Tricep Extensions
3 sets: 8-10 reps

Wrist/Forearm
Wrist Rollers—2 sets

Neck
Neck Machine—1 set: 10 reps

Static Stretch Routine

THURSDAY

Abs
Hanging Leg Raises—2 sets: 20 reps
Medicine Ball Stack Crunches
2 sets: 20 reps

Power
Hang Snatch (Speed!)
4 sets: 3 reps

Legs
Speed Squats (50 percent of max)
4 sets: 5 reps

Back
Pullups (vary grip)
3 sets: 5-10 reps
Lying Dumbbell Pullovers
2 sets: 12 reps

Lower Back/Hamstrings
Back Extensions or Glute Ham Raises
3 sets: 10 reps

Calf
Standing Calf Raises—2 sets: 15 reps
Seated Calf Raises—2 sets: 15 reps

PNF Partner Stretch

FRIDAY

Abs
Hokie Leg Raises—1 set: 20 reps
Figure Four Double Crunches
(each side)—2 sets: 10 reps

Power
Push Jerks (warmup—3 reps)
55%—3 reps
61%—3 reps
67%—3 reps
73%—3 reps
79%—3 reps

Chest
Dumbbell Bench Press
(stop and stab)—3 sets: 6 reps

Shoulder
Seated Plate Raises—2 sets: 20 reps

Bicep
Standing Alternate Dumbbell Curls
3 sets: 8 reps

Tricep
Weighted Dips or Bench Dips
3 sets: 8 reps

Forearms
Grippers—2 round trips

Neck
Neck Machine—1 set: 10 reps

Static Stretch Routine

237

INTERMEDIATE PRESEASON　　　SPEED AGILITY QUICKNESS CONDITIONING SCHEDULE　　　WEEK 5 PHASE 3

MONDAY	TUESDAY	WEDNESDAY	THURSDAY	FRIDAY
Pre-Strength Workout	**Pre-Strength Workout**	**Active Rest**	**Pre-Strength Workout**	**Pre-Strength Workout**
Dot Drills 10-15 seconds 1. In and Out 2. Figure 8—both feet right side 3. Figure 8—both feet left side 4. In and Out—turns 5. Make up your own pattern **Post-Strength Workout** **PNF Partner Stretch** **Speed Development** 1. Heel-to-Butt Kicks 　1 set: 20 yards 2. A Marches 　1 set: 20 yards 3. A Skips 　1 set: 20 yards 4. A Runs 　1 set: 20 yards	**Jump Rope** with movement 1. Running—1 set: 20 yards 2. Double Leg Hops Forward 　1 set: 20 yards 3. Double Leg Lateral Hops Right—1 set: 20 yards 4. Double Leg Lateral Hops Left—1 set: 20 yards 5. Running—1 set: 20 yards **Post-Strength Workout** **Static Stretch Routine** **Conditioning** 10 110s Linemen—18 seconds TE, LB, QB, Spec, FB, DE 16 seconds WR, TB, DB—15 seconds Work-to-Rest Ratio—1:3	**Competitive Games** Basketball Volleyball Tag Football Racquetball, etc.	**Speed Ladder** 5-7 sets 1. Run Through High Knees 2. Lateral 2 Feet in, 2 Feet out 3. Slalom Jumps 4. Backward Slalom Jumps 5. Ickey Shuffle 6. Make up your own pattern **Post-Strength Workout** **PNF Partner Stretch** **Programmable Agility** 1. Four-Corner Drill—4 sets 2. Hourglass Drill—4 sets	**Dynamic Warmup** 2 set: 20 yards 1. Walking/Skipping Knee Ups 2. Walking/Skipping Toe Touches 3. Low Shuffle 4. Starts—Football Stance 4-6 sets **Post-Strength Workout** **Static Stretch Routine** **Conditioning** 4-5 Modified Suicides 　10 yards and back 　15 yards and back 　20 yards and back Linemen—22 seconds TE, LB, QB, Spec, FB, DE 20 seconds WR, TB, DB—18 seconds Work-to-Rest Ratio—1:3
Stretch Lower Back, Hamstrings	Stretch Lower Back, Hamstrings	Stretch Lower Back, Hamstrings	Stretch Lower Back, Hamstrings	Stretch Lower Back, Hamstrings

INTERMEDIATE PRESEASON
Phase 3

WEEK 5

MONDAY	TUESDAY	THURSDAY	FRIDAY
Speed Ladder—5-7 sets	Jump Rope—4-5 sets – 15 seconds	Dot Drills—4-5 sets – 15 reps	Jump Rope—4-5 sets – 15 seconds
Abs Hanging Leg Raises—2 sets: 20 reps Twisting Stack Crunches 2 sets; 20 reps	**Abs** Flutterkicks—30 seconds Bicycle Abs—30 seconds Dying Cockroach—30 seconds	**Abs** Hanging Leg Raises—2 sets: 20 reps Medicine Ball Stack Crunches 2 sets: 20 reps	**Abs** Hokie Leg Raises—1 set; 20 reps Figure Four Double Crunches (each side)—2 sets: 10 reps
Power Hang Cleans (warmup—3 reps) 55%—3 reps 64%—3 reps 70%—3 reps 76%—3 reps 82%—3 reps	**Power** Olympic Deadlifts to Knee 3 sets: 3 reps Clean Pulls from Floor 3 sets: 3 reps	**Power** Hang Snatch (Speed!) 4 sets: 3 reps	**Power** Push Jerks (warmup—3 reps) 55%—3 reps 64%—3 reps 70%—3 reps 76%—3 reps 82%—3 reps
Legs Back Squats (warmup—8 reps) 55%—3 reps 64%—3 reps 70%—3 reps 76%—3 reps 82%—3 reps 88%—3 reps	**Chest** Bench Press (warmup—8 reps) 61%—3 reps 67%—3 reps 73%—3 reps 79%—3 reps 85%—3 reps 91%—3 reps	**Legs** Speed Squats (50 percent of max) 4 sets: 5 reps	**Chest** Dumbbell Bench Press (stop and stab) 3 sets: 6 reps
Back Seated Cable Rows 8-6-6 reps Pullups—3 sets: 5-10 reps	Dumbbell Alternate Bench Press 3 sets: 5 reps	**Back** Pullups (vary grip) 3 sets: 5-10 reps Lying Dumbbell Pullovers 2 sets: 12 reps	**Shoulder** Seated Plate Raises—2 sets: 20 reps
Lower Back/Hamstrings Reverse Hyperextensions 2 sets: 15 reps	**Shoulder** Dumbbell 21s—1-2 sets: 7 reps each (front raise, lat raise, bent over lateral)	**Lower Back/Hamstrings** Back Extensions or Glute Ham Raises 3 sets: 10 reps	**Bicep** Standing Alternate Dumbbell Curls 3 sets: 8 reps
Calf Standing Calf Raises—3 sets: 15 reps	**Bicep** Barbell Curls or Cable Curls 3 sets: 8-10 reps	**Calf** Standing Calf Raises—2 sets: 15 reps Seated Calf Raises—2 sets: 15 reps	**Tricep** Weighted Dips or Bench Dips 3 sets: 8 reps
Flexibility—Grip Bar Hang—60 seconds	**Tricep** Straight Bars or Curl Bars 3 sets: 8-10 reps		**Forearm** Grippers—2 round trips
	Wrist/Forearm Wrist Rollers—2 sets		**Neck** Neck Machine—1 set: 10 reps
	Neck Neck Machine—1 set: 10 reps		
PNF Partner Stretch	Static Stretch Routine	PNF Partner Stretch	Static Stretch Routine

INTERMEDIATE PRESEASON   SPEED AGILITY QUICKNESS CONDITIONING SCHEDULE   WEEK 6 PHASE 3

MONDAY	TUESDAY	WEDNESDAY	THURSDAY	FRIDAY
Pre-Strength Workout	Pre-Strength Workout	Active Rest	Pre-Strength Workout	Pre-Strength Workout
Dot Drills 10-15 seconds 1. In and Out 2. Figure 8—both feet right side 3. Figure 8—both feet left side 4. In and Out—turns 5. Make up your own pattern **Post-Strength Workout** **PNF Partner Stretch** **Speed Development** 1. Downhill Runs—6-8 sets: slight grade 30-40 yards (sprint down, walk back)	**Jump Rope** with movement 1. Running—1 set: 20 yards 2. Double Leg Hops Forward 1 set: 20 yards 3. Double Leg Lateral Hops Right—1 set: 20 yards 4. Double Leg Lateral Hops Left—1 set: 20 yards 5. Running—1 set: 20 yards **Post-Strength Workout** **Static Stretch Routine** **Conditioning** 10 110s Linemen—20 seconds TE, LB, QB, Spec, FB, DE 18 seconds WR, TB, DB—16 seconds Work-to-Rest Ratio—1:3	**Competitive Games** Basketball Volleyball Tag Football Racquetball, etc.	**Speed Ladder** 5-7 sets 1. Run Through High Knees 2. Lateral 2 Feet in, 2 Feet out 3. Slalom Jumps 4. Backward Slalom Jumps 5. Ickey Shuffle 6. Make up your own pattern **Post-Strength Workout** **PNF Partner Stretch** **Programmable Agility** 1. Texas-Drill—2-4 sets 2. 20-yard Shuttle 3-4 sets: record best time	**Dynamic Warmup** 2 sets: 20 yards 1. Walking/Skipping Knee Ups 2. Walking/Skipping Toe Touches 3. Low Shuffle 4. Starts—Football Stance 4-6 sets **Post-Strength Workout** **Static Stretch Routine** **Conditioning** 4-5 Modified Suicides 10 yards and back 15 yards and back 20 yards and back Linemen—22 seconds TE, LB, QB, Spec, FB, DE 20 seconds WR, TB, DB—18 seconds Work-to-Rest Ratio—1:3
Stretch Lower Back, Hamstrings	Stretch Lower Back, Hamstrings	Stretch Lower Back, Hamstrings	Stretch Lower Back, Hamstrings	Stretch Lower Back, Hamstrings

WEEK 6

INTERMEDIATE PRESEASON
Phase 3

MONDAY	TUESDAY	THURSDAY	FRIDAY
Speed Ladder—5-7 sets	Jump Rope—4-5 sets – 15 seconds	Dot Drills—4-5 sets – 15 reps	Jump Rope—4-5 sets – 15 seconds

Abs
Hanging Leg Raises—2 sets: 20 reps
Twisting Stack Crunches
  2 sets: 20 reps
	Abs
	Flutterkicks—30 seconds
	Bicycle Abs—30 seconds
	Dying Cockroach—30 seconds
		Abs
		Hanging Leg Raises—2 sets: 20 reps
		Medicine Ball Stack Crunches
		  2 sets: 20 reps
			Abs
			Hokie Leg Raises—1 set: 20 reps
			Figure Four Double Crunches
			  (each side)—2 sets: 10 reps

Power
Hang Cleans (warmup—3 reps)
55%—3 reps
64%—3 reps
70%—3 reps
76%—3 reps
82%—1 rep
	Power
	Olympic Deadlifts to Knee
	  3 sets: 3 reps
	Clean Pulls from Floor
	  3 sets: 3 reps
		Power
		Hang Snatch (Speed!)
		  4 sets: 3 reps
			Power
			Push Jerks (warmup—3 reps)
			55%—3 reps
			64%—3 reps
			70%—3 reps
			76%—3 reps
			82%—1 rep

Legs
Back Squats (warmup—8 reps)
55%—3 reps
61%—3 reps
67%—3 reps
73%—3 reps
79%—3 reps
	Chest
	Bench Press (warmup—8 reps)
	55%—3 reps
	64%—3 reps
	70%—3 reps
	76%—3 reps
	82%—3 reps
	Dumbbell Alternate Bench Press
	  3 sets: 5 reps
		Legs
		Speed Squats (50 percent of max)
		  4 sets: 5 reps
			Chest
			Dumbbell Bench Press
			  (stop and stab)
			  3 sets: 6 reps

Back
Seated Cable Rows
  3 sets: 6 reps
Pullups—3 sets: 5-10 reps
	Shoulder
	Dumbbell 21s—1 set: 7 reps each
	  (front raise, lat raise,
	  bent over lateral)
		Back
		Pullups (vary grip)
		  3 sets: 5-10 reps
		Lying Dumbbell Pullovers
		  2 sets: 12 reps
			Shoulder
			Seated Plate Raises—2 sets: 20 reps

Lower Back/Hamstrings
Reverse Hyperextensions
  2 sets: 15 reps
	Bicep
	Barbell Curls or Cable Curls
	  3 sets: 8-10 reps
		Lower Back/Hamstrings
		Back Extensions or Glute Ham Raises
		  3 sets: 10 reps
			Bicep
			Standing Alternate Dumbbell Curls
			  3 sets: 8 reps

Calf
Standing Calf Raises—3 sets: 15 reps
	Tricep
	Straight Bars or Curl Bars
	  3 sets: 8-10 reps
		Calf
		Standing Calf Raises—2 sets: 15 reps
		Seated Calf Raises—2 sets: 15 reps
			Tricep
			Weighted Dips or Bench Dips
			  3 sets: 8 reps

Flexibility—Grip Bar Hang—60 seconds	**Wrist/Forearm** Wrist Rollers—2 sets		**Forearm** Grippers—2 round trips
	Neck Neck Machine—1 set: 10 reps		**Neck** Neck Machine—1 set: 10 reps
PNF Partner Stretch	Static Stretch Routine	PNF Partner Stretch	Static Stretch Routine

INTERMEDIATE PRESEASON   SPEED AGILITY QUICKNESS CONDITIONING SCHEDULE   WEEK 7 PHASE 3

MONDAY	TUESDAY	WEDNESDAY	THURSDAY	FRIDAY
Pre-Strength Workout	**Pre-Strength Workout**	**Active Rest**	**Pre-Strength Workout**	**Pre-Strength Workout**

Dot Drills
 10-15 seconds
 1. In and Out
 2. Figure 8—both feet right side
 3. Figure 8—both feet left side
 4. In and Out—turns
 5. Make up your own pattern
	Jump Rope with movement
	 1. Running—1 set: 20 yards
	 2. Double Leg Hops Forward
	   1 set: 20 yards
	 3. Double Leg Lateral Hops Right—1 set: 20 yards
	 4. Double Leg Lateral Hops Left—1 set: 20 yards
	 5. Running—1 set: 20 yards
		Competitive Games
		 Basketball
		 Volleyball
		 Tag Football
		 Racquetball, etc.
			Speed Ladder
			 5-7 sets
			 1. Run Through High Knees
			 2. Lateral 2 Feet in, 2 Feet out
			 3. Slalom Jumps
			 4. Backward Slalom Jumps
			 5. Ickey Shuffle
			 6. Make up your own pattern
				Dynamic Warmup
				 2 sets: 20 yards
				 1. Walking/Skipping Knee Ups
				 2. Walking/Skipping Toe Touches
				 3. Low Shuffle
				 4. Starts—Football Stance
				   4-6 sets

Post-Strength Workout	**Post-Strength Workout**		**Post-Strength Workout**	**Post-Strength Workout**
PNF Partner Stretch	**Static Stretch Routine**		**PNF Partner Stretch**	**Static Stretch Routine**

Speed Development
 1. Fast Arms Drill
   1 set: 15 seconds
 2. Heel-to-Butt Kicks
   1 set: 20 yards
 3. A Marches
   1 set: 20 yards
 4. A Skips
   1 set: 20 yards
	Conditioning
	 10 110s
	 Linemen—19 seconds
	 TE, LB, QB, Spec, FB, DE
	   17 seconds
	 WR, TB, DB—15 seconds
	 Work-to-Rest Ratio—1:3
			Programmable Agility
			 1. Star Drill—2 sets
			 Reactive Agility
			 1. Eight-Cone Reaction Drill visual cues
			   4 sets: 10-15 second
				Competitive Drills
				 1. Shark in a Tank
				   6-8 sets: 8-10 seconds

Stretch Lower Back, Hamstrings	Stretch Lower Back, Hamstrings	Stretch Lower Back, Hamstrings	Stretch Lower Back, Hamstrings	Stretch Lower Back, Hamstrings

WEEK 7
TESTING WEEK

INTERMEDIATE PRESEASON
Phase 3

Testing and Evaluation

MONDAY	TUESDAY	THURSDAY	FRIDAY
Speed Ladder—5-7 sets	Jump Rope—4-5 sets – 15 seconds	Dot Drills—4-5 sets – 15 reps	Jump Rope—4-5 sets – 15 seconds
Abs Hanging Leg Raises—2 sets: 20 reps Twisting Stack Crunches 2 sets: 20 reps	**Abs** Flutterkicks—30 seconds Bicycle Abs—30 seconds Dying Cockroach—30 seconds	**Abs** Hanging Leg Raises—2 sets: 20 reps Medicine Ball Stack Crunches 2 sets: 20 reps	**Abs** Hokie Leg Raises—1 set: 20 reps Figure Four Double Crunches (each side)—2 sets: 20 reps
TEST—Vertical Jump	**TEST**—10-yard Sprint (electronically timed)	**TEST**—Back Squats 3 rep max, convert to 1 RM	**TEST**—Push Jerks 1 rep max
TEST—Hang Cleans 1 rep max	**TEST**—20-yard Shuttle best of three trials		**TEST**—Body Weight Dips max reps
TEST—Max Pullups max reps	**TEST**—Bench Press—3 rep max convert to 1 RM		
Get Body Weight	**TEST**—Get Sit and Reach Flexibility Test		
PNF Partner Stretch	Static Stretch Routine	PNF Partner Stretch	Static Stretch Routine

Advanced: Off-Season/Preseason Program

ADVANCED
Off-Season Cycles

BENCH PRESS

Week 1	67% - 10 reps
Week 2	70% - 8 reps
Week 3	76% - 6 reps - 2 sets
Week 4	82% - 5 reps
Week 5	85% - 3 reps - 2 sets
Week 6	88% - 3 reps
Week 7	91% - 1 rep - 3 sets
Week 8	**MAX** - 1 rep
Week 9	ACTIVE REST - TEST-Vertical Jump, 10-yard shuttle, 40, etc.

SQUAT

50% - 20 reps - 2 sets
70% - 8 reps
76% - 6 reps
79% - 5 reps
85% - 3 reps
88% - 3 reps
91% - 1 rep - 3 sets
MAX - 3 reps

Preseason Cycles

Week 1	64% - 10 reps	61% - 10 reps
Week 2	67% - 10 reps	64% - 10 reps
Week 3	70% - 8 reps	67% - 8 reps
Week 4	76% - 5 reps **UNLOAD**	73% - 5 reps **UNLOAD**
Week 5	79% - 5 reps	76% - 5 reps
Week 6	82% - 5 reps	79% - 5 reps
Week 7	85% - 3 reps - 2 sets	85% - 3 reps - 1 set
Week 8	88% - 3 reps	88% - 2 reps - 2 sets
Week 9	91% - 1 rep - 3 sets	91% - 1 rep
Week 10	**MAX**	**MAX**

ASSISTANCE

10 reps
10 reps
10 reps
8 reps
8 reps
8 reps
5-8 reps
5-8 reps
5-8 reps

ACTIVE REST—TEST—Vertical Jump, 10-yard Shuttle, 40 etc., Sit and Reach, etc.

ADVANCED
Off-Season Cycles

POWER CLEAN

Week 1	Hang Cleans below Knee	64% - 5 reps
Week 2	Hang Cleans below Knee	67% - 3 reps - 2 sets
Week 3	Power Cleans	73% - 3 reps
Week 4	Power Cleans	76% - 3 reps - 2 sets
Week 5	Power Cleans	79% - 3 reps - 2 sets
Week 6	Power Cleans	82-85% - 1 rep - 3 sets
Week 7	Power Cleans	79% - 2 reps
Week 8	MAX	1 rep
Week 9	ACTIVE REST - TEST—Vertical Jump, 10-yard Shuttle, 40, etc.	

Preseason Cycles

Week 1	Hang Clean FS Combo	58% - 3 reps - 2 sets
Week 2	Hang Clean FS Combo	61% - 3 reps
Week 3	Power Cleans	70% - 3 reps - 2 sets
Week 4	Power Cleans	65% - 3 reps
Week 5	Power Cleans	79% - 3 reps
Week 6	Power Cleans	85% - 2 reps
Week 7	Power Cleans	88% - 1 rep - 2 sets
Week 8	Power Cleans	91% - 1 rep - 2 sets
Week 9	Power Cleans	85% - 1 rep **UNLOAD**
Week 10	MAX 1 rep	

PUSH JERK

67% - 5 reps
70% - 5 reps
73% - 5 reps
76% - 3 reps - 2 sets
79% - 3 reps - 2 sets
82% - 3 reps - 2 sets
85% - 1 rep - 3 sets
MAX - 1 rep

70% - 5 reps
73% - 5 reps
76% - 3 reps - 2 sets
76% - 1 rep - 3 sets **UNLOAD**
79% - 3 reps
82% - 3 reps
85% - 2 reps - 2 sets
91% - 1 rep - 3 sets
85% - 1 rep **UNLOAD**

Advanced: Off-Season/Preseason Program
LOS and LB

Advanced OFF SEASON   SPEED AGILITY QUICKNESS CONDITIONING SCHEDULE   WEEK 1 PHASE 1 LOS and LB

MONDAY	TUESDAY	WEDNESDAY	THURSDAY	FRIDAY
Pre-Strength Workout	**Pre-Strength Workout**	**Active Rest**	**Pre-Strength Workout**	**Pre-Strength Workout**
Dot Drills 4-5 sets: 10-15 seconds 1. In and Out 2. Figure 8—both feet right side 3. Figure 8—both feet left side 4. In and Out Spins 5. Make up your own pattern	**Jump Rope** with movement 20 yards 1. Running 2. Double Leg Hops Forward and Lateral 3. Single Leg Hops Right and Left 4. Running	**Competitive Games** Basketball Volleyball Tag Football Racquetball, etc.	**Speed Ladder** 5-7 sets 1. Run Through 2. Lateral 2 Feet in, 2 Feet out 3. Lateral Shuffle 4. Slalom Jumps 5. Hop Scotch 6. Ickey Shuffle	**Jump Rope**—stationary 10-20 seconds 1. Both Feet 2. Alternate Feet 3. 2 on Right, 2 on Left Foot 4. Speed Jump
Post-Strength Workout	**Post-Strength Workout**		**Post-Strength Workout**	**Post-Strength Workout**
PNF Partner Stretch Routine	**Static Stretch Routine**		**PNF Partner Stretch Routine**	**Static Stretch Routine**
Programmable Agility 1. Four-Cone Drill—4 sets (include back-pedal, shuffle, carioca, sprint)	**Conditioning** Punch—Heavy Bag 3 rounds—30 seconds Work-to-Rest Ratio—1:1		**Programmable Agility** 1. 20-yard Shuttle 4 sets: record best time	**Conditioning** 4 Modified Suicides 10 yards and back 15 yards and back 20 yards and back
Reactive Agility 1. Two-Point and Four-Point Wave Drill—2-3 sets each	**Team Builders** Two-Minute Push-ups (1 push-up every 10 seconds) Any breakdown starts group over.		**Reactive Agility** 1. Four-Cone Reaction Drill verbal cue 4-6 sets: 10-15 seconds	Linemen—22 seconds LB, TE, DE, FB, QB, Spec 20 seconds WR, DB, TB—18 seconds Work-to-Rest Ratio—1:3
Stretch Lower Back, Hamstrings	Stretch Lower Back, Hamstrings	Stretch Lower Back, Hamstrings	Stretch Lower Back, Hamstrings	Stretch Lower Back, Hamstrings

Advanced OFF SEASON Phase 1

LOS and LB WEEK 1

Strength Power Workout

MONDAY	TUESDAY	THURSDAY	FRIDAY
Dot Drills—4-5 sets – 10-15 seconds	Jump Rope—4-5 sets - 15 seconds	Speed Ladder—5-7 sets	Jump Rope—1½ minutes
Abs Hanging Leg Raises—2 sets: 20 reps Medicine Ball Stack Crunches 2 sets: 20 reps **Power** Push Jerks (warmup—5 reps) 61%—5 reps 64%—5 reps 67%—5 reps **Legs** Lateral Squats—2 sets: 6 reps Back Squats (man makers) (warmup—10 reps) 50%—0—2 sets **Traps** Kazmeyer Shrugs (10-10-10)—2 sets **Lats** Pullups—3 sets: 5 reps **Lowerback, Glutes, Hamstrings** Romanian Deadlifts—3 sets: 6 reps	**Abs** Flutterkicks—30 seconds Bicycle Abs—30 seconds **Power** Box Jumps—3 sets: 5 reps **Chest, Shoulder, Arm** Bench Press (warmup—10 reps) 61%—10 reps 64%—10 reps 67%—10 reps Incline Dumbbell Bench Press (stop and stab) 3 sets: 8 reps **Tricep** Weighted Dips—3 set: 8 reps **Bicep, Forearm** Dumbbell Hammer Curls 3 sets: 8 reps **Flexibility—Grip** Bar Hang—1:00 **Neck** Neck Iso with partner 1 set: 6 reps	**Abs** Hanging Leg Raises—2 sets: 20 reps Medicine Ball Stack Crunches 2 sets: 20 reps **Power** Olympic Deadlifts to Knee 3 sets: 3 reps Hang Cleans below Knee warmup—5 reps Clean Pulls from Floor 64%—3 reps 67%—3 reps 70%—10 reps **Legs** Front Squats—4 sets: 6 reps **Lats** Lat Pulldowns (front, underhand) 3 sets: 10 reps **Lowerback, Glutes** Reverse Hyperextensions 2 sets: 20 reps	**Abs** Hokie Leg Raises—1 set: 20 reps ABC Sit-Ups—1 set: 10 reps **Power** Hang Snatch (Speed!) 4 sets: 3 reps **Chest, Shoulder, Tricep** Incline Bench Press 3 sets: 10 reps Dumbbell Bench Press (stop and stab) 3 sets: 10 reps **Tricep** Lying Tricep Extensions (with curl or straight bar) 3 sets: 10 reps **Bicep** Barbell Curls (6-6-6)—3 sets **Flexibility—Grip** Bar Hang—minute **Neck** Neck Machine—1 set: 10 reps
PNF Partner Stretch See Agility Conditioning Schedule	**PNF Partner Stretch** See Agility Conditioning Schedule	**PNF Partner Stretch** See Agility Conditioning Schedule	**PNF Partner Stretch** See Agility Conditioning Schedule

Advanced OFF SEASON   SPEED AGILITY QUICKNESS CONDITIONING SCHEDULE   WEEK 2 PHASE 1 LOS and LB

MONDAY	TUESDAY	WEDNESDAY	THURSDAY	FRIDAY
Pre-Strength Workout	**Pre-Strength Workout**	**Active Rest**	**Pre-Strength Workout**	**Pre-Strength Workout**
<u>Dot Drills</u> 4-5 sets: 10-15 seconds 1. In and Out 2. Figure 8—both feet right side 3. Figure 8—both feet left side 4. In and Out Spins 5. Make up your own pattern **Post-Strength Workout** **PNF Partner Stretch Routine** <u>Programmable Agility</u> Bag Drills 1. Run Through 2. Lateral Shuffle 3. Double Leg Hops 4. Zig-Zag 5. Run Through <u>Reactive Agility</u> 1. Four-Cone Reaction Drill visual cues 4-6 sets: 10 seconds	**Jump Rope** <u>with movement</u> 20 yards 1. Running 2. Double Leg Hops Forward and Lateral 3. Single Leg Hops Right and Left 4. Running **Post-Strength Workout** **Static Stretch Routine** <u>Conditioning</u> Starts—Football Stance 4-6 sets Bear Crawls (all variations—forward lateral, backward, etc.) 2 sets: 10 yards each <u>Team Builders</u> Big 5—5 "perfect" push-ups, 5 "perfect" sit-ups (then 4 and 4, 3 and 3, etc.)	**Competitive Games** Basketball Volleyball Tag Football Racquetball, etc.	<u>Speed Ladder</u> 5-7 sets 1. Run Through 2. Lateral 2 Feet in, 2 Feet out 3. Lateral Shuffle 4. Slalom Jumps 5. Hop Scotch 6. Ickey Shuffle **Post-Strength Workout** **PNF Partner Stretch Routine** <u>Programmable Agility</u> 1. Four Corner Drill 4 sets <u>Reactive Agility</u> 1. Four-Cone Reaction Drill verbal cue 4-6 sets: 10-15 seconds	**Jump Rope**—stationary 10-20 seconds 1. Both Feet 2. Alternate Feet 3. 2 on Right, 2 on Left Foot 4. Speed Jump **Post-Strength Workout** **Static Stretch Routine** <u>Conditioning</u> 5 Modified Suicides 10 yards and back 15 yards and back 20 yards and back Linemen—22 seconds LB, TE, DE, FB, QB, Spec 20 seconds WR, DB, TB—18 seconds Work-to-Rest Ratio—1:3
Stretch Lower Back, Hamstrings	Stretch Lower Back, Hamstrings	Stretch Lower Back, Hamstrings	Stretch Lower Back, Hamstrings	Stretch Lower Back, Hamstrings

Advanced OFF SEASON
Phase 1

Strength Power
Workout

LOS and LB
WEEK 2

MONDAY	TUESDAY	THURSDAY	FRIDAY
Dot Drills—4-5 sets – 10-15 seconds	Jump Rope—4-5 sets - 15 seconds	Speed Ladder—5-7 sets	Jump Rope—1½ minutes
Abs Hanging Leg Raises—2 sets: 20 reps Medicine Ball Stack Crunches 2 sets: 20 reps	**Abs** Flutterkicks—30 seconds Bicycle Abs—30 seconds	**Abs** Hanging Leg Raises—2 sets: 20 reps Medicine Ball Stack Crunches 2 sets: 20 reps	**Abs** Hokie Leg Raises—1 set: 20 reps ABC Sit-Ups—1 set: 10 reps
Power Push Jerks (warmup—5 reps) 61%—5 reps 64%—5 reps 67%—5 reps 70%—5 reps	**Power** Box Jumps—3 sets: 5 reps	**Power** Olympic Deadlifts to Knee 3 sets: 3 reps Hang Cleans below Knee (warmup—5 reps) 61%—3 reps 64%—3 reps 67%—3 reps—2 sets Clean Pulls from Floor 67%—3 reps 70%—3 reps 73%—3 reps	**Power** Hang Snatch (Speed!) 4 sets: 3 reps
Legs Lateral Squats—2 sets: 6 reps Back Squats (warmup—10 reps) 61%—8 reps 64%—8 reps 67%—8 reps 70%—8 reps	**Chest, Shoulder, Arm** Bench Press (warmup—8 reps) 61%—8 reps 64%—8 reps 67%—8 reps 70%—8 reps Incline Dumbbell Bench Press (stop and stab) 3 sets: 8 reps	**Legs** Front Squats—4 sets: 6 reps	**Chest, Shoulder, Tricep** Incline Bench Press 3 sets: 8 reps Dumbbell Bench Press (stop and stab) 3 sets: 8 reps
Traps Kazmeyer Shrugs (10-10-10)—2 sets	**Tricep** Weighted Dips—3 set: 8 reps	**Lats** Lat Pulldowns (to front, underhand) 3 sets: 10 reps	**Tricep** Lying Tricep Extensions (with curl or straight bar) 3 sets: 10 reps
Lats Pullups—3 sets: 5 reps	**Bicep, Forearm** Dumbbell Hammer Curls 3 sets: 8 reps	**Lowerback, Glutes** Reverse Hyperextensions 2 sets: 20 reps	**Bicep** Barbell Curls (6-6-6)—3 sets
Lowerback, Glutes, Hamstrings Romanian Deadlifts—3 sets: 6 reps	**Flexibility—Grip** Bar Hang—1 minute		**Flexibility—Grip** Bar Hang—1 minute
	Neck Neck Iso with partner 1 set: 6 reps		**Neck** Neck Machine—1 set: 10 reps
PNF Partner Stretch See Agility Conditioning Schedule	**PNF Partner Stretch** See Agility Conditioning Schedule	**PNF Partner Stretch** See Agility Conditioning Schedule	**PNF Partner Stretch** See Agility Conditioning Schedule

Advanced OFF SEASON   SPEED AGILITY QUICKNESS CONDITIONING SCHEDULE   WEEK 3 PHASE 1 LOS and LB

MONDAY	TUESDAY	WEDNESDAY	THURSDAY	FRIDAY
Pre-Strength Workout	**Pre-Strength Workout**	**Active Rest**	**Pre-Strength Workout**	**Pre-Strength Workout**
Dot Drills 4-5 sets: 10-15 seconds 1. In and Out 2. Figure 8—both feet right side 3. Figure 8—both feet left side 4. In and Out Spins 5. Make up your own pattern	**Jump Rope** with movement 20 yards 1. Running 2. Double Leg Hops Forward and Lateral 3. Single Leg Hops Right and Left 4. Running	**Competitive Games** Basketball Volleyball Tag Football Racquetball, etc.	**Speed Ladder** 5-7 sets 1. Run Through 2. Lateral 2 Feet in, 2 Feet out 3. Lateral Shuffle 4. Slalom Jumps 5. Hop Scotch 6. Ickey Shuffle	**Jump Rope**—stationary 10-20 seconds 1. Both Feet 2. Alternate Feet 3. 2 on Right, 2 on Left Foot 4. Speed Jump
Post-Strength Workout	**Post-Strength Workout**		**Post-Strength Workout**	**Post-Strength Workout**
PNF Partner Stretch Routine	**Static Stretch Routine**		**PNF Partner Stretch Routine**	**Static Stretch Routine**
Programmable Agility 1. 20-yard Shuttle 4 sets: record best time	**Conditioning** 1. Bear Crawls (all variations—forward lateral, backward, etc.) 2 sets: 20 yards each		**Programmable Agility** 1. Pattern Runs include speed cuts, and power cuts 4-6 sets: 20 yards	**Conditioning** 5 Modified Suicides 10 yards and back 15 yards and back 20 yards and back Linemen—22 seconds LB, TE, DE, FB, QB, Spec 20 seconds WR, DB, TB—18 seconds Work-to-Rest Ratio—1:3
Reactive Agility 1. Eight-Cone Reaction Drill visual cues 4-6 sets: 10 seconds	**Team Builders** 1. Big 8-8 "perfect" push-ups, 8 "perfect" sit-ups, 8 "perfect" up-downs		**Acceleration** 1. Acceleration Ladder 6 sets: 20 yards	
Stretch Lower Back, Hamstrings	Stretch Lower Back, Hamstrings	Stretch Lower Back, Hamstrings	Stretch Lower Back, Hamstrings	Stretch Lower Back, Hamstrings

**LOS and LB
WEEK 3**

**Advanced OFF SEASON
Phase 1**

**Strength Power
Workout**

MONDAY	TUESDAY	THURSDAY	FRIDAY
Dot Drills—4-5 sets – 10-15 seconds	Jump Rope—4-5 sets - 15 seconds	Speed Ladder—5-7 sets	Jump Rope—1½ minutes
Abs Hanging Leg Raises—2 sets: 20 reps Medicine Ball Stack Crunches 2 sets: 20 reps	**Abs** Flutterkicks—30 seconds Bicycle Abs—30 seconds	**Abs** Hanging Leg Raises—2 sets: 20 reps Medicine Ball Stack Crunches 2 sets: 20 reps	**Abs** Hokie Leg Raises—1 set: 20 reps ABC Sit-Ups—1 set: 10 reps
Power Push Jerks (warmup—5 reps) 61%—5 reps 64%—5 reps 67%—5 reps 73%—5 reps	**Power** Box Jumps—3 sets: 4 reps	**Power** Olympic Deadlifts to Knee 2 sets: 3 reps Push Jerks (warmup—5 reps) 61%—3 reps 64%—3 reps 67%—3 reps 73%—3 reps	**Power** Hang Snatch (Speed!) 4 sets: 3 reps
Legs Lateral Squats—2 sets: 6 reps Back Squats (warmup—8 reps) 58%—6 reps 64%—6 reps 70%—6 reps 76%—6 reps	**Chest, Shoulder, Arm** Bench Press (warmup—8 reps) 58%—6 reps 64%—6 reps 70%—6 reps 76%—6 reps—2 sets Incline Dumbbell Bench Press (stop and stab) 4 sets: 6 reps	Clean Pulls from Floor 76%—3 reps 79%—3 reps	**Chest, Shoulder, Tricep** Incline Bench Press 4 sets: 6 reps Dumbbell Bench Press (stop and stab) 4 sets: 6 reps
Traps Kazmeyer Shrugs (10-10-10)—2 sets	**Tricep** Weighted Dips—3 set: 8 reps	**Legs** Front Squats—4 sets: 6 reps	**Tricep** Lying Tricep Extensions (with curl or straight bar) 4 sets: 8 reps
Lats Pullups—3 sets: 5 reps	**Bicep, Forearm** Dumbbell Hammer Curls 3—sets: 8 reps	**Lats** Lat Pulldowns (front, underhand) 3 sets: 8 reps	**Bicep** Barbell Curls—3 sets : 10 reps
Lowerback, Glutes, Hamstrings Romanian Deadlifts—3 sets: 6 reps	**Flexibility—Grip** Bar Hang—1-1:30 minutes	**Lowerback, Glutes** Glute Ham Raises 2 sets: 6-8 reps	**Flexibility—Grip** Bar Hang—1-1:30 minutes
	Neck Neck Iso with partner 1—set: 6 reps		**Neck** Neck Machine—1 set: 10 reps
PNF Partner Stretch See Agility Conditioning Schedule	**PNF Partner Stretch** See Agility Conditioning Schedule	**PNF Partner Stretch** See Agility Conditioning Schedule	**PNF Partner Stretch** See Agility Conditioning Schedule

Advanced OFF SEASON   SPEED AGILITY QUICKNESS CONDITIONING SCHEDULE   WEEK 4 PHASE 2 LOS and LB

MONDAY	TUESDAY	WEDNESDAY	THURSDAY	FRIDAY
Pre-Strength Workout	**Pre-Strength Workout**	**Active Rest**	**Pre-Strength Workout**	**Pre-Strength Workout**
Dot Drills 4-5 sets—10-15 seconds 1. In and Out 2. Figure 8—both feet right side 3. Figure 8—both feet left side 4. In and Out Spins 5. Make up your own pattern	**Jump Rope** with movement 20 yards 1. Running 2. Double Leg Hops Forward and Lateral 3. Single Leg Hops Right and Left 4. Running	**Competitive Games** Basketball Volleyball Tag Football Racquetball, etc.	**Speed Ladder** 5-7 sets 1. Run Through 2. Lateral 2 Feet in, 2 Feet out 3. Lateral Shuffle 4. Slalom Jumps 5. Hop Scotch 6. Ickey Shuffle	**Jump Rope**—stationary 10-20 seconds 1. Both Feet 2. Alternate Feet 3. 2 on Right, 2 on Left Foot 4. Speed Jump
Post-Strength Workout	**Post-Strength Workout**		**Post-Strength Workout**	**Post-Strength Workout**
PNF Partner Stretch Routine	**Static Stretch Routine**		**PNF Partner Stretch Routine**	**Static Stretch Routine**
Programmable Agility 1. Carolina Drill—4 sets	**Conditioning** Punch Heavy Bag 3-4 rounds—30 seconds Work-to-Rest Ratio—1:1		**Programmable Agility** 1. Texas-Drill—4 sets	**Conditioning** 5 Modified Suicides 10 yards and back 15 yards and back 20 yards and back Linemen—22 seconds LB, TE, DE, FB, QB, Spec 20 seconds WR, DB, TB—18 seconds Work-to-Rest Ratio—1:3
Reactive Agility 1. Two-Point and Four-Point Wave Drill 2-3 sets each	**Acceleration** 1. Sled Pulls 4-6 sets: 20 yards (50 pounds max weight on sled)		**Reactive Agility** 1. Four-Cone Reaction Drill verbal cues 4 sets: 4 seconds	
Competitive Drill 1. Get Up and Sprint (vary start) 4-6 sets: 20 yards				
Stretch Lower Back, Hamstrings	Stretch Lower Back, Hamstrings	Stretch Lower Back, Hamstrings	Stretch Lower Back, Hamstrings	Stretch Lower Back, Hamstrings

LOS and LB
WEEK 4

Advanced OFF SEASON
Phase 2

Strength Power
Workout

MONDAY	TUESDAY	THURSDAY	FRIDAY
Dot Drills—4-5 sets – 10-15 seconds	Jump Rope—Running, Hops	Speed Ladder—5-7 sets	Jump Rope—1½ minutes

Abs
Timed Leg Throws—30 seconds
Timed Sit-Ups—30 seconds
 	
Power
Push Jerks (warmup—5 reps)
  61%—5 reps
  64%—5 reps
  70%—5 reps
  76%—3 reps—2 sets
 	
Legs
Extended Squats—2 sets: 6 reps
Back Squats (warmup—8 reps)
  61%—5 reps
  67%—5 reps
  73%—5 reps
  79%—5 reps
 	
Traps
Dumbbell Shrugs
3 sets: 10 reps
 	
Lats
Bent Over Rows—4 sets: 6 reps
 	
Lower Back, Glutes, Hamstrings
Reverse Hyperextensions
2 sets: 15 reps
	Abs
	Hanging Leg Raises—2 sets: 20 reps
	Medicine Ball Stack Crunches
	2 sets: 20 reps
	
	Power
	Explosive Box Stepups
	3 sets: 4 reps
	
	Chest, Shoulder, Tricep
	Bench Press (warmup—8 reps)
	  64%—5 reps
	  70%—5 reps
	  76%—5 reps
	  82%—5 reps
	Alternate Incline Dumbbell Bench
	Press (stop and stab)
	3 sets: 5 reps
	
	Shoulder
	Seated Plate Raises—2 sets: 20 reps
	
	Bicep
	Incline Dumbbell Curls
	3 sets: 8 reps
	
	Flexibility—Grip
	Bar Hang—1-1:30 minutes
	
	Neck
	Neck Iso with partner—1 set: 6 reps
	or
	Neck Machine—1 set: 10 reps
		Abs
		Flutterkicks—30 seconds
		Twisting Sit-Ups—1 set: 20 reps
		
		Power
		Olympic Deadlifts to Knee
		2 sets: 3 reps
		Push Jerks (warmup—3 reps)
		  58%—3 reps
		  64%—3 reps
		  70%—3 reps
		  76%—3 reps—2 sets
		Clean Pulls from Floor
		  79%—3 reps
		  82%—3 reps
		
		Legs
		Speed Squats (pause at bottom)
		50% of max—4 sets: 5 reps
		Lateral Squats—2 sets: 6 reps
		
		Lats
		Pullups (vary grip)
		3 sets: 5 reps
		
		Lowerback, Glutes, Hamstrings
		Glute Ham Raises
		2 sets: 6-8 reps
			Abs
			Big 40s—1 set
			Twisting Stack Crunches
			2 sets: 20 reps
			
			Power
			Hang Snatch (Speed!)
			4 sets: 3 reps
			
			Chest, Shoulder, Tricep
			Close Grip Bench Press
			(stop and stab)
			5 sets: 5 reps
			
			Shoulder
			Dumbbell Seated Alternate
			Shoulder Press
			3 sets: 6 reps
			
			Tricep
			Dumbbell Tricep Extensions
			(15-second rest between sets)
			5 sets: 8 reps
			
			Bicep
			Curlbar Curls—3 sets: 10 reps
			
			Flexibility—Grip
			Grippers—2 round trips
			
			Neck
			Neck Machine—1 set: 10 reps
			or
			Neck Iso—1 set: 6 reps

PNF Partner Stretch See Agility Conditioning Schedule	**PNF Partner Stretch** See Agility Conditioning Schedule	**PNF Partner Stretch** See Agility Conditioning Schedule	**PNF Partner Stretch** See Agility Conditioning Schedule

Advanced OFF SEASON — SPEED AGILITY QUICKNESS CONDITIONING SCHEDULE — WEEK 5 PHASE 2 LOS and LB

MONDAY	TUESDAY	WEDNESDAY	THURSDAY	FRIDAY
Pre-Strength Workout	**Pre-Strength Workout**	**Active Rest**	**Pre-Strength Workout**	**Pre-Strength Workout**
Dot Drills 4-5 sets: 10-15 seconds 1. In and Out 2. Figure 8—both feet right side 3. Figure 8—both feet left side 4. In and Out Spins 5. Make up your own pattern	**Jump Rope** with movement 20 yards 1. Running 2. Double Leg Hops Forward and Lateral 3. Single Leg Hops Right and Left 4. Running	**Competitive Games** Basketball Volleyball Tag Football Racquetball, etc.	**Speed Ladder** 5-7 sets 1. Run Through 2. Lateral 2 Feet in, 2 Feet out 3. Lateral Shuffle 4. Slalom Jumps 5. Hop Scotch 6. Ickey Shuffle	**Jump Rope**—stationary 10-20 seconds 1. Both Feet 2. Alternate Feet 3. 2 on Right, 2 on Left Foot 4. Speed Jump
Post-Strength Workout	**Post-Strength Workout**		**Post-Strength Workout**	**Post-Strength Workout**
PNF Partner Stretch Routine	**Static Stretch Routine**		**PNF Partner Stretch Routine**	**Static Stretch Routine**
Programmable Agility 1. 20-yard Shuttle 4 sets: record best time	**Acceleration** 1. Acceleration Ladder 6 sets: 20 yards Starts—Football Stance 4-6 sets		**Programmable Agility** 1. Carolina Drill—4 sets	**Conditioning** 5 Modified Suicides 10 yards and back 15 yards and back 20 yards and back Linemen—22 seconds LB, TE, DE, FB, QB, Spec 20 seconds WR, DB, TB—18 seconds Work-to-Rest Ratio—1:3
Reactive Agility 1. Tennis Ball Drills (all variations) 8-10 sets	**Competitive Drill** 1. Shark in a Tank 6-8 sets: 10 seconds		**Acceleration** 1. Sled Pulls 6 sets: 20 yards	
			Team Builders 1. Two-Minute Push-ups 1 push-up every 10 seconds (One man breaks all men repeat.)	
Stretch Lower Back, Hamstrings	Stretch Lower Back, Hamstrings	Stretch Lower Back, Hamstrings	Stretch Lower Back, Hamstrings	Stretch Lower Back, Hamstrings

LOS and LB WEEK 5 — Advanced OFF SEASON Phase 2 — Strength Power Workout

MONDAY	TUESDAY	THURSDAY	FRIDAY
Dot Drills—4-5 sets – 10-15 seconds	Jump Rope—Running, Hops	Speed Ladder—5-7 sets	Jump Rope—1½ minutes
Abs Timed Leg Throws—30 seconds Timed Sit-Ups—30 seconds **Power** Push Jerks (warmup—5 reps) 61%—3 reps 67%—3 reps 73%—3 reps 79%—3 reps—2 sets **Legs** Extended Squats—2 sets: 5 reps Back Squats (warmup—8 reps) 61%—3 reps 67%—3 reps 73%—3 reps 79%—3 reps 85%—3 reps **Traps** Dumbbell Shrugs 3 sets: 10 reps **Lats** Bent Over Rows—4 sets: 6 reps **Lower Back, Glutes, Hamstrings** Reverse Hyperextensions 2 sets: 15 reps	**Abs** Hanging Leg Raises—2 sets: 20 reps Medicine Ball Stack Crunches 2 sets: 20 reps **Power** Explosive Box Stepups 3 sets: 4 reps **Chest, Shoulder, Tricep** Bench Press (warmup—8 reps) 61%—5 reps 67%—5 reps 73%—3 reps 79%—3 reps 85%—3 reps—2 sets Alternate Incline Dumbbell Bench Press (stop and stab) 3 sets: 5 reps **Shoulder** Seated Plate Raises—2 sets: 20 reps **Bicep** Incline Dumbbell Curls 3 sets: 8 reps **Flexibility—Grip** Bar Hang—1-1:30 minutes **Neck** Neck Iso with partner—1 set: 6 reps or Neck Machine—1 set: 10 reps	**Abs** Flutterkicks—30 seconds Twisting Sit-Ups—1 set: 20 reps **Power** Olympic Deadlifts to Knee 2 sets: 3 reps Power Cleans (warmup—3 reps) 61%—3 reps 67%—3 reps 73%—3 reps 79%—3 reps—2 sets Clean Pulls from Floor 2 sets—3 reps 82%—3 reps 85%—3 reps **Legs** Speed Squats (pause at bottom) 50% of max—4 sets: 5 reps Lateral Squats—2 sets: 5 reps **Lats** Pullups (vary grip) 3 sets: 5 reps **Lower Back, Glutes, Hamstrings** Glute Ham Raises 3 sets: 6-8 reps	**Abs** Big 40s—1 set Twisting Stack Crunches 2 sets: 20 reps **Power** Power Snatch 4 sets: 3 reps **Chest, Shoulder, Tricep** Close Grip Bench Press (stop and stab) 5 sets: 5 reps **Shoulder** Dumbbell Seated Alternate Shoulder Press 4 sets: 5 reps **Tricep** Dumbbell Tricep Extensions (15-second rest between sets) 5 sets: 8 reps **Bicep** Curls—3 sets: 8-10 reps **Flexibility—Grip** Grippers—2 round trips **Neck** Neck Machine—1 set: 10 reps or Neck Iso—1 set: 6 reps
PNF Partner Stretch	**PNF Partner Stretch**	**PNF Partner Stretch**	**PNF Partner Stretch**
See Agility Conditioning Schedule	See Agility Conditioning Schedule	See Agility Conditioning Schedule	See Agility Conditioning Schedule

257

Advanced OFF SEASON   SPEED AGILITY QUICKNESS CONDITIONING SCHEDULE   WEEK 6 PHASE 2 LOS and LB

MONDAY	TUESDAY	WEDNESDAY	THURSDAY	FRIDAY
Pre-Strength Workout	**Pre-Strength Workout**	**Active Rest**	**Pre-Strength Workout**	**Pre-Strength Workout**
Dot Drills 4–5 sets: 10-15 seconds 1. In and Out 2. Figure 8—both feet right side 3. Figure 8—both feet left side 4. In and Out Spins 5. Make up your own pattern	**Jump Rope** with movement 20 yards 1. Running 2. Double Leg Hops Forward and Lateral 3. Single Leg Hops Right and Left 4. Running	**Competitive Games** Basketball Volleyball Tag Football Racquetball, etc.	**Speed Ladder** 5-7 sets 1. Run Through 2. Lateral 2 Feet in, 2 Feet out 3. Lateral Shuffle 4. Slalom Jumps 5. Hop Scotch 6. Ickey Shuffle	**Jump Rope**—stationary 10-20 seconds 1. Both Feet 2. Alternate Feet 3. 2 on Right, 2 on Left Foot 4. Speed Jump
Post-Strength Workout	**Post-Strength Workout**		**Post-Strength Workout**	**Post-Strength Workout**
PNF Partner Stretch Routine	**Static Stretch Routine**		**PNF Partner Stretch Routine**	**Static Stretch Routine**

Programmable Agility
1. Hourglass Drill—4 sets
	Reactive Agility
	1. Eight-Cone Reaction Drill visual cues
	45 sets: 10 seconds
			Acceleration
			Starts—Football Stance
			4-6 sets
				Conditioning
				5 Modified Suicides
				    10 yards and back
				    15 yards and back
				    20 yards and back
				Linemen,—22 seconds
				LB, TE, DE, FB, QB, Spec 20 seconds
				WR, DB, TB—18 seconds
				Work-to-Rest Ratio—1:3

Reactive Agility 1. Two-Point and Four-Point Wave Drill 2-3 sets each	**Acceleration** 1. Sled Pulls 6 sets: 20 yards (50 pounds max weight on sled) or 2. Uphill Runs 6-8 sets: 30 yards (sprint up, walk down)		**Programmable Agility** Bag Drills 1. Run Through 2. Lateral Shuffle 3. Double Leg Hops 4. Zig-Zag 5. Run Through	
Competitive Drill 1. Get Up and Sprint (vary start) 4-6 sets: 20 yards			**Team Builders** Big 10—10 "perfect" push-ups, 10 "perfect" sit-ups, 10 "perfect" up-downs (One man breaks all men repeat.)	
Stretch Lower Back, Hamstrings	Stretch Lower Back, Hamstrings	Stretch Lower Back, Hamstrings	Stretch Lower Back, Hamstrings	Stretch Lower Back, Hamstrings

LOS and LB
WEEK 6

Advanced OFF SEASON
Phase 2

Strength Power
Workout

MONDAY	TUESDAY	THURSDAY	FRIDAY
Dot Drills—4-5 sets – 10-15 seconds	Jump Rope—Running, Hops	Speed Ladder—5-7 sets	Jump Rope—1½ minutes
Abs Timed Leg Throws—30 seconds Timed Sit-Ups—30 seconds **Power** Push Jerks (warmup—5 reps) 64%—3 reps 70%—3 reps 76%—3 reps 82%—3 reps—2 sets **Legs** Extended Squats—2 sets: 5 reps Back Squats (warmup—5 reps) 64%—5 reps 70%—3 reps 76%—3 reps 82%—3 reps 88%—3 reps **Traps** Dumbbell Shrugs—3 sets: 10 reps Dumbbell Rows—3 sets: 8 reps **Lats** Lat Pulldowns—3 sets: 10 reps **Neck** Neck Machine—1 set: 10 reps	**Abs** Hanging Leg Raises—2 sets: 20 reps Medicine Ball Stack Crunches 2 sets: 20 reps **Power** Bear Jumps—3 sets: 4 reps **Chest, Shoulder, Tricep** Bench Press (warmup—8 reps) 64%—5 reps 70%—3 reps 76%—3 reps 82%—3 reps 88%—3 reps Alternate Incline Dumbbell Bench Press (stop and stab) 4 sets: 5 reps **Shoulder** Weighted Dips—4 sets: 6 reps **Bicep** Straight Bar Curls 3 sets: 10 reps **Neck** Neck Iso with partner—1 set: 6 reps	**Abs** Flutterkicks—30 seconds Twisting Sit-Ups—1 set: 20 reps **Power** Olympic Deadlifts to Knee 2 sets: 3 reps Power Cleans (warmup—3 reps) 61%—3 reps 67%—3 reps 73%—3 reps 79%—3 reps 82-85%—1 rep Clean Pulls from Floor 2 sets—3 reps 88%—3 reps 91%—3 reps **Legs** Box Stepups—4 sets: 5 reps Lateral Squats—2 sets: 5 reps **Lats** Pullups (vary grip) 3 sets: 5 reps **Lower Back, Glutes, Hamstrings** Glute Ham Raises—3 sets: 6-8 reps or Reverse Hyperextensions 2 sets: 15 reps	**Abs** Big 40s—1 set Twisting Stack Crunches 2 sets: 20 reps **Power** Power Snatch (Speed!) 4 sets: 3 reps **Chest, Shoulder, Tricep** Close Grip Bench Press (stop and stab) 5 sets: 5 reps **Shoulder** Dumbbell Seated Alternate Shoulder Press 4 sets: 6 reps **Tricep** Dumbbell Tricep Extensions (15-second rest between sets) 5 sets: 8 reps **Bicep** Curls—3 sets: 8-10 reps **Flexibility—Grip** Grippers—2 round trips **Neck** Neck Machine—1 set: 10 reps or Neck Iso with partner 1 set: 6 reps
PNF Partner Stretch See Agility Conditioning Schedule	**PNF Partner Stretch** See Agility Conditioning Schedule	**PNF Partner Stretch** See Agility Conditioning Schedule	**PNF Partner Stretch** See Agility Conditioning Schedule

Advanced OFF SEASON   SPEED AGILITY QUICKNESS CONDITIONING SCHEDULE   WEEK 7 PHASE 2 LOS and LB

MONDAY	TUESDAY	WEDNESDAY	THURSDAY	FRIDAY
Pre-Strength Workout	**Pre-Strength Workout**	**Active Rest**	**Pre-Strength Workout**	**Pre-Strength Workout**
Dot Drills 4-5 sets—10-15 seconds 1. In and Out 2. Figure 8—right foot only right side 3. Figure 8—left foot only left side 4. Make up your own pattern	**Jump Rope** with movement 20 yards 1. Running 2. Double Leg Hops Forward and Lateral 3. Single Leg Hops Right and Left 4. Running	**Competitive Games** Basketball Volleyball Tag Football Racquetball, etc.	**Speed Ladder** 5-7 sets 1. Run Through 2. Lateral Shuffle 3. Hop Scotch 4. Slalom Jumps 5. Backward Slalom Jumps 6. Ickey Shuffle 7. Backward Ickey Shuffle	**Jump Rope**—stationary 10-20 seconds 1. Both Feet 2. Right Foot 3. Left Foot 4. Alternate Feet 5. 2 on Right, 2 on Left Foot 6. Speed Jump
Post-Strength Workout	**Post-Strength Workout**		**Post-Strength Workout**	**Post-Strength Workout**
PNF Partner Stretch Routine	**Static Stretch Routine**		**PNF Partner Stretch Routine**	**Static Stretch Routine**
Programmable Agility 1. Texas-Drill—3-4 sets	**Reactive** 1. Crazy Ball Drills (all variations) 8-10 sets		**Programmable Agility** 1. Four-Cone Drill—4 sets (include back-pedal, shuffle, carioca, sprint)	**Conditioning** 5 Modified Suicides 10 yards and back 15 yards and back 20 yards and back Linemen—22 seconds LB, TE, DE, FB, QB, Spec 20 seconds WR, DB, TB—18 seconds Work-to-Rest Ratio—1:3
Reactive Agility 1. Four-Cone Reaction Drill verbal cues 3-4 sets: 10 seconds	**Acceleration** 1. Uphill Runs 8-10 hills—30 yards (sprint up, walk down)		**Team Builders** 1. Two-Minute Push-ups 1 push up every 10 seconds (One man breaks all men repeat.)	
Competitive Drill 1. Shark in a Tank 6-8 sets: 10 seconds				
Stretch Lower Back, Hamstrings	Stretch Lower Back, Hamstrings	Stretch Lower Back, Hamstrings	Stretch Lower Back, Hamstrings	Stretch Lower Back, Hamstrings

Strength Power Workout

Advanced OFF SEASON Phase 2

LOS and LB WEEK 7

MONDAY	TUESDAY	THURSDAY	FRIDAY
Dot Drills—4-5 sets – 10-15 seconds	Jump Rope—Running, Hops	Speed Ladder—5-7 sets	Jump Rope—1½ minutes
Abs Timed Leg Throws—30 seconds Timed Sit-Ups—30 seconds	**Abs** Hanging Leg Raises—2 sets: 20 reps Medicine Ball Stack Crunches 2 sets: 20 reps	**Abs** Flutterkicks—30 seconds Twisting Sit-Ups—1 set: 20 reps	**Abs** Big 40s—1 set Twisting Stack Crunches 2 sets: 20 reps
Power Push Jerks (warmup—5 reps) 61%—3 reps 67%—3 reps 73%—3 reps 79%—2 reps 85%—1 rep	**Power** Bear Jumps—3 sets: 4 reps	**Power** Olympic Deadlifts to Knee 2 sets: 3 reps Power Cleans (warmup—3 reps) 61%—3 reps 67%—3 reps 73%—3 reps 79%—3 reps Clean Pulls from Floor 2 sets: 3 reps 82%—3 reps 85%—3 reps	**Power** Power Snatch (Speed!) 4 sets: 3 reps
Legs Extended Squats—2 sets: 5 reps Back Squats (warmup—8 reps) 61%—3 reps 67%—3 reps 73%—3 reps 79%—3 reps 85%—2 reps 91%—1 rep—3 sets	**Chest, Shoulder, Tricep** Bench Press (warmup—8 reps) 61%—3 reps 67%—3 reps 73%—3 reps 79%—3 reps 85%—2 reps 91%—1 rep—3 sets Alternate Incline Dumbbell Bench Press (stop and stab) 4 sets: 5 reps	**Legs** Box Stepups—4 sets: 5 reps Lateral Squats—2 sets : 5 reps	**Chest, Shoulder, Tricep** Close Grip Bench Press (stop and stab) 5 sets: 5 reps
Traps Dumbbell Shrugs 3 sets: 10 reps Dumbbell Rows—3 sets: 8 reps	**Shoulder** Weighted Dips—4 sets: 6 reps	**Lats** Pullups (vary grip) 3 sets: 5 reps	**Shoulder** Dumbbell Seated Alternate Shoulder Press 4 sets: 6 reps
Lats Lat Pulldowns—3 sets: 10 reps	**Bicep** Straight Bar Curls 3 sets: 10 reps	**Lower Back, Glutes, Hamstrings** Glute Ham Raises—3 sets: 6-8 reps or Reverse Hyperextensions 2 sets: 15 reps	**Tricep** Dumbbell Tricep Extensions (15-second rest between sets) 5 sets: 8 reps
Neck Neck Machine—1 set: 10 reps	**Neck** Neck Iso with partner—1 set: 6 reps		**Bicep** Curls—3 sets: 8-10 reps
	Flexibility—Grip Bar Hang—1-1:30 minutes		**Flexibility—Grip** Grippers—2 round trips
			Neck Neck Machine—1 set: 10 reps or Neck Iso with partner 1 set: 6 reps
PNF Partner Stretch See Agility Conditioning Schedule	**PNF Partner Stretch** See Agility Conditioning Schedule	**PNF Partner Stretch** See Agility Conditioning Schedule	**PNF Partner Stretch** See Agility Conditioning Schedule

Advanced OFF SEASON   SPEED AGILITY QUICKNESS CONDITIONING SCHEDULE   WEEK 8 PHASE 2 LOS and LB

MONDAY	TUESDAY	WEDNESDAY	THURSDAY	FRIDAY
Pre-Strength Workout	**Pre-Strength Workout**	**Active Rest**	**Pre-Strength Workout**	**Pre-Strength Workout**
Dot Drills 4-5 sets—10-15 seconds 1. In and Out 2. Figure 8—both feet right side 3. Figure 8—both feet left side 4. In and Out with Spin	**Jump Rope** with movement 1. Running 2. Single Leg Hops Right and Left 3. Double Leg Hops Forward and Lateral 4. Running	**Test** Vertical Jump Test Sit and Reach Flexibility Test 10-yard Sprint Test 20-yard Shuttle Test	**Speed Ladder** 5-6 sets 1. Run Through 2. Lateral Shuffle 3. Hop Scotch 4. Ickey Shuffle 5. Backward Ickey Shuffle	**Jump Rope**—stationary 10-20 seconds 1. Both Feet 2. Right Foot 3. Left Foot 4. Alternate Feet 5. Speed Jump
Post-Max Testing	**Post-Max Testing**	Record all results.	**Post-Max Testing**	**Post-Strength Workout**
PNF Partner Stretch Routine	**Static Stretch Routine**		**PNF Partner Stretch Routine**	**Static Stretch Routine**
Programmable Agility 1. 20-yard Shuttle 3-4 sets	**Reactive Agility** 1. Eight-Cone Reaction Drill visual cues 3-4 sets: 10 seconds		**Programmable Agility** 1. Carolina Drill—3-4 sets	**Conditioning** 5 Modified Suicides 10 yards and back 15 yards and back 20 yards and back Linemen—22 seconds LB, TE, DE, FB, QB, Spec 20 seconds WR, DB, TB—18 seconds Work-to-Rest Ratio—1:3
Reactive Agility 1. Four-Cone Reaction Drill visual cues 3-4 sets: 10 seconds	**Acceleration** 1. 8 Sled Pulls 6 sets: 20 yards (50 pounds max weight on sled)		**Team Builders** 1. Big 10—10 "perfect" push-ups, 10 "perfect" sit-ups, 10 "perfect" up-downs (One man breaks all men repeat.)	
Competitive Drill 1. Get Up and Sprint (vary starting positions) 4-6 sets: 20 yards				
Stretch Lower Back, Hamstrings	Stretch Lower Back, Hamstrings	Stretch Lower Back, Hamstrings	Stretch Lower Back, Hamstrings	Stretch Lower Back, Hamstrings

LOS and LB
WEEK 8

ADVANCED OFF SEASON
Phase 2

Strength Power
MAX TESTING

MONDAY	TUESDAY	WEDNESDAY	THURSDAY	FRIDAY
Pre-Strength Workout	Pre-Strength Workout	TEST	Pre-Strength Workout	Pre-Strength Workout
Dot Drills 4-5 sets: 10-15 seconds **Abs** Figure Four Double Crunches 2 sets: 10 reps (switch crossover legs at 10 and repeat) **Test**—Back Squats (warmup—8 reps) 55%—5 reps 64%—3 reps 73%—3 reps 82%—1 rep 88%—1 rep Begin 3 rep max attempts.	**Jump Rope** with movement **Abs** Big 40s—1 set Medicine Ball Stack Crunches 2 sets: 20 yards **Test**—Push Jerks (warmup—3 reps) 55%—3 reps 64%—1 rep 73%—1 rep 82%—1 rep 88%—1 rep Begin 1 rep max attempts.	**Test**—Vertical Jump **Test**—Sit and Reach, Hamstring Stretch **Test**—10-yard (electronically timed) **Test**—20-yard Shuttle (electronically timed) Record all results.	**Speed Ladder** **Abs** Vertical Figure Eights (hold small dumbbell between feet while doing the exercise) 1 set: 10 reps **Test**—Power Cleans (warmup—3 reps) 55%—3 reps 64%—1-2 reps 73%—1 rep 82%—1 rep 88-91%—1 rep Begin 1 rep max attempts.	**Jump Rope** with movement **Abs** Hokie Leg Raises 2 sets: 20 reps Twisting Stack Crunches 2 sets: 20 reps **Test**—Bench Press (warmup—8 reps) 55%—5 reps 64%—3 reps 73%—1 rep 82%—1 rep 88%—1 rep 94%—1 rep Begin 1 rep max attempts.
Stretch Lower Back, Hamstrings	Stretch Lower Back, Hamstrings	Stretch Lower Back, Hamstrings	Stretch Lower Back, Hamstrings	Stretch Lower Back, Hamstrings

Advanced OFF SEASON   SPEED AGILITY QUICKNESS CONDITIONING SCHEDULE   WEEK 9 PHASE 2 LOS and LB

MONDAY	TUESDAY	WEDNESDAY	THURSDAY	FRIDAY
Pre-Strength Workout	Pre-Strength Workout	Active Rest	Pre-Strength Workout	Pre-Strength Workout

Active Rest

Play basketball, volleyball, tag, football, racquetball, etc.

STAY OUT OF THE WEIGHT ROOM!

| Stretch Lower Back, Hamstrings | Stretch Lower Back, Hamstrings | Stretch Lower Back, Hamstrings | Stretch Lower Back, Hamstrings | Stretch Lower Back, Hamstrings |

LOS and LB
WEEK 9

ADVANCED OFF SEASON
Phase 2

Strength Power
MAX TESTING

MONDAY	TUESDAY	WEDNESDAY	THURSDAY	FRIDAY
Pre-Strength Workout	Pre-Strength Workout	TEST	Pre-Strength Workout	Pre-Strength Workout
Stretch Lower Back, Hamstrings	Stretch Lower Back, Hamstrings	Stretch Lower Back, Hamstrings	Stretch Lower Back, Hamstrings	Stretch Lower Back, Hamstrings

Active Rest

Play basketball, volleyball, tag, football, racquetball, etc.

STAY OUT OF THE WEIGHT ROOM!

Advanced PRESEASON   SPEED AGILITY QUICKNESS CONDITIONING SCHEDULE   WEEK 1 PHASE 1 LOS and LB

MONDAY	TUESDAY	WEDNESDAY	THURSDAY	FRIDAY
Pre-Strength Workout	Pre-Strength Workout	Active Rest	Pre-Strength Workout	Pre-Strength Workout

Dynamic Warmup
Walking Toe Touches
Backward High Knees
Power Skips
Low Shuffle
2 sets: 20 yards
 	
Foot Speed
Dot Drills
3-4 sets: 10-15 seconds
 	
Post-Strength Workout
 	
Static Stretch Routine
 	
Programmable Agility
1. Texas-Drill—3 sets
2. 20-yard Shuttle
3-4 sets: record best time
 	
Reactive Agility
1. Two-Point and Four-Point
  Wave Drill
4 sets: 10-15 seconds
 	
Conditioning
Punch Heavy Bag
3 rounds—30 seconds
Work-to-Rest Ratio—1:1
	Dynamic Warmup
	Walking Knee Hugs
	High Knee Crossovers
	Backward Skips
	Starts—Football Stance
	2 sets: 20 yards
	
	Foot Speed
	Jump Rope—moving
	1. Running
	2. Double Leg Hops
	3. Single Leg Hops
	4. Lateral Double Leg Hops
	5. Running
	
	Post-Strength Workout
	
	PNF Partner Stretch
	
	Conditioning
	400 meters—3
	OL, DT—1:50 minutes
	DE, LB, TE—1:35 minutes
	Rest 4 minutes between 400s.
		Competitive Games
		Basketball
		Racquetball
		Tag Football
		Martial Arts, etc.
		
		or
		
		Choose 1-2:
		  Programmable Agility
		  Drills and 1-2 Reactive
		  Agility Drills and 1-2
		  Position Specific Drills
			Dynamic Warmup
			Walking/Skipping Toe
			  Touches
			Walking/Skipping Knee
			  Hugs
			Backward High Knees
			Low Carioca
			Starts—Football Stance
			2 sets: 20 yards
			
			Foot Speed
			Speed Ladder—5-6 sets
			
			Post-Strength Workout
			
			PNF Partner Stretch
			
			Programmable Agility
			1. Pattern Runs—4 sets
			  (include speed cuts,
			  power cuts, and spins)
			
			Reactive Agility
			1. Four-Cone Reaction Drill
			  visual cues
			3-4 sets: 10-15 seconds
			
			Competitive Drill
			1. Shark in a Tank
			6-7 sets: 10 seconds
				Dynamic Warmup
				Walking Toe Touches
				Skipping Toe Touches
				High Knee Crossovers
				Backward Skips
				Low Shuffle
				2 sets: 20 yards
				
				Foot Speed
				Jump Rope—stationary
				4-6 sets: 10-20 seconds
				
				Post-Strength Workout
				
				Static Stretch Routine
				
				Conditioning
				400 meters—3
				OL, DT—1:50 minutes
				DE, LB, TE—1:35
				  minutes
				Rest 4 minutes between
				400s.

Stretch Lower Back, Hamstrings	Stretch Lower Back, Hamstrings	Stretch Lower Back, Hamstrings	Stretch Lower Back, Hamstrings	Stretch Lower Back, Hamstrings

ADVANCED PRESEASON
Phase 1

WRITE DOWN YOUR GOALS
VISUALIZE SUCCESS!

LOS and LB
WEEK 1

MONDAY	TUESDAY	WEDNESDAY	THURSDAY	FRIDAY
Dot Drills - 4 sets - 10-15 seconds	Jump Rope—Running, Hops, etc.	Active Rest	Speed Ladder—5-7 sets	Jump Rope—1½ minutes
Abdominal Exercises Hanging Leg Raises 2 sets: 20 reps Medicine Ball Stack Crunches 2 sets: 20 reps **Push Jerks** (warmup—5 reps) 55%—5 reps 61%—5 reps 67%—5 reps 70%—5 reps **Back Squats** (warmup—10 reps) 55%—10 reps 61%—10 reps—(2 sets) **Lateral Squats** 2 sets: 6 reps **One-Arm Dumbbell Rows** 3 sets: 10 reps **Offense: Reverse Hyperextensions** 2 sets: 15 reps **Defense: Glute Ham Raises** 2 sets: 10 reps **Bear Calf Raises** 1 set: 20 reps	**Abdominal Exercises** Hokie Leg Raises 1 set: 20 reps Twisting Sit-Ups 1 set: 20 reps ABC Sit-Ups 1 set: 10 reps **Hang Clean-Front Squat Combo** (warmup 5 reps) 50%—3 reps 55%—3 reps 58%—3 reps—(2 sets) **Power Shrugs** 3 sets: 8 reps **Bench Press** (warmup—10 reps) 55%—10 reps 61%—10 reps 64%—10 reps **Incline Dumbbell Bench Press** (stop and stab) 3 sets: 10 reps **Straight Bar Curls** 3 sets: 10 reps **Straight Bar Lying Tricep Ext.** 3 sets: 20, 15, 12 reps **Medicine Ball Plyo Push-ups** 1 set: 10 reps **Neck Iso with partner** 1 set: 6 reps	Play basketball, racquetball, tennis. Do martial arts. or Choose 1-2 Programmable Agility Drills. Choose 1-2 Reactive Agility Drills. Choose 1-2 Position-Specific Drills.	**Abdominal Exercises** Flutterkicks—30 seconds Bicycle Abs—30 seconds Dying Cockroach 30 seconds **Olympic Deadlifts to Knee** 2 sets: 5 reps **Clean Pulls—(Floor)** 3 sets: 5 reps 73% of Clean max **Barbell Lunges** 3 sets: 5 reps **Box Stepups** 3 sets: 5 reps **Pullups (vary grip)** 3 sets: 5-10reps **Offense: Glute Ham Raises** 2 sets: 10 reps **Defense: Reverse HyperExt.** 2 sets: 15 reps **Bear Calf Raises** 1 set: 20 reps **Bar Hang** 1 minute	**Abdominal Exercises** Denver Bronco Abs with partner (see Ab Menu) **Hang Snatch Combo** Jump Shrugs—3 sets: 2 reps Snatch High Pulls 3 sets: 2 reps Hang Snatch—3 sets: 2 reps **Incline Bench Press** 4 sets: 10 reps **Dumbbell Bench Press** (stop and stab) 3 sets: 10 reps **Incline Dumbbell Curls** 3 sets: 10 reps **Weighted Dips** 3 sets: 10 reps **Clapping Push-ups** 1 set: 10 reps **Neck Machine** 1 set: 10 reps
Stretch See Conditioning Schedule	Stretch See Conditioning Schedule	Stretch	Stretch See Conditioning Schedule	Stretch See Conditioning Schedule

Advanced PRESEASON   SPEED AGILITY QUICKNESS CONDITIONING SCHEDULE   WEEK 2 PHASE 1 LOS and LB

MONDAY	TUESDAY	WEDNESDAY	THURSDAY	FRIDAY
Pre-Strength Workout	Pre-Strength Workout	Active Rest	Pre-Strength Workout	Pre-Strength Workout
Dynamic Warmup Walking Toe Touches Backward High Knees Power Skips Low Shuffle 2 sets: 20 yards **Foot Speed** Dot Drills 3-4 sets: 10-15 seconds **Post-Strength Workout** Static Stretch Routine **Programmable Agility** 1. Carolina Box Drill—3 sets 2. Pattern Runs—4-6 sets (include speed cuts, power cuts, and spins) **Reactive Agility** 1. Two-Point and Four-Point Wave Drill 3-4 sets: 10-15 seconds (include jumps, shuffle, "Hit It," etc.) **Competitive Drill** 1. Get Up and Sprint 4-6 sets (vary starting positions)	**Dynamic Warmup** Walking Knee Hugs High Knee Crossovers Backward Skips Starts—Football Stance 2 sets: 20 yards **Foot Speed** Jump Rope—moving 1. Running 2. Double Leg Hops 3. Single Leg Hops 4. Lateral Double Leg Hops 5. Running **Post-Strength Workout** **PNF Partner Stretch** **Conditioning** Metabolic Speed Pac 3 quarters (rest 2 minutes between quarters)	**Competitive Games** Basketball Racquetball Tag Football Martial Arts, etc. or Choose 1-2: Programmable Agility Drills and 1-2 Reactive Agility Drills and 1-2 Position-Specific Drills	**Dynamic Warmup** Walking/Skipping Toe Touches Walking/Skipping Knee Hugs Backward High Knees Low Carioca Starts—Football Stance 2 sets: 20 yards **Foot Speed** Speed Ladder—5-6 sets **Post-Strength Workout** **PNF Partner Stretch** **Programmable Agility** 1. 20-yard Shuttle 4 sets: record best time **Reactive Agility** 1. Eight-Cone Reaction Drill visual cues 3-4 sets: 10-15 seconds **Conditioning** Punch Heavy Bag 3 rounds—30 seconds Work-to-Rest Ratio—1:1	**Dynamic Warmup** Walking Toe Touches Skipping Toe Touches High Knee Crossovers Backward Skips Low Shuffle 2 sets: 20 yards **Foot Speed** Jump Rope—stationary 4-6 sets: 10-20 seconds **Post-Strength Workout** Static Stretch Routine **Conditioning** 400 meters—3 OL, DT—1:45 minutes DE, LB, TE—1:30 minutes Rest 3:45 minutes between 400s
Stretch Lower Back, Hamstrings	Stretch Lower Back, Hamstrings	Stretch Lower Back, Hamstrings	Stretch Lower Back, Hamstrings	Stretch Lower Back, Hamstrings

LOS and LB WEEK 2

ADVANCED PRESEASON Phase 1

YOU DO NOT NEED A MAP IF YOU ARE NOT GOING ANYWHERE. WINNERS HAVE GOALS!

MONDAY	TUESDAY	WEDNESDAY	THURSDAY	FRIDAY
Dot Drills—4 sets - 10-15 seconds	Jump Rope—Running, Hops, etc.	Active Rest	Speed Ladder—5-7 sets	Jump Rope—1½ minutes
Abdominal Exercises Hanging Leg Raises 2 sets: 20 reps Medicine Ball Stack Crunches 2 sets: 20 reps	**Abdominal Exercises** Hokie Leg Raises 1 set: 20 reps Twisting Sit-Ups 1 set: 20 reps ABC Sit-Ups 1 set: 10 reps	Play basketball, racquetball, tennis. Do martial arts, etc. or Choose 1-2 Programmable Agility Drills.	**Abdominal Exercises** Flutterkicks—30 seconds Bicycle Abs—30 seconds Dying Cockroach 30 seconds	**Abdominal Exercises** Denver Bronco Abs with partner
Push Jerks (warmup—5 reps) 55%—5 reps 61%—5 reps 67%—5 reps 73%—5 reps	**Hang Clean-Front Squat Combo** (warmup 5 reps) 55%—3 reps 58%—3 reps 61%—3 reps	Choose 1-2 Reactive Agility Drills. Choose 1-2 Position-Specific Drills.	**Olympic Deadlifts to Knee** 2 sets: 5 reps	**Hang Snatch Combo** Jump Shrugs—3 sets: 2 reps Snatch High Pulls 3 sets: 2 reps Hang Snatch—3 sets: 2 reps
Back Squats (warmup—10 reps) 55%—10 reps 58%—10 reps 61%—10 reps 64%—10 reps	**Bench Press** (warmup—10 reps) 55%—10 reps 61%—10 reps 64%—10 reps 67%—10 reps		**Clean Pulls from Floor** 3 sets: 3 reps (up to 79% of Clean max)	**Incline Bench Press** 4 sets: 10 reps
Lateral Squats 2 sets: 6 reps	**Power Shrugs** 3 sets: 8 reps		**Barbell Lunges** 3 sets: 5 reps	**Dumbbell Bench Press** (stop and stab) 3 sets: 10 reps
One-Arm Dumbbell Rows 3 sets: 10 reps	**Incline Dumbbell Bench Press** (stop and stab) 3 sets: 10 reps		**Box Stepups** 3 sets: 5 reps	**Incline Dumbbell Curls** 3 sets: 10 reps
Offense: Reverse HyperExt. 2 sets: 15 reps	**Straight Bar Curls** 3 sets: 10 reps		**Pullups (vary grip)** 3 sets: 5-10reps	**Weighted Dips** 3 sets: 10 reps
Defense: Glute Ham Raises 2 sets: 10 reps	**Straight Bar Lying Tricep Ext.** 3 sets: 15, 12, 10 reps		**Offense: Glute Ham Raises** 2 sets: 10 reps	**Clapping Push-ups** 1 set: 10 reps
Bear Calf Raises 1 set: 20 reps	**Medicine Ball Plyo Push-ups** 1 set: 10 reps		**Defense: Reverse HyperExt.** 2 sets: 12 reps	**Neck Machine** 1 set: 10 reps
Bar Hang 1:05 minutes	**Neck Iso with partner** 1 set: 6 reps		**Bear Calf Raises** 1 set: 20 reps	
			Bar Hang 1:05 minutes	
Stretch See Conditioning Schedule	Stretch See Conditioning Schedule	Strretch	Stretch See Conditioning Schedule	Stretch See Conditioning Schedule

269

Advanced PRESEASON   SPEED AGILITY QUICKNESS CONDITIONING SCHEDULE   WEEK 3 PHASE 1 LOS and LB

MONDAY	TUESDAY	WEDNESDAY	THURSDAY	FRIDAY
Pre-Strength Workout	**Pre-Strength Workout**	**Active Rest**	**Pre-Strength Workout**	**Pre-Strength Workout**

Dynamic Warmup
Walking Toe Touches
Backward High Knees
Power Skips
Low Shuffle
2 sets: 20 yards
	Dynamic Warmup
	Walking Knee Hugs
	High Knee Crossovers
	Backward Skips
	Starts—Football Stance
	2 sets: 20 yards
		Competitive Games
		Basketball
		Racquetball
		Tag Football
		Martial Arts, etc.
		
		or
		
		Choose 1-2:
		  Programmable Agility
		  Drills and 1-2 Reactive
		  Agility Drills and 1-2
		  Position-Specific
		  Drills
			Dynamic Warmup
			Walking/Skipping Toe
			  Touches
			Walking/Skipping Knee
			  Hugs
			Backward High Knee
			Low Carioca
			Starts—Football Stance
			2 sets: 20 yards
				Dynamic Warmup
				Walking Toe Touches
				Skipping Toe Touches
				High Knee Crossovers
				Backward Skips
				Low Shuffle
				2 sets: 20 yards

Foot Speed Dot Drills 3-4 sets: 10-15 seconds	**Foot Speed** Jump Rope—moving 1. Running 2. Double Leg Hops 3. Single Leg Hops 4. Lateral Double Leg Hops 5. Running		**Foot Speed** Speed Ladder—5-6 sets	**Foot Speed** Jump Rope—stationary 4-6 sets: 10-20 seconds
Post-Strength Workout	**Post-Strength Workout**		**Post-Strength Workout**	**Post-Strength Workout**
Static Stretch Routine	**PNF Partner Stretch**		**PNF Partner Stretch**	**Static Stretch Routine**

Programmable Agility
1. Carolina Box Drill
   3 sets
2. Hourglass Drill—3 sets
	Conditioning
	400 meters—3
	OL, DT - 1:40 minutes
	DE, LB, TE - 1:30 minutes
	Rest 3:30 minutes between
	400s.
			Programmable Agility
			1. Texas-Drill—3 sets
			2. 20-yard Shuttle
			   3-4 sets: record best time
				Conditioning
				Metabolic Speed Pac
				3 quarters
				Rest 2 minutes between
				quarters.
				(See Appendix for
				details)

Reactive Agility
1. Tennis Ball Drills
   (all variations)
   8-10 sets
			Reactive Agility
			1. Four-Cone Agility Drill
			   verbal cues
			   3-4 sets: 10-15 seconds	

Competitive Drill
1. Capture the Flag
   4-6 sets
			Competitive Drill
			1. Get Up and Sprint
			   (vary starting positions)
			   5-6 sets: 30 yards	

Stretch Lower Back, Hamstrings	Stretch Lower Back, Hamstrings	Stretch Lower Back, Hamstrings	Stretch Lower Back, Hamstrings	Stretch Lower Back, Hamstrings

ADVANCED PRESEASON
Phase 1

STAY HYDRATED
REVIEW YOUR GOALS!

LOS and LB
WEEK 3

MONDAY	TUESDAY	WEDNESDAY	THURSDAY	FRIDAY
Dot Drills—4 sets - 10-15 seconds	Jump Rope—Running, Hops, etc.	Active Rest	Speed Ladder—5-7 sets	Jump Rope—1½ minutes
Abdominal Exercises Hanging Leg Raises 2 sets: 20 reps Medicine Ball Stack Crunches 2 sets: 20 reps	**Abdominal Exercises** Hokie Leg Raises 1 set: 20 reps Twisting Sit-Ups 1 set: 20 reps ABC Sit-Ups 1 set: 10 reps	Play basketball, racquetball, tennis. Do martial arts, etc. or Choose 1-2 Programmable Agility Drills.	**Abdominal Exercises** Flutterkick—30 seconds Bicycle Abs—30 seconds Dying Cockroach 30 seconds	**Abdominal Exercises** Denver Bronco Abs with partner
Push Jerks (warmup—3 reps) 58%—3 reps 64%—3 reps 70%—3 reps 76%—3 reps—(2 sets)	**Olympic Deadlifts to Knee** 2 sets: 3 reps	Choose 1-2 Reactive Agility Drills.	**Olympic Deadlifts to Knee** 2 sets: 5 reps	**Hang Snatch Combo** Jump Shrugs—3 sets: 2 reps Snatch High Pulls 3 sets: 2 reps Hang Snatch—3 sets: 2 reps
Back Squats (warmup—8 reps) 50%—8 reps 58%—8 reps 64%—8 reps 70%—8 reps	**Power Cleans** (warmup 3 reps) 55%—3 reps 61%—3 reps 67%—3 reps 70% - 3 reps—(2 sets)	Choose 1-2 Position-Specific Drills.	**Clean Pulls** 3 sets: 3 reps (up to 82% of Clean max)	**Incline Bench Press** 4 sets: 8 reps
Lateral Squats 2 sets: 6 reps	**Bench Press** (warmup—8 reps) 61%—8 reps 64%—8 reps 67%—8 reps 70%—8 reps		**Barbell Lunges** 3 sets: 5 reps	**Dumbbell Bench Press** (stop and stab) 3 sets: 8 reps
One-Arm Dumbbell Rows 3 sets: 8 reps	**Incline Dumbbell Bench Press** (stop and stab) 3 sets: 8 reps		**Box Stepups** 3 sets: 5 reps	**Incline Dumbbell Curls** 3 sets: 8 reps
Offense: Reverse HyperExt. 2 sets: 15 reps	**Straight Bar Curls** 3 sets: 10 reps		**Pullups (vary grip)** 3 sets: 5-10 reps	**Weighted Dips** 3 sets: 8 reps
Defense: Glute Ham Raises 2 sets: 10 reps	**Straight Bar Lying Tricep Ext.** 3 sets: 15, 12, 10 reps,		**Offense: Glute Ham Raises** 2 sets: 10 reps	**Clapping Push-ups** 1 set: 10 reps
Bear Calf Raises 1 set: 20 reps	**Medicine Ball Plyo Push-ups** 1 set: 10 reps		**Defense: Reverse HyperExt.** 2 sets: 15 reps	**Neck Machine** 1 set: 10 reps
Bar Hang 1:10 minutes	**Neck Iso with partner** 1 set: 6 reps		**Bear Calf Raises** 1 set: 20 reps	
			Bar Hang 1:05 minutes	
Stretch See Conditioning Schedule	Stretch See Conditioning Schedule	Strtech	Stretch See Conditioning Schedule	Stretch See Conditioning Schedule

Advanced PRESEASON SPEED AGILITY QUICKNESS CONDITIONING SCHEDULE WEEK 4 PHASE 2 LOS and LB

MONDAY	TUESDAY	WEDNESDAY	THURSDAY	FRIDAY
Pre-Strength Workout	Pre-Strength Workout	Active Rest	Pre-Strength Workout	Pre-Strength Workout
Dynamic Warmup Walking/Skipping Knee Hugs Walking/Skipping Toe Touches Low Shuffle Starts—Football Stance 2 sets: 20 yards	**Dynamic Warmup** High Knee Crossovers Backward Skips Duckwalk Backward Duckwalk 2 sets: 20 yards	**Competitive Games** Basketball Volleyball Tag Football Martial Arts, etc. or	**Dynamic Warmup** Walking Knee Hugs Skipping Toe Touches Low Carioca Starts—Football Stance 2 sets: 20 yards	**Dynamic Warmup** Walking Toe Touches Skipping Knee Hugs Low Shuffle Starts—Football Stance 2 sets: 20 yards
Foot Speed Dot Drills 3-4 sets: 10-15 seconds	**Foot Speed** Jump Rope—moving 1. Running 2. Double Leg Hops Forward and Lateral 3. Single Leg Hops 4. Running	Choose 1-2: Programmable Agility Drills and 1-2 Reactive Agility Drills and 1-2 Position-Specific Drills	**Foot Speed** Speed Ladder—5-6 sets	**Foot Speed** Jump Rope—stationary 4-6 sets: 10-20 seconds
Post-Strength Workout	**Post-Strength Workout**		**Post-Strength Workout**	**Post-Strength Workout**
Static Stretch Routine	**PNF Partner Stretch**		**PNF Partner Stretch**	**Static Stretch Routine**

Programmable Agility
1. Texas-Drills—3-4 sets
2. Four-Cone Perimeter Drill
   4 sets: (include back-pedal, shuffle, carioca, sprints)
	Conditioning
	400 meters—3
	OL, DT—1:40 minutes
	DE, LB, TE—1:30 minutes
	Rest 3:30 minutes between 400s.
			Programmable Agility
			1. 20-yard Shuttle
			   3-4 sets: record best time
			2. Carolina Drill—3-4 sets
				Conditioning
				5 Modified Suicides
				   10 yards and back
				   15 yards and back
				   20 yards and back
				OL, DT—22 seconds
				TE, LB, DE—20 seconds
				Work-to-Rest Ratio—1:3

Reactive Agility
1. Crazy Ball Drills
   (all variations)
   8-10 sets
			Reactive Agility
			1. Four-Cone Agility Drill
			   visual cues
			   3-4 sets: 10-15 seconds	

Competitive Drill
1. Shark in a Tank
   6-7 sets: 10 seconds
			Competitive Drill
			1. Get Up and Sprint
			   4-6 sets	

Stretch Lower Back, Hamstrings	Stretch Lower Back, Hamstrings	Stretch Lower Back, Hamstrings	Stretch Lower Back, Hamstrings	Stretch Lower Back, Hamstrings

LOS and LB WEEK 4

ADVANCED PRESEASON Phase 2

ATTITUDE!

MONDAY	TUESDAY	WEDNESDAY	THURSDAY	FRIDAY
Dot Drills—4 sets - 10-15 seconds	Jump Rope—Running, Hops, etc.	Active Rest	Speed Ladder—5-7 sets	Jump Rope—1½ minutes
Abdominal Exercises Big 40s—1 set Figure Four Double Crunches 2 sets: 10 reps—each way	**Abdominal Exercises** Partner Leg Throws—30 seconds Sit-Ups—30 seconds	Play basketball, racquetball, tennis. Do martial arts, etc.	**Abdominal Exercises** Hanging Leg Raises 2 sets: 20 reps Twisting Stack Crunches 2 sets: 20 reps	**Abdominal Exercises** Captain's Choice
Push Jerks Unload (warmup—3 reps) 58%—3 reps 64%—3 reps 70%—3 reps 76%—1 rep—(3 sets)	**Hang Snatch** 4 sets: 3 reps	or	**Olympic Deadlifts to Knee** 2 sets: 3 reps	**Lateral Box Jumps** 3 sets: 15 seconds
Back Squats Unload (warmup—8 reps) 55%—5 reps 61%—5 reps 67%—5 reps 73%—5 reps	**Bench Press Unload** (warmup—8 reps) 58%—5 reps 64%—5 reps 70%—5 reps 76%—5 reps	Choose 1-2 Programmable Agility Drills.	**Power Cleans** (warmup—3 reps) 58%—3 reps 64%—3 reps 70%—3 reps 76%—3 reps	**Close Grip Chain Bench** Press—5 sets: 5 reps
Extended Squats 2 sets: 5 reps	**Bench Rack (close grip)** **Lockouts—6-Inch Lockout** 3 sets: 3 reps	Choose 1-2 Reactive Agility Drills.	**Clean Pulls** 3 sets: 3 reps (up to 85% of Clean max)	**Seated Plate Raises** 2 sets: 20 reps
Seated Cable Rows or Iso Rows—3 sets: 8 reps	**Seated Dumbbell Shoulder Press** 4 sets: 6 reps	Choose 1-2 Position-Specific Drills.	**Front Squat** 4 sets: 6 reps	**Curls (your choice)** 3-4 sets: 8-10 reps
Offense: Reverse HyperExt. 2 sets: 15 reps	**Barbell Curls** 6-6-6 (3 sets)		**Lat Pulldowns** (front, underhand) 3 sets: 10 reps	**Dumbbell Tricep Ext.** 5 sets: 8 reps (15 second rest between sets)
Defense: Glute Ham Raises 2 sets: 10 reps	**Medicine Ball Plyo Press** 2 sets: 10 reps		**Offense: Glute Ham Raises** 2 sets: 10 reps	**Cinder Block Push-Ups with weight** 2 sets: 10 reps
Bear Calf Raises 1 set: 20 reps	**Neck Iso with partner** 1 set: 6 reps		**Defense: Reverse HyperExt.** 2 sets: 15 reps	**Grippers**—2 round trips
Bar Hang 1:15 minutes			**Bear Calf Raises** 1 set: 20 reps	**Neck Machine** 1 set: 10 reps
Stretch See Conditioning Schedule	Stretch See Conditioning Schedule	Stretch	Stretch See Conditioning Schedule	Stretch See Conditioning Schedule

273

Advanced PRESEASON   SPEED AGILITY QUICKNESS CONDITIONING SCHEDULE   WEEK 5 PHASE 2 LOS and LB

MONDAY	TUESDAY	WEDNESDAY	THURSDAY	FRIDAY
Pre-Strength Workout	Pre-Strength Workout	Active Rest	Pre-Strength Workout	Pre-Strength Workout

Dynamic Warmup
Walking Toe Touches
Skipping Toe Touches
Backward High Knees
Heel-to-Butt Kicks
Low Shuffle
  2 sets: 20 yards
 	
Foot Speed
Dot Drills
  3-4 sets: 10-15 seconds
 	
Post-Strength Workout
 	
Static Stretch Routine
 	
Programmable Agility
1. 20-yard Shuttle
  3-4 sets: record best time
 	
Reactive Agility
1. Four-Cone Reaction Drill
  verbal cues
  3-4 sets: 10-15 seconds
 	
Competitive Drill
1. Shark in a Tank
  4-6 sets: 10 seconds
	Dynamic Warmup
	Walking Knee Hugs
	Skipping Knee Hugs
	High Knee Crossovers
	Backward Skips
	Duckwalk
	Starts—Football Stance
	  2 sets: 20 yards
	
	Foot Speed
	Jump Rope—moving
	1. Running
	2. Double Leg Hops
	3. Single Leg Hops
	4. Running
	  2 sets: 20 yards
	
	Post-Strength Workout
	
	PNF Partner Stretch
	
	Conditioning
	Metabolic Speed Pac
	3 quarters
	(Rest 2 minutes between
	  quarters.)
	(See Appendix for
	  details)
		Competitive Games
		Basketball
		Volleyball
		Racquetball
		Martial Arts, etc.
		
		or
		
		Choose 1-2:
		  Programmable Agility
		  Drills and 1-2 Reactive
		  Agility Drills and 1-2
		  Position-Specific
		  Drills
			Dynamic Warmup
			Walking/Skipping Toe
			  Touches
			Walking/Skipping Knee
			  Hugs
			Low Carioca
			Starts—Football Stance
			  2 sets: 20 yards
			
			Foot Speed
			Speed Ladder—5-6 sets
			
			Post-Strength Workout
			
			PNF Partner Stretch
			
			Programmable Agility
			1. Star Drill—3-4 sets
			  (include speed cuts,
			  power cuts, and spins)
			
			Reactive Agility
			1. Tennis Ball Drills
			  (all variations)
			  8-10 sets
			
			Conditioning
			Punch Heavy Bag
			3 rounds—30 seconds
			Work-to-Rest Ratio—1:1
				Dynamic Warmup
				Walking Toe Touches
				Skipping Toe Touches
				High Knee Crossovers
				Backward Skips
				Low Shuffle
				  2 sets: 20 yards
				
				Foot Speed
				Jump Rope—stationary
				  5-6 sets: 15-20 seconds
				
				Post-Strength Workout
				
				PNF Partner Stretch
				
				Conditioning
				200 meters—6
				OL, DT—45 seconds
				DE, LB, TE—40 seconds
				Rest 1:30 minutes between
				  200s.

Stretch Lower Back, Hamstrings	Stretch Lower Back, Hamstrings	Stretch Lower Back, Hamstrings	Stretch Lower Back, Hamstrings	Stretch Lower Back, Hamstrings

ADVANCED PRESEASON
Phase 2

LOS and LB
WEEK 5

SPEED KILLS;
STRENGTH PUNISHES!

MONDAY	TUESDAY	WEDNESDAY	THURSDAY	FRIDAY
Dot Drills—4 sets - 10-15 seconds	Jump Rope—Running, Hops, etc.	Active Rest	Speed Ladder—5-7 sets	Jump Rope—1½ minutes
Abdominal Exercises Big 40s—1 set Figure Four Double Crunches 2 sets: 10 reps (each way)	**Abdominal Exercises** Partner Leg Throws—30 seconds Sit-Ups—30 seconds	Play basketball, racquetball, tennis. Do martial arts, etc.	**Abdominal Exercises** Hanging Leg Raises 2 sets: 20 reps Twisting Stack Crunches 2 sets: 20 reps	**Abdominal Exercises** Captain's Choice
Push Jerks (warmup—3 reps) 55%—3 reps 61%—3 reps 67%—3 reps 73%—3 reps 79%—3 reps	**Hang Snatch** 4 sets: 3 reps	or	**Olympic Deadlifts to Knee** 2 sets: 3 reps	**Lateral Box Jumps** 3 sets: 15 seconds
	Bench Press (warmup—8 reps) 55%—5 reps 61%—5 reps 67%—5 reps 73%—5 reps 79%—5 reps	Choose 1-2 Programmable Agility Drills.	**Power Cleans** (warmup—3 reps) 55%—3 reps 61%—3 reps 67%—3 reps 73%—3 reps 79%—3 reps	**Close Grip Chain Bench Press**—5 sets: 5 reps
Back Squats (warmup—8 reps) 58%—5 reps 64%—5 reps 70%—5 reps 76%—5 reps	**Bench Rack (close grip)**	Choose 1-2 Reactive Agility Drills.	**Clean Pulls** 3 sets: 3 reps (up to 88% of Clean max)	**Seated Plate Raises** 2 sets: 20 reps
Extended Squats 2 sets: 5 reps	**Lockouts—6-Inch Lockout** 3 sets: 3 reps	Choose 1-2 Position-Specific Drills.	**Front Squats** 4 sets: 6 reps	**Curls (your choice)** 3-4 sets: 8-10 reps
Seated Cable Rows or **Hammer Iso Rows** 3 sets: 8 reps	**Seated Dumbbell Shoulder Press** 4 sets: 6 reps		**Lat Pulldowns** (front, underhand) 3 sets: 10 reps	**Dumbbell Tricep Ext.** 5 sets: 8 reps (15 second rest between sets)
Offense: Reverse HyperExt. 2 sets: 15 reps	**Barbell Curls** 6-6-6 (3 sets)		**Offense: Glute Ham Raises** 2 sets: 10 reps	**Cinder Block Push-Ups with weight** 2 sets: 10 reps
Defense: Glute Ham Raises 2 sets: 10 reps	**Medicine Ball Plyo Press** 2 sets: 10 reps		**Defense: Reverse HyperExt.** 2 sets: 15 reps	**Grippers**—2 round trips
Bear Calf Raises 1 set: 20 reps	**Neck Iso with partner** 1 set: 6 reps		**Bear Calf Raises** 1 set: 20 reps	**Neck Machine** 1 set: 10 reps
Bar Hang 1:15 minutes				
Stretch See Conditioning Schedule	Stretch See Conditioning Schedule	Stretch	Stretch See Conditioning Schedule	Stretch See Conditioning Schedule

275

Advanced PRESEASON   SPEED AGILITY QUICKNESS CONDITIONING SCHEDULE   WEEK 6 PHASE 2 LOS and LB

MONDAY	TUESDAY	WEDNESDAY	THURSDAY	FRIDAY
Pre-Strength Workout	Pre-Strength Workout	Active Rest	Pre-Strength Workout	Pre-Strength Workout
Dynamic Warmup Walking Toe Touches Skipping Toe Touches Backward High Knees Heel-to-Butt Kicks Low Shuffle 2 sets: 20 yards **Foot Speed** Dot Drills 3-4 sets: 10-15 seconds **Post-Strength Workout** **PNF Partner Stretch** **Conditioning** 110s—10 OL, DT—20 seconds DE, LB, TE—18 seconds (rest 45 seconds between 110s)	**Dynamic Warmup** Walking Knee Hugs Skipping Knee Hugs High Knee Crossovers Backward Skips Duckwalk Starts—Football Stance 2 sets: 20 yards **Foot Speed** Jump Rope—moving 1. Running 2. Double Leg Hops 3. Single Leg Hops 4. Running 2 sets: 20 yards **Post-Strength Workout** **PNF Partner Stretch** **Programmable Agility** 1. 20-yard Shuttle 3-4 sets: record best time **Reactive Agility** 1. Tennis Ball Drills 8-10 sets (all variations) **Acceleration/Conditioning** 1. Sled Pulls—6 sets: 30 yards (50 pounds max weight on sled) or 2. Sand Sprints—6 sets: 40 yards (sprint 40 yards, walk back)	**Competitive Games** Basketball Volleyball Racquetball Martial Arts, etc. or Choose 1-2: Programmable Agility Drills and 1-2 Reactive Agility Drills and 1-2 Position-Specific Drills	**Dynamic Warmup** Walking/Skipping Toe Touches Walking/Skipping Knee Hugs Low Carioca Starts—Football Stance 2 sets: 20 yards **Foot Speed** Speed Ladder—5-6 sets **Post-Strength Workout** **Static Stretch Routine** **Conditioning** Metabolic Speed Pac 4 quarters Rest 2 minutes between quarters (See Appendix for details)	**Dynamic Warmup** Walking Toe Touches Skipping Toe Touches High Knee Crossovers Backward Skips Low Shuffle 2 sets: 20 yards **Foot Speed** Jump Rope—stationary 5-6 sets: 15-20 seconds **Post-Strength Workout** **PNF Partner Stretch** **Programmable Agility** 1. Four-Cone Perimeter Drill 4 sets 2. Carolina Drill—3 sets **Competitive Drill** 1. Get Up and Sprint (vary starting position) 4-6 sets: 30 yards
Stretch Lower Back, Hamstrings	Stretch Lower Back, Hamstrings	Stretch Lower Back, Hamstrings	Stretch Lower Back, Hamstrings	Stretch Lower Back, Hamstrings

ADVANCED PRESEASON
Phase 2

IMPROVISE, ADAPT, OVERCOME!

LOS and LB
WEEK 6

MONDAY	TUESDAY	WEDNESDAY	THURSDAY	FRIDAY
Dot Drills—4 sets - 10-15 seconds	Jump Rope—Running, Hops, etc.	Active Rest	Speed Ladder—5-7 sets	Jump Rope—1½ minutes
Abdominal Exercises Big 40s—1 set Figure Four Double Crunches 2 sets: 15 reps (each way) **Push Jerks** (warmup—3 reps) 58%—3 reps 64%—3 reps 70%—3 reps 76%—3 reps 82%—3 reps **Back Squats** (warmup—8 reps) 61%—5 reps 67%—5 reps 73%—5 reps 79%—5 reps **Extended Squats** 2 sets: 5 reps **Seated Cable Rows** or **Hammer Iso Rows** 3 sets: 8 reps **Offense: Reverse HyperExt.** 2 sets: 15 reps **Defense: Glute Ham Raises** 2 sets: 10 reps **Bear Calf Raises** 1 set: 20 reps **Bar Hang** 1:15 minutes	**Abdominal Exercises** Partner Leg Throws—30 seconds Sit-Ups—30 seconds **Hang Snatch** 4 sets: 3 reps **Bench Press** (warmup—8 reps) 55%—5 reps 64%—5 reps 70%—5 reps 76%—5 reps 82%—5 reps **Bench Rack (close grip)** **Lockouts—6-Inch Lockout** 3 sets: 3 reps **Seated Dumbbell Shoulder Press** 4 sets: 6 reps **Barbell Curls** 6-6-6 (3 sets) **Medicine Ball Plyo Press** 2 sets: 10 reps **Neck Iso with partner** 1 set: 6 reps	Play basketball, racquetball, tennis. Do martial arts, etc. or Choose 1-2 Programmable Agility Drills. Choose 1-2 Reactive Agility Drills. Choose 1-2 Position-Specific Drills.	**Abdominal Exercises** Hanging Leg Raises 2 sets: 20 reps Twisting Stack Crunches 2 sets: 20 reps **Olympic Deadlifts to Knee** 2 sets: 3 reps **Power Cleans** (warmup—3 reps) 61%—3 reps 67%—3 reps 73%—3 reps 79%—3 reps 85%—2 reps **Clean Pulls** 3 sets: 3 reps (up to 91% of Clean max) **Front Squats** 4 sets: 5 reps **Lat Pulldowns** (front, underhand) 3 sets: 8 reps **Offense: Glute Ham Raises** 2 sets: 10 reps **Defense: Reverse HyperExt.** 2 sets: 15 reps **Bear Calf Raises** 1 set: 20 reps	**Abdominal Exercises** Captain's Choice **Lateral Box Jumps** 3 sets: 15 seconds **Close Grip Chain Bench Press**—5 sets: 5 reps **Seated Plate Raises** 2 sets: 20 reps **Curls (your choice)** 3-4 sets: 8-10 reps **Dumbbell Tricep Ext.** 5 sets: 8 reps (15 second rest between sets) **Cinder Block Push-Ups with weight** 2 sets: 10 reps **Grippers**—2 round trips **Neck Machine** 1 set: 10 reps
Stretch See Conditioning Schedule	Stretch See Conditioning Schedule	Stretch	Stretch See Conditioning Schedule	Stretch See Conditioning Schedule

Advanced PRESEASON SPEED AGILITY QUICKNESS CONDITIONING SCHEDULE WEEK 7 PHASE 3 LOS and LB

MONDAY	TUESDAY	WEDNESDAY	THURSDAY	FRIDAY
Pre-Strength Workout	**Pre-Strength Workout**	**Active Rest**	**Pre-Strength Workout**	**Pre-Strength Workout**
Dynamic Warmup Walking Toe Touches Skipping Toe Touches Backward High Knees Heel-to-Butt Kicks Low Shuffle 2 sets: 20 yards **Foot Speed** Dot Drills 3-4 sets: 10-15 seconds **Post-Strength Workout** **PNF Partner Stretch** **Conditioning** 12—110s OL, DT—19 seconds DE, LB, TE—17 seconds (Rest 45 seconds between 110s.)	**Dynamic Warmup** Walking Knee Hugs Skipping Knee Hugs High Knee Crossovers Backward Skips Duckwalk Starts—Football Stance 2 sets: 20 yards **Foot Speed** Jump Rope—moving 1. Running 2. Double Leg Hops 3. Single Leg Hops 4. Running 2 sets: 20 yards **Post-Strength Workout** **PNF Partner Stretch** **Programmable Agility** 1. Texas-Drill—3 sets **Reactive Agility** 1. Crazy Ball Drills—8-10 sets (all variations) **Competitive Drill** 1. Shark in a Tank 4-5 sets: 10 seconds	**Competitive Games** Basketball Volleyball Racquetball Martial Arts, etc. or Choose 1-2: Programmable Agility Drills and 1-2 Reactive Agility Drills and 1-2 Position-Specific Drills	**Dynamic Warmup** Walking/Skipping Toe Touches Walking/Skipping Knee Hugs Low Carioca Starts—Football Stance 2 sets: 20 yards **Foot Speed** Speed Ladder—5-6 sets **Post-Strength Workout** **Static Stretch Routine** **Conditioning** 14—110s OL, DT—19 seconds DE, LB, TE—17 seconds (Rest 45 seconds between 110s.)	**Dynamic Warmup** Walking Toe Touches Skipping Toe Touches High Knee Crossovers Backward Skips Low Shuffle 2 sets: 20 yards **Foot Speed** Jump Rope—stationary 5-6 sets: 15-20 seconds **Post-Strength Workout** **PNF Partner Stretch** **Programmable Agility** 1. Star Drill—4 sets (include speed cuts, power cuts, and spins) **Reactive Agility** 1. Eight-Cone Reaction Drill visual cues 3 sets: 10-15 seconds **Competitive Drill** 1. Get Up and Sprint (vary starting position) 4-6 sets: 30 yards
Stretch Lower Back, Hamstrings	Stretch Lower Back, Hamstrings	Strtech Lower Back, Hamstrings	Stretch Lower Back, Hamstrings	Stretch Lower Back, Hamstrings

ADVANCED PRESEASON
Phase 3

IF IT WERE EASY,
EVERYONE WOULD DO IT!

LOS and LB
WEEK 7

MONDAY	TUESDAY	WEDNESDAY	THURSDAY	FRIDAY
Dot Drills—4 sets - 10-15 seconds	Jump Rope—Running, Hops, etc.	Active Rest	Speed Ladder—5-7 sets	Jump Rope—1½ minutes
Abdominal Exercises Figure Eights—2 sets: 10 reps ABC Sit-Ups—2 sets: 10 reps	**Abdominal Exercises** Denver Bronco Ab Program	Play basketball, racquetball, tennis. Do martial arts, etc.	**Abdominal Exercises** Hanging Leg Raises 2 sets: 20 reps Medicine Ball Stack Crunches 2 sets: 20 reps	**Abdominal Exercises** Captain's Choice
Power Snatch 4 sets: 3 reps	**Olympic Deadlifts to Knee** 2 sets: 3 reps	or	**Explosive Bear Jumps** Defense: Sight Cue Offense: Sound Cue 3 sets: 4 reps	**Push Jerks** (warmup—3 reps) 55%—3 reps 61%—3 reps 67%—3 reps 73%—3 reps 79%—3 reps 85%—2 reps—(2 sets)
Bench Press (warmup—8 reps) 61%—5 reps 67%—3 reps 73%—3 reps 79%—3 reps 85%—3 reps—(2 sets)	**Power Cleans** (warmup—3 reps) 64%—3 reps 70%—3 reps 76%—3 reps 82%—2 reps 88%—1 rep—(2 sets)	Choose 1-2 Programmable Agility Drills.	**Incline Bench Press** 4 sets: 6 reps	**Back Squats** (warmup—8 reps) 61%—5 reps 67%—5 reps 73%—5 reps 79%—3 reps 85%—3 reps
Swiss Ball Alternate Dumbbbell Press 3 sets: 6 reps	**Clean Pulls** 3 sets: 2 reps (up to 94% of Clean max)	Choose 1-2 Reactive Agility Drills.	**Decline Dumbbell Bench Press** 3 sets: 8 reps	**One-Arm Dumbbell Rows** 3 sets: 8 reps
Seated Shoulder Press 3 sets: 10 reps	**Speed Squats** (50% of max) 4 sets: 5 reps	Choose 1-2 Position-Specific Drills.	**Swiss Ball Curls** 3 sets: 10 reps	**Lat Pulldowns** (front, underhand) 3 sets: 8-10 reps
Curls (your choice) 3-4 sets: 8-10 reps	**Pullups (vary grip)** 3 sets: 5-10 reps		**Straight Bar Lying Tricep Extensions** 3 sets: 10 reps	**Offense: Glute Ham Raises** 2 sets: 10 reps
Weighted Dips 3 sets: 8 reps	**Offense: Reverse HyperExt.** 2 sets: 15 reps		**Wrist Rollers** 2 sets	**Defense: Reverse HyperExt.** 2 sets: 15 reps
Dominator Punch 2 sets: 5 reps	**Defense: Glute Ham Raises** 2 sets: 10 reps		**Neck Iso**—1 set: 6 reps or	**Bear Calf Raises** 1 set: 20 reps
Neck Iso—1 set: 6 reps or **Neck Machine** 1 set: 10 reps	**Dominator Throws** (each way) 1 set: 5 reps		**Neck Machine** 1 set: 10 reps	
	Bar Hang 1:15 minutes		**Medicine Ball Pullover Throws** 1 set: 10 reps	
Stretch See Conditioning Schedule	Stretch See Conditioning Schedule	Stretch	Stretch See Conditioning Schedule	Stretch See Conditioning Schedule

Advanced PRESEASON   SPEED AGILITY QUICKNESS CONDITIONING SCHEDULE   WEEK 8 PHASE 3 LOS and LB

MONDAY	TUESDAY	WEDNESDAY	THURSDAY	FRIDAY
Pre-Strength Workout	**Pre-Strength Workout**	**Active Rest**	**Pre-Strength Workout**	**Pre-Strength Workout**

Dynamic Warmup
Walking Toe Touches
Skipping Toe Touches
Backward High Knees
Heel-to-Butt Kicks
Low Shuffle
  2 sets: 20 yards
 	
Foot Speed
Dot Drills
3-4 sets—10-15 seconds
 	
Post-Strength Workout
 	
PNF Partner Stretch
 	
Conditioning
Metabolic Speed Pac
4 quarters
(Rest 2 minutes between quarters.)
(See Appendix for details)
	Dynamic Warmup
	Walking Knee Hugs
	Skipping Knee Hugs
	High Knee Crossovers
	Backward Skips
	Duckwalk
	Starts—Football Stance
	  2 sets: 20 yards
	
	Foot Speed
	Jump Rope—moving
	1. Running
	2. Double Leg Hops
	3. Single Leg Hops
	4. Running
	  2 sets: 20 yards
	
	Post-Strength Workout
	
	PNF Partner Stretch
	
	Programmable Agility
	1. Carolina Drill—3 sets
	2. Bag Drills—2 sets: 6-8 bags
	3. Run Through
	4. Lateral Shuffle
	5. Double Hops
	6. Zig-Zag
	7. Run Through
	
	Reactive Agility
	1. Two-Point and Four-Point Wave Drill
	  2 sets: 10-15 seconds
		Competitive Games
		Basketball
		Volleyball
		Racquetball
		Martial Arts, etc.
		
		or
		
		Choose 1-2:
		Programmable Agility Drills and 1-2 Reactive Agility Drills and 1-2 Position-Specific Drills
			Dynamic Warmup
			Walking/Skipping Toe Touches
			Walking/Skipping Knee Hugs
			Low Carioca
			Starts—Football Stance
			  2 sets: 20 yards
			
			Foot Speed
			Speed Ladder—5-6 sets
			
			Post-Strength Workout
			
			Static Stretch Routine
			
			Conditioning
			16—110s
			OL, DT—19 seconds
			DE, LB, TE—17 seconds
			(Rest 45 seconds between 110s.)
				Dynamic Warmup
				Walking Toe Touches
				Skipping Toe Touches
				High Knee Crossovers
				Backward Skips
				Low Shuffle
				  2 sets: 20 yards
				
				Foot Speed
				Jump Rope—stationary
				5-6 sets: 15-20 seconds
				
				Post-Strength Workout
				
				PNF Partner Stretch
				
				Programmable Agility
				1. Pattern Runs—6 sets: 20 yards
				(include speed cuts, power cuts, and spins)
				
				Reactive Agility
				1. Crazy Ball Drills (all variations)
				8-10 sets
				
				Competitive Drill
				1. Get Up and Sprint (vary starting position)
				4-6 sets: 30 yards

Stretch Lower Back, Hamstrings	Stretch Lower Back, Hamstrings	Stretch Lower Back, Hamstrings	Stretch Lower Back, Hamstrings	Stretch Lower Back, Hamstrings

MANY SPECTATE; FEW COMPETE!

LOS and LB WEEK 8

ADVANCED PRESEASON Phase 3

MONDAY	TUESDAY	WEDNESDAY	THURSDAY	FRIDAY
Dot Drills—4 sets - 10-15 seconds	Jump Rope—Running, Hops, etc.	Active Rest	Speed Ladder—5-7 sets	Jump Rope—1½ minutes
Abdominal Exercises Figure Eights—2 sets: 10 reps ABC Sit-Ups—2 sets: 10 reps	**Abdominal Exercises** Denver Bronco Ab Program	Play basketball, racquetball, tennis. Do martial arts, etc.	**Abdominal Exercises** Hanging Leg Raises 2 sets: 20 reps Medicine Ball Stack Crunches 2 sets: 20 reps	**Abdominal Exercises** Captain's Choice
Power Snatch 4 sets—3 reps	**Olympic Deadlifts to Knee** 2 sets: 3 reps	or	**Explosive Bear Jumps** Defense: Sight Cue Offense: Sound Cue 3 sets: 4 reps	**Push Jerks** (warmup—3 reps) 61%—3 reps 67%—3 reps 73%—3 reps 78%—3 reps 85%—2 reps 91%—1 rep—(2 sets)
Bench Press (warmup—8 reps) 55%—3 reps 64%—3 reps 70%—3 reps 76%—3 reps 82%—3 reps 88%—3 reps	**Power Cleans** warmup—3 reps 61%—3 reps 67%—3 reps 73%—3 reps 79%—3 reps 85%—2 reps 91%—1 rep—(2 sets)	Choose 1-2 Programmable Agility Drills.	**Incline Bench Press** 4 sets: 6 reps	**Back Squats** (warmup—8 reps) 64%—5 reps 70%—5 reps 76%—3 reps 82%—3 reps 88%—2 reps—(2 sets)
Swiss Ball Alternate Dumbbell Press 3 sets: 6 reps	**Clean Pulls** 3 sets: 2 reps (up to 97% of Clean max)	Choose 1-2 Reactive Agility Drills.	**Decline Dumbbell Bench Press** 3 sets: 8 reps	**One-Arm Dumbbell Rows** 3 sets: 8 reps
Seated Shoulder Press 3 sets: 10 reps	**Speed Squats (50% of max)** 4 sets: 5 reps	Choose 1-2 Position-Specific Drills.	**Swiss Ball Curls** 3 sets: 10 reps	**Lat Pulldowns** (front, underhand) 3 sets: 8-10 reps
Curls (your choice) 3-4 sets: 8-10 reps	**Pullups (vary grip)** 3 sets: 5-10 reps		**Straight Bar Lying Tricep Extensions** 3 sets: 10 reps	**Offense: Glute Ham Raises** 2 sets: 10 reps
Weighted Dips 3 sets: 8 reps	**Offense: Reverse HyperExt.** 2 sets: 15 reps		**Wrist Rollers** 2 sets	**Defense: Reverse HyperExt.** 2 sets: 15 reps
Dominator Punches 2 sets: 5 reps	**Defense: Glute Ham Raises** 2 sets: 10 reps		**Neck Iso**—1 set: 6 reps or **Neck Machine** 1 set: 10 reps	**Bear Calf Raises** 1 set: 20 reps
Neck Iso—1 set: 6 reps or **Neck Machine** 1 set: 10 reps	**Dominator Throws** (each way) 1 set: 5 reps		**Medicine Ball Pullover Throws** 1 set: 10 reps	
	Bar Hang 1:15 minutes			
Stretch See Conditioning Schedule	Stretch See Conditioning Schedule	Strretch	Stretch See Conditioning Schedule	Stretch See Conditioning Schedule

Advanced PRESEASON   SPEED AGILITY QUICKNESS CONDITIONING SCHEDULE   WEEK 9 PHASE 3 LOS and LB

MONDAY	TUESDAY	WEDNESDAY	THURSDAY	FRIDAY
Pre-Strength Workout	**Pre-Strength Workout**	**Active Rest**	**Pre-Strength Workout**	**Pre-Strength Workout**

Dynamic Warmup
Walking Toe Touches
Skipping Toe Touches
Backward High Knees
Heel-to-Butt Kicks
Low Shuffle
  2 sets: 20 yards
	Dynamic Warmup
	Walking Knee Hugs
	Skipping Knee Hugs
	High Knee Crossovers
	Backward Skips
	Duckwalk
	Starts—Football Stance
	  2 sets: 20 yards
		Competitive Games
		Basketball
		Volleyball
		Racquetball
		Martial Arts, etc.
		
		or
		
		Choose 1-2:
		  Programmable Agility
		  Drills and 1-2 Reactive
		  Agility Drills and 1-2
		  Position-Specific
		  Drills
			Dynamic Warmup
			Walking/Skipping Toe
			  Touches
			Walking/Skipping Knee
			  Hugs
			Low Carioca
			Starts—Football Stance
			  2 sets: 20 yards
				Dynamic Warmup
				Walking Toe Touches
				Skipping Toe Touches
				High Knee Crossovers
				Backward Skips
				Low Shuffle
				  2 sets: 20 yards

Foot Speed
Dot Drills
  3-4 sets: 10-15 seconds
	Foot Speed
	Jump Rope—moving
	1. Running
	2. Double Leg Hops
	3. Single Leg Hops
	4. Running
	  2 sets: 20 yards
			Foot Speed
			Speed Ladder—5-6 sets
				Foot Speed
				Jump Rope—stationary
				  5-6 sets: 15-20 seconds

Post-Strength Workout	**Post-Strength Workout**		**Post-Strength Workout**	**Post-Strength Workout**
PNF Partner Stretch	**PNF Partner Stretch**		**Static Stretch Routine**	**PNF Partner Stretch**

Conditioning
110s—18
OL, DT—19 seconds
DE, LB, TE—17 seconds
(rest 45 seconds between
110s)
(See Appendix for
details)
	Programmable Agility
	1. Texas-Drill—3-4 sets
	2. 20-yard Shuttle
	  3-4 sets: record best time
			Conditioning
			110s—16
			OL, DT—19 seconds
			DE, LB, TE—17 seconds
			(rest 45 seconds between
			110s)
				Programmable Agility
				1. Pattern Runs—6 sets: 20
				  yards
				  (include speed cuts,
				  power cuts, and spins)

	Reactive Agility
	1. Four-Cone Reaction Drill
	  verbal cues
	  3-4 sets: 10-15 seconds
				Reactive Agility
				1. Crazy Ball Drills
				  (all variations)
				  8-10 sets

	Competitive Drill
	1. Shark in a Tank
	  5-7 sets: 10-15 seconds
				Competitive Drill
				1. Get Up and Sprint
				  (vary starting position)
				  4-6 sets: 30 yards

Stretch Lower Back, Hamstrings	Stretch Lower Back, Hamstrings	Stretch Lower Back, Hamstrings	Stretch Lower Back, Hamstrings	Stretch Lower Back, Hamstrings

THE HARDER YOU WORK, THE LUCKIER YOU GET!

ADVANCED PRESEASON
Phase 3

LOS and LB
WEEK 9

MONDAY	TUESDAY	WEDNESDAY	THURSDAY	FRIDAY
Dot Drills - 4 sets - 10-15 seconds	Jump Rope—Running, Hops, etc.	Active Rest	Speed Ladder—5-7 sets	Jump Rope—1½ minutes
Abdominal Exercises Partner Medicine Ball Sit-Ups/Throws 2 sets: 30 throws	**Abdominal Exercises** Hanging Leg Raises 2 sets: 20 reps Twisting Stack Crunches 2 sets: 20 reps	Play basketball, racquetball, tennis. Do martial arts, etc.	**Abdominal Exercises** Flutterkicks—30 seconds Bicycle Abs—30 seconds Dying Cockroach 30 seconds	**Abdominal Exercises** Captain's Choice
Power Snatch 4 sets: 3 reps	**Olympic Deadlifts to Knee** 2 sets: 3 reps	or	**Explosive Box Stepups** (each leg) 3 sets: 4 reps	**Push Jerk Unload** (warmup—3 reps) 55%—3 reps 64%—1 rep 73%—1 rep 79%—1 rep 85%—1 rep
Bench Press (warmup—8 reps) 61%—3 reps 67%—3 reps 73%—3 reps 79%—3 reps 85%—3 reps 91%—1 rep—(3 sets)	**Power Cleans Unload** (warmup—3 reps) 61%—3 reps 67%—3 reps 73%—3 reps 79%—3 reps 85%—1 rep	Choose 1-2 Programmable Agility Drills.	**Close Grip Bench with Chains** 5 sets: 5 reps	**Back Squats** (warmup—8 reps) 64%—5 reps 70%—5 reps 76%—5 reps 82%—3 reps 85%—2 reps 91%—1 rep
Dumbbell Incline Bench Press (stop and stab) 3 set: 6 reps	**Clean Pulls** 3 sets: 2 reps (100% of clean max)	Choose 1-2 Reactive Agility Drills.	**Seated Plate Raises** 2 sets: 20 reps	**Seated Cable Rows** or **Hammer Iso Rows** 3 sets: 8 reps
Cinder Block Push-Ups with weight 3 sets: 8 reps	**Bear Squats** 3 sets: 10 reps	Choose 1-2 Position-Specific Drills.	**Curls (your choice)** 3-4 sets: 8-10 reps	**Lat Pulldowns (vary grip)** 3 sets: 10 reps
Curls (your choice) 3-4 sets: 8-10 reps	**Pullups (vary grip)** 3 sets: 5-10 reps		**Dumbbell Lying Tricep Ext.** (heavy) 3 sets: 10 reps	**Offense: Glute Ham Raises** 2 sets: 10 reps
Neck Iso—1 set: 6 reps or **Neck Machine** 1 set: 10 reps	**Offense: Reverse HyperExt.** 2 sets: 15 reps		**Grippers**—2 round trips	**Defense: Reverse HyperExt.** 2 sets: 15 reps
	Defense: Glute Ham Raises 2 sets: 10 reps		**Clapping Push-Ups** 1 sets: 10 reps	**Bear Calf Raises** 1 set: 20 reps
	Dominator Throws (each way) 1 set: 5 reps		**Neck Iso**—1 set: 6 reps or **Neck Machine** 1 set: 10 reps	
Stretch See Conditioning Schedule	Stretch See Conditioning Schedule	Stretch	Stretch See Conditioning Schedule	Stretch See Conditioning Schedule

Advanced PRESEASON   SPEED AGILITY QUICKNESS CONDITIONING SCHEDULE   WEEK 10 PHASE 3 LOS and LB

MONDAY	TUESDAY	WEDNESDAY	THURSDAY	FRIDAY
Pre-Strength Workout	Pre-Strength Workout	Pre-Strength Workout	Pre-Strength Workout	Pre-Strength Workout
Dot Drills 3-5 sets: 10-15 seconds **Post-Strength Workout** **PNF Partner Stretch Routine** **Conditioning** 8—110s Unload QB, Spec, FB—17 seconds WR, DB, TB—15 seconds (Rest 45 seconds between 110s.)	**Post-Testing** **PNF Partner Stretch Routine** **Competitive Drill** 1. Shark in a Tank 6-8 sets: 10 seconds	**Speed Ladder** 5-7 sets **Post-Strength Workout** **PNF Partner Stretch Routine** **Conditioning** 8—110s Unload QB, Spec, FB—17 seconds WR, DB, TB—15 seconds (Rest 45 seconds between 110s.)	OFF	OFF
Stretch Lower Back, Hamstrings	Stretch Lower Back, Hamstrings	Stretch Lower Back, Hamstrings	Stretch Lower Back, Hamstrings	Stretch Lower Back, Hamstrings

LOS and LB
WEEK 10

ADVANCED PRESEASON
Phase 3

Strength Power
MAX TESTING

MONDAY	TUESDAY	WEDNESDAY	THURSDAY	FRIDAY
Dot Drills		Speed Ladder		Jump Rope
Power Cleans (warmup—3-5 reps) 61%—3 reps 70%—2 reps 79%—1 rep 85%—1 rep 91%—1 rep Begin 1 rep max attempts	**TEST**—Vertical Jump **TEST**—10-yard Spring (electronically timed) **TEST**—20-yard shuttle **TEST**—Sit and Reach Flex Get Body Weight	**Push Jerks** (warmup—3-5 reps) 61%—3 reps 70%—2 reps 79%—1 rep 85%—1 rep 91%—1 rep Begin 1 rep max attempts.	OFF	OFF
Bench Press (warmup—8 reps) 61%—5 reps 70%—3 reps 79%—1 rep 88%—1 rep 94%—1 rep Begin 1 rep max attempts.		**Back Squats** (warmup—8 reps) 61%—5 reps 70%—3 reps 79%—1 rep 88%—1 rep Begin 3 rep max attempts.		
Stretch Lower Back, Hamstrings	Stretch Lower Back, Hamstrings	Stretch Lower Back, Hamstrings	Stretch Lower Back, Hamstrings	Stretch Lower Back, Hamstrings

Advanced: Off-Season/Preseason Program

SKILL POSITIONS

WR, DB, QB, RB, Specialist

Advanced OFF SEASON   SPEED AGILITY QUICKNESS CONDITIONING SCHEDULE   WEEK 1 PHASE 1 Skill Positions

MONDAY	TUESDAY	WEDNESDAY	THURSDAY	FRIDAY
Pre-Strength Workout	**Dynamic Warmup**	**Pre-Strength Workout**	**Dynamic Warmup**	**Pre-Strength Workout**
Dot Drills 10-15 seconds 1. In and Out 2. Figure 8—both feet right side 3. Figure 8—both feet left side 4. Make up your own pattern	Walking Toe Touches 2 sets: 20 yards Skipping Toe Touches 2 sets: 20 yards Backward Skips 2 sets: 20 yards High Knee Crossovers 2 sets: 20 yards	**Speed Ladder** 5-7 sets 1. Run Through 2. Lateral Shuffle 3. Hop Scotch 4. Slalom Jumps 5. Ickey Shuffle 6. Backward Ickey Shuffle	Walking Knee Hugs 2 sets: 20 yards Skipping Knee Hugs 2 sets: 20 yards High Knee Crossovers 2 sets: 20 yards Backward Skips 2 sets: 20 yards	**Jump Rope** 10-20 seconds 1. Both Feet 2. Right Foot 3. Left Foot 4. Alternate Feet 5. 2 on Right, 2 on Left Foot 6. Speed Jump
Post-Strength Workout	**PNF Partner Stretch Routine**	**Post-Strength Workout**	**PNF Partner Stretch Routine**	**Post-Strength Workout**
Static Stretch Routine	**Speed Development** 1. Heel-to-Butt Kick 2 sets: 20 yards 2. A Marches 2 sets: 20 yards 3. A Skips 2 sets: 20 yards 4. A Runs 2 sets: 20 yards	**Static Stretch Routine**	**Speed Development** 1. Fast Arms Drill 2 sets: 15 seconds 2. Heel-to-Butt Kicks 2 sets: 15 yards 3. A Marches 2 sets: 20 yards 4. A Skips 2 sets: 20 yards 5. A Runs 2 sets: 20 yards	**Static Stretch Routine**
Programmable Agility 1. 20-yard Shuttle 4 trials—record best time	**Acceleration** 1. Acceleration Ladder 6 sets: 20 seconds	**Programmable Agility** 1. Carolina Drill—4 sets	**Programmable Agility** 1. 20-yard Shuttle 4 trials—record best time	**Conditioning** 5 Modified Suicides 10 yards and back 15 yards and back 20 yards and back Linemen—22 seconds LB, TE, DE, FB, QB, Spec 20 seconds WR, DB, TB—18 seconds Work-to-Rest Ratio—1:3
Reactive Agility 1. Two-Point Wave Drill 4-5 sets: 10-15 seconds	**Programmable Agility** 1. Pattern Runs 4-6 sets: 20 yards (include speed cuts, power cuts, and spins) 2. Active—Isolation	**Reactive Agility** 1. Crazy Ball Drills (all variations) 8-10 sets	**Reactive Agility** 1. Four-Cone Reaction Drill verbal cues—4 sets	
Competitive Drill 1. Get Up and Sprint 4-5 sets				
Stretch Lower Back, Hamstrings	Stretch Lower Back, Hamstrings	Stretch Lower Back, Hamstrings	Stretch Lower Back, Hamstrings	Stretch Lower Back, Hamstrings

Strength Power Workout

Advanced OFF SEASON
Phase 1

Skill Positions
WEEK 1

MONDAY	WEDNESDAY	FRIDAY
Dot Drills — 4-5 sets — 10-15 reps	Speed Ladder — 5-7 sets	Jump Rope — 1½ minutes

MONDAY

Dot Drills — 4-5 sets — 10-15 reps

Abs
Hanging Leg Raises—2 sets: 20 reps
Twisting Stack Crunches—2 sets: 20 reps

Power
Push Jerks (warmup—5 reps)
61%—5 reps
64%—5 reps
67%—5 reps

Legs
Back Squats—man makers (warmup—10 reps)
50%—20 reps: 2 sets

Chest, Shoulder, Tricep
Close Grip Bench Press (stob and stab)
4 sets: 8 reps

Tricep
Dips—30 total reps
2 sets: 10 reps

Lower Back, Glutes
Reverse Hyperextensions
2 sets: 15 reps

Neck
Neck Machine—1 set: 10 reps

Flexibility—Grip
Bar Hang—1 minute

PNF Partner Stretch
See Agility Conditioning Schedule

WEDNESDAY

Speed Ladder — 5-7 sets

Abs
Flutterkicks—30 seconds
Bicycle Abs—30 seconds

Power
Olympic Deadlifts to Knee—2 sets: 5 reps
Below Knee Hang Cleans (warmup—5 reps)
58%—5 reps
61%—5 reps
64%—5 reps

Legs
Dumbbell Walking Lunges
2 round trips—20 yards

Chest/Shoulder
Incline Bench Press—4 sets: 8 reps

Back
Towel Pullups—3 sets: 10 reps

Tricep
Dumbbell Tricep Extensions
5 sets: 8 reps (15-second rest between sets)

Neck
Neck Iso with partner
1 set: 6 reps

PNF Partner Stretch
See Agility Conditioning Schedule

FRIDAY

Jump Rope — 1½ minutes

Abs
Hokie Leg Raises—1 set: 20 reps
ABC Sit-Ups—1 set: 10 reps
Dying Cockroach—30 seconds

Power
Hang Snatch—4 sets: 5 reps

Legs
Extended Squats—2 set: 5 reps
Front Squats—4 sets: 5 reps

Chest
Bench Press (warmup—10 reps)
61%—10 reps
64%—10 reps
67%—10 reps

Tricep
Weighted Dips—3 sets: 8 reps

Lower Back, Glutes, Hamstrings
Glute Ham Raises—2 sets: 10 reps

Neck
Neck Machine—1 set: 10 reps
or
Neck Iso—1 set: 6 reps

Flexibility—Grip
Bar Hang—1 minute

PNF Partner Stretch
See Agility Conditioning Schedule

Advanced OFF SEASON   SPEED AGILITY QUICKNESS CONDITIONING SCHEDULE   WEEK 2 PHASE 1 Skill Positions

MONDAY	TUESDAY	WEDNESDAY	THURSDAY	FRIDAY
Pre-Strength Workout	**Dynamic Warmup**	**Pre-Strength Workout**	**Dynamic Warmup**	**Pre-Strength Workout**
Dot Drills 10-15 seconds 1. In and Out 2. Figure 8—both feet right side 3. Figure 8—both feet left side 4. Make up your own pattern	Walking/Skipping Toe Touches 2 sets: 20 yards Walking/Skipping Knee Hugs 2 sets: 20 yards Low Shuffle 2 sets: 20 yards Starts 2 sets: 20 yards	**Speed Ladder** 5-7 sets 1. Run Through 2. Lateral 2 Feet in, 2 Feet out 3. Lateral Shuffle 4. Slalom Jumps 5. Hop Scotch 6. Ickey Shuffle	Walking/Skipping Toe Touches 2 sets: 20 yards Walking/Skipping Knee Hugs 2 sets: 20 yards Low Carioca 2 sets: 20 yards Power Skips 2 sets: 20 yards	**Jump Rope** 10-20 seconds 1. Both Feet 2. Alternate Feet 3. 2 on Right, 2 on Left Foot 4. Make up your own pattern 5. Speed Jump
Post-Strength Workout	**PNF Partner Stretch Routine**	**Post-Strength Workout**	**PNF Partner Stretch Routine**	**Post-Strength Workout**
Static Stretch Routine	**Speed Development** 1. Heel-to-Butt Kick 2 sets: 20 yards 2. A Marches 2 sets: 20 yards 3. A Skips 2 sets: 20 yards 4. A Runs 2 sets: 20 yards	**Static Stretch Routine**	**Speed Development** 1. Fast Arms Drill 2 sets: 10-15 seconds 2. A Marches 2 sets: 15 yards 3. A Skips 2 sets: 20 yards 4. A Runs 2 sets: 20 yards	**Static Stretch Routine**
Programmable Agility 1. Texas-Drill—4 sets	**Programmable Agility** Pattern Runs 4-6 sets: 20 yards (include speed cuts, power cuts, and spins)	**Programmable Agility** 1. Carolina Drill—4 sets	**Acceleration** 1. Bullet Belts 4-6 sets: 20 yards	**Conditioning** 5 Modified Suicides 10 yards and back 15 yards and back 20 yards and back Linemen—22 seconds LB, TE, DE, FB, QB, Spec 20 seconds WR, DB, TB—18 seconds Work-to-Rest Ratio—1:3
Reactive Agility 1. Four-Cone Reaction Drill visual cues 4-6 sets: 10 seconds	**Acceleration** 1. Sled Pulls 6 sets: 20 yards (50 pounds max weight on sleds) 2. Active—Isolation	**Reactive Agility** 1. Tennis Ball Drills (all variations) 8-10 sets	**Programmable Agility** 1. 20-yard Shuttle 3-4 trials—record best time	
Competitive Drill 1. Shark in a Tank 6-8 sets: 10 seconds			**Reactive Agility** 1. Two-Point Wave Drill (includes jumps, shuffle, and "Hit It") 2. Active—Isolation	
Stretch Lower Back, Hamstrings	Stretch Lower Back, Hamstrings	Stretch Lower Back, Hamstrings	Stretch Lower Back, Hamstrings	Stretch Lower Back, Hamstrings

Skill Positions
WEEK 2

Advanced OFF SEASON
Phase 1

Strength Power
Workout

MONDAY	WEDNESDAY	FRIDAY
Dot Drills—4-5 sets – 10-15 reps	Speed Ladder—5-7 sets	Jump Rope—1½ minutes

MONDAY

Abs
Hanging Leg Raises—2 sets: 20 reps
Twisting Stack Crunches—2 sets: 20 reps

Power
Push Jerks (warmup—5 reps)
61%—5 reps
64%—5 reps
67%—5 reps
70%—5 reps

Legs
Back Squats—(warmup—10 reps)
61%—8 reps
64%—8 reps
67%—8 reps
70%—8 reps

Chest, Shoulder, Tricep
Close Grip Bench Press (stob and stab)
4 sets: 6 reps

Tricep
Dips—35 total reps

Lower Back, Glutes
Reverse Hyperextensions
2 sets: 15 reps

Neck
Neck Machine—1 set: 10 reps

Flexibility—Grip
Bar Hang—1:10 minutes

PNF Partner Stretch
See Agility Conditioning Schedule

WEDNESDAY

Abs
Flutterkicks—30 seconds
Bicycle Abs—30 seconds

Power
Olympic Deadlifts to Knee—2 sets: 5 reps
Below Knee Hang Cleans (warmup—3 reps)
61%—3 reps
64%—3 reps
67%—3 reps—2 sets

Legs
Dumbbell Walking Lunges
2 round trips—20 yards

Chest, Shoulder, Tricep
Incline Bench Press—4 sets: 6 reps

Back, Wrist, Hand
Towel Pullups—3 sets: 10 reps

Tricep
Dumbbell Tricep Extensions
5 sets: 8 reps (15-second rest between sets)

Neck
Neck Iso with partner
1 set: 6 reps

PNF Partner Stretch
See Agility Conditioning Schedule

FRIDAY

Abs
Hokie Leg Raises—1 set: 20 reps
ABC Sit-Ups—1 set: 10 reps
Dying Cockroach—30 seconds

Power
Hang Snatch (Speed!)—4 sets: 3 reps

Legs
Extended Squats—2 set: 5 reps
Front Squats—4 sets: 5 reps

Chest, Shoulder, Tricep
Bench Press (warmup—5 reps)
61%—8 reps
64%—8 reps
67%—8 reps
70%—8 reps

Tricep
Weighted Dips—3 sets: 8 reps

Lower Back, Glutes, Hamstrings
Glute Ham Raises—2 sets: 10 reps

Neck
Neck Machine—1 set: 10 reps
or
Neck Iso—1 set: 6 reps

Flexibility—Grip
Bar Hang—1:10

PNF Partner Stretch
See Agility Conditioning Schedule

Advanced OFF SEASON   SPEED AGILITY QUICKNESS CONDITIONING SCHEDULE   WEEK 3 PHASE 1 Skill Positions

MONDAY	TUESDAY	WEDNESDAY	THURSDAY	FRIDAY
Pre-Strength Workout	**Dynamic Warmup**	**Pre-Strength Workout**	**Dynamic Warmup**	**Pre-Strength Workout**
Dot Drills 10-15 seconds 1. In and Out 2. Figure 8—both feet right side 3. Figure 8—both feet left side 4. Spins 5. Make up your own pattern	Walking/Skipping Toe Touches 2 sets: 20 yards Walking/Skipping Knee Hugs 2 sets: 20 yards Low Shuffle 2 sets: 20 yards Starts—Football Stance 4-6 sets	**Speed Ladder** 5-7 sets 1. Run Through 2. Lateral 2 Feet in, 2 Feet out 3. Lateral Shuffle 4. Slalom Jumps 5. Hop Scotch 6. Ickey Shuffle	High Knees 2 sets: 20 yards Backward High Knees 2 sets: 20 yards High Knee Crossovers 2 sets: 20 yards Backward Skips 2 sets: 20 yards	**Jump Rope** 10-20 seconds 1. Both Feet 2. Alternate Feet 3. 2 on Right, 2 on Left Foot 4. Make up your own pattern 5. Speed Jump
Post-Strength Workout	**PNF Partner Stretch Routine**	**Post-Strength Workout**	**PNF Partner Stretch Routine**	**Post-Strength Workout**
Static Stretch Routine	**Plyometrics** 1. Standing Long Jumps (series of 5 jumps each set) 2 sets 2. Single Leg Hops 2 sets: 20 yards 3. Power Skips 2 sets: 20 yards 4. Bounding—2 sets: 20 yards	**Static Stretch Routine**	**Speed Development** 1. Heel-to-Butt Kicks 2 set: 20 yards 2. A Marches 2 sets: 20 yards 3. A Skips 2 sets: 20 yards 4. A Runs 2 sets: 20 yards	**Static Stretch Routine**
Programmable Agility 1. Star Drill 2-4 sets (include speed cuts, power cuts, and spins)	**Programmable Agility** 1. Carolina Drill 3-4 sets	**Programmable Agility** 20-yard Shuttle 4 sets: record best time	**Acceleration** Acceleration Ladder 6 sets: 20 yards	**Conditioning** 5 Modified Suicides 10 yards and back 15 yards and back 20 yards and back Linemen—22 seconds LB, TE, DE, FB, QB, Spec 20 seconds WR, DB, TB—18 seconds Work-to-Rest Ratio—1:3
Reactive Agility 1. Eight-Point Reactive Cone Drill visual cues	**Reactive Agility** 1. Four-Cone Reaction Drill verbal cues 4-6 sets	**Reactive Agility** 1. Four-Cone Reaction Drill verbal cues 4-5 sets	**Reactive Agility** 1. Tennis Ball Drills (all variations) 8-10 sets	
Competitve Drill 1. Get Up and Sprint (various starting positions) 4-6 sets	2. Active—Isolation	**Conditioning** Punching Bag (heavy) 3 sets: 30 seconds Work-to-Rest Ratio—1:1	2. Active—Isolation	
Stretch Lower Back, Hamstrings	Stretch Lower Back, Hamstrings	Stretch Lower Back, Hamstrings	Stretch Lower Back, Hamstrings	Stretch Lower Back, Hamstrings

Skill Positions
WEEK 3

Advanced OFF SEASON
Phase 1

Strength Power
Workout

MONDAY

Dot Drills—4-5 sets – 10-15 reps

Abs
Hanging Leg Raises—2 sets: 20 reps
Twisting Stack Crunches—2 sets: 20 reps

Power
Push Jerks (warmup—5 reps)
  61%—5 reps
  64%—5 reps
  67%—5 reps
  73%—5 reps

Legs
Back Squats (warmup—8 reps)
  58%—6 reps
  64%—6 reps
  70%—6 reps
  76%—6 reps

Chest, Shoulder, Arm
Close Grip Bench Press (stob and stab)
4 sets: 6 reps

Tricep
Dips—40 total reps

Lower Back, Glutes
Reverse Hyperextensions
2 sets: 15 reps

Neck
Neck Machine—1 set: 10 reps

Flexibility—Grip
Bar Hang—1:15 minutes

PNF Partner Stretch
See Agility Conditioning Schedule

WEDNESDAY

Speed Ladder—5-7 sets

Abs
Flutterkicks—30 seconds
Bicycle Abs—30 seconds

Power
Olympic Deadlifts to Knee—2 sets: 3 reps
Power Cleans (warmup—5 reps)
  61%—5 reps
  64%—5 reps
  67%—3 reps
  73%—3 reps

Legs
Dumbbell Walking Lunges
2 round trips—20 yards

Chest, Shoulder, Tricep
Incline Bench Press—4 sets: 6 reps

Back—Grip
Towel Pullups—3 sets: 10 reps

Tricep
Dumbbell Tricep Extensions
5 sets: 8 reps (15-second rest between sets)

Neck
Neck Iso with partner
1 set: 6 reps

PNF Partner Stretch
See Agility Conditioning Schedule

FRIDAY

Jump Rope—1½ minutes

Abs
Hokie Leg Raises—1 set: 20 reps
ABC Sit-Ups—1 set: 10 reps
Dying Cockroach—30 seconds

Power
Hang Snatch (Speed!)—4 sets: 3 reps

Legs
Extended Squats—2 set: 5 reps
Front Squats—4 sets: 5 reps

Chest, Shoulder, Tricep
Bench Press (warmup—8 reps)
  58%—6 reps
  64%—6 reps
  70%—6 reps
  76%—6 reps—2 sets

Tricep
Weighted Dips—4 sets: 6 reps

Lower Back, Glutes, Hamstrings
Glute Ham Raises—2 sets: 12 reps

Neck
Neck Machine—1 set: 10 reps
or
Neck Iso—1 set: 6 reps

Flexibility—Grip
Bar Hang—1:20 minutes

PNF Partner Stretch
See Agility Conditioning Schedule

Advanced OFF SEASON   SPEED AGILITY QUICKNESS CONDITIONING SCHEDULE   WEEK 4 PHASE 2 Skill Positions

MONDAY	TUESDAY	WEDNESDAY	THURSDAY	FRIDAY
Pre-Strength Workout	**Dynamic Warmup**	**Pre-Strength Workout**	**Dynamic Warmup**	**Pre-Strength Workout**
Dot Drills 10–15 seconds	Walking Knee Hugs 2 sets: 20 yards	**Speed Ladder** 5–7 sets	Walking/Skipping Knee Hugs 2 sets: 20 yards	**Jump Rope** 10–20 seconds
1. In and Out	Skipping Toe Touches 2 sets: 20 yards	1. Run Through	Walking/Skipping Toe Touches 2 sets: 20 yards	1. Both Feet
2. Figure 8—both feet right side	Low Shuffle 2 sets: 20 yards	2. Lateral 2 Feet in, 2 Feet out	Low Carioca 2 sets: 20 yards	2. Alternate Feet
3. Figure 8—both feet left side	Starts—Football Stance 4–6 sets	3. Lateral Shuffle	**PNF Partner Stretch Routine**	3. 2 on Right, 2 on Left Foot
4. Spins	**PNF Partner Stretch Routine**	4. Slalom Jumps	**Plyometrics**	4. Make up your own pattern
5. Make up your own pattern	**Speed Development**	5. Hop Scotch	1. Single Leg Hops 2 set: 20 yards	5. Speed Jump
Post-Strength Workout	1. Fast Arms 2 sets: 15 seconds	6. Ickey Shuffle	2. Power Skips 2 sets: 20 yards	**Post-Strength Workout**
Static Stretch Routine	2. A Marches 2 sets: 20 yards	**Post-Strength Workout**	3. Bounding 2 sets: 20 yards	**Static Stretch Routine**
Programmable Agility Pattern Runs 6 sets: 20 yards (include speed cuts, power cuts, and spins)	3. A Skips 2 sets: 20 yards	**Static Stretch Routine**	**Acceleration**	**Conditioning** 5 Modified Suicides
Reactive Agility	4. A Runs 2 sets: 20 yards	**Programmable Agility**	1. Acceleration Ladder 6 sets: 20 yards	10 yards and back
1. Two-Point Wave Drill 4–6 sets	5. Fast Leg Drill—right and left	1. Four-Cone Drill 2 sets each side (include back-pedal, shuffle, carioca, and sprint)	**Programmable Agility**	15 yards and back
	Reactive Agility	**Competitive Drill**	1. 20-yard Shuttle 4 sets: record best time	20 yards and back
	1. Eight-Point Cone Reaction Drill visual cues 4–6 sets: 10 seconds	1. Get Up and Sprint (vary starting positions) 6–8 sets	**Competitive Drill**	Linemen—22 seconds LB, TE, DE, FB, QB, Spec. 20 seconds WR, DB, TB—18 seconds
	Acceleration		1. Shark in a Tank 4–8 sets: 10 seconds	Work-to-Rest Ratio—1:3
	1. Sled Pulls 6 sets: 20 yards (50 pounds max weight on sled)		2. Active—Isolation	
	2. Active—Isolation			
Stretch Lower Back, Hamstrings	Stretch Lower Back, Hamstrings	Stretch Lower Back, Hamstrings	Stretch Lower Back, Hamstrings	Stretch Lower Back, Hamstrings

Skill Positions
WEEK 4

Advanced OFF SEASON
Phase 2

Strength Power
Workout

MONDAY

Dot Drills—4-5 sets – 10-15 reps

Abs
Timed Leg Throws (with partner)—30 seconds
Timed Sit-Ups (with partner)—30 seconds

Power
Push Jerks (warmup—5 reps)
61%—3 reps
64%—3 reps
70%—3 reps
76%—3 reps—2 sets

Legs
Lateral Squats—2 sets: 6 reps
Back Squats—(warmup—8 reps)
61%—5 reps
67%—5 reps
73%—5 reps
79%—5 reps

Chest, Shoulder, Tricep
Dumbbell Bench Press (stop and stab)
4 sets: 6 reps

Tricep
Weighted Dips—3 sets: 8 reps

Lats
Pullups (vary grip)—3 sets: 10 reps

Neck
Neck Machine—1 set: 10 reps

PNF Partner Stretch
See Agility Conditioning Schedule

WEDNESDAY

Speed Ladder—5-7 sets

Abs
Hanging Leg Raises—2 sets: 20 reps
Medicine Ball Stack Crunches—2 set: 20 reps

Power
Olympic Deadlifts to Knee—2 sets: 3 reps
Power Cleans (warmup—3 reps)
58%—3 reps
64%—3 reps
70%—3 reps
76%—3 reps—2 sets
Clean Pulls—2 sets: 3 reps

Legs
Box Stepups—4 sets: 5 reps

Shoulder, Tricep
Seated Shoulder Press—8, 6, 5, 5

Lats
Seated Cable Rows—3 sets: 8 reps
or
Dumbbell Rows—3 sets: 8 reps

Lower Back, Glutes, Hamstrings
Glute Ham Raises—2 sets: 12 reps

Neck
Neck Iso with partner
1 set: 6 reps

Flexibility—Grip
Bar Hang—1:20 minutes

PNF Partner Stretch
See Agility Conditioning Schedule

FRIDAY

Jump Rope—1½ minutes

Abs
Flutterkicks—30 seconds
Twisting Sit-Ups—1 set: 20 reps

Power
Powersnatch (Speed!)—4 sets: 3 reps

Legs
Extended Squats—2 set: 6 reps
Speed Squats (50% of max)—4 sets: 5 reps

Chest, Shoulder, Tricep
Bench Press (warmup—8 reps)
64%—5 reps
70%—5 reps
76%—5 reps
82%—5 reps

Tricep
Straight Bar Tricep Extensions
4 sets: 8 reps

Lats
Lat Pulldowns (front, underhand)
3 sets: 10 reps

Lower Back, Glutes, Hamstrings
Glute Ham Raises—2 sets: 12 reps
or

Lower Back, Glutes
Reverse Hyperextensions—2 sets: 15 reps

Neck
Neck Machine—1 set: 10 reps
or
Neck Iso—1 set: 6 reps

PNF Partner Stretch
See Agility Conditioning Schedule

Advanced OFF SEASON   SPEED AGILITY QUICKNESS CONDITIONING SCHEDULE   WEEK 5 PHASE 2 Skill Positions

MONDAY	TUESDAY	WEDNESDAY	THURSDAY	FRIDAY
Pre-Strength Workout	**Dynamic Warmup**	**Pre-Strength Workout**	**Dynamic Warmup**	**Pre-Strength Workout**
Dot Drills 10-15 seconds 1. In and Out 2. Figure 8—both feet right side 3. Figure 8—both feet left side 4. Spins 5. Make up your own pattern	Walking Toe Touches 2 sets: 20 yards Skipping Knee Hugs 2 sets: 20 yards Low Carioca 2 sets: 20 yards Lunge Walk 2 sets: 20 yards	**Speed Ladder** 5-7 sets 1. Run Through 2. Lateral 2 Feet in, 2 Feet out 3. Lateral Shuffle 4. Slalom Jumps 5. Hop Scotch 6. Ickey Shuffle	Walking/Skipping Knee Hugs 2 sets: 20 yards Walking/Skipping Toe Touches 2 sets: 20 yards High Knee Crossovers 2 sets: 20 yards Backward High Knees 2 sets: 20 yards	**Jump Rope** 10-20 seconds 1. Both Feet 2. Alternate Feet 3. 2 on Right, 2 on Left Foot 4. Make up your own pattern 5. Speed Jump
Post-Strength Workout Static Stretch Routine	**PNF Partner Stretch Routine**	**Post-Strength Workout** Static Stretch Routine	**PNF Partner Stretch Routine**	**Post-Strength Workout** Static Stretch Routine
Programmable Agility 1. Star Drill—2-4 sets (include speed cuts, power cuts, and spins) 2. Bag Drills (include Run Through, High Knee Hop variations, and Lateral Shuffle)	**Speed Development** 1. Heel-to-Butt Kicks 2 sets: 20 yards 2. A Marches 2 sets: 20 yards 3. A Skips 2 sets: 20 yards 4. A Runs 2 sets: 20 yards 5. Fast Leg Drill—right and left	**Programmable Agility** 1. 20-yard Shuttle 4 sets: record best time	**Plyometrics** 1. Standing Long Jumps 2 sets: 5 jumps 2. Single Leg Speed Hops 2 sets: 20 yards 3. Power Skips 2 sets: 20 yards 4. Bounding—2 sets: 20 yards	**Conditioning** 5 Modified Suicides 10 yards and back 15 yards and back 20 yards and back Linemen—22 seconds LB, TE, DE, FB, QB, Spec 20 seconds WR, DB, TB—18 seconds Work-to-Rest Ratio—1:3
Reactive Agility 1. Two-Point Wave Drill 4-6 sets	**Programmable Agility** 1. Texas-Drill—4 sets	**Reactive Agility** 1. Tennis Ball Drills (all variations) 8-10 sets	**Acceleration** Sled Pulls—6 sets: 20 yards or Uphill Runs 6-8 sets: 30 yards	
	Acceleration 1. Acceleration Ladder 6 sets: 20 yards		**Competitive Drill** 1. Capture the Flag 2. Active—Isolation	
	Competitive Drill 1. Get Up and Sprint—4-6 sets: (vary start position) 2. Active—Isolation			
Stretch Lower Back, Hamstrings	Stretch Lower Back, Hamstrings	Stretch Lower Back, Hamstrings	Stretch Lower Back, Hamstrings	Stretch Lower Back, Hamstrings

Skill Positions
WEEK 5

Advanced OFF SEASON
Phase 2

Strength Power Workout

MONDAY

Dot Drills—4-5 sets – 10-15 reps

Abs
Timed Leg Throws (with partner)—30 seconds
Timed Sit-Ups (with partner)—30 seconds

Power
Push Jerks (warmup—5 reps)
61%—3 reps
67%—3 reps
73%—3 reps
79%—3 reps—2 sets

Legs
Lateral Squats—2 sets: 6 reps
Back Squats—(warmup—8 reps)
61%—3 reps
67%—3 reps
73%—3 reps
79%—3 reps
85%—3 reps

Chest, Shoulder, Tricep
Dumbbell Bench Press (stop and stab)
5 sets: 5 reps

Tricep
Weighted Dips—4 sets: 6 reps

Lats
Pullups (vary grip)—3 sets: 10 reps

Neck
Neck Machine—1 set: 10 reps

PNF Partner Stretch
See Agility Conditioning Schedule

WEDNESDAY

Speed Ladder—5-7 sets

Abs
Hanging Leg Raises—2 sets: 20 reps
Medicine Ball Stack Crunches—2 set: 20 reps

Power
Olympic Deadlifts to Knee—2 sets: 3 reps
Power Cleans (warmup—3 reps)
61%—3 reps
67%—3 reps
73%—3 reps
79%—3 reps—2 sets
Clean Pulls—2 sets: 3 reps

Legs
Box Stepups—4 sets: 5 reps

Shoulder, Tricep
Seated Shoulder Press—8, 6, 6, 5, 5

Lats
Seated Cable Rows—3 sets: 8 reps
or
Dumbbell Rows—3 sets: 8 reps

Lower Back, Glutes, Hamstrings
Glute Ham Raises—2 sets: 12 reps

Neck
Neck Iso with partner
1 set: 6 reps

Flexibility—Grip
Bar Hang—1:20 minutes

PNF Partner Stretch
See Agility Conditioning Schedule

FRIDAY

Jump Rope—1½ minutes

Abs
Flutterkicks—30 seconds
Twisting Sit-Ups—1 set: 20 reps

Power
Power Snatch (Speed!)—4 sets: 3 reps

Legs
Extended Squats—2 set: 6 reps
Speed Squats (50% of max)—4 sets: 5 reps

Chest, Shoulder, Tricep
Bench Press (warmup—8 reps)
61%—5 reps
67%—5 reps
73%—3 reps
79%—3 reps
85%—3 reps—2 sets
Straight Bar Tricep Extensions
4 sets: 8 reps

Lats
Lat Pulldowns (front, underhand)
3 sets: 10 reps

Lower Back, Glutes, Hamstrings
Glute Ham Raises—2 sets: 12 reps
or
Lower Back, Glutes
Reverse Hyperextensions—2 sets: 15 reps

Neck
Neck Machine—1 set: 10 reps
or
Neck Iso—1 set: 6 reps

PNF Partner Stretch
See Agility Conditioning Schedule

Advanced OFF SEASON   SPEED AGILITY QUICKNESS CONDITIONING SCHEDULE   WEEK 6 PHASE 2 Skill Positions

MONDAY	TUESDAY	WEDNESDAY	THURSDAY	FRIDAY
Pre-Strength Workout	Dynamic Warmup	Pre-Strength Workout	Dynamic Warmup	Pre-Strength Workout
Dot Drills 10-15 seconds 1. In and Out 2. Figure 8—both feet right side 3. Figure 8—both feet left side 4. Spins 5. Make up your own pattern	Walking/Skipping Knee Hugs 2 sets: 20 yards Walking/Skipping Toe Touches 2 sets: 20 yards Low Shuffle 2 sets: 20 yards Starts 4-6 sets	**Speed Ladder** 5-7 sets 1. Run Through 2. Lateral 2 Feet in, 2 Feet out 3. Lateral Shuffle 4. Slalom Jumps 5. Hop Scotch 6. Ickey Shuffle	Walking Toe Touches 2 sets: 20 yards Skipping Knee Hugs 2 sets: 20 yards High Knee Crossovers 2 sets: 20 yards Backward Skips 2 sets: 20 yards	**Jump Rope** 10-20 seconds 1. Both Feet 2. Alternate Feet 3. 2 on Right, 2 on Left Foot 4. Make up your own pattern 5. Speed Jump
Post-Strength Workout Static Stretch Routine	PNF Partner Stretch Routine	Post-Strength Workout Static Stretch Routine	PNF Partner Stretch Routine	Post-Strength Workout Static Stretch Routine
Programmable Agility 1. 20-yard Shuttle 4 sets: record best time	**Speed Development** 1. A Marches 2 sets: 20 yards 2. A Skips—2 sets: 20 yards 3. A Runs—2 sets: 20 yards 4. Fast Leg Drill-Right and Left 2 sets: 20 yards (alternate legs)	**Acceleration** Sled Pulls 6 sets: 20 yards or Uphill Runs 6-8 hills—20-30 yards	**Speed Development** 1. Fast Arms 2 sets: 15 seconds 2. Heel-to-Butt Kicks 2 sets: 20 yards 3. A Skips 2 sets: 20 yards 4. A Runs 2 sets: 20 yards	**Conditioning** 5 Modified Suicides 10 yards and back 15 yards and back 20 yards and back Linemen—22 seconds LB, TE, DE, FB, QB, Spec 20 seconds WR, DB, TB—18 seconds Work-to-Rest Ratio—1:3
Reactive Agility 1. Four-Cone Reaction Drill verbal cues 4-6 sets: 10-15 seconds	**Programmable Agility** Bag Drills 1. Run Through 2. Lateral Shuffle 3. Lateral Double Leg Hops 4. Zig-Zag 5. Run Through		**Reactive Agility** 1. Two-Point Wave Drill 4-6 sets: 10-15 seconds (include one player as leader for other to mirror)	
	Reactive Agility 1. Crazy Ball Drills (all variations) 2. Active—Isolation		**Competitive Drill** 1. Shark in a Tank 4-6 sets: 10 seconds 2. Active—Isolation	
Stretch Lower Back, Hamstrings	Stretch Lower Back, Hamstrings	Stretch Lower Back, Hamstrings	Stretch Lower Back, Hamstrings	Stretch Lower Back, Hamstrings

Skill Positions
WEEK 6

Advanced OFFSEASON
Phase 2

Strength Power
Workout

MONDAY	WEDNESDAY	FRIDAY
Dot Drills—4-5 sets – 10-15 reps	Speed Ladder—5-7 sets	Jump Rope—1½ minutes

MONDAY

Dot Drills—4-5 sets – 10-15 reps

Abs
Timed Leg Throws (with partner)—30 seconds
Timed Sit-Ups (with partner)—30 seconds

Power
Push Jerks (warmup—5 reps)
64%—3 reps
70%—3 reps
76%—3 reps
82%—3 reps—2 sets

Legs
Lateral Squats—2 sets: 6 reps
Back Squats—(warmup—8 reps)
64%—5 reps
70%—3 reps
76%—3 reps
82%—3 reps
88%—3 reps

Chest, Shoulder, Tricep
Alternate Dumbbell Press
4 sets: 5 reps

Tricep
Weighted Dips—4 sets: 6 reps

Lats
Pullups (vary grip)—3 sets: 10 reps

Neck
Neck Machine—1 set: 10 reps

PNF Partner Stretch
See Agility Conditioning Schedule

WEDNESDAY

Speed Ladder—5-7 sets

Abs
Hanging Leg Raises—2 sets: 20 reps
Medicine Ball Stack Crunches—2 set: 20 reps

Power
Olympic Deadlifts to Knee—2 sets: 3 reps
Power Cleans (warmup—3 reps)
61%—3 reps
67%—3 reps
73%—3 reps
79%—3 reps
82-85%—1 rep—3 sets
Clean Pulls—2 sets: 3 reps

Legs
Box Stepups—4 sets: 5 reps

Shoulder, Tricep
Incline Bench Press—4 sets: 5 reps

Lats
Seated Cable Rows—3 sets: 8 reps
or
Dumbbell Rows—3 sets: 8 reps

Lower Back, Glutes, Hamstrings
Glute Ham Raises—2 sets: 12 reps

Neck
Neck Iso with partner
1 set: 6 reps

Flexibility—Grip
Bar Hang—1:30 minutes

PNF Partner Stretch
See Agility Conditioning Schedule

FRIDAY

Jump Rope—1½ minutes

Abs
Flutterkicks—30 seconds
Twisting Sit-Ups—1 set: 20 reps

Power
Power Snatch (Speed!)—4 sets: 3 reps

Legs
Extended Squats—2 set: 6 reps
Speed Squats (50% of max)—4 sets: 5 reps

Chest, Shoulder, Tricep
Bench Press (warmup—8 reps)
64%—5 reps
70%—3 reps
76%—3 reps
82%—3 reps
88%—3 reps
Straight Bar Tricep Extensions
4 sets: 8 reps

Lats
Lat Pulldowns (front, underhand)
3 sets: 10 reps

Lower Back, Glutes, Hamstrings
Glute Ham Raises—2 sets: 12 reps
or

Lower Back, Glutes
Reverse Hyperextensions—2 sets: 15 reps

Neck
Neck Machine—1 set: 10 reps
or
Neck Iso—1 set: 6 reps

PNF Partner Stretch
See Agility Conditioning Schedule

Advanced OFF SEASON   SPEED AGILITY QUICKNESS CONDITIONING SCHEDULE   WEEK 7 PHASE 2 Skill Positions

MONDAY	TUESDAY	WEDNESDAY	THURSDAY	FRIDAY
Pre-Strength Workout	Dynamic Warmup	Pre-Strength Workout	Dynamic Warmup	Pre-Strength Workout

MONDAY

Pre-Strength Workout

Dot Drills
1. In and Out
2. Figure 8—both feet right side
3. Figure 8—both feet left side
4. Make up your own pattern
3–4 sets: 10–15 seconds

Post-Strength Workout

Static Stretch Routine

Programmable Agility
1. Four-Cone Perimeter Drill
4 sets each side (include back-pedal, shuffle, carioca, and sprint)

Reactive Agility
1. Tennis Ball Drills (all variations)
8–10 sets

Conditioning
3 Modified Suicides
QB, FB, Spec.—20 seconds
WR, DB, TB—18 seconds
Work-to-Rest Ratio—1:3

Stretch
Lower Back, Hamstrings

TUESDAY

Dynamic Warmup

Walking Toe Touches
2 sets: 20 yards
Skipping Knee Hugs
2 sets: 20 yards
High Knee Crossovers
2 sets: 20 yards
Backward Skips
2 sets: 20 yards

Speed Development
1. A Marches
2 sets: 20 yards
2. A Skips
2 sets: 20 yards
3. A Runs
2 sets: 20 yards
4. Bounding
2 sets: 20 yards

Programmable Agility
1. Carolina Drill—4 sets

Reactive Agility
1. Two-Point Wave Drill (includes jumps, shuffle, and "Hit It")
4 sets: 10–15 seconds

Aceleration Drill
1. Build Ups—6 sets: 60 yards (graduated sprint out, walk back for recovery)

Stretch
Lower Back, Hamstrings

WEDNESDAY

Pre-Strength Workout

Speed Ladder
5–7 sets
1. Run Through
2. Lateral Shuffle
3. Hop Scotch
4. Slalom Jumps
5. Ickey Shuffle

Post-Strength Workout

Static Stretch Routine

Acceleration
1. Uphill Runs
6–8 sets—20–30 yards (sprint uphill, walk down)

Stretch
Lower Back, Hamstrings

THURSDAY

Dynamic Warmup

Walking Knee Hugs
2 sets: 20 yards
Skipping Toe Touches
2 sets: 20 yards
Low Shuffle
2 sets: 20 yards
Starts—Football Stance
2 sets: 20 yards

Speed Development
1. Heel-to-Butt Kicks
2 sets: 20 yards
2. A Marches
2 sets: 20 yards
3. A Skips
2 sets: 20 yards
4. A Runs—2 sets: 20 yard
5. Power Skips
2 sets: 20 yards

Acceleration
1. Sled Pulls
6 sets: 20 yards (50 pounds max weight on sled)

Programmable Agility
1. 20-yard Shuttle
3–4 sets: record best time

Stretch
Lower Back, Hamstrings

FRIDAY

Pre-Strength Workout

Jump Rope—stationary
10–20 seconds
1. Both Feet
2. Right Foot Only
3. Left Foot Only
4. Alternate Feet
5. Speed Jump

Post-Strength Workout

Static Stretch Routine

Conditioning
5 Modified Suicides
10 yards and back
15 yards and back
20 yards and back
Linemen—22 seconds
FB, QB, Spec.
20 seconds
WR, DB, TB—18 seconds
Work-to-Rest Ratio—1:3

Stretch
Lower Back, Hamstrings

Skill Positions
WEEK 7

Advanced OFF SEASON
Phase 2

Strength Power
Workout

MONDAY

Dot Drills—4-5 sets – 10-15 reps

Abs
Timed Leg Throws (with partner)—30 seconds
Timed Sit-Ups (with partner)—30 seconds

Power
Push Jerks (warmup—5 reps)
61%—3 reps
67%—3 reps
73%—3 reps
79%—2 reps
85%—1 rep—3 sets

Legs
Lateral Squats—2 sets: 6 reps
Back Squats—(warmup—8 reps)
61%—3 reps
67%—3 reps
73%—3 reps
79%—3 reps
85%—2 reps
91%—1 rep—3 sets

Chest, Shoulder, Tricep
Alternate Dumbbell Bench Press (stop and stab)
4 sets: 5 reps

Tricep
Weighted Dips—4 sets: 6 reps

Lats
Pullups (vary grip)—3 sets: 10 reps

Neck
Neck Machine—1 set: 10 reps

PNF Partner Stretch
See Agility Conditioning Schedule

WEDNESDAY

Speed Ladder—5-7 sets

Abs
Hanging Leg Raises—2 sets: 20 reps
Medicine Ball Stack Crunches—2 set: 20 reps

Power
Olympic Deadlifts to Knee—2 sets: 3 reps
Power Cleans (warmup—3 reps)
61%—3 reps
67%—3 reps
73%—3 reps
79%—2 reps
Clean Pulls—2 sets: 3 reps

Legs
Box Stepups—4 sets: 5 reps

Shoulder, Tricep
Incline Bench Press—4 sets: 5 reps

Lats
Seated Cable Rows—3 sets: 8 reps
or
Dumbbell Rows—3 sets: 8 reps

Lower Back, Glutes, Hamstrings
Glute Ham Raises—2 sets: 12 reps

Neck
Neck Iso with partner
1 set: 6 reps

Flexibility—Grip
Bar Hang—1:30 minutes

PNF Partner Stretch
See Agility Conditioning Schedule

FRIDAY

Jump Rope—1½ minutes

Abs
Flutterkicks—30 seconds
Twisting Sit-Ups—1 set: 20 reps

Power
Power Snatch (Speed!)—4 sets: 3 reps

Legs
Extended Squats—2 set: 6 reps
Speed Squats (50% of max)—4 sets: 5 reps

Chest, Shoulder, Tricep
Bench Press (warmup—8 reps)
61%—3 reps
67%—3 reps
73%—3 reps
79%—3 reps
85%—2 reps
91%—1 rep—3 sets
Straight Bar Tricep Extensions
4 sets: 8 reps

Lats
Lat Pulldowns (front, underhand)
3 sets: 10 reps

Lower Back, Glutes, Hamstrings
Glute Ham Raises—2 sets: 12 reps
or

Lower Back, Glutes
Reverse Hyperextensions—2 sets: 10 reps

Neck
Neck Machine—1 set: 10 reps
or
Neck Iso—1 set: 6 reps

PNF Partner Stretch
See Agility Conditioning Schedule

Advanced OFF SEASON   SPEED AGILITY QUICKNESS CONDITIONING SCHEDULE   WEEK 8 PHASE 2 Skill Positions

MONDAY	TUESDAY	WEDNESDAY	THURSDAY	FRIDAY
Pre-Strength Workout	**Dynamic Warmup**	**Pre-Strength Workout**	**Dynamic Warmup**	**Pre-Strength Workout**

<u>Dot Drills</u>
3-5 sets: 10-15 seconds
1. In and Out
2. Figure 8—right side right foot only
3. Figure 8—left side left foot only
4. In and Out with Spin
5. Make up your own pattern
 	
Post-Strength Workout
 	
PNF Partner Stretch Routine
	Walking Toe Touches
	Skipping Toe Touches
	Backward Skips
	High Knee Crossovers
	2 sets: 20 yards
	
	<u>Speed Development</u>
	1. A Marches
	   2 sets: 20 yards
	2. A Skips
	   2 sets: 20 yards
	3. A Runs
	   2 sets: 20 yards
	
	PNF Partner Stretch Routine
	
	<u>Programmable Agility</u>
	1. Pattern Runs (include speed cuts, power cuts, and spins)
	   6 sets: 20 yards
	2. Carolina Box Drill
	   3-4 sets
	
	<u>Reactive Agility</u>
	1. Four-Cone Reaction Drill (visual cues)
	   3-4 sets: 10-15 seconds
	
	<u>Acceleration</u>
	1. Build Ups
	   6 sets: 60 yards (graduated sprint out, walk back for recovery)
		<u>Speed Ladder</u>
		5-7 sets
		1. Run Through
		2. Lateral 2 Feet in, 2 Feet out
		3. Slalom Jumps
		4. Backward Slalom Jumps
		5. Ickey Shuffle
		
		Post-Strength Workout
		
		Static Stretch Routine
		
		<u>Acceleration</u>
		1. Uphill Runs
		   6-8 sets: 30 yards (sprint up, walk down)
		
		or
		
		2. Sand Runs
		   6-8 sets: 40 yards (sprint 40 yards, walk back for recovery)
		
		or
		
		3. Short Stadium Sprint
		   6-8 sets: 30 yards (sprint up, walk down)
			Walking Toe Touches
			Skipping Toe Touches
			Backward High Knees
			   2 sets: 20 yards
			
			<u>Speed Development</u>
			1. A Marches
			   2 sets: 20 yards
			2. A Skips
			   2 sets: 20 yards
			3. A Runs
			   2 sets: 20 yards
			4. Bounding
			   2 sets: 20 yards
			
			PNF Partner Stretch Routine
			
			TEST
			Vertical Jump
			Sit and Reach Flexibility Test
			10-yard Sprint
				<u>Jump Rope</u>—stationary
				10-20 seconds
				1. Both Feet
				2. Right Foot
				3. Left Foot
				4. Alternate Feet
				5. 2 on Right, 2 on Left
				
				Post-Strength Workout
				
				PNF Partner Stretch Routine
				
				<u>Conditioning</u>
				5 Modified Suicides
				   10 yards and back
				   15 yards and back
				   20 yards and back
				FB, QB, Spec.
				   20 seconds
				WR, DB, TB—18 seconds
				Work-to-Rest Ratio—1:3

Stretch Lower Back, Hamstrings	Stretch Lower Back, Hamstrings	Stretch Lower Back, Hamstrings	Stretch Lower Back, Hamstrings	Stretch Lower Back, Hamstrings

Skill Positions
WEEK 8

Advanced OFF SEASON
Phase 2

MAX
TESTING

MONDAY	WEDNESDAY	FRIDAY
Dot Drills—4-5 sets – 10-15 reps	Speed Ladder—5-7 sets	Jump Rope—1½ minutes

MONDAY

Test—Push Jerks Max
(warmup—3 reps)
55%—3 reps
64%—1 rep
73%—1 rep
82%—1 rep
88%—1 rep
Begin 1 rep max test!

Back Squats Max
(warmup—8 reps)
61%—3-5 reps
70%—3 reps
79%—1 rep
85-88%—1 rep
Begin 3 rep max test!

Stretch
Lower back, Hamstrings
See Agility Conditioning Schedule

WEDNESDAY

Test—Power Cleans Max
(warmup—3 reps)
55%—3 reps
64%—1-2 reps
73%—1 rep
82%—1 rep
88%—1 rep
Begin 1 rep max test!

Stretch
Lower back, Hamstrings
See Agility Conditioning Schedule

FRIDAY

Test—Bench Press Max
(warmup—6-8 reps)
61%—5 reps
70%—3 reps
79%—1 rep
85%—1 rep
91%—1 rep
Begin 1 rep max test!

Stretch
Lower back, Hamstrings
See Agility Conditioning Schedule

Advanced OFF SEASON   SPEED AGILITY QUICKNESS CONDITIONING SCHEDULE   WEEK 9 PHASE 2 Skill Positions

MONDAY	TUESDAY	WEDNESDAY	THURSDAY	FRIDAY
Pre-Strength Workout	Dynamic Warmup	Pre-Strength Workout	Dynamic Warmup	Pre-Strength Workout

Active Rest

Play basketball, volleyball, tag, football, racquetball, etc.

STAY OUT OF THE WEIGHT ROOM!

Stretch Lower Back, Hamstrings	Stretch Lower Back, Hamstrings	Stretch Lower Back, Hamstrings	Stretch Lower Back, Hamstrings	Stretch Lower Back, Hamstrings

Skill Positions
WEEK 9

Advanced OFF SEASON
CPhase 2

ACTIVE
REST

MONDAY	WEDNESDAY	FRIDAY
Dot Drills—4-5 sets — 10-15 reps	Speed Ladder—5-7 sets	Jump Rope—1½ minutes

Active Rest

Play basketball, volleyball, tag, football, racquetball, etc.

STAY OUT OF THE WEIGHT ROOM!

MONDAY	WEDNESDAY	FRIDAY
Stretch Lower back, Hamstrings	Stretch Lower back, Hamstrings	Stretch Lower back, Hamstrings

Advanced PRESEASON   SPEED AGILITY QUICKNESS CONDITIONING SCHEDULE   WEEK 1 PHASE 1 Skill Positions

MONDAY	TUESDAY	WEDNESDAY	THURSDAY	FRIDAY
Pre-Strength Workout	**Pre-Strength Workout**	**Active Rest**	**Pre-Strength Workout**	**Pre-Strength Workout**

Dot Drills
3-5 sets: 10-15 seconds
1. In and Out
2. Figure 8—right side both feet
3. Figure 8—left side both feet
4. Make up your own pattern
 	
Post-Strength Workout
 	
PNF Partner Stretch Routine
 	
Conditioning
Metabolic Speed Pac
3 quarters
(Rest 2 minutes between quarters.)
(see Appendix for details)
	Walking/Skipping Knee Hugs
	Walking/Skipping Toe Touches
	High Knee Crossovers
	Backward Skips
	2 sets: 20 yards
	
	Speed Development
	1. A Marches—2 sets: 20 yards
	2. A Skips—2 sets: 20 yards
	3. A Runs—2 sets: 20 yards
	4. Fast Leg Drills
	2 sets: 20 yards
	  a. Right leg
	  b. Left leg
	  c. Alternate legs
	
	PNF Partner Stretch Routine
	
	Programmable Agility
	1. Pattern Runs (include speed cuts, power cuts, and spins)
	6-8 sets: 20 yards
	2. Bag Drills
	2 sets each—6-8 bags
	  a. Run Through
	  b. Lateral Shuffle
	  c. Lateral Hops
	  d. Zig-Zag
	  e. Run Through
	3. 20-yard Shuttle
	3-4 sets: record best time
	
	Reactive Agility
	1. Tennis Ball Drills (all variations)
	8-10 sets
		Speed Ladder
		5-7 sets
		1. Run Through
		2. Lateral Shuffle
		3. Double Leg Hops
		4. Hop Scotch
		5. Ickey Shuffle
		6. Backward Ickey Shuffle
		
		Post-Strength Workout
		
		Static Stretch Routine
		
		Acceleration
		1. Uphill Runs
		6-8 sets: 30 yards (sprint up, walk down)
		or
		2. Sand Runs
		6-8 sets: 40 yards (sprint 40 yards, walk back for recovery)
		or
		3. Stadium Sprint
		6-8 sets: 30 yards (sprint up, walk down)
			Walking/Skipping Toe Touches
			Walking/Skipping Knee Hugs
			Backward Skips
			High Knee Crossovers
			2 sets: 20 yards
			
			Speed Development
			1. A Marches—2 sets: 20 yards
			2. A Skips—2 sets: 20 yards
			3. A Runs—2 sets: 20 yards
			4. Fast Leg Drills
			2 sets: 20 yards
			  a. Right leg
			  b. Left leg
			  c. Alternate legs
			
			PNF Partner Stretch Routine
			
			Plyometric
			1. Speed Hops
			2 sets: 20 yards
			2. Power Skips
			2 sets: 20 yards
			
			Acceleration
			Acceleration Ladder
			6 sets: 20 yards
			
			Programmable Agility
			1. Hourglass Drill—4 sets
			
			Reactive Agility
			1. Two-Point Wave Drill (include jumps, shuffle, "Hit It," etc.)
			4 sets: 10-15 seconds
			
			Acceleration/Conditioning
			1. Sled Pulls
			6 sets: 20-30 yards
			or
			2. Sand Runs—6 sets: 40 yards
				Jump Rope—stationary
				10-20 seconds
				1. Both Feet
				2. Alternate Feet
				3. 2 on Right, 2 on Left
				4. Something Different
				5. Speed Jump
				
				Post-Strength Workout
				
				PNF Partner Stretch Routine
				
				Conditioning
				3—440s
				QB, Spec, FB—1:30 minutes
				WR, DB, TB—1:25 minutes
				(Rest 3:45 minutes between 400s.)

Stretch Lower Back, Hamstrings	Stretch Lower Back, Hamstrings	Stretch Lower Back, Hamstrings	Stretch Lower Back, Hamstrings	Stretch Lower Back, Hamstrings

ADVANCED PRESEASON
Phase 1

COMMIT YOUR PLANS TO THE LORD AND THEN YOUR PLANS WILL SUCCEED. Proverbs 16:3

Skill Positions
WEEK 1

MONDAY	TUESDAY	WEDNESDAY	THURSDAY	FRIDAY
Dot Drills		Speed Ladder		Jump Rope
Abdominal Exercises Hanging Leg Raises 2 sets: 20 reps Medicine Ball Stack Crunches 2 sets: 20 reps	**Speed Development** (see Conditioning Schedule)	**Abdominal Exercises** Flutterkicks—30 seconds Bicycle Abs—30 seconds Dying Cockroach 30 seconds	**Speed Development** (see Conditioning Schedule)	**Abdominal Exercises** Denver Bronco Ab Program
Hang Snatch Combo Jump Shrugs—3 sets: 2 reps Snatch High Pulls 3 sets: 2 reps Hang Snatch—3 sets: 2 reps		**Push Jerks** (warmup—5 reps) 55%—5 reps 61%—5 reps 67%—5 reps 73%—5 reps		**Hang Clean/Front Squat Combo** (warmup—5 reps) 55%—3 reps 58%—3 reps 61%—3 reps
Box Stepups 3 sets: 5 reps		**Back Squats** (warmup—10 reps) 55%—10 reps 58%—10 reps 61%—10 reps 64%—10 reps		**Leg Press** 3 sets: 10 reps
Barbell Lunges 3 sets: 5 reps		**Incline Dumbbell Three-Level Bench Press** 3 sets: 6-6-6 reps each set		**Close Grip Bench** (stop and stab) 4 sets: 10 reps
Bench Press (warmup—10 reps) 55%—10 reps 61%—10 reps 67%—10 reps		**Towel Pullups** 3 sets: 8-10 reps		**Seated Cable Rows** 3 sets: 10 reps or **One-Arm Dumbbell Rows** 3 sets: 10 reps
Weighted Dips 3 sets: 10 reps		**Bench Dips** 3 sets: 15, 12, 10 reps		**Offense: Reverse HyperExt.** 2 sets: 15 reps
Lat Pulldowns (front, underhand) 3 sets: 10 reps		**Offense: Glute Ham Raises** 2 sets: 10 reps		**Defense: Glute Ham Raises** 2 sets: 10 reps
Neck Machine 1 set: 10 reps		**Defense: Reverse HyperExt.** 2 sets: 15 reps		**Curls** 3-4 sets: 8-10 reps
Bar Hang 1:05 minutes		**Neck Iso with partner** 1 set: 6 reps		**Neck Machine** 1 set: 10 reps
Stretch See Conditioning Schedule	Stretch	Stretch See Conditioning Schedule	Stretch	Stretch See Conditioning Schedule

Advanced PRESEASON   SPEED AGILITY QUICKNESS CONDITIONING SCHEDULE   WEEK 2 PHASE 1 Skill Positions

MONDAY	TUESDAY	WEDNESDAY	THURSDAY	FRIDAY
Pre-Strength Workout	Pre-Strength Workout	Active Rest	Pre-Strength Workout	Pre-Strength Workout

Dot Drills
3-4 sets: 10-15 seconds
1. In and Out
2. Figure 8—right side both feet
3. Figure 8—left side both feet
4. Make up your own pattern
 	
Post-Strength Workout
 	
PNF Partner Stretch Routine
 	
Conditioning
<u>3—440s</u>
QB, Spec, FB—1:30
WR, DB, TB—1:25
(rest 3:30 minutes between 440s)
	Walking/Skipping Knee Hugs
	Walking/Skipping Toe Touches
	High Knee Crossovers
	Backward Skips
	2 sets: 20 yards
	
	Speed Development
	1. A Marches—2 sets: 20 yards
	2. A Skips—2 sets: 20 yards
	3. A Runs—2 sets: 20 yards
	4. Fast Leg Drills
	  2 sets: 20 yards
	  a. Right leg
	  b. Left leg
	  c. Alternate legs
	
	PNF Partner Stretch Routine
	
	Programmable Agility
	1. Star Drill—2 sets each (include speed cuts, power cuts, and spins)
	2. 20-yard Shuffle
	  4 sets: record best time
	3. Bag Drills
	  a. Run Through
	  b. Lateral Shuffle
	  c. Double Leg Hops
	  d. Zig-Zag
	  e. Run Through
	  2 sets each—6-8 bags
	
	Plyometric
	1. Power Skips—2 sets: 20 yards
	2. Bounding—2 sets: 20 yards
	
	Competitive Drill
	1. Get Up and Sprint (vary starting position)
	5-6 sets
		Speed Ladder
		<u>5-7 sets</u>
		1. Run Through
		2. Lateral Shuffle
		3. Double Leg Hops
		4. Hop Scotch
		5. Ickey Shuffle
		6. Backward Ickey Shuffle
		
		Post-Strength Workout
		
		Static Stretch Routine
		
		Acceleration
		1. Uphill Runs
		  6-8 sets: 30 yards (sprint up, walk down)
		or
		2. Sand Runs
		  6-8 sets: 40 yards (sprint 40 yards, walk back for recovery)
		or
		3. Stadium Sprint
		  6-8 sets: 30 yards (sprint up, walk down)
			Walking/Skipping Toe Touches
			Walking/Skipping Knee Hugs
			Backward Skips
			High Knee Crossovers
			2 sets: 20 yards
			
			Speed Development
			1. A Marches—2 sets: 20 yards
			2. A Skips—2 sets: 20 yards
			3. A Runs—2 sets: 20 yards
			4. Fast Leg Drills
			  2 sets: 20 yards
			  a. Right leg
			  b. Left leg
			  c. Alternate legs
			
			PNF Partner Stretch Routine
			
			Acceleration
			Acceleration Ladder
			6 sets: 20 yards
			
			Programmable Agility
			1. Hourglass Drill—4 sets
			
			Reactive Agility
			1. Eight-Cone Reaction Drill visual cues
			4 sets: 10-15 seconds
			
			Acceleration/Conditioning
			1. Sled Pulls
			  6-8 sets: 20 yards (50 pounds max weight on sled)
			or
			2. Uphill Runs
			  6-8 sets: 30 yards (sprint up, walk down)
				Jump Rope—stationary
				10-20 seconds
				1. Both Feet
				2. Alternate Feet
				3. 2 on Right, 2 on Left
				4. Something Different
				5. Speed Jump
				
				Post-Strength Workout
				
				PNF Partner Stretch Routine
				
				Conditioning
				Metabolic Speed Pac
				3 quarters
				(Rest 2 minutes between quarters.)
				(see Appendix for details)

Stretch Lower Back, Hamstrings	Stretch Lower Back, Hamstrings	Stretch Lower Back, Hamstrings	Stretch Lower Back, Hamstrings	Stretch Lower Back, Hamstrings

WINNERS EXPECT TO WIN IN ADVANCE
WINNERS PREPARE TO WIN!

ADVANCED PRESEASON
Phase 1

Skill Positions
WEEK 2

MONDAY	TUESDAY	WEDNESDAY	THURSDAY	FRIDAY
Dot Drills		Speed Ladder		Jump Rope
Abdominal Exercises Hanging Leg Raises 2 sets: 20 reps Medicine Ball Stack Crunches 2 sets: 20 reps	**Speed Development** (see Conditioning Schedule)	**Abdominal Exercises** Flutterkicks—30 seconds Bicycle Abs—30 seconds Dying Cockroach 30 seconds	**Speed Development** (see Conditioning Schedule)	**Abdominal Exercises** Denver Bronco Ab Program
Hang Snatch Combo Jump Shrugs—3 sets: 2 reps Snatch High Pulls 3 sets: 2 reps Hang Snatch—3 sets: 2 reps		**Push Jerks** (warmup—3 reps) 58%—3 reps 64%—3 reps 70%—3 reps 76%—3 reps—(2 sets)		**Olympic Deadlifts to Knee** 2 sets: 5 reps
Box Stepups 3 sets: 5 reps		**Back Squats** (warmup—8 reps) 50%—8 reps 58%—8 reps 61%—8 reps 67%—8 reps		**Power Cleans** (warmup—3 reps) 55%—3 reps 61%—3 reps 67%—3 reps 70%—3 reps—(2 sets)
Barbell Lunges 3 sets: 5 reps		**Incline Dumbbell Three-Level Bench Press** 3 sets: 6-6-6 reps each set		**Clean Pulls** 3 sets: 3 reps (Up to 82% of Clean max)
Bench Press (warmup—8 reps) 61%—8 reps 64%—8 reps 67%—8 reps 70%—8 reps		**Towel Pullups** 3 sets: 8-10 reps		**Leg Press** 3 sets: 10 reps
Weighted Dips 3 sets: 8 reps		**Bench Dips** 3 sets: 15, 12, 10		**Close Grip Bench** (stop and stab) 4 sets: 8 reps
Lat Pulldowns (front, underhand) 3 sets: 8-10 reps		**Offense: Glute Ham Raises** 2 sets: 10 reps		**Seated Cable Rows** or **One-Arm Dumbbell Rows** 3 sets: 8 reps
Neck Machine 1 set: 10 reps		**Defense: Reverse HyperExt.** 2 sets: 15 reps		**Curls** 3-4 sets: 8-10 reps
Bar Hang 1:10 minutes		**Neck Iso with partner** 1 set: 6 reps		**Neck Machine** 1 set: 10 reps
Stretch See Conditioning Schedule	Stretch	Stretch See Conditioning Schedule	Stretch	Stretch See Conditioning Schedule

Advanced PRESEASON   SPEED AGILITY QUICKNESS CONDITIONING SCHEDULE   WEEK 3 PHASE 2 Skill Positions

MONDAY	TUESDAY	WEDNESDAY	THURSDAY	FRIDAY
Pre-Strength Workout	**Pre-Strength Workout**	**Active Rest**	**Pre-Strength Workout**	**Pre-Strength Workout**

Dot Drills
3-4 sets: 10-15 seconds
1. In and Out
2. Figure 8—right side both feet
3. Figure 8—left side both feet
4. Make up your own pattern
 	
Post-Strength Workout
 	
PNF Partner Stretch Routine
 	
Conditioning
5—440s
QB, Spec, FB—1:30 minutes
WR, DB, TB—1:20 minutes
(rest 3:30 minutes between 440s)
	Walking/Skipping Knee Hugs
	Walking/Skipping Toe Touches
	High Knee Crossovers
	Backward Skips
	2 sets: 20 yards
	
	Speed Development
	1. A Marches—2 sets: 20 yards
	2. A Skips—2 sets: 20 yards
	3. A Runs—2 sets: 20 yards
	4. Fast Leg Drills
	2 sets: 20 yards
	  a. Right leg
	  b. Left leg
	  c. Alternate legs
	
	PNF Partner Stretch Routine
	
	Programmable Agility
	1. Pattern Runs (include speed cuts, power cuts, and spins)
	6 sets: 20 yards
	2. Bag Drills
	2 sets each: 6-8 bags
	  a. Run Through
	  b. Double Leg Hops Forward
	  c. Double Leg Hops Lateral
	  d. Lateral Shuffle
	  e. Zig-Zag
	  f. Run Through
	
	Competitive Drill
	1. Shark in a Tank
	5-6 sets: 10 seconds
		Speed Ladder
		5-7 sets
		1. Run Through
		2. Lateral Shuffle
		3. Double Leg Hops
		4. Hop Scotch
		5. Ickey Shuffle
		6. Backward Ickey Shuffle
		
		Post-Strength Workout
		
		Static Stretch Routine
		
		Acceleration
		1. Uphill Runs
		6-8 sets: 30 yards (sprint up, walk down)
		or
		2. Sand Runs
		6-8 sets: 40 yards (sprint 40 yards; walk back for recovery)
		or
		3. Stadium Sprint
		6-8 sets: 30 yards (sprint up, walk down)
			Walking/Skipping Toe Touches
			Walking/Skipping Knee Hugs
			Backward Skips
			High Knee Crossovers
			2 sets: 20 yards
			
			Speed Development
			1. A Marches—2 sets: 20 yards
			2. A Skips—2 sets: 20 yards
			3. A Runs—2 sets: 20 yards
			4. Fast Leg Drills
			2 sets: 20 yards
			  a. Right leg
			  b. Left leg
			  c. Alternate legs
			
			PNF Partner Stretch Routine
			
			Acceleration
			1. Acceleration Ladder
			6 sets: 20 yards
			
			Programmable Agility
			1. Star Drill—6 sets (include speed cuts, power cuts, and spins)
			
			Reactive Agility
			1. Four-Cone Reaction Drill verbal cues
			4 sets: 40 seconds
			
			Competitive Drill
			1. Get Up and Sprint (vary start position)
			5-6 sets: 30 yards
				Jump Rope—stationary
				10-20 seconds
				1. Both Feet
				2. Alternate Feet
				3. 2 on Right, 2 on Left
				4. Something Different
				5. Speed Jump
				
				Post-Strength Workout
				
				PNF Partner Stretch Routine
				
				Conditioning
				6 220s
				QB, Spec, FB—40 seconds
				WR, DB, TB—35 seconds
				(rest 1:30 minutes between 220s)

Stretch Lower Back, Hamstrings	Stretch Lower Back, Hamstrings	Strtech Lower Back, Hamstrings	Stretch Lower Back, Hamstrings	Stretch Lower Back, Hamstrings

Skill Positions
WEEK 3

ADVANCED PRESEASON
Phase 2

NOTHING GREAT WAS EVER
ACHIEVED WITHOUT ENTHUSIASM

MONDAY	TUESDAY	WEDNESDAY	THURSDAY	FRIDAY
Dot Drills		Speed Ladder		Jump Rope
Abdominal Exercises Big 40s—1 set Figure Four Double Crunches 2 sets: 10 reps (each way)	**Speed Development** (see Conditioning Schedule)	**Abdominal Exercises** Hanging Leg Raises 2 sets: 20 reps Twisting Stack Crunches 2 sets: 20 reps	**Speed Development** (see Conditioning Schedule)	**Abdominal Exercises** Captain's Choice
Power Snatch 4 sets: 3 reps		**Push Jerks Unload** (warmup—5 reps) 58%—3 reps 64%—3 reps 70%—3 reps 76%—1 rep—(3 sets)		**Olympic Deadlifts to Knee** 2 sets: 3 reps
Single-Leg Leg Squats 4 sets: 5 reps (each leg)		**Back Squats Unload** (warmup—8 reps) 55%—5 reps 61%—5 reps 67%—5 reps 73%—5 reps		**Power Cleans** (warmup—3 reps) 58%—3 reps 64%—3 reps 70%—3 reps 76%—3 reps
Lateral Squats 2 sets: 6 reps		**Extended Squats** 2 sets: 5 reps		**Clean Pulls** 3 sets: 3 reps (Up to 85% of Clean max)
Bench Press Unload (warmup—8 reps) 58%—6 reps 64%—6 reps 70%—6 reps 76%—6 reps		**Dumbbell Alternate Bench Press** (stop and stab) 4 sets: 6 reps		**Front Squats** 4 sets: 6 reps
Pullups—(vary grip) 3 sets: 8-10 reps		**Dumbbell Pullovers** 2 sets: 12 reps		**Incline Bench Press** 4 sets: 8 reps
Incline Dumbbell Curls 3 sets: 8 reps		**Offense: Reverse HyperExt.** 2 sets: 15 reps		**Body Weighted Dips** 30 total reps
Dumbbell Tricep Extensions (15-second rest between sets) 5 sets: 8 reps		**Defense: Glute Ham Raises** 2 sets: 10 reps		**Pullups—(vary grip)** 3 sets: 10 reps
Neck Machine 1 set: 10 reps		**Bear Calf Raises** 2 sets: 15 reps		**Offense: Glute Ham Raises** 2 sets: 10 reps
		Neck Iso—1 set: 6 reps		**Defense: Reverse HyperExt.** 2 sets: 15 reps
				Neck Machine 1 set: 10 reps
Strrtch See Conditioning Schedule	Stretch	Stretch See Conditioning Schedule	Stretch	Stretch See Conditioning Schedule

Advanced PRESEASON   SPEED AGILITY QUICKNESS CONDITIONING SCHEDULE   WEEK 4 PHASE 2 Skill Positions

MONDAY	TUESDAY	WEDNESDAY	THURSDAY	FRIDAY
Pre-Strength Workout	**Pre-Strength Workout**	**Active Rest**	**Pre-Strength Workout**	**Pre-Strength Workout**

Dot Drills
3-4 sets: 10-15 seconds
1. In and Out
2. Figure 8—right side both feet
3. Figure 8—left side both feet
4. Make up your own pattern
 	
Post-Strength Workout
 	
PNF Partner Stretch Routine
 	
Conditioning
Metabolic Speed Pac
3 quarters
(Rest 2 minutes between quarters.)
(see Appendix for details)
	Walking/Skipping Knee Hugs
	Walking/Skipping Toe Touches
	High Knee Crossovers
	Backward Skips
	  2 sets: 20 yards
	
	Speed Development
	1. A Marches—2 sets: 20 yards
	2. A Skips—2 sets: 20 yards
	3. A Runs—2 sets: 20 yards
	4. Fast Leg Drills
	  2 sets: 20 yards
	  a. Right leg
	  b. Left leg
	  c. Alternate legs
	
	PNF Partner Stretch Routine
	
	Acceleration
	1. Starts—Football Stance
	  4-6 sets
	2. Bullet Belts
	  6 sets: 20 yards
	
	Programmable Agility
	1. 20-yard Shuttle
	  4 sets: record best time
	2. Bag Drills
	  2 sets each: 6-8 bags
	  a. Run Through
	  b. Double Leg Hops
	  c. Lateral Shuffle
	  d. Zig-Zag
	  e. Run Through
	
	Competitive Drill
	Get Up and Sprint
	(vary start position)
	  4-6 sets
		Speed Ladder
		  5-7 sets
		1. Run Through
		2. Lateral Shuffle
		3. Double Leg Hops
		4. Hop Scotch
		5. Ickey Shuffle
		6. Backward Ickey Shuffle
		
		Post-Strength Workout
		
		Static Stretch Routine
		
		Acceleration
		1. Uphill Runs
		  6-8 sets: 30 yards
		  (sprint up, walk down)
		
		or
		2. Sand Runs
		  6-8 sets: 40 yards
		  (sprint 40 yards; walk back for recovery)
		
		or
		3. Stadium Sprint
		  6-8 sets: 30 yards
		  (sprint up, walk down)
			Walking /Skipping Toe Touches
			Walking/Skipping Knee Hugs
			Backward Skips
			High Knee Crossovers
			  2 sets: 20 yards
			
			Speed Development
			1. A Marches—2 sets: 20 yards
			2. A Skips—2 sets: 20 yards
			3. A Runs—2 sets: 20 yards
			4. Fast Leg Drills
			  2 sets: 20 yards
			  a. Right leg
			  b. Left leg
			  c. Alternate legs
			
			PNF Partner Stretch Routine
			
			Plyometric
			1. Standing Long Jumps
			  2 sets: 5 jumps
			  record best set distance
			2. Single Leg Speed Hops
			  2 sets: 20 yards
			3. Power Skips
			  2 sets: 20 yards
			4. Bounding—2 sets: 20 yards
			
			Programmable Agility
			1. Carolina Drill—3 sets
			
			Reactive Agility
			1. Tennis Ball Drills
			  (all variations)
			  8-10 sets
				Jump Rope—stationary
				  10-20 seconds
				1. Both Feet
				2. Alternate Feet
				3. 2 on Right, 2 on Left
				4. Something Different
				5. Speed Jump
				
				Post-Strength Workout
				
				PNF Partner Stretch Routine
				
				Conditioning
				6 220s
				QB, Spec, FB—45 seconds
				WR, DB, TB—40 seconds
				(rest 1:30 minutes between 220s)

Stretch Lower Back, Hamstrings	Stretch Lower Back, Hamstrings	Stretch Lower Back, Hamstrings	Stretch Lower Back, Hamstrings	Stretch Lower Back, Hamstrings

ADVANCED PRESEASON
Phase 2

Skill Positions
WEEK 4

EXCELLENCE IS NOT A MATTER OF CHANCE, IT IS A MATTER OF CHOICE.

MONDAY	TUESDAY	WEDNESDAY	THURSDAY	FRIDAY
Dot Drills		Speed Ladder		Jump Rope
Abdominal Exercises Big 40s—1 set Figure Four Double Crunches 2 sets: 15 reps (each way)	**Speed Development** (see Conditioning Schedule)	**Abdominal Exercises** Hanging Leg Raises 2 sets: 20 reps Twisting Stack Crunches 2 sets: 20 reps	**Speed Development** (see Conditioning Schedule)	**Abdominal Exercises** Captain's Choice
Power Snatch 4 sets: 3 reps		**Push Jerks** (warmup—3 reps) 55%—3 reps 61%—3 reps 67%—3 reps 73%—3 reps 79%—3 reps		**Olympic Deadlifts to Knee** 2 sets: 3 reps
Single-Leg Leg Squats 4 sets: 5 reps (each leg)		**Back Squats** (warmup—8 reps) 58%—5 reps 64%—5 reps 70%—5 reps 76%—5 reps		**Power Cleans** (warmup—3 reps) 55%—3 reps 61%—3 reps 67%—3 reps 73%—3 reps 79%—3 reps
Lateral Squats 2 sets: 6 reps		**Extended Squats** 2 sets: 5 reps		**Clean Pulls** 3 sets: 3 reps (Up to 88% of Clean max)
Bench Press (warmup—8 reps) 55%—5 reps 61%—5 reps 67%—5 reps 73%—5 reps 79%—5 reps		**Dumbbell Alternate Bench Press** (stop and stab) 4 sets: 5 reps		**Front Squats** 4 sets: 5 reps
Pullups—(vary grip) 3 sets: 10 reps		**Dumbbell Pullovers** 2 sets: 12 reps		**Incline Bench Press** 4 sets: 6 reps
Incline Dumbbell Curls 3 sets: 8 reps		**Offense: Reverse HyperExt.** 2 sets: 15 reps		**Body Weighted Dips** 35 total reps
Dumbbell Tricep Extensions (15-second rest between sets) 5 sets: 8 reps		**Defense: Glute Ham Raises** 2 sets: 10 reps		**Pullups—(vary grip)** 3 sets: 10 reps
Neck Machine 1 set: 10 reps		**Neck Iso**—1 set: 6 reps		**Offense: Glute Ham Raises** 2 sets: 10 reps
				Defense: Reverse HyperExt. 2 sets: 15 reps
				Neck Machine 1 set: 10 reps
Stretch See Conditioning Schedule	Stretch	Stretch See Conditioning Schedule	Stretch	Stretch See Conditioning Schedule

Advanced PRESEASON   SPEED AGILITY QUICKNESS CONDITIONING SCHEDULE   WEEK 5 PHASE 2 Skill Positions

MONDAY	TUESDAY	WEDNESDAY	THURSDAY	FRIDAY
Pre-Strength Workout	**Pre-Strength Workout**	**Active Rest**	**Pre-Strength Workout**	**Pre-Strength Workout**

Dot Drills 3-4 sets—10-15 seconds
1. In and Out
2. Figure 8—right side both feet
3. Figure 8—left side both feet
4. Make up your own pattern
 	
Post-Strength Workout
 	
PNF Partner Stretch Routine
 	
<u>Conditioning</u>
10 110s
QB, Spec, FB—18 seconds
WR, DB, TB—16 seconds
(Rest 45 seconds between 110s.)
	Walking/Skipping Knee Hugs
	Walking/Skipping Toe Touches
	High Knee Crossovers
	Backward Skips
	2 sets: 20 yards
	
	<u>**Speed Development**</u>
	1. A Marches—2 sets: 20 yards
	2. A Skips—2 sets: 20 yards
	3. A Runs—2 sets: 20 yards
	4. Fast Leg Drills
	2 sets: 20 yards
	  a. Right leg
	  b. Left leg
	  c. Alternate legs
	
	PNF Partner Stretch Routine
	
	<u>Acceleration</u>
	1. Starts—Football Stance
	4-6 sets
	
	<u>Programmable Agility</u>
	1. Star Drill—6 sets
	(include speed cuts, power cuts, and spins)
	2. Texas-Drill—4 sets
	3. 20-yard Shuttle
	4 sets: record best time
	
	<u>Reactive Agility</u>
	1. Eight-Cone Reactive Cone Drill visual cue
	
	<u>Acceleration/Conditioning</u>
	1. Sand Runs—6-8 sets: 40 yards
	(sprint 40 yards; walk back for recovery)
	or
	2. Sled Pulls
	6 sets: 30 yards
	(50 pounds max weight on sled)
		<u>**Speed Ladder**</u>
		5-7 sets
		1. Run Through
		2. Lateral Shuffle
		3. Double Leg Hops
		4. Hop Scotch
		5. Ickey Shuffle
		6. Backward Ickey Shuffle
		
		Post-Strength Workout
		
		Static Stretch Routine
		
		<u>**Competitive Drill**</u>
		1. Get Up and Sprint
		(vary starting position)
		8-10 sets: 30 yards
			Walking/Skipping Toe Touches
			Walking/Skipping Knee Hugs
			Backward Skips
			High Knee Crossovers
			2 sets: 20 yards
			
			<u>**Speed Development**</u>
			1. A Marches
			2 sets—20 yards
			2. A Skips—2 sets: 20 yards
			3. A Runs—2 sets: 20 yards
			4. Fast Leg Drills
			2 sets: 20 yards
			  a. Right leg
			  b. Left leg
			  c. Alternate legs
			
			PNF Partner Stretch Routine
			
			<u>Acceleration</u>
			1. Bullet Belts
			6-8 sets: 30 yards
			
			<u>Programmable Agility</u>
			1. 90 Power Cut/Spin Drill
			4 sets
			
			<u>**Competitive Drill**</u>
			1. Shark in a Tank
			6-8 sets: 10-15 seconds
				<u>**Jump Rope**</u>—stationary
				10-20 seconds
				1. Both Feet
				2. Alternate Feet
				3. 2 on Light, 2 on Left
				4. Something Different
				5. Speed Jump
				
				Post-Strength Workout
				
				PNF Partner Stretch Routine
				
				<u>Conditioning</u>
				6 220s
				QB, Spec, FB—45 seconds
				WR, DB, TB—40 seconds
				(rest 1:30 minutes between 220s)
				
				or
				
				Metabolic Speed Pac
				3 quarters
				(Rest 2 minutes between quarters.)
				(see Appendix for details)

Stretch Lower Back, Hamstrings	Stretch Lower Back, Hamstrings	Stretch Lower Back, Hamstrings	Stretch Lower Back, Hamstrings	Stretch Lower Back, Hamstrings

SAMPLE PROGRAMS

LEADERS WALK THE TALK. LEAD BY DEED.

Skill Positions
WEEK 5

ADVANCED PRESEASON
Phase 2

MONDAY	TUESDAY	WEDNESDAY	THURSDAY	FRIDAY
Dot Drills		Speed Ladder		Jump Rope
Abdominal Exercises Big 40s—1 set Figure Four Double Crunches 2 sets: 15 reps (each way)	**Speed Development** (see Conditioning Schedule)	**Abdominal Exercises** Hanging Leg Raises 2 sets: 20 reps Twisting Stack Crunches 2 sets: 20 reps	**Speed Development** (see Conditioning Schedule)	**Abdominal Exercises** Captain's Choice
Power Snatch 4 sets: 3 reps		**Push Jerks** (warmup—3 reps) 58%—3 reps 64%—3 reps 70%—3 reps 76%—3 reps 82%—3 reps		**Olympic Deadlifts to Knee** 2 sets: 3 reps
Single-Leg Leg Squats 4 sets: 5 reps (each leg)		**Back Squats** (warmup—8 reps) 61%—5 reps 67%—5 reps 73%—5 reps 79%—5 reps		**Power Cleans** (warmup—3 reps) 58%—3 reps 64%—3 reps 70%—3 reps 76%—3 reps 82%—2 reps—(2 sets)
Lateral Squats 2 sets: 6 reps		**Extended Squats** 2 sets: 5 reps		**Clean Pulls** 3 sets: 3 reps (Up to 91% of Clean max)
Bench Press (warmup—8 reps) 55%—5 reps 64%—5 reps 70%—5 reps 76%—5 reps 82%—5 reps		**Seated Cable Rows** or **Dumbbell Rows** 3 sets: 8 reps		**Front Squats** 4 sets: 5 reps
Pullups—(vary grip) 3 sets: 10 reps		**Offense: Reverse HyperExt.** 2 sets: 12 reps		**Incline Bench Press** 4 sets: 6 reps
Incline Dumbbell Curls 3 sets: 8 reps		**Defense: Glute Ham Raises** 2 sets: 10 reps		**Body Weighted Dips** 40 total reps
Dumbbell Tricep Extensions (15-second rest between sets) 5 sets: 8 reps		**Neck Iso**—1 set: 6 reps or **Neck Machine** 1 set: 10 reps		**Pullups—(vary grip)** 3 sets: 10 reps
Neck Machine 1 set: 10 reps				**Offense: Glute Ham Raises** 2 sets: 10 reps
				Defense: Reverse HyperExt. 2 sets: 15 reps
				Neck Machine 1 set: 10 reps
Stretch See Conditioning Schedule	Stretch	Stretch See Conditioning Schedule	Stretch	Stretch See Conditioning Schedule

Advanced PRESEASON   SPEED AGILITY QUICKNESS CONDITIONING SCHEDULE   WEEK 6 PHASE 3 Skill Positions

MONDAY	TUESDAY	WEDNESDAY	THURSDAY	FRIDAY
Pre-Strength Workout	**Pre-Strength Workout**	**Active Rest**	**Pre-Strength Workout**	**Pre-Strength Workout**
<u>Dot Drills</u> 3-5 sets: 10-15 seconds **Post-Strength Workout** **Static Stretch Routine** <u>Acceleration</u> 1. Acceleration Ladder 6 sets: 20 yards <u>Programmable Agility</u> 1. Four-Cone Perimeter Drill (include back-pedal, shuffle, carioca, and sprint) <u>Reactive Agility</u> 1. Two-Point Wave Drill (include jumps, shuffle, and "Hit It") <u>Competitive Drill</u> 1. Shark in a Tank 6-8 sets: 10 seconds	Walking Toe Touches High Knee Crossovers Backward Skips Low Carioca 2 sets—20 yards **Speed Development** 1. A Skips 2 sets: 20 yards 2. A Runs 2 sets: 20 yards 3. Fast Leg Drills 2 sets: 20 yards **PNF Partner Stretch Routine** <u>Conditioning</u> 110s—12 QB, Spec, FB—17 seconds WR, DB, TB—15 seconds (Rest 45 seconds between 110s.)	<u>Speed Ladder</u> 5-7 sets **Post-Strength Workout** **Static Stretch Routine** Starts—Football Stance 4-6 sets <u>Programmable Agility</u> 1. Star Drill—6 sets (include speed cuts, power cuts, and spins) <u>Reactive Agility</u> 1. Eight-Cone Reaction Drill visual cue <u>Conditioning</u> Punch Heavy Bag 3 rounds—30 seconds (Rest 30 seconds between rounds.)	Walking/Skipping Knee Hugs Walking/Skipping Toe Touches Low Shuffle Starts—Football Stance 2 sets: 20 yards **PNF Partner Stretch Routine** <u>Conditioning</u> 14 110s QB, Spec, FB—17 seconds WR, DB, TB—15 seconds (Rest 45 seconds between 110s.)	<u>Jump Rope</u>—stationary 5-6 sets: 15-30 seconds **Post-Strength Workout** **Static Stretch Routine** <u>Programmable Agility</u> 1. Carolina Drill—4 sets 2. 20-yard Shuttle 4 sets: record best time <u>Reactive Agility</u> 1. Crazy Ball Drills (all variations) 8-10 sets <u>Competitive Drill</u> 1. Get Up and Sprint 6-8 sets: 30 yards
Stretch Lower Back, Hamstrings	Stretch Lower Back, Hamstrings	Stretch Lower Back, Hamstrings	Stretch Lower Back, Hamstrings	Stretch Lower Back, Hamstrings

Skill Positions WEEK 6

ADVANCED PRESEASON Phase 3

DO THE BEST YOU CAN WITH WHAT YOU HAVE, WHERE YOU ARE

MONDAY	TUESDAY	WEDNESDAY	THURSDAY	FRIDAY
Dot Drills		Speed Ladder		Jump Rope
Abdominal Exercises Medicine Ball Partner Throws 2 sets: 30 reps **Olympic Deadlifts to Knee** 2 sets: 3 reps **Power Cleans Unload** (warmup—3 reps) 61%—3 reps 67%—3 reps 73%—3 reps 79%—3 reps 85%—2 reps **Clean Pulls** 3 sets: 2 reps (Up to 94% of Clean max) **Speed Squats** 4 sets: 5 reps (50% of max) **Bench Press** (warmup—8 reps) 61%—3 reps 67%—3 reps 73%—3 reps 79%—3 reps 85%—3 reps—(2 sets) **Bench Dips** 3 sets: 15, 12, 10 **Dumbbell Curls** 3 set: 8-10 reps **Neck Iso with partner** 1 set: 6 reps	<u>Conditioning</u> 12 110s QB, FB, Spec—17 seconds WR, DB, TE—15 seconds (Rest 45 seconds between 110s.)	**Abdominal Exercises** Figure Eights—2 sets: 10 reps Medicine Ball Stack Crunches 2 sets: 20 reps **Push Jerks** (warmup—3 reps) 55%—3 reps 61%—3 reps 67%—3 reps 73%—3 reps 79%—3 reps 85%—2 reps—(2 sets) **Single-Leg Leg Press** 3 sets: 10 reps (each leg) **Incline Alternate Dumbbell Bench Press** (stop and stab) 4 sets: 5 reps **Pullups—(vary grip)** 3 sets: 10 reps **Straight Bar Lying Tricep Ext.** 3 sets: 10 reps **Bear Calf Raises** 2 sets: 15-20 reps **Neck Machine** 1 set: 10 reps **Bar Hang** 1:15 minutes	<u>Conditioning</u> 14—110s QB, FB, Spec—17 seconds WR, DB, TE—15 seconds (Rest 45 seconds between 110s.)	**Abdominal Exercises** Captain's Choice **Weighted Box Jumps** 3 sets: 5 reps **Back Squats** (warmup—8 reps) 61%—5 reps 67%—5 reps 73%—5 reps 79%—3 reps 85%—3 reps **Close Grip Chain Bench Press** (stop and stab) 4 sets: 5 reps **Lat Pulldowns** (front, underhand) 3 sets: 8-10 reps **Seated Plate Raises** 2 sets: 20 reps **Glute Ham Raises** 2 sets: 10 reps or **Reverse Hyperextensions** 2 sets: 15 reps **Swiss Ball Curls** 3 sets: 10 reps **Neck Iso** 1 sets: 6 reps or **Neck Machine** 1 set: 10 reps
Stretch See Conditioning Schedule	Strtetch	Stretch See Conditioning Schedule	Stretch	Stretch See Conditioning Schedule

Advanced PRESEASON SPEED AGILITY QUICKNESS CONDITIONING SCHEDULE   WEEK 7 PHASE 3 Skill Positions

MONDAY	TUESDAY	WEDNESDAY	THURSDAY	FRIDAY
Pre-Strength Workout	**Pre-Strength Workout**	**Active Rest**	**Pre-Strength Workout**	**Pre-Strength Workout**
Dot Drills 3-5 sets: 10-15 seconds	Walking Toe Touches High Knee Crossovers Backward Skips Low Carioca 2 sets: 20 yards	**Speed Ladder** 5-7 sets	Walking/Skipping Knee Hugs Walking/Skipping Toe Touches Low Shuffle Starts—Football Stance 2 sets: 20 yards	**Jump Rope**—stationary 5-6 sets: 15-30 seconds

Post-Strength Workout	**Speed Development**
	1. A Skips
	   2 sets: 20 yards
	2. A Runs
	   2 sets: 20 yards
	3. Fast Leg Drills
	   2 sets: 20 yards
		Post-Strength Workout	**PNF Partner Stretch Routine**	**Post-Strength Workout**

Static Stretch Routine		**Static Stretch Routine** Starts—Football Stance 4-6 sets	**Conditioning** 110s—16 QB, Spec, FB—17 seconds WR, DB, TB—15 seconds (Rest 45 seconds between 110s.)	**Static Stretch Routine**

Programmable Agility
1. Texas-Drill—4 sets
	PNF Partner Stretch Routine	**Acceleration**
		1. Bullet Belts
		   6-8 sets: 20 yards
				Programmable Agility
				1. Pattern Runs
				   (include speed cuts, power cuts, and spins)
				   6 sets: 20 yards
				2. Four-Cone Perimeter Drill
				   4 sets

Reactive Agility
1. Tennis Ball Drills
   (all variations)
   8-10 sets
	Conditioning
	Metabolic Speed Pac
	4 quarters
	(Rest 2 minutes between quarters.)
	(see Appendix for details)
		Agility/Acceleration
		1. Sand Pit Work
		   a. Zig-Zag Course
		   b. Backpedal
		   c. Low Shuffle
		   2 sets: 40 yards each
		   d. Sprints—4 sets: 40 yards
				Competitive Drill
				1. Get Up and Sprint
				   6-8 sets: 30 yards

Competitive Drill 1. Shark in a Tank 8-10 sets: 10-15 seconds				
Stretch Lower Back, Hamstrings	Stretch Lower Back, Hamstrings	Stretch Lower Back, Hamstrings	Stretch Lower Back, Hamstrings	Stretch Lower Back, Hamstrings

Skill Positions
WEEK 7

ADVANCED PRESEASON
Phase 3

NONE OF US IS AS
STRONG AS ALL OF US

MONDAY	TUESDAY	WEDNESDAY	THURSDAY	FRIDAY
Dot Drills		Speed Ladder		Jump Rope

MONDAY

Abdominal Exercises
Medicine Ball Partner Throws
2 sets: 30 reps

Olympic Deadlifts to Knee
2 sets: 3 reps

Power Cleans
(warmup—3 reps)
55%—3 reps
64%—3 reps
70%—3 reps
76%—3 reps
82%—3 reps
88%—1 rep—(2 sets)

Clean Pulls—3 sets: 2 reps
(Up to 97% of max)

Speed Squats
4 sets: 5 reps
(50% of max)

Bench Press
(warmup—8 reps)
64%—5 reps
70%—5 reps
76%—3 reps
82%—3 reps
88%—3 reps

Bench Dips
3 sets: 15, 12, 10

Dumbbell Curls
3 set: 10 reps

Neck Iso with partner
1 set: 6 reps

Stretch
See Conditioning Schedule

TUESDAY

Conditioning
Metabolic Speed Pac
4 quarters

Stretch

WEDNESDAY

Abdominal Exercises
Figure Eights—2 sets: 10 reps
Medicine Ball Stack Crunches
2 sets: 20 reps

Push Jerks
(warmup—3 reps)
61%—3 reps
67%—3 reps
73%—3 reps
79%—3 reps
85%—2 reps
91%—1 rep (3 sets)

Single-Leg Leg Press
3 sets: 10 reps (each leg)

**Incline Alternate Dumbbell
Bench Press** (stop and stab)
4 sets: 5 reps

Pullups—(vary grip)
3 sets: 10 reps

**Straight Bar Lying Tricep
Extensions**—3 sets: 10 reps

Bear Calf Raises
2 sets: 15-20 reps

Neck Machine
1 set: 10 reps

Bar Hang
1:20 minutes

Stretch
See Conditioning Schedule

THURSDAY

Conditioning
16 110s

QB, FB, Spec—17 seconds
WR, DB, TE—15 seconds
(Rest 45 seconds between
110s.)

Stretch

FRIDAY

Abdominal Exercises
Captain's Choice

Weighted Box Jumps
3 sets: 5 reps

Back Squats
(warmup—8 reps)
64%—5 reps
70%—5 reps
76%—5 reps
82%—3 reps
88%—2 reps—(2 sets)

**Close Grip Chain Bench
Press**
(stop and stab)
4 sets: 5 reps

Lat Pulldowns
(front, underhand)
3 sets: 8-10 reps

Seated Plate Raises
2 sets: 20 reps

Glute Ham Raises
2 sets: 10 reps
or

Reverse Hyperextensions
2 sets: 15 reps

Swiss Ball Curls
3 sets: 10 reps

Neck Iso
1 sets: 6 reps
or

Neck Machine
1 set: 10 reps

Stretch
See Conditioning Schedule

Advanced PRESEASON   SPEED AGILITY QUICKNESS CONDITIONING SCHEDULE   WEEK 8 PHASE 3 Skill Positions

MONDAY	TUESDAY	WEDNESDAY	THURSDAY	FRIDAY
Pre-Strength Workout	Pre-Strength Workout	Active Rest	Pre-Strength Workout	Pre-Strength Workout
Dot Drills 3-5 sets: 10-15 seconds **Post-Strength Workout** **Static Stretch Routine** **Programmable Agility** 1. Carolina Drill—4 sets **Reactive Agility** 1. Four-Cone Reaction Drill verbal cue 4 sets: 10 seconds **Competitive Drill** 1. Shark in a Tank 6-8 sets: 30 yards	Walking Toe Touches High Knee Crossovers Backward Skips Low Carioca 2 sets: 20 yards **Speed Development** 1. A Skips 2 sets: 20 yards 2. A Runs 2 sets: 20 yards 3. Fast Leg Drills 2 sets: 20 yards **PNF Partner Stretch Routine** **Conditioning** 18 110s QB, Spec, FB—17 seconds WR, DB, TB—15 seconds (Rest 45 seconds between 110s.)	**Speed Ladder** 5-7 sets **Post-Strength Workout** **Static Stretch Routine** Starts—Football Stance 4-6 sets **Acceleration** 1. Acceleration Ladder 4-6 sets: 20 yards **Programmable Agility** 1. 20-yard Shuttle 4 sets: record best time **Reactive Agility** 1. Two-Point Wave Drill 4 sets: 10-15 seconds	Walking/Skipping Knee Hugs Walking/Skipping Toe Touches Low Shuffle Starts—Football Stance 2 sets: 20 yards **PNF Partner Stretch Routine** **Conditioning** Metabolic Speed Pac 5 quarters (Rest 2 minutes between quarters.) (see Appendix for details)	**Jump Rope**—stationary 5-6 sets: 15-30 seconds **Post-Strength Workout** **Static Stretch Routine** **Programmable Agility** 1. Texas-Drill—4 sets **Reactive Agility** 1. Eight-Cone Reaction Drill visual cues 4 sets: 10 seconds **Competitive Drill** 1. Get Up and Sprint 6-8 sets: 30 yards
Stretch Lower Back, Hamstrings	Stretch Lower Back, Hamstrings	Stretch Lower Back, Hamstrings	Stretch Lower Back, Hamstrings	Stretch Lower Back, Hamstrings

THE GREATER THE CHALLENGE,
THE GREATER THE REWARDS.

ADVANCED PRESEASON
Phase 3

Skill Positions
WEEK 8

MONDAY	TUESDAY	WEDNESDAY	THURSDAY	FRIDAY
Dot Drills		Speed Ladder		Jump Rope
Abdominal Exercises Medicine Ball Partner Throws 2 sets: 30 reps	**Conditioning** 18 110s QB, FB, Spec—17 seconds WR, DB, TE—15 seconds (Rest 45 seconds between 110s.)	**Abdominal Exercises** Big 40s—2 sets Twisting Stack Crunches 2 sets: 20 reps	**Conditioning** Metabolic Speed Pac 5 quarters	**Abdominal Exercises** Captain's Choice
Olympic Deadlifts to Knee 2 sets: 3 reps		**Series Box Jumps** 4 sets: 6-7 boxes		**Push Jerks Unload** (warmup—3 reps) 61%—3 reps 67%—3 reps 73%—3 reps 79%—3 reps 85%—3 reps
Power Cleans Unload (warmup—3 reps) 61%—3 reps 67%—3 reps 73%—3 reps 79%—3 reps 85%—1 rep		**Single-Leg Leg Press** 3 sets: 10 reps (each leg)		**Back Squats** (warmup—8 reps) 61%—5 reps 67%—5 reps 73%—5 reps 79%—3 reps 85%—3 reps 91%—1 rep
Clean Pulls 3 sets: 2 reps (Up to 100% of Clean max)		**Dumbbell Bench Press** (stop and stab) 4 sets: 5 reps		**Close Grip Chain Bench Press** (stop and stab) 4 sets: 5 reps
Speed Squats 4 sets: 5 reps (50% of max)		**Pullups—(vary grip)** 3 sets: 10 reps		**Lat Pulldowns (vary grip)** 3 sets: 10 reps
Bench Press (warmup—8 reps) 61%—3 reps 67%—3 reps 73%—3 reps 79%—3 reps 85%—3 reps 91%—1 rep—(3 sets)		**Straight Bar Lying Tricep Extensions** 3 sets: 10 reps		**Seated Plate Raises** 2 sets: 20 reps
Weighted Dips 3 sets: 6 reps		**Bear Calf Raises** 2 sets: 15-20 reps		**Glute Ham Raises** 2 sets: 10 reps or
Straight Bar Curls 3 set: 10 reps		**Neck Machine** 1 set: 10 reps		**Reverse Hyperextensions** 2 sets: 15 reps
Neck Iso with partner 1 set: 6 reps		**Bar Hang** 1:20 minutes		**Neck Iso** 1 set: 6 reps or **Neck Machine** 1 set: 10 reps
Stretch See Conditioning Schedule	Stretch	Stretch See Conditioning Schedule	Stretch	Stretch See Conditioning Schedule

321

Advanced PRESEASON   SPEED AGILITY QUICKNESS CONDITIONING SCHEDULE   WEEK 9 PHASE 3 Skill Positions

MONDAY	TUESDAY	WEDNESDAY	THURSDAY	FRIDAY
Pre-Strength Workout	**Pre-Strength Workout**	**Active Rest**	**Pre-Strength Workout**	**Pre-Strength Workout**
Dot Drills 3-5 sets: 10-15 seconds	Walking Toe Touches High Knee Crossovers Backward Skips Low Carioca 2 sets: 20 yards	**Speed Ladder** 5-7 sets	Walking/Skipping Knee Hugs Walking/Skipping Toe Touches Low Shuffle Starts—Football Stance 2 sets: 20 yards	**Jump Rope**—stationary 5-6 sets: 15-30 seconds
Post-Strength Workout	**Speed Development** 1. A Skips—2 sets: 20 yards 2. A Runs—2 sets: 20 yards 3. Fast Leg Drills 2 sets: 20 yards	**Post-Strength Workout**	**PNF Partner Stretch Routine**	**Post-Strength Workout**
Static Stretch Routine		**Static Stretch Routine**		**Static Stretch Routine**
Speed Development 1. A Marches 2 sets: 20 yards 2. A Skips 2 sets: 20 yards 3. A Runs 2 sets: 20 yards	**PNF Partner Stretch Routine**	**Programmable Agility** 1. Four-Cone Perimeter Drill 4 sets	**Conditioning** 16 110s QB, Spec, FB—17 seconds WR, DB, TB—15 seconds (Rest 45 seconds between 110s.)	**Programmable Agility** 1. Carolina Drill—3 sets
Programmable Agility 1. 20-yard Shuttle 4 sets: record best time	**Conditioning** 8 110s Unload QB, Spec, FB—17 seconds WR, DB, TB—15 seconds (Rest 45 seconds between 110s.)	**Reactive Agility** 1. Two-Point Wave Drill (include jumps, shuffle, "Hit It," etc.)		**Reactive Agility** 1. Four-Cone Reaction Drill visual cues 3-4 sets: 10 seconds
Reactive Agility 1. Tennis Ball Drills (all variations) 8-10 sets		**Accleration** 1. Sand Runs 6 sets: 40 yards (sprint 40 yards; walk back for recovery)		**Competitive Drill** 1. Get Up and Sprint 4 sets: 30 yards
Competitive Drill 1. Shark in a Tank 8-10 sets: 10 seconds		or 2. Uphill Runs 6 sets: 30 yards (sprint up, walk down)		
Stretch Lower Back, Hamstrings	Stretch Lower Back, Hamstrings	Stretch Lower Back, Hamstrings	Stretch Lower Back, Hamstrings	Stretch Lower Back, Hamstrings

**Skill Positions
WEEK 9**

**ADVANCED PRESEASON
Phase 3**

**THE HARDER YOU WORK,
THE LUCKIER YOU GET!**

MONDAY	TUESDAY	WEDNESDAY	THURSDAY	FRIDAY
Dot Drills		Speed Ladder		Jump Rope
Abdominal Exercises Medicine Ball Partner Throws 2 sets: 30 reps	**Conditioning** 18 110s Upload QB, FB, Spec.—17 seconds WR, DB, TE—15 seconds (Rest 45 seconds between 110s.)	**Abdominal Exercises** Big 40s—2 sets Twisting Stack Crunches 2 sets: 20 reps	**Conditioning** Metabolic Speed Pac 5 quarters 16 110s QB, Spec.—17 seconds WR, DB, TB—17 seconds (Rest 45 seconds between 110s.)	**Abdominal Exercises** Captain's Choice
Olympic Deadlifts to Knee 2 sets: 3 reps		**Series Box Jumps** 4 sets: 6-7 boxes		**Push Jerks Unload** (warmup—3 reps) 61%—3 reps 67%—3 reps 73%—3 reps 79%—3 reps 85%—1 rep
Power Cleans Unload (warmup—3 reps) 61%—3 reps 67%—3 reps 73%—3 reps 79%—3 reps 85%—1 rep		**Single-Leg Leg Press** 3 sets: 10 reps (each leg)		**Back Squats** (warmup—8 reps) 61%—5 reps 67%—5 reps 73%—5 reps 79%—3 reps 85%—3 reps 91%—1 rep
Clean Pulls 3 sets: 2 reps (100% clean max)		**Dumbbell Bench Press** (stop and stab) 4 sets: 5 reps		**Close Grip Chain Bench Press** (stop and stab) 4 sets: 5 reps
Speed Squats 4 sets: 5 reps (50% of max)		**Pullups—(vary grip)** 3 sets: 10 reps		**Lat Pulldowns (vary grip)** 3 sets: 10 reps
Bench Press (warmup—8 reps) 61%—3 reps 67%—3 reps 73%—3 reps 79%—3 reps 85%—3 reps 91%—1 rep—(3 sets)		**Straight Bar Lying Tricep Extensions** 3 sets: 10 reps		**Seated Plate Raises** 2 sets: 20 reps
Weighted Dips 3 sets: 6 reps		**Bear Calf Raises** 2 sets: 15-20 reps		**Glute Ham Raises** 2 sets: 10 reps or
Straight Bar Curls 3 sets: 10 reps		**Neck Machine** 1 set: 10 reps		**Reverse Hyperextensions** 2 sets: 15 reps
Neck Iso with partner 1 set: 6 reps		**Bar Hang** 1:20 minutes		**Neck Iso** 1 set: 6 reps or
				Neck Machine 1 set: 10 reps
Stretch See Conditioning Schedule	Stretch	Stretch See Conditioning Schedule	Stretch	Stretch See Conditioning Schedule

Advanced PRESEASON TEST WEEK   SPEED AGILITY QUICKNESS CONDITIONING SCHEDULE   WEEK 10 PHASE 3 Skill Positions

MONDAY	TUESDAY	WEDNESDAY	THURSDAY	FRIDAY
Pre-Strength Workout	Pre-Strength Workout	Active Rest	Pre-Strength Workout	Pre-Strength Workout
Dot Drills 3-5 sets: 10-15 seconds **Post-Strength Workout** **PNF Partner Stretch Routine** **Conditioning** 8 110s Unload QB, Spec, FB—17 seconds WR, DB, TB—15 seconds (Rest 45 seconds between 110s.)	**Post-Testing** **PNF Partner Stretch Routine** **Competitive Drill** 1. Shark in a Tank 6-8 sets: 10 seconds	**Speed Ladder** 5-7 sets **Post-Strength Workout** **PNF Partner Stretch Routine** **Conditioning** 6-8 110s Unload QB, Spec, FB—17 seconds WR, DB, TB—15 seconds (Rest 45 seconds between 110s.)	OFF	OFF
Stretch Lower Back, Hamstrings	Stretch Lower Back, Hamstrings	Stretch Lower Back, Hamstrings	Stretch Lower Back, Hamstrings	Stretch Lower Back, Hamstrings

Skill Positions
WEEK 10

ADVANCED PRESEASON
Phase 3

TEST WEEK
LUCK FAVORS THE PREPARED!

	MONDAY	TUESDAY	WEDNESDAY	THURSDAY	FRIDAY
	Dot Drills	Get Body Weight	Speed Ladder	OFF	Jump Rope
	Power Cleans (warmup—3-5 reps) 61%—3 reps 70%—2 reps 79%—1 rep 85%—1 rep 91%—1 rep Begin 1 rep max attempts.	**TEST**—Vertical Jump **TEST**—10-yard Sprint (electronically timed) **TEST**—20-yard Shuttle **TEST**—Sit and Reach Flex	**Push Jerks** (warmup—3-5 reps) 61%—3 reps 70%—2 reps 79%—1 rep 85%—1 rep 91%—1 rep Begin 1 rep max attempts.		OFF
	Bench Press (warmup—8 reps) 61%—5 reps 70%—3 reps 79%—1 rep 88%—1 rep 94%—1 rep Begin 1 rep max attempts.		**Back Squats** (warmup—8 reps) 61%—5 reps 70%—3 reps 79%—1 rep 88%—1 rep Begin 3 rep max attempts.		
	Stretch Lower back, Hamstrings	Stretch Lower back, Hamstrings	Stretch Lower back, Hamstrings	Stretch Lower back, Hamstrings	Stretch Lower back, Hamstrings

325

IN-SEASON TRAINING

IN-SEASON CONDITIONING MENU

Choose 1 Exercise

1st Day

1. 5th-S—1 lap around field including end zones, typical volume 4-5 reps
    Linemen—75 seconds
    DE, TE, LB, FB, QB, Specialist—70 seconds
    WR, DB, TB—65 seconds
  Work-to-Rest Ratio—1:3

2. Full Gassers—across the field and back, twice—220 total yards, typical volume 3-5 reps
    Lineman—45 seconds
    DE, TE, FB, QB, Specialist, LB—40 seconds
    TB, WR, DB—35 seconds
  Work-to-Rest Ratio—1:3

3. 1/2 Gassers—across the field and back—110 total yards, typical volume 6-8 reps
  Work-to-Rest Ratio—1:3

Choose 1 Exercise

2nd Day

1. 1/2 Gassers—across the field and back—110 total yards, typical volume 6-8 reps
  Work-to-Rest Ratio—1:3

2. 30-30-30s, typical volume 6-8 reps—stride 30 yards, sprint 30 yards, stride 30 yards,

3. 110s—sprint 110 yards, typical volume 6-8 reps
    Linemen—18-20 seconds
    TE, LB, DE, QB, Specialist, FB—16-18 seconds
    WR, DB, TB—15-16 seconds
  Work-to-Rest Ratio—1:3

4. Hash Sprint—sprint from sideline to far hash, stride or jog to opposite sideline,
    typical volume 6-8 reps
  Work-to-Rest Ratio—1:3

5. Perfect 40s—full speed, typical volume 6 reps
    Work-to-Rest Ratio—1:3
    Plus makeups for non-perfect 40s

Choose 1 Exercise

3rd Day

1. Perfect 40s—full speed, typical volume 6 reps
    Work-to-Rest Ratio—1:3

2. 20s—full speed, typical volume 6-8 reps
    Work-to-Rest Ratio—1:3

or

Football-Specific Conditioning

1. Perfect Plays—offense must execute full speed play against air, typical volume 10-15 plays

2. Pursuit Drills—defense must execute proper pursuit angles while chasing the ball full speed, typical volume 10-15 plays

3. Scramble Drills—offense executes QB scramble rules with all players, typical volume 10-15 plays

4. Deep Balls—WRs and DBs work on executing and defending the long pass, typical volume 10-15 plays

IN-SEASON CONDITIONING
Sample Week

Monday   **4 Full Gassers**
            OL, DT—45 seconds
            TE, LB, DE, QB, Specialist, FB—40 seconds
            WR, DB, TB—35 seconds
            Work-to-Rest Ratio—1:3

Tuesday   **6½ Gassers**
            OL, DT—20 seconds
            TE, LB, DE, QB, Specialist, FB—18 seconds
            WR, DB, TB—16 seconds
            Work-to-Rest Ratio—1:3

Wednesday   **Football-Specific Drills**
            Offense—Perfect Plays—10-15 plays
            Defense—Pursuit Drills—10-15 plays

Thursday   **No Conditioning**

Friday   **No Conditioning**

Saturday   WIN GAME!

BEGINNER
TRAINING

Phase 1—4 Weeks

DAY 1

Foot Speed
Dot Drills—3-4 sets: 10-15 seconds

Abs
Flutterkicks—30 seconds
Regular Sit-Ups—1 set: 15-20 reps

Power
Dumbbell Jump Shrugs
(very light weight) 3 sets: 5 reps

Lower-Body Strength
Back Squats—5 sets: 5 reps
warmup—5 reps, 55%, 64%, 70%, 73%,
76%

Upper-Body Strength
Bench Press—5 sets: 5 reps
warmup—5 reps, 55%, 64%, 70%, 76%,
79%

Assistance/Isolation Exercises
Pullups (vary grip)
2 sets: 5-10 reps

Lying Tricep Extensions with Barbell
2 sets: 10 reps

Barbell Curls
2 sets: 10 reps

Hamstring Curls—seated or prone
2 sets: 10 reps

Four-Way Neck Machine—1 set: 10 reps
or
Four-Way Neck Isolation with partner—1 set: 6 reps

Upper-Body Plyometrics
Supine Medicine Ball Plyometric Press
(light weight) 1-2 sets: 10 reps

STRETCH
Static Stretch
Lower Back, Hamstrings

DAY 2

Foot Speed
Jump Rope—4-5 sets: 20-30 seconds

Abs
Reverse Crunches—1 set: 15-20 reps
Regular Sit-Ups—1 sets: 20 reps

Power
Box Jumps—2-3 sets: 5 reps
(jump up, step down)
(set box height at appropriate level)

Lower-Body Strength
Leg Press—3 sets: 10 reps

Upper-Body Strength
Incline Bench Press
4 sets: 6 reps

Assistance/Isolation Exercises
Lat Pulldowns (front, underhand)
2 sets: 10 reps

Body Weight Dips—2 sets: 10 reps

Dumbbell Curls—2 sets: 10 reps

Hamstring Curls—seated or prone
2 sets: 10 reps

Four-Way Neck Machine—1 set: 10 reps
or
Four-Way Neck Isolation with partner—1 set: 6 reps

Upper-Body Plyometrics
Clapping Push-Ups
2 sets: 5-10 reps

STRETCH
Static Stretch
Lower Back, Hamstrings

Phase 2—4 Weeks

BEGINNER IN-SEASON Workout

DAY 1	DAY 2

DAY 1

Foot Speed
Jump Rope—4-5 sets: 20-30 seconds

Abs
Reverse Crunches—1 set: 20 reps
Rocky Sit-Ups—1 set: 20 reps

Power
Barbell Jump Shrugs
      (light weight) 3 sets: 5 reps
or
Hammer Jammer—3 sets: 5 reps

Lower-Body Strength
Speed Squats
      warmup—5 reps, 4 sets: 5 reps at 50%

Upper-Body Strength
Incline Bench Press
      5 sets: 5 reps

Assistance/Isolation Exercises
Seated Cable Rows
      2 sets: 8-10 reps
or
One-Arm Dumbbell Rows
      2 sets: 8-10 reps

Dumbbell Tricep Extensions
      2 sets: 8-10 reps

Hamstring Curls—Seated or Prone
      2 sets—8-10 reps

Four-Way Neck Machine—1 set: 10 reps
or
Four-Way Neck Isolation with partner—1 set: 6 reps

Upper-Body Plyometrics
Medicine Ball Push-Ups—2 sets: 5 reps

STRETCH
Static Stretch
Lower Back, Hamstrings

DAY 2

Foot Speed
Speed Ladder—4-5 sets

Abs
Flutterkicks—30 seconds
ABC Sit-Ups—1 set: 10 reps

Power
Explosive Box Stepups (no weight)
      3 sets: 5 reps (each leg)

Lower-Body Strength
Front Squats—4 sets: 5 reps

Upper-Body Strength
Close Grip Bench Press
      (stop and stab) 4 sets: 6 reps

Assistance/Isolation Exercises
Lat Pulldowns (front, underhand)
      2 sets: 10 reps
or
Pullups—2 sets: 5-10 reps

Dumbbell Shoulder 21s—1 set

Glute Ham Raises—2 sets: 6-10 reps

Four-Way Neck Machine—1 set: 10 reps
or
Four-Way Neck Isolation with partner—1 set: 6 reps

Upper-Body Plyometrics
Clapping Push-Ups
      2 sets: 5-10 reps

STRETCH
Static Stretch
Lower Back, Hamstrings

Phase 3—4 Weeks

BEGINNER
IN-SEASON Workout

DAY 1	DAY 2
Foot Speed Speed Ladder—4-5 sets	**Foot Speed** Dot Drills—3-4 sets: 10-15 seconds
Abs Figure Eights—1 set: 10 reps Rocky Sit-Ups—1 set: 20 reps	**Abs** Big 40s—1 set Dying Cockroach—1 set: 30 seconds
Power Barbell or Dumbbell Jump Shrugs (light weight) 3 sets: 5 reps	**Power** Box Jumps—2-3 sets: 5 reps (jump up, step down) (set box height at appropriate level)
Lower-Body Strength Interval Back Squats warmup—8 reps, 6 sets: 3 reps at 61% 1-minute rest interval between sets	**Lower-Body Strength** Single-Leg Leg Press 3 sets: 10 reps (each leg)
Upper-Body Strength Barbell Seated Shoulder Press 4 sets: 6 reps	**Upper-Body Strength** Close Grip Bench Press (stop and stab) 4 sets: 5 reps
Assistance/Isolation Exercises One-Arm Dumbbell Rows 2 sets: 8-10 reps Bench Dips (unweighted) 2 sets: 10-15 reps Standing Dumbbell Alternate Curls 2 sets: 10 reps Glute Ham Raises—2 sets: 6-10 reps Four-Way Neck Machine—1 set: 10 reps or Four-Way Neck Isolation with partner—1 set: 6 reps	**Assistance/Isolation Exercises** Pullups—(vary grip) 2 sets: 5-10 reps Body Weight Dips 2 sets: 10-15 reps Dumbbell Hammer Curls 2 sets: 10 reps Hamstring Curls—seated or prone 2 sets: 10 reps Four-Way Neck Machine—1 set: 10 reps or Four-Way Neck Isolation with partner—1 set: 6 reps
Upper-Body Plyometrics Medicine Ball Push-Ups—2 sets: 5 reps	**Upper-Body Plyometrics** Clapping Push-Ups 2 sets: 5-10 reps
STRETCH Static Stretch Lower Back, Hamstrings	**STRETCH** Static Stretch Lower Back, Hamstrings

INTERMEDIATE
IN-SEASON

Phase 1—4 Weeks

INTERMEDIATE
IN-SEASON Workout

DAY 1	DAY 2
Foot Speed Dot Drills—3-4 sets: 10-15 seconds	**Foot Speed** Jump Rope—4-5 sets: 20-30 seconds
Abs Flutterkicks—1 set: 30 seconds Dying Cockroach—30 seconds	**Abs** Hanging Reverse Crunches 1 set: 20 reps Twisting Stack Crunches—1 set: 20 reps

Power
Hang Snatch Combo—4 sets
Jump Shrugs—1 set; 1 rep
Snatch High Pulls—1 set: 1 rep
Hang Snatch—1 set: 1 rep
	Power
	Box Jumps—3 sets: 5 reps
	    (jump up, step down)
	    (use appropriate height box)

Lower-Body Strength
Back Squats—warmup—8 reps
    55%—5 reps, 61%—5 reps,
    67%—5 reps, 73%—5 reps
	Lower-Body Strength
	Leg Press—3 sets: 10 reps

Upper-Body Strength
Incline Bench Press
    5 sets: 5 reps
	Upper-Body Strength
	Close Grip Bench Press
	    4 sets: 6 reps (stop and stab)

Assistance/Isolation Exercises
Dumbbell Bench Press—2 sets: 6 reps
 	
Pullups—2 sets: 5-10 reps
 	
Lying Tricep Extensions (with barbell)
    2 sets: 8-10 reps
 	
Dumbbell Standing Alternate Curls
    2 sets: 10 reps
 	
Seated or Prone Leg Curls—2 sets: 10 reps
 	
Four-Way Neck Machine—1 set: 10 reps
	Assistance/Isolation Exercises
	Seated Dumbbell Shoulder Press
	    2 sets: 8 reps
	
	Body Weight Dips
	    2 sets: 10-15 reps (stop and stab)
	
	Seated Cable Rows
	    2 sets: 10 reps
	
	Four-Way Neck Isolation with partner—1 set: 6 reps

Upper-Body Plyometrics
Supine Medicine Ball Plyometric Press
    2 sets: 10 reps
	Upper-Body Plyometrics
	Supine Medicine Ball Pullover Throws
	    1 set: 10 reps

STRETCH Static or A-I Stretch Lower Back, Hamstrings	**STRETCH** Static or A-I Stretch Lower Back, Hamstrings

Phase 2—4 Weeks

INTERMEDIATE IN-SEASON Workout

DAY 1	DAY 2
Foot Speed Jump Rope—4-5 sets: 20-30 seconds	**Foot Speed** Speed Ladder—4-5 sets
Abs Reverse Crunches—1 set: 20 reps ABC Sit-Ups—1 set: 10 reps	**Abs** Bicycle Abs—1 set: 30 seconds Dying Cockroach—1 sets: 30 seconds
Power Explosive Box Stepups (no weight)—3 sets: 5 reps (each leg)	**Power** Hang Snatch Combo—4 sets Jump Shrugs—1 set: 1 rep Hang Cleans High Pulls—1 set: 1 rep Hang Cleans—1 set: 1 rep
Lower-Body Strength Front Squats—4 sets: 6 reps	**Lower-Body Strength** Box Stepups—2 sets: 5 reps (each leg) Barbell Lunges—2 sets: 5 reps (each leg)
Upper-Body Strength Bench Press—warmup—10 reps 61%—8 reps, 70%—6 reps, 79%—4 reps, 85%—2 reps 64%—8 reps	**Upper-Body Strength** Seated Barbell Shoulder Press 4 sets: 6 reps
Assistance/Isolation Exercises Incline Dumbbell Alternate Bench Press 2 sets: 6 reps Lat Pulldowns (front, underhand) 2 sets: 8-10 reps Dumbbell Lying Tricep Extensions 2 sets: 10 reps Four-Way Neck Isolation with partner 1 set: 6 reps	**Assistance/Isolation Exercises** Dumbbell Bench Press 2 sets: 6 reps (stop and stab) One-Arm Dumbbell Rows 2 sets: 8 reps Barbell Curls—2 sets: 10 reps Glute Ham Raises—2 sets: 6-10 reps Four-Way Neck Machine—1 set: 10 reps
Upper-Body Plyometrics Clapping Push-Ups 2 sets: 6 reps	**Upper-Body Plyometrics** Medicine Ball Push-Ups 1 set: 6-8 reps
STRETCH Static or A-I Stretch Lower Back, Hamstrings	**STRETCH** Static or A-I Stretch Lower Back, Hamstrings

Phase 3—4 Weeks

INTERMEDIATE
IN-SEASON Workout

DAY 1	DAY 2

DAY 1

Foot Speed
Speed Ladder—5-6 sets

Abs
Flutterkicks—1 set: 30 seconds
Figure Four Double Crunches
　　　1 set: 10 reps (each leg)

Power
Hang Snatch (Speed!)
　　　4 sets: 3 reps

Lower-Body Strength
Speed Back Squats
　　　warmup—8 reps—4 sets: 5 reps at 50%
　　　(pause at bottom, explode up)

Upper-Body Strength
Interval Bench Press
　　　warmup—8 reps—8 sets: 3 reps at 64%
　　　(45-second to 1-minute rest between intervals)

Assistance/Isolation Exercises
Dumbbell Seated Alternate Shoulder Press
　　　2 sets: 6 reps

Pullups—2 sets: 6-10 reps

Weighted Dips—2 sets: 8 reps

Reverse Hyperextension Machine
　　　1 set: 20 reps

Four-Way Neck Machine
　　　1 set: 10 reps

Upper-Body Plyometrics
Supine Medicine Ball Plyometric Press
　　　2 sets: 10 reps

DAY 2

Foot Speed
Dot Drills—3-4 sets: 10-15 seconds each set

Abs
Hanging Reverse Crunches—1 set: 20 reps
Medicine Ball Stack Crunches—1 set: 20 reps

Power
Hang Cleans
　　　warmup—5 reps
　　　55%—3 reps, 61%—3 reps,
　　　67%—3 reps, 73%—3 reps

Lower-Body Strength
Single-Leg Leg Press
　　　3 sets: 10 reps (each leg)

Upper-Body Strength
Incline Dumbbell Bench Press
　　　4 sets: 6 reps

Assistance/Isolation Exercises
Dumbbell Alternate Bench Press
　　　2 sets: 6 reps (stop and stab)

Leg Curls—seated or prone
　　　2 sets: 10 reps

Dumbbell Lying Tricep Extensions
　　　2 sets: 10 reps

Four-Way Neck Machine
　　　1 set: 10 reps

Upper-Body Plyometrics
Clapping Push-Ups
　　　2 sets: 8 reps

STRETCH
Static or A-I Stretch
Lower Back, Hamstrings

STRETCH
Static or A-I Stretch
Lower Back, Hamstrings

ADVANCED
IN-SEASON
L.O.S. and LB

Phase 1—4 Weeks

ADVANCED
IN-SEASON Workout

OL, DL, LB, TE

DAY 1	DAY 2	DAY 3

Foot Speed
Jump Rope—4-5 sets:
  20-30 seconds
	Foot Speed
	Dot Drills—3-4 sets:
	  10-15 seconds
		Foot Speed
		Speed Ladder

Abs
Hanging Reverse Crunches
  1 set: 20 reps
Twisting Stack Crunches
  1 set: 20 reps
	Abs
	Figure Eights—1 set: 10 reps
	Medicine Ball Stack Crunches
	  1 set: 20 reps
		Abs
		Big 40s—1 set
		Swiss Ball Crunches
		  1 sets: 20 reps

Power
Hang Snatch
  (Speed!)
  4 sets: 3 reps
	Power
	Hammer Jammer
	  3 sets: 5 reps
		Power
		Hang Cleans or Power Cleans
		  warmup—5 reps, 61%—3
		  reps, 64%—3 reps, 67%—3
		  reps, 70%—3 reps

Lower-Body Strength
Back Squats
  warmup—10 reps
  61%—5 reps, 67%—5 reps,
  73%—5 reps, 76-79%—3 reps
	Upper-Body Strength
	Seated Barbell Shoulder Press
	  1 set: 8 reps, 1 set: 6 reps,
	  2 sets: 5 reps
		Lower-Body Strength
		Front Squats—4 set: 5 reps

Upper-Body Strength
Bench Press—warmup—10 reps
  64%—8 reps, 73%—5 reps,
  79%—3 reps, 82%—3 reps
	Dumbbell Bench Press
	  (stop and stab)
	  1 set: 8 reps, 2 sets: 6 reps
		Upper-Body Strength
		Close Grip Bench Press
		  (stop and stab)
		  4 sets: 5 reps

Assistance/Isolation Exercises
Pullups—3 sets: 5-10 reps
Weighted Dips—3 sets: 8 reps
Grip Builders—2 sets: 20 yards
  (bumper plate carrys, one
  in each hand)
Four-Way Neck Machine
  1 set: 10 reps
	Seated Cable Rows
	  1 set: 8 reps, 2 sets: 6 reps
		Assistance/Isolation Exercises
		Lat Pulldowns
		  (front, underhand)
		  3 sets: 10 reps

	Assistance/Isolation Exercises
	Leg Extension Machine
	  2 sets: 10 reps
		Lying Dumbbell Tricep Extensions
		  3 sets: 8-10 reps

Upper-Body Plyometrics
Supine Medicine Ball Plyometric
  Press
  2 sets: 10 reps
	Leg Curl Machine—seated or
	  prone
	  2 sets: 10 reps
		Four-Way Neck Machine
		  1 set: 10 reps

	Standing Dumbbell Alternate
	  Curls
	  3 sets: 10 reps
		Grip Builders—2 sets: 20 yards
		  (bumper plate carrys, one in
		  each hand)

	Reverse Hyperextension Machine
	  1 set: 20 reps
		Upper-Body Plyometrics
		Supine Medicine Ball Plyometric
		  Press
		  2 sets: 10 reps

	Upper-Body Plyometrics Clapping Push-Ups 2 sets: 6-10 reps	
STRETCH Static or A-I Stretch Lower Back, Hamstrings	STRETCH Static or A-I Stretch Lower Back, Hamstrings	STRETCH Static or A-I Stretch Lower Back, Hamstrings

ADVANCED
IN-SEASON Workout

Phase 2—4 Weeks

OL, DL, LB, TE

DAY 1	DAY 2	DAY 3

Foot Speed
Jump Rope
    4-5 sets: 20-30 seconds
	Foot Speed
	Dot Drills—3-4 sets:
	    10-15 seconds
		Foot Speed
		Speed Ladder—5-6 sets

Abs
Flutterkicks—30 seconds
ABC Sit-Ups—10 reps
	Abs
	Bicycle Abs—30 seconds
	Dying Cockroach Position
	    3 seconds
		Abs
		Hanging Reverse Crunches
		    1 set: 20 reps
		Medicine Ball Stack Crunches
		    1 set: 20 reps

Power
Power Snatch
    (Speed!)
    4 sets: 3 reps
	Power
	Push Jerks
	    warmup—3 reps,
	    61%—3 reps, 67%—3 reps,
	    70%—3 reps, 73%—3 reps
		Power
		Hang Cleans or Power Cleans
		    warmup—5 reps, 61%—3
		    reps, 67%—3 reps, 70%—3
		    reps, 76%—3 reps

Lower-Body Strength
Interval Back Squats
    warmup—8 reps, 61-64%—
    5 sets: 3 reps
    (45-60 seconds rest interval
    between sets)
	Lower-Body Strength
	Single-Leg Leg Press
	    3 sets: 10 reps each leg
		Lower-Body Strength
		Speed Back Squats
		    warmup—8 reps
		    4 sets: 5 reps
		    (50% pause at bottom—
		    explode up!)

Upper-Body Strength
Bench Press
    warmup—10 reps
    64%—8 reps, 73%—6 reps,
    79%—4 reps, 88%—2 reps,
    70%—8 reps
	Upper-Body Strength
	Alternate Dumbbell Bench Press
	    (stop and stab)
	    4 sets: 5 reps
		Upper-Body Strength
		Close Grip Bench Press
		    (stop and stab)
		    4 sets: 5 reps

Assistance/Isolation Exercises
Pullups (vary grip)
    3 sets: 5-10 reps
	Assistance/Isolation Exercises
	Seated Cable Rows
	    1 set: 8 reps, 2 sets: 6 reps
		Assistance/Isolation Exercises
		Incline Dumbbell Bench Press
		    4 sets: 5 reps

Lying Tricep Extensions with Curl
Bar
    4 sets: 6 reps
	Weighted Dips—3 sets: 6 reps	Lying Dumbbell Tricep Extensions
		    5 sets: 8 reps

Barbell Bicep Curls
    3 sets: 8 reps
	Incline Alternate Dumbbell Curls
	    3 sets: 8 reps
		Upper-Body Plyometrics
		Supine Medicine Ball Plyometric
		Press
		    2 sets: 10 reps

Glute Ham Raises
    2 sets: 8-10 reps
	Grip Builders
	    2 sets: 20 yards
	    (bumper plate carrys, one in
	    each hand)	

Wrist Roller (up and down)
    2 sets
	Upper-Body Plyometrics
	Clapping Push-Ups
	    2 sets: 10 reps	

Four-Way Neck Isolation
    with partner
    1 set: 6 reps		

Upper-Body Plyometrics Medicine Ball Push-Ups 2 sets: 5-8 reps		
STRETCH Static or A-I Stretch Lower Back, Hamstrings	STRETCH Static or A-I Stretch Lower Back, Hamstrings	STRETCH Static or A-I Stretch Lower Back, Hamstrings

Phase 3—4 Weeks

ADVANCED
IN-SEASON Workout

OL, DL, LB, TE

DAY 1	DAY 2	DAY 3

Foot Speed
Speed Ladder—5-6 sets
	Foot Speed
	Dot Drills—3-4 sets
	  10-15 seconds
		Foot Speed
		Jump Rope—4-5 sets:
		  20-30 seconds

Abs
Flutterkicks—30 seconds
Figure Four Double Crunches
  1 set: 10 reps (each side)
	Abs
	Hanging Reverse Crunches
	  1 set: 20 reps
	Medicine Ball Stack Crunches
	  1 set: 20 reps
		Abs
		Reverse Crunches—1 set: 20 reps
		Quick Crunches—1 set: 25 reps

Power
Hang Cleans or Power Cleans
  warmup—3 reps, 55%—3
  reps, 61%—3 reps, 67%—3
  reps, 73-76%—3 reps
	Power
	Explosive Box Stepups
	(no weight)
	  3 sets: 3 reps (each leg)
		Power
		Hang Snatch or Power Snatch
		  (Speed!)
		  4 sets: 3 reps

Lower-Body Strength
Back Squats—warmup—10 reps
  61%—5 reps, 67%—5 reps,
  73%—5 reps, 76-79%—3 reps
	Lower-Body Strength
	Box Stepups
	  3 sets: 5 reps (each leg)
		Lower-Body Strength
		Speed Back Squats
		  warmup—8 reps
		  4 sets: 5 reps at 50%

Upper-Body Strength
Incline Bench Press
  3 sets: 5 reps, 1 set: 3 reps
	Upper-Body Strength
	Close Grip Bench Press
	(stop and stab)
	  4 sets: 5 reps
		Upper-Body Strength
		Close Grip Bench Press
		  (stop and stab) 4 sets: 5 reps
		  (use chains, 20 pounds each)

Assistance/Isolation Exercises
Seated Cable Rows or Bent Over
  Barbell Rows
  3 sets: 6 reps
	Assistance/Isolation Exercises
	Seated Dumbbell Shoulder Press
	  3 sets: 6 reps
		Assistance/Isolation Exercises
		Lat Pulldowns
		  (front, underhand)
		  3 sets: 10 reps

Dumbbell Bench Press
  (stop and stab)
  3 sets: 5 reps
	Lat Pulldowns
	(front, underhand)
	  2 sets: 8-10 reps
		or
		Pullups (vary grip)
		  3 sets: 5-10 reps

Weighted Dips—3 sets: 5 reps	One Arm Bent Over Dumbbell
	  Rows
	  2 sets: 8 reps
		Body Weight Dips (stop and stab)
		  2 sets: 10-15 reps

Reverse Hyperextension Machine
  1 set: 20 reps
	Strict Barbell Curls
	  3 sets: 10 reps
		Grip Builders
		  2 sets: 20 yards
		  (bumper plate carrys, one in
		  each hand)

Upper-Body Plyometrics
Medicine Ball Push-Ups
  2 sets: 6-10 reps
	Barbell Wrist Curls
	  2 sets: 10-15 reps
		Four-Way Neck Machine
		  1 set: 10 reps

	Tricep Pushdown Machine
	  2 sets: 20 reps
		or
		Four-Way Neck Isolation with
		  partner
		  1 set: 6 reps

	Upper-Body Plyometrics
	Clapping Push-Ups
	  2 sets: 8-10 reps
		Upper-Body Plyometrics
		Supine Medicine Ball Plyometric
		  Press
		  2 sets: 10 reps

STRETCH Static or A-I Stretch Lower Back, Hamstrings	STRETCH Static or A-I Stretch Lower Back, Hamstrings	STRETCH Static or A-I Stretch Lower Back, Hamstrings

ADVANCED
IN-SEASON
SKILL POSITIONS
WR, DB, QB, RB, Specialist

Phase 1—4 Weeks   ADVANCED   QB, Specialist, RB, DB, WR
                      IN-SEASON Workout

DAY 1

Foot Speed
Speed Ladder—4-5 sets

Abs
Flutterkicks—1 set: 30 seconds
Dying Cockroach—1 set: 30 seconds

Power
Hang Snatch (Speed!)
    4 sets: 3 reps

Lower-Body Strength
Back Squats
    warmup—10 reps
    61%—5 reps, 67%—5 reps, 73%—5 reps
    76-79%—3 reps

Upper-Body Strength
Incline Bench Press
    4 sets: 5 reps

Assistance/Isolation Exercises
Lateral Squats
    1 set: 6 reps (each leg)

Glute Ham Raises
    2 sets: 10 reps

Dumbbell Tricep Extensions
    2 sets: 10 reps

Towel Pullups—1 set: 10 reps

Four-Way Neck Machine—1 set: 10 reps

QB's Option
Tricep Pushdowns—2 sets: 10 reps
Dumbbell Shoulder 21s—1 set

Upper-Body Plyometrics
Clapping Push-Ups—3 sets: 5 reps

STRETCH
Static or A-I Stretch
Lower Back, Hamstrings

DAY 2

Foot Speed
Dot Drills—3-4 sets: 10-15 seconds

Abs
Big 40s—1 set
Medicine Ball Stack Crunches
    1 set—20 reps

Power
Hang Cleans
    warmup—5 reps
    61%—3 reps, 64%—3 reps,
    67%—3 reps, 70%—3 reps

Lower-Body Strength
Box Stepups
    2 sets: 5 reps (each leg)
Barbell Lunges
    2 sets: 5 reps (each leg)

Upper-Body Strength
Bench Press
    warmup—10 reps
    61%—8 reps, 67%—5 reps,
    73%—5 reps, 79%—3 reps

Assistance/Isolation Exercises
Weighted Dips
    2 sets: 10 reps

Four-Way Neck Machine—1 set: 10 reps
or
Four-Way Neck Isolation with partner—1 set: 6 reps

QB's Option
Rotator Cuff Dumbbell Exercises
Lying on Side—1 set: 20 reps (each arm)
Standing Partner Medicine Ball Twisting
Handoffs—1 set: 20 reps (each direction)

Upper-Body Plyometrics
Medicine Ball Push-Ups
    2 sets: 6 reps

STRETCH
Static or A-I Stretch
Lower Back, Hamstrings

ADVANCED
IN-SEASON Workout

Phase 2—4 Weeks

QB, Specialist, RB, DB, WR

DAY 1

Foot Speed
Jump Rope—4-5 sets: 20-30 seconds

Abs
Hanging Reverse Crunches—1 set: 20 reps
Twisting Stack Crunches—1 set: 20 reps

Power
Power Snatch (Speed!)
    4 sets: 3 reps

Lower-Body Strength
Interval Back Squats
    warmup—8 reps, 5 sets: 3 reps at 64%
    (45-second to 1-minute rest interval between
    sets)

Upper-Body Strength
Bench Press
    warmup—10 reps
    64%—8 reps, 70%—6 reps, 76%—4 reps,
    82%—2 reps, 70%—8 reps

Assistance/Isolation Exercises
Lateral Squats
    1 set: 6 reps (each leg)

Pullups—(vary grip)
    3 sets: 8-10 reps

Dumbbell Tricep Extensions
    4 sets: 8 reps
    (15-second rest interval between sets)

Four-Way Neck Machine—1 set: 10 reps
or
Four-Way Neck Isolation with partner—1 set: 6 reps

QB's Option
Dumbbell Pullovers—1 set: 12 reps
Dumbbell Lying Rotator Cuff Exercises
    1 set: 20 reps (each arm)

Upper-Body Plyometrics
Supine Medicine Ball Plyometric Press
    2 sets: 10 reps

STRETCH
Static or A-I Stretch
Lower Back, Hamstrings

DAY 2

Foot Speed
Dot Drills—3-4 sets: 10-15 seconds (each set)

Abs
Figure Eights—1 set: 10 reps
Medicine Ball Stack Crunches—1 set: 20 reps

Power
Push Jerks—warmup—3 reps
    55%—3 reps, 61%—3 reps
    67%—3 reps, 70%—3 reps

Lower-Body Strength
Single-Leg Leg Press—3 sets: 10 reps

Upper-Body Strength
Close Grip Bench Press
    (stop and stab) 4 sets: 5 reps

Assistance/Isolation Exercises
Incline Dumbbell Press
    3 sets: 5 reps

Towel Pullups—2 sets: 10 reps

Reverse Hyperextensions
    2 sets: 15 reps

Four-Way Neck Machine—1 set: 10 reps

QB's Option
Dumbbell Shoulder 21s—1 set
Tricep Kickbacks (slow and controlled)
    2 sets: 15 reps

Upper-Body Plyometrics
Clapping Push-Ups
    2 sets: 6-10 reps

STRETCH
Static or A-I Stretch
Lower Back, Hamstrings

Phase 3—4 Weeks   ADVANCED
                    IN-SEASON Workout   QB, Specialist, RB, DB, WR

DAY 1

Foot Speed
Speed Ladder—5-6 sets

Abs
Flutterkicks—1 set: 30 seconds
Figure Four Double Crunches
      1 set: 10 reps (each side)

Power
Hang Cleans—warmup—3 reps
      55%—3 reps, 61%—3 reps,
      67%—3 reps, 73%—2-3 reps

Lower-Body Strength
Speed Squats—warmup—5 reps
      4 sets: 5 reps
      (50% pause at bottom—explode up!)

Upper-Body Strength
Incline Bench Press
      4 sets: 5 reps, 1 set: 3 reps

Assistance/Isolation Exercises
Seated Cable Rows—3 sets: 8 reps

Weighted Dips—3 sets: 8 reps

Glute Ham Raises—2 sets: 10 reps

Four-Way Neck Machine—1 set: 10 reps
or
Four-Way Neck Isolation with partner—1 set: 6 reps

QB's Option
Dumbbell Pullovers—1-2 sets: 10 reps
Dumbbell Lying Rotator Cuff Exercises
      1 set: 20 reps

Upper-Body Plyometrics
Supine Medicine Ball Pullover Throws
      1 set: 10 reps

STRETCH
Static or A-I Stretch
Lower Back, Hamstrings

DAY 2

Foot Speed
Dot Drills—3-4 sets: 10-15 seconds

Abs
Hanging Reverse Crunches
      1 set: 20 reps
Medicine Ball Stack Crunches—1 set: 20 reps

Power
Explosive Box Stepups (no weight)
      3 sets: 4 reps (each leg)
or
Hammer Jammer—3 sets: 4 reps

Lower-Body Strength
Box Stepups
      3 sets: 5 reps

Upper-Body Strength
Bench Press—warmup—10 reps
      64%—5 reps, 73%—5 reps,
      79%—3 reps, 82-85%—3 reps

Assistance/Isolation Exercises
Dumbbell Shoulder 21s—1 set

Towel Pullups—2 sets: 8-10 reps

Reverse Hyperextensions
      2 sets: 15 reps

Four-Way Neck Machine—1 set: 10 reps
or
Four-Way Neck Isolation with partner—1 set: 6 reps

QB's Option
Tricep Pushdowns (slow)
      1 set: 20 reps
Dumbbell Lying Rotator Cuff Exercises
      1 set: 20 reps (each arm)

STRETCH
Static or A-I Stretch
Lower Back, Hamstrings

Appendix

Glossary

Acceleration – The process of achieving maximum speed when starting from a dead stop or running at a slower speed.

Accommodation – The decreased strength gains due to an unchanging workout routine. This may be appropriate for a maintenance cycle, in-season, but is to be avoided when increasing strength is the goal.

Actin – The thin protein filament found in the muscle cell, to which myosin (another protein filament) attaches allowing the muscle cell to shorten or contract.

Adenosinetriphosphate (ATP) – Often called the currency of work, it is the basic source of energy for the muscle. It links the energy requiring functions of the muscle cell to the available energy taken from fats, carbohydrates, and protein.

Agility – The ability to react and control one's body athletically in an open skill sport. This would include change of direction, accelerating, and decelerating in a precise manner depending upon the game situation.

Anaerobic glycolysis – The process of breaking down the simplest form or carbohydrate (glucose) and extracting energy during high-intensity activity. The process is anaerobic since oxygen is not used in the process, and with high-intensity activity lactic acid is the end product.

Core strength development – Improvements in the integrity of key muscle groups in the hips, thighs, and torso that provide balance and stability to the entire musculoskeletal system.

Cortisol – The hormone that initiates the protein breakdown process in the muscle cell. If the training and rest cycles are planned correctly, increases in cortisol levels are a desirable result, critical to the remodeling process in the muscle. If cortisol levels get too high, as in the case of overtraining, muscle hypertrophy is negatively affected.

Delayed transformation — Changing the training loads (number of repetitions, sets, amount of resistance used and time between sets) performed in a workout from cycle to cycle, which often results in deferring the goal of maximizing specificity of training relative to training intensity and volume.

Delayed transmutation – Changing the lifts or exercises performed in a workout from cycle to cycle, which often results in deferring the goal of maximizing specificity of training.

Dorsiflexion – Describes the position of the ankle joint in which the toe is higher than the heel (toes up).

Elastin – The connective tissue found in muscles and tendons that allows them to be stretched.

Explosive strength deficit – The difference between the maximum amount of force a muscle can generate in unlimited time and the amount that can be generated in sport performance in which there is a time limit.

Fast twitch muscle fiber – Muscle cells that can reach full force rapidly and are typically only recruited with high levels of resistance. These tend to be large and capable of generating large amounts of force, but also tend to fatigue rapidly.

Glucose – A digested form of all carbohydrates that is absorbed into the blood and eventually absorbed by the cells.

Glycemic index – The speed at which carbohydrates are digested into glucose and absorbed into the blood stream.

Glycogen – The stored form of carbohydrate, stored in both muscle and liver cells. The muscle glycogen is used locally when needed while the liver glycogen is available when the blood glucose levels are low.

Golgi tendon organ – The sensory structure found in our tendons that protect the tendon from excessive force by limiting the number of motor units that we can recruit in the muscle.

Human growth hormone – A protein-Building hormone that facilitates increases in muscle size. Research shows that this hormone is secreted during high-volume resistance training and during the deepest levels of sleep.

Insulin – The hormone produced by the pancreas that allows muscle and liver cells to take in glucose (a simple form of carbohydrate).

Intensity – The training variable that describes the amount of weight used in resistance training as well as the speed of a lift or plyometric exercise.

Lactic acid – The by-product of anaerobic glycolysis during high-intensity exercise. The high acidity is a major contributor to muscle fatigue.

Motor unit – The motor nerve (nerve sending the signal from the brain and spinal column to the muscle) and the group of muscle cells it supplies or stimulates. Each motor unit has a threshold level of activation that can be described as "low," meaning that light resistance can activate it, or "high," meaning that a heavy resistance is required for activation.

Muscle hypertrophy – The increase in the size of the muscle cell through the addition of contractile proteins (actin and myosin).

Muscle spindle – A sensory structure in the muscle that detects the rate and extent of stretch being placed on that muscle. In an effort to protect the muscle from tearing, the muscle spindle causes a reflex contraction or shortening of the muscle called the stretch eflex.

Myosin – A thick contractile protein filament with golf club-shaped structures that attaches to another contractile protein (actin) and, through a pulling action, cause the muscle cells to contract.

Periodization – The Eastern European concept of breaking the year down into short training cycles in which the acute training variables such as exercise choice, training intensity and training volume are changed from cycle to cycle. This provides variety and good quality rest periods to maximize gains.

Plyometrics – Describes a type of exercise that uses eccentric muscle actions (negatives) followed by explosive muscle contractions to develop speed specific adaptations. The most typical plyometric exercises involve explosive jumps.

Power – Work divided by time. In sport performance this would translate into the ability to generate the most strength in a sport-related movement, in the shortest period of time.

Rate coding – The increase in muscle firing frequency, through increased neural stimulation, which eventually leads to greater force production inside the muscle cell.

Slow twitch muscle fiber – Muscle cells that take a relatively long time to reach full force, but are easily recruited with minimal resistance and tend to have high endurance capabilities in repeated muscle contractions.

Specificity of training – The concept that states that the human body will adapt in a precise way based on the type of demand placed upon it through systematic exercise.

Speed – Applying maximum power to specific athletic techniques, such as sprinting, with the goal of attaining maximum velocity.

Strength – The maximum amount of force that can be generated in a muscle with one voluntary muscle contraction.

Synovial fluid – The fluid in the joints that lubricates surfaces to allow the moving parts to slide, thereby reducing friction and preventing inflammation.

Target adaptation – Specific physical changes that occur as a result of placing a high priority on a precise type of training. Ideally the training variables are selected to meet explicit goals based on the timing of the training phase.

Testosterone – The hormone most responsible for protein building in the muscle (Anabolism). Both males and females produce this hormone, but males produce about 10 times the amount as females. In addition to muscle building, this hormone is responsible for secondary male sexual characteristics such increases in facial hair, the deepening of the voice, and other changes males experience during puberty.

Training effects – The specific adaptations that occur in the body as a result of long-term systematic exercise.

Transfer specificity – How well a training adaptation gained in a workout program translates to performance in the game.

Volume — The training variable that describes the total amount of work performed in a given time period. In resistance training this includes the number of sets and repetitions, time between sets, and number of workouts.

FOOTBALL WEIGHT-LIFTING GOALS

	AWARD LEVELS	SQUAT	BENCH	POWER CLEAN	PUSH JERK	POWER CLEAN TOTAL
Lineman	IRON HOKIE	575	400	315	340	1630
	HOKIE	525	370	295	320	1510
	ORANGE	500	349	275	295	1410
	MAROON	470	320	250	265	1305
TE, ILB, DE, FB	IRON HOKIE	525	355	300	320	1500
	HOKIE	500	340	280	300	1420
	ORANGE	475	320	260	280	1335
	MAROON	450	300	235	260	1245
WHIP, LB, TB, DB	IRON HOKIE	475	340	275	305	1395
	HOKIE	450	320	255	285	1320
	ORANGE	425	300	235	265	1235
	MAROON	400	280	215	245	1150
QB, WR, SPEC	IRON HOKIE	450	320	265	275	1310
	HOKIE	425	300	245	255	1225
	ORANGE	400	275	225	235	1135
	MAROON	375	250	205	215	1045

REQUIREMENTS:

1) Each level must reach total weight.

2) **_All_ maroon requirements must be met before receiving maroon award or any higher award.**

3) Orange must meet or exceed *three* lift requirements and total.

4) Hokie must meet *two* lift requirements and total.

5) Iron Hokie must meet *one* lift requirement and total.

6) Super Iron Hokie must meet *all* Iron Hokie lift requirements and total.

7) You must pass the 16 110s conditioning test to be eligible for any award in fall testing.

VIRGINIA TECH OFFENSIVE LINE PERFORMANCE SCALE

POINTS	BENCH	SQUAT	CLEAN	JERK	VERTICAL	40-YARD	10-YARD	NFL SHUTTLE	FLEX	RATING
100	435	635	350	370	36.0	4.80	1.70	4.30	-9.00	
98.5	430	625	345	365	35.5	4.82	1.71	4.33	-8.70	
97	425	615	340	360	35.0	4.84	1.72	4.35	-8.40	Superior
95.5	420	605	335	355	34.5	4.86	1.73	4.38	-8.10	
94	415	595	330	350	34.0	4.88	1.74	4.40	-7.80	
92.5	410	585	325	345	33.5	4.90	1.75	4.43	-7.50	
91	405	575	320	340	33.0	4.92	1.76	4.45	-7.20	
89.5	400	565	315	335	32.5	4.94	1.77	4.48	-6.90	
88	395	555	310	330	32.0	4.96	1.78	4.50	-6.60	Excellent
86.5	390	545	305	325	31.5	4.98	1.79	4.53	-6.30	
85	385	535	300	320	31.0	5.00	1.80	4.55	-6.00	
83.5	380	525	295	315	30.5	5.02	1.81	4.58	-5.70	
82	375	515	290	310	30.0	5.04	1.82	4.60	-5.40	
80.5	370	505	285	305	29.5	5.06	1.83	4.63	-5.10	
79	365	495	280	300	29.0	5.08	1.84	4.65	-4.80	Good
77.5	360	485	275	295	28.5	5.10	1.85	4.68	-4.50	
76	355	475	270	290	28.0	5.12	1.86	4.70	-4.20	
74.5	350	465	265	285	27.5	5.14	1.87	4.73	-3.90	
73	345	455	260	280	27.0	5.16	1.88	4.75	-3.60	
71.5	340	445	255	275	26.5	5.18	1.89	4.78	-3.30	
70	335	435	250	270	26.0	5.20	1.90	4.80	-3.00	Average
68.5	330	425	245	265	25.5	5.22	1.91	4.83	-2.70	
67	325	415	240	260	25.0	5.24	1.92	4.85	-2.40	
65.5	320	405	235	255	24.5	5.26	1.93	4.88	-2.10	
64	315	395	230	250	24.0	5.28	1.94	4.90	-1.80	
62.5	310	385	225	245	23.5	5.30	1.95	4.93	-1.50	Below
61	305	375	220	240	23.0	5.32	1.96	4.95	-1.20	Average
59.5	300	365	215	235	22.5	5.34	1.97	4.98	-0.90	
58	295	355	210	230	22.0	5.36	1.98	5.00	-0.60	
56.5	290	345	205	225	21.5	5.38	1.99	5.03	-0.30	
55	285	335	200	220	21.0	5.40	2.00	5.05	0.00	
53.5	280	325	195	215	20.5	5.42	2.01	5.08	0.30	
52	275	315	190	210	20.0	5.44	2.02	5.10	0.60	
50.5	270	305	185	205	19.5	5.46	2.03	5.13	0.90	
49	265	295	180	200	19.0	5.48	2.04	5.15	1.20	
47.5	260	285	175	195	18.5	5.50	2.05	5.18	1.50	Poor
46	255	275	170	190	18.0	5.52	1.06	5.20	1.80	
44.5	250	265	165	185	17.5	5.54	2.07	5.23	2.10	
43	245	255	160	180	17.0	5.56	2.08	5.25	2.40	
41.5	240	245	155	175	16.5	5.58	2.09	5.28	2.70	
40	235	235	150	170	16.0	5.60	2.10	5.30	3.00	

VIRGINIA TECH QUARTERBACK PERFORMANCE SCALE

POINTS	BENCH	SQUAT	CLEAN	JERK	VERTICAL	40-YARD	10-YARD	NFL SHUTTLE	FLEX	RATING
100	360	520	305	310	38.0	4.43	1.54	4.00	-11.00	
98.5	355	510	300	305	37.5	4.45	1.55	4.03	-10.70	
97	350	500	295	300	37.0	4.47	1.56	4.05	-10.40	Superior
95.5	345	490	290	295	36.5	4.49	1.57	4.08	-10.10	
94	340	480	285	290	36.0	4.51	1.58	4.10	-9.80	
92.5	335	470	280	285	35.5	4.53	1.59	4.13	-9.50	
91	330	460	275	280	35.0	4.55	1.60	4.15	-9.20	
89.5	325	450	270	275	34.5	4.57	1.61	4.18	-8.90	
88	320	440	265	270	34.0	4.59	1.62	4.20	-8.60	Excellent
86.5	315	430	260	265	33.5	4.61	1.63	4.23	-8.30	
85	310	420	255	260	33.0	4.63	1.64	4.25	-8.00	
83.5	305	410	250	255	32.5	4.65	1.65	4.28	-7.70	
82	300	400	245	250	32.0	4.67	1.66	4.30	-7.40	
80.5	295	390	240	245	31.5	4.69	1.67	4.33	-7.10	
79	290	380	235	240	31.0	4.71	1.68	4.35	-6.80	Good
77.5	285	370	230	235	30.5	4.73	1.69	4.38	-6.50	
76	280	360	225	230	30.0	4.75	1.70	4.40	-6.20	
74.5	275	350	220	225	29.5	4.77	1.71	4.43	-5.90	
73	270	340	215	220	29.0	4.79	1.72	4.45	-5.60	
71.5	265	330	210	215	28.5	4.81	1.73	4.48	-5.30	
70	260	320	205	210	28.0	4.83	1.74	4.50	-5.00	Average
68.5	255	310	200	205	27.5	4.85	1.75	4.53	-4.70	
67	250	300	195	200	27.0	4.87	1.76	4.55	-4.40	
65.5	245	290	190	195	26.5	4.89	1.77	4.58	-4.10	
64	240	280	185	190	26.0	4.91	1.78	4.60	-3.80	
62.5	235	270	180	185	25.5	4.93	1.79	4.63	-3.50	Below
61	230	260	175	180	25.0	4.95	1.80	4.65	-3.20	Average
59.5	225	250	170	175	24.5	4.97	1.81	4.68	-2.90	
58	220	240	165	170	24.0	4.99	1.82	4.70	-2.60	
56.5	215	230	160	165	23.5	5.01	1.83	4.73	-2.30	
55	210	225	155	160	23.0	5.03	1.84	4.75	-2.00	
53.5	205	220	150	155	22.5	5.05	1.85	4.78	-1.70	
52	200	215	145	150	22.0	5.07	1.86	4.80	-1.40	
50.5	195	210	140	145	21.5	5.09	1.87	4.83	-1.10	
49	190	205	135	140	21.0	5.11	1.88	4.85	-0.80	Poor
47.5	185	200	130	135	20.5	5.13	1.89	4.88	-0.50	
46	180	195	125	130	20.0	5.15	1.90	4.90	-0.20	
44.5	175	190	120	125	19.5	5.17	1.91	4.93	0.10	
43	170	185	115	120	19.0	5.19	1.92	4.95	0.40	
41.5	165	180	110	115	18.5	5.21	1.93	4.98	0.70	
40	160	175	105	110	18	5.23	1.94	5.00	1.00	

VIRGINIA TECH TAILBACK and WHIP LB PERFORMANCE SCALE

POINTS	BENCH	SQUAT	CLEAN	JERK	VERTICAL	40-YARD	10-YARD	NFL SHUTTLE	FLEX	RATING
100	385	555	320	330	40.0	4.32	1.49	3.95	-11.00	
98.5	380	545	315	325	39.5	4.34	1.50	3.98	-10.70	
97	375	535	310	320	39.0	4.35	1.51	4.00	-10.40	Superior
95.5	370	525	305	315	38.5	4.37	1.52	4.03	-10.10	
94	365	515	300	310	38.0	4.38	1.53	4.05	-9.80	
92.5	360	505	295	305	37.5	4.40	1.54	4.08	-9.50	
91	355	495	290	300	37.0	4.41	1.55	4.10	-9.20	
89.5	350	485	285	295	36.5	4.43	1.56	4.13	-8.90	
88	345	475	280	290	36.0	4.44	1.57	4.15	-8.60	Excellent
86.5	340	465	275	285	35.5	4.46	1.58	4.18	-8.30	
85	335	455	270	280	35.0	4.47	1.59	4.20	-8.00	
83.5	330	445	265	275	34.5	4.49	1.60	4.23	-7.70	
82	325	435	260	270	34.0	4.50	1.61	4.25	-7.40	
80.5	320	425	255	265	33.5	4.52	1.62	4.28	-7.10	
79	315	415	250	260	33.0	4.53	1.63	4.30	-6.80	Good
77.5	310	405	245	255	32.5	4.55	1.64	4.33	-6.50	
76	305	395	240	250	32.0	4.56	1.65	4.35	-6.20	
74.5	300	385	235	245	31.5	4.57	1.66	4.38	-5.90	
73	295	375	230	240	31.0	4.59	1.67	4.40	-5.60	
71.5	290	365	225	235	30.5	4.60	1.68	4.43	-5.30	
70	285	355	220	230	30.0	4.62	1.69	4.45	-5.00	Average
68.5	280	345	215	225	29.5	4.63	1.70	4.48	-4.70	
67	275	335	210	220	29.0	4.65	1.71	4.50	-4.40	
65.5	270	325	205	215	28.5	4.66	1.72	4.53	-4.10	
64	265	315	200	210	28.0	4.68	1.73	4.55	-3.80	
62.5	260	305	195	205	27.5	4.69	1.74	4.58	-3.50	Below
61	255	295	190	200	27.0	4.71	1.75	4.60	-3.20	Average
59.5	250	285	185	195	26.5	4.72	1.76	4.63	-2.90	
58	245	275	180	190	26.0	4.74	1.77	4.65	-2.60	
56.5	240	265	175	185	25.5	4.75	1.78	4.68	-2.30	
55	235	260	170	180	25.0	4.77	1.79	4.70	-2.00	
53.5	230	255	165	175	24.5	4.78	1.80	4.73	-1.70	
52	225	250	160	170	24.0	4.80	1.81	4.75	-1.40	
50.5	220	245	155	165	23.5	4.81	1.82	4.78	-1.10	
49	215	240	150	160	23.0	4.83	1.83	4.80	-0.80	Poor
47.5	210	235	145	155	22.5	4.84	1.84	4.83	-0.50	
46	205	230	140	150	22.0	4.86	1.85	4.85	-0.20	
44.5	200	225	135	145	21.5	4.87	1.86	4.88	0.10	
43	195	220	130	140	21.0	4.89	1.87	4.90	0.40	
41.5	190	215	125	135	20.5	4.90	1.88	4.93	0.70	
40	185	210	120	130	20.0	4.92	1.89	4.95	1.00	

VIRGINIA TECH WIDE RECEIVER PERFORMANCE SCALE

POINTS	BENCH	SQUAT	CLEAN	JERK	VERTICAL	40-YARD	10-YARD	NFL SHUTTLE	FLEX	RATING
100	360	520	305	310	42.0	4.28	1.48	3.95	-11.00	
98.5	355	510	300	305	41.5	4.30	1.49	3.98	-10.70	
97	350	500	295	300	41.0	4.31	1.50	4.00	-10.40	Superior
95.5	345	490	290	295	40.5	4.33	1.51	4.03	-10.10	
94	340	480	285	290	40.0	4.34	1.52	4.05	-9.80	
92.5	335	470	280	285	39.5	4.36	1.53	4.08	-9.50	
91	330	460	275	280	39.0	4.37	1.54	4.10	-9.20	
89.5	325	450	270	275	38.5	4.39	1.55	4.13	-8.90	
88	320	440	265	270	38.0	4.40	1.56	4.15	-8.60	Excellent
86.5	315	430	260	265	37.5	4.42	1.57	4.18	-8.30	
85	310	420	255	260	37.0	4.43	1.58	4.20	-8.00	
83.5	305	410	250	255	36.5	4.45	1.59	4.23	-7.70	
82	300	400	245	250	36.0	4.46	1.60	4.25	-7.40	
80.5	295	390	240	245	35.5	4.48	1.61	4.28	-7.10	
79	290	380	235	240	35.0	4.49	1.62	4.30	-6.80	Good
77.5	285	370	230	235	34.5	4.51	1.63	4.33	-6.50	
76	280	360	225	230	34.0	4.52	1.64	4.35	-6.20	
74.5	275	350	220	225	33.5	4.53	1.65	4.38	-5.90	
73	270	340	215	220	33.0	4.55	1.66	4.40	-5.60	
71.5	265	330	210	215	32.5	4.56	1.67	4.43	-5.30	
70	260	320	205	210	32.0	4.58	1.68	4.45	-5.00	Average
68.5	255	310	200	205	31.5	4.59	1.69	4.48	-4.70	
67	250	300	195	200	31.0	4.61	1.70	4.50	-4.40	
65.5	245	290	190	195	30.5	4.62	1.71	4.53	-4.10	
64	240	280	185	190	30.0	4.64	1.72	4.55	-3.80	
62.5	235	270	180	185	29.5	4.65	1.73	4.58	-3.50	Below
61	230	260	175	180	29.0	4.67	1.74	4.60	-3.20	Average
59.5	225	250	170	175	28.5	4.68	1.75	4.63	-2.90	
58	220	240	165	170	28.0	4.70	1.76	4.65	-2.60	
56.5	215	230	160	165	27.5	4.71	1.77	4.68	-2.30	
55	210	225	155	160	27.0	4.73	1.78	4.70	-2.00	
53.5	205	220	150	155	26.5	4.74	1.79	4.73	-1.70	
52	200	215	145	150	26.0	4.76	1.80	4.75	-1.40	
50.5	195	210	140	145	25.5	4.77	1.81	4.78	-1.10	
49	190	205	135	140	25.0	4.79	1.82	4.80	-0.80	Poor
47.5	185	200	130	135	24.5	4.80	1.83	4.83	-0.50	
46	180	195	125	130	24.0	4.82	1.84	4.85	-0.20	
44.5	175	190	120	125	23.5	4.83	1.85	4.88	0.10	
43	170	185	115	120	23.0	4.85	1.86	4.90	0.40	
41.5	165	180	110	115	22.5	4.86	1.87	4.93	0.70	
40	160	175	105	110	22.0	4.88	1.88	4.95	1.00	

VIRGINIA TECH DEFENSIVE BACK PERFORMANCE SCALE

POINTS	BENCH	SQUAT	CLEAN	JERK	VERTICAL	40-YARD	10-YARD	NFL SHUTTLE	FLEX	RATING
100	375	545	315	325	42.0	4.30	1.49	3.95	-11.00	
98.5	370	535	310	320	41.5	4.32	1.50	3.98	-10.70	
97	365	525	305	315	41.0	4.33	1.51	4.00	-10.40	Superior
95.5	360	515	300	310	40.5	4.35	1.52	4.03	-10.10	
94	355	505	295	305	40.0	4.36	1.53	4.05	-9.80	
92.5	350	495	290	300	39.5	4.38	1.54	4.08	-9.50	
91	345	485	285	295	39.0	4.39	1.55	4.10	-9.20	
89.5	340	475	280	290	38.5	4.41	1.56	4.13	-8.90	
88	335	465	275	285	38.0	4.42	1.57	4.15	-8.60	Excellent
86.5	330	455	270	280	37.5	4.44	1.58	4.18	-8.30	
85	325	445	265	275	37.0	4.45	1.59	4.20	-8.00	
83.5	320	435	260	270	36.5	4.47	1.60	4.23	-7.70	
82	315	425	255	265	36.0	4.48	1.61	4.25	-7.40	
80.5	310	415	250	260	35.5	4.50	1.62	4.28	-7.10	
79	305	405	245	255	35.0	4.51	1.63	4.30	-6.80	Good
77.5	300	395	240	250	34.5	4.53	1.64	4.33	-6.50	
76	295	385	235	245	34.0	4.54	1.65	4.35	-6.20	
74.5	290	375	230	240	33.5	4.55	1.66	4.38	-5.90	
73	285	365	225	235	33.0	4.57	1.67	4.40	-5.60	
71.5	280	355	220	230	32.5	4.58	1.68	4.43	-5.30	
70	275	345	215	225	32.0	4.60	1.69	4.45	-5.00	Average
68.5	270	335	210	220	31.5	4.61	1.70	4.48	-4.70	
67	265	325	205	215	31.0	4.63	1.71	4.50	-4.40	
65.5	260	315	200	210	30.5	4.64	1.72	4.53	-4.10	
64	255	305	195	205	30.0	4.66	1.73	4.55	-3.80	
62.5	250	295	190	200	29.5	4.67	1.74	4.58	-3.50	Below
61	245	285	185	195	29.0	4.69	1.75	4.60	-3.20	Average
59.5	240	275	180	190	28.5	4.70	1.76	4.63	-2.90	
58	235	265	175	185	28.0	4.72	1.77	4.65	-2.60	
56.5	230	255	170	180	27.5	4.73	1.78	4.68	-2.30	
55	225	250	165	175	27.0	4.75	1.79	4.70	-2.00	
53.5	220	245	160	170	26.5	4.76	1.80	4.73	-1.70	
52	215	240	155	165	26.0	4.78	1.81	4.75	-1.40	
50.5	210	235	150	160	25.5	4.79	1.82	4.78	-1.10	
49	205	230	145	155	25.0	4.81	1.83	4.80	-0.80	Poor
47.5	200	225	140	150	24.5	4.82	1.84	4.83	-0.50	
46	195	220	135	145	24.0	4.84	1.85	4.85	-0.20	
44.5	190	215	130	140	23.5	4.85	1.86	4.88	0.10	
43	185	210	125	135	23.0	4.87	1.87	4.90	0.40	
41.5	180	205	120	130	22.5	4.88	1.88	4.93	0.70	
40	175	200	115	125	22.0	4.90	1.89	4.95	1.00	

VIRGINIA TECH SPECIALIST PERFORMANCE SCALE

POINTS	BENCH	SQUAT	CLEAN	JERK	VERTICAL	40-YARD	10-YARD	NFL SHUTTLE	FLEX	RATING
100	360	520	305	310	38.0	4.43	1.54	4.00	-11.00	
98.5	355	510	300	305	37.5	4.45	1.55	4.03	-10.70	
97	350	500	295	300	37.0	4.47	1.56	4.05	-10.40	Superior
95.5	345	490	290	295	36.5	4.49	1.57	4.08	-10.10	
94	340	480	285	290	36.0	4.51	1.58	4.10	-9.80	
92.5	335	470	280	285	35.5	4.53	1.59	4.13	-9.50	
91	330	460	275	280	35.0	4.55	1.60	4.15	-9.20	
89.5	325	450	270	275	34.5	4.57	1.61	4.18	-8.90	
88	320	440	265	270	34.0	4.59	1.62	4.20	-8.60	Excellent
86.5	315	430	260	265	33.5	4.61	1.63	4.23	-8.30	
85	310	420	255	260	33.0	4.63	1.64	4.25	-8.00	
83.5	305	410	250	255	32.5	4.65	1.65	4.28	-7.70	
82	300	400	245	250	32.0	4.67	1.66	4.30	-7.40	
80.5	295	390	240	245	31.5	4.69	1.67	4.33	-7.10	
79	290	380	235	240	31.0	4.71	1.68	4.35	-6.80	Good
77.5	285	370	230	235	30.5	4.73	1.69	4.38	-6.50	
76	280	360	225	230	30.0	4.75	1.70	4.40	-6.20	
74.5	275	350	220	225	29.5	4.77	1.71	4.43	-5.90	
73	270	340	215	220	29.0	4.79	1.72	4.45	-5.60	
71.5	265	330	210	215	28.5	4.81	1.73	4.48	-5.30	
70	260	320	205	210	28.0	4.83	1.74	4.50	-5.00	Average
68.5	255	310	200	205	27.5	4.85	1.75	4.53	-4.70	
67	250	300	195	200	27.0	4.87	1.76	4.55	-4.40	
65.5	245	290	190	195	26.5	4.89	1.77	4.58	-4.10	
64	240	280	185	190	26.0	4.91	1.78	4.60	-3.80	
62.5	235	270	180	185	25.5	4.93	1.79	4.63	-3.50	Below
61	230	260	175	180	25.0	4.95	1.80	4.65	-3.20	Average
59.5	225	250	170	175	24.5	4.97	1.81	4.68	-2.90	
58	220	240	165	170	24.0	4.99	1.82	4.70	-2.60	
56.5	215	230	160	165	23.5	5.01	1.83	4.73	-2.30	
55	210	225	155	160	23.0	5.03	1.84	4.75	-2.00	
53.5	205	220	150	155	22.5	5.05	1.85	4.78	-1.70	
52	200	215	145	150	22.0	5.07	1.86	4.80	-1.40	
50.5	195	210	140	145	21.5	5.09	1.87	4.83	-1.10	
49	190	205	135	140	21.0	5.11	1.88	4.85	-0.80	Poor
47.5	185	200	130	135	20.5	5.13	1.89	4.88	-0.50	
46	180	195	125	130	20.0	5.15	1.90	4.90	-0.20	
44.5	175	190	120	125	19.5	5.17	1.91	4.93	0.10	
43	170	185	115	120	19.0	5.19	1.92	4.95	0.40	
41.5	165	180	110	115	18.5	5.21	1.93	4.98	0.70	
40	160	175	105	110	18	5.23	1.94	5.00	1.00	

VIRGINIA TECH DEFENSIVE LINE PERFORMANCE SCALE

POINTS	BENCH	SQUAT	CLEAN	JERK	VERTICAL	40-YARD	10-YARD	NFL SHUTTLE	FLEX	RATING
100	435	635	350	370	38.0	4.62	1.65	4.20	-9.00	
98.5	430	625	345	365	37.5	4.64	1.66	4.23	-8.70	
97	425	615	340	360	37.0	4.66	2.67	4.25	-8.40	Superior
95.5	420	605	335	355	36.5	4.68	1.68	4.28	-8.10	
94	415	595	330	350	36.0	4.70	1.69	4.30	-7.80	
92.5	410	585	325	345	35.5	4.72	1.70	4.33	-7.50	
91	405	575	320	340	35.0	4.74	1.71	4.35	-7.20	
89.5	400	565	315	335	34.5	4.76	1.72	4.38	-6.90	
88	395	555	310	330	34.0	4.78	1.73	4.40	-6.60	Excellent
86.5	390	545	305	325	33.5	4.80	1.74	4.43	-6.30	
85	385	535	300	320	33.0	4.82	1.75	4.45	-6.00	
83.5	380	525	295	315	32.5	4.84	1.76	4.48	-5.70	
82	375	515	290	310	32.0	4.86	1.77	4.50	-5.40	
80.5	370	505	285	305	31.5	4.88	1.7	4.53	-5.10	
79	365	495	280	300	31.0	4.90	1.79	4.55	-4.80	Good
77.5	360	485	275	295	30.5	4.92	1.80	4.58	-4.50	
76	355	475	270	290	30.0	4.94	1.81	4.60	-4.20	
74.5	350	465	265	285	29.5	4.96	1.82	4.63	-3.90	
73	345	455	260	280	29.0	4.98	183	4.65	-3.60	
71.5	340	445	255	275	28.5	5.00	1.84	4.68	-3.30	
70	335	435	250	270	28.0	5.02	1.85	4.70	-3.00	Average
68.5	330	425	245	265	27.5	5.04	1.86	4.73	-2.70	
67	325	415	240	260	27.0	5.06	1.87	4.75	-2.40	
65.5	320	405	235	255	26.5	5.08	1.88	4.78	-2.10	
64	315	395	230	250	26.0	5.10	1.89	4.80	-1.80	
62.5	310	385	225	245	25.5	5.12	1.90	4.83	-1.50	Below
61	305	375	220	240	25.0	5.14	1.91	4.85	-1.20	Average
59.5	300	365	215	235	24.5	5.16	1.92	4.88	-0.90	
58	295	355	210	230	24.0	5.18	1.93	4.90	-0.60	
56.5	290	345	205	225	23.5	5.20	1.94	4.93	-0.30	
55	285	335	200	220	23.0	5.22	1.95	4.95	0.00	
53.5	280	325	195	215	22.5	5.24	1.96	4.98	0.30	
52	275	315	190	210	22.0	5.26	1.97	5.00	0.60	
50.5	270	305	185	205	21.5	5.28	1.98	5.03	0.90	
49	265	295	180	200	21.0	5.30	1.99	5.05	1.20	Poor
47.5	260	285	175	195	20.5	5.32	2.00	5.08	1.50	
46	255	275	170	190	20.0	5.34	2.01	5.10	1.80	
44.5	250	265	165	185	19.5	5.36	2.02	5.13	2.10	
43	245	255	160	180	19.0	5.38	2.03	5.15	2.40	
41.5	240	245	155	175	18.5	5.40	2.04	5.18	2.70	
40	235	235	150	170	18.0	5.42	2.05	5.20	3.00	

VIRGINIA TECH DE, LB, TE, and FB PERFORMANCE SCALE

POINTS	BENCH	SQUAT	CLEAN	JERK	VERTICAL	40-YARD	10-YARD	NFL SHUTTLE	FLEX	RATING
100	400	600	340	355	39.0	4.45	1.55	4.00	-10.00	
98.5	395	590	335	350	38.5	4.47	1.56	4.03	-9.70	
97	390	580	330	345	38.0	4.49	1.57	4.05	-9.40	Superior
95.5	385	570	325	340	37.5	4.51	1.58	4.08	-9.10	
94	380	560	320	335	37.0	4.53	1.59	4.10	-8.80	
92.5	375	550	315	330	36.5	4.55	1.60	4.13	-8.50	
91	370	540	310	325	36.0	4.57	1.61	4.15	-8.20	
89.5	365	530	305	320	35.5	4.59	1.62	4.18	-7.90	
88	360	520	300	315	35.0	4.61	1.63	4.20	-7.60	Excellent
86.5	355	510	295	310	34.5	4.63	1.64	4.23	-7.30	
85	350	500	290	305	34.0	4.65	1.65	4.25	-7.00	
83.5	345	490	285	300	33.5	4.67	1.66	4.28	-6.70	
82	340	480	280	295	33.0	4.69	1.67	4.30	-6.40	
80.5	335	470	275	290	32.5	4.71	1.68	4.33	-6.10	
79	330	460	270	285	32.0	4.73	1.69	4.35	-5.80	Good
77.5	325	450	265	280	31.5	4.75	1.70	4.38	-5.50	
76	320	440	260	275	31.0	4.77	1.71	4.40	-5.20	
74.5	315	430	255	270	30.5	4.79	1.72	4.43	-4.90	
73	310	420	250	265	30.0	4.81	1.73	4.45	-4.60	
71.5	305	410	245	260	29.5	4.83	1.74	4.48	-4.30	
70	300	400	240	255	29.0	4.85	1.75	4.50	-4.00	Average
68.5	295	390	235	250	28.5	4.87	1.76	4.53	-3.70	
67	290	380	230	245	28.0	4.89	1.77	4.55	-3.40	
65.5	285	370	225	240	27.5	4.91	1.78	4.58	-3.10	
64	280	360	220	235	27.0	4.93	1.79	4.60	-2.80	
62.5	275	350	215	230	26.5	4.95	1.80	4.63	-2.50	Below
61	270	340	210	225	26.0	4.97	1.81	4.65	-2.20	Average
59.5	265	330	205	220	25.5	4.99	1.82	4.68	-1.90	
58	260	320	200	215	25.0	5.01	1.83	4.70	-1.60	
56.5	255	310	195	210	24.5	5.03	1.84	4.73	-1.30	
55	250	300	190	205	24.0	5.05	1.85	4.75	-1.00	
53.5	245	290	185	200	23.5	5.07	1.86	4.78	-0.70	
52	240	280	180	195	23.0	5.09	1.87	4.80	-0.40	
50.5	235	270	175	190	22.5	5.11	1.88	4.83	-0.10	
49	230	260	170	185	22.0	5.13	1.89	4.85	0.20	Poor
47.5	225	250	165	180	21.5	5.15	1.90	4.88	0.50	
46	220	240	160	175	21.0	5.17	1.91	4.90	0.80	
44.5	215	230	155	170	20.5	5.19	1.92	4.93	1.10	
43	210	220	150	165	20.0	5.21	1.93	4.95	1.40	
41.5	205	210	145	160	19.5	5.23	1.94	4.98	1.70	
40	200	200	140	155	19.0	5.25	1.95	5.00	2.00	

PREDICTED MAXIMUM

# Repetitions	%
1	1.000
2	.955
3	.917
4	.885
5	.857
6	.832
7	.809
8	.788
9	.769
10	.752
11	.736
12	.721

Sample: Maximum of 5 reps with 280 pounds

280/.857 = 325 predicted max

LBS	49%	52%	55%	58%	61%	64%	67%	70%	73%	76%	79%	82%	85%	88%	91%	94%	97%	103%	106%	109%	112%
50	25	25	30	30	30	30	35	35	35	40	40	40	45	45	45	45	50	50	55	55	55
55	25	30	30	30	35	35	35	40	40	40	45	45	45	50	50	50	55	55	60	60	60
60	30	30	35	35	35	40	40	40	45	45	45	50	50	55	55	55	60	60	65	65	65
65	30	35	35	40	40	40	45	45	45	50	50	55	55	55	60	60	65	65	70	70	75
70	35	35	40	40	45	45	45	50	50	55	55	55	60	60	65	65	70	70	75	75	80
75	35	40	40	45	45	50	50	55	55	55	60	60	65	65	70	70	75	75	80	80	85
80	40	40	45	45	50	50	55	55	60	60	65	65	70	70	75	75	80	80	85	85	90
85	40	45	45	50	50	55	55	60	60	65	65	70	70	75	75	80	80	90	90	95	95
90	45	45	50	50	55	60	60	65	65	70	70	75	75	80	80	85	85	95	95	100	100
95	45	50	50	55	60	60	65	65	70	70	75	80	80	85	85	90	90	100	100	105	105
100	50	50	55	60	60	65	65	70	75	75	80	80	85	90	90	95	95	105	105	110	110
105	50	55	60	60	65	65	70	75	75	80	85	85	90	90	95	100	100	110	110	115	120
110	55	55	60	65	65	70	75	75	80	85	85	90	95	95	100	105	105	115	115	120	125
115	55	60	65	65	70	75	75	80	85	85	90	95	100	100	105	110	110	120	120	125	130
120	60	60	65	70	75	75	80	85	90	90	95	100	100	105	110	115	115	125	125	130	135
125	60	65	70	75	75	80	85	90	90	95	100	105	105	110	115	120	120	130	135	135	140
130	65	70	70	75	80	85	85	90	95	100	105	105	110	115	120	120	125	135	140	140	145
135	65	70	75	80	80	85	90	95	100	105	105	110	115	120	120	125	130	140	145	145	150
140	70	75	75	80	85	90	95	100	100	105	110	115	120	125	125	130	135	145	150	150	155
145	70	75	80	85	90	95	95	100	105	110	115	120	125	130	130	135	140	150	155	160	160
150	75	80	85	85	90	95	100	105	110	115	120	125	130	130	135	140	145	155	160	165	170
155	75	80	85	90	95	100	105	110	115	120	120	125	130	135	140	145	150	160	165	170	175
160	80	85	90	95	100	100	105	110	115	120	125	130	135	140	145	150	155	165	170	175	180
165	80	85	90	95	100	105	110	115	120	125	130	135	140	145	150	155	160	170	175	180	185
170	85	90	95	100	105	110	115	120	125	130	135	140	145	150	155	160	165	175	180	185	190
175	85	90	95	100	105	110	115	125	130	135	140	145	150	155	160	165	170	180	185	190	195
180	90	95	100	105	110	115	120	125	130	135	140	150	155	160	165	170	175	185	190	195	200
185	90	95	100	105	115	120	125	130	135	140	145	150	155	165	170	175	180	190	195	200	205
190	95	100	105	110	115	120	125	135	140	145	150	155	160	165	175	180	185	195	200	205	215
195	95	100	105	115	120	125	130	135	140	150	155	160	165	170	175	185	190	200	205	215	220
200	100	105	110	115	120	130	135	140	145	150	160	165	170	175	180	190	195	205	210	220	225
205	100	105	115	120	125	130	135	145	150	155	160	170	175	180	185	195	200	210	215	225	230
210	105	110	115	120	130	135	140	145	155	160	165	170	180	185	190	195	205	215	225	230	235
215	105	110	120	125	130	140	145	150	155	165	170	175	185	190	195	200	210	220	230	235	240
220	110	115	120	125	135	140	145	155	160	165	175	180	185	195	200	205	215	225	235	240	245
225	110	115	125	130	135	145	150	160	165	170	180	185	190	200	205	210	220	230	240	245	250
230	115	120	125	135	140	145	155	160	170	175	180	190	195	200	210	215	225	235	245	250	260
235	115	120	130	135	145	150	155	165	170	180	185	195	200	205	215	220	230	240	250	255	265
240	120	125	130	140	145	155	160	170	175	180	190	195	205	210	220	225	235	245	255	260	270
245	120	125	135	140	150	155	165	170	180	185	195	200	210	215	225	230	240	250	260	265	275
250	125	130	140	145	155	160	170	175	185	190	200	205	215	220	230	235	245	260	265	275	280
255	125	135	140	150	155	165	170	180	185	195	200	210	215	225	230	240	245	265	270	280	285

LBS	49%	52%	55%	58%	61%	64%	67%	70%	73%	76%	79%	82%	85%	88%	91%	94%	97%	103%	106%	109%	112%
260	125	135	145	150	160	165	175	180	190	200	205	215	220	230	235	245	250	270	275	285	290
265	130	140	145	155	160	170	180	185	195	200	210	215	225	235	240	250	255	275	280	290	295
270	130	140	150	155	165	175	180	190	195	205	215	220	230	240	245	255	260	280	285	295	300
275	135	145	150	160	170	175	185	195	200	210	215	225	235	240	250	260	265	285	290	300	310
280	135	145	155	160	170	180	190	195	205	215	220	230	240	245	255	265	270	290	295	305	315
285	140	150	155	165	175	180	190	200	210	215	225	235	240	250	260	270	275	295	300	310	320
290	140	150	160	170	175	185	195	205	210	220	230	240	245	255	265	275	280	300	305	315	325
295	145	155	160	170	180	190	200	205	215	225	235	240	250	260	270	275	285	305	315	320	330
300	145	155	165	175	185	190	200	210	220	230	235	245	255	265	275	280	290	310	320	325	335
305	150	160	170	175	185	195	205	215	225	230	240	250	260	270	280	285	295	315	325	330	340
310	150	160	170	180	190	200	210	215	225	235	245	255	265	275	280	290	300	320	330	340	345
315	155	165	175	185	190	200	210	220	230	240	250	260	270	275	285	295	305	325	335	345	355
320	155	165	175	185	195	205	215	225	235	245	255	260	270	280	290	300	310	330	340	350	360
325	160	170	180	190	200	210	220	230	235	245	255	265	275	285	295	305	315	335	345	355	365
330	160	170	180	190	200	210	220	230	240	250	260	270	280	290	300	310	320	340	350	360	370
335	165	175	185	195	205	215	225	235	245	255	265	275	285	295	305	315	325	345	355	365	375
340	165	175	185	195	205	220	230	240	250	260	270	280	290	300	310	320	330	350	360	370	380
345	170	180	190	200	210	220	230	240	250	260	275	285	295	305	315	325	335	355	365	375	385
350	170	180	195	205	215	225	235	245	255	265	275	285	300	310	320	330	340	360	370	380	390
355	175	185	195	205	215	225	240	250	260	270	280	290	300	310	325	335	345	365	375	385	400
360	175	185	200	210	220	230	240	250	265	275	285	295	305	315	330	340	350	370	380	390	405
365	180	190	200	210	225	235	245	255	265	275	290	300	310	320	330	345	355	375	385	400	410
370	180	190	205	215	225	235	250	260	270	280	290	305	315	325	335	350	360	380	390	405	415
375	185	195	205	220	230	240	250	265	275	285	295	310	320	330	340	355	365	385	400	410	420
380	185	200	210	220	230	245	255	265	275	290	300	310	325	335	345	355	370	390	405	415	425
385	190	200	210	225	235	245	260	270	280	295	305	315	325	340	350	360	375	395	410	420	430
390	190	205	215	225	240	250	260	275	285	295	310	320	330	345	355	365	380	400	415	425	435
395	195	205	215	230	240	255	265	275	290	300	310	325	335	350	360	370	385	405	420	430	440
400	195	210	220	230	245	255	270	280	290	305	315	330	340	350	365	375	390	410	425	435	450
405	200	210	225	235	245	260	270	285	295	310	320	330	345	355	370	380	395	415	430	440	455
410	200	215	225	240	250	260	275	285	300	310	325	335	350	360	375	385	400	420	435	445	460
415	205	215	230	240	255	265	280	290	305	315	330	340	355	365	380	390	405	425	440	450	465
420	205	220	230	245	255	270	280	295	305	320	330	345	355	370	380	395	405	435	445	460	470
425	210	220	235	245	260	270	285	300	310	325	335	350	360	375	385	400	410	440	450	465	475
430	210	225	235	250	260	275	290	300	315	325	340	350	365	380	390	405	415	445	455	470	480
435	215	225	240	250	265	280	290	305	320	330	345	355	370	385	395	410	420	450	460	475	485
440	215	230	240	255	270	280	295	310	320	335	350	360	375	385	400	415	425	455	465	480	495
445	220	230	245	260	270	285	300	310	325	340	350	365	380	390	405	420	430	460	470	485	500
450	220	235	250	260	275	290	300	315	330	340	355	370	385	395	410	425	435	465	475	490	505
455	225	235	250	265	280	290	305	320	330	345	360	375	385	400	415	430	440	470	480	495	510
460	225	240	255	265	280	295	310	320	335	350	365	375	390	405	420	430	445	475	490	500	515
465	230	240	255	270	285	300	310	325	340	355	365	380	395	410	425	435	450	480	495	505	520

LBS	49%	52%	55%	58%	61%	64%	67%	70%	73%	76%	79%	82%	85%	88%	91%	94%	97%	103%	106%	109%	112%
470	230	245	260	275	285	300	315	330	345	355	370	385	400	415	430	440	455	485	500	510	525
475	235	245	260	275	290	305	320	335	345	360	375	390	405	420	430	445	460	490	505	520	530
480	235	250	265	280	295	305	320	335	350	365	380	395	410	420	435	450	465	495	510	525	540
485	240	250	265	280	295	310	325	340	355	370	385	400	410	425	440	455	470	500	515	530	545
490	240	255	270	285	300	315	330	345	360	370	385	400	415	430	445	460	475	505	520	535	550
495	245	255	270	285	300	315	330	345	360	375	390	405	420	435	450	465	480	510	525	540	555
500	245	260	275	290	305	320	335	350	365	380	395	410	425	440	455	470	485	515	530	545	560
505	245	265	280	295	310	325	340	355	370	385	400	415	430	445	460	475	490	520	535	550	565
510	250	265	280	295	310	325	340	355	370	390	405	420	435	450	465	480	495	525	540	555	570
515	250	270	285	300	315	330	345	360	375	390	405	420	440	455	470	485	500	530	545	560	575
520	255	270	285	300	315	335	350	365	380	395	410	425	440	460	475	490	505	535	550	565	580
525	255	275	290	305	320	335	350	370	385	400	415	430	445	460	480	495	510	540	555	570	590
530	260	275	290	305	325	340	355	370	385	405	420	435	450	465	480	500	515	545	560	580	595
535	260	280	295	310	325	340	360	375	390	405	425	440	455	470	485	505	520	550	565	585	600
540	265	280	295	315	330	345	360	380	395	410	425	445	460	475	490	510	525	555	570	590	605
545	265	285	300	315	330	350	365	380	400	415	430	445	465	480	495	510	530	560	580	595	610
550	270	285	305	320	335	350	370	385	400	420	435	450	470	485	500	515	535	565	585	600	615
555	270	290	305	320	340	355	370	390	405	420	440	455	470	490	505	520	540	570	590	605	620
560	275	290	310	325	340	360	375	390	410	425	440	460	475	495	510	525	545	575	595	610	625
565	275	295	310	330	345	360	380	395	410	430	445	465	480	500	515	530	550	580	600	615	635
570	280	295	315	330	350	365	380	400	415	435	450	465	485	500	520	535	555	585	605	620	640
575	280	300	315	335	350	370	385	405	420	435	455	470	490	505	525	540	560	590	610	625	645
580	285	300	320	335	355	370	390	405	425	440	460	475	495	510	530	545	565	595	615	630	650
585	285	305	320	340	355	375	390	410	425	445	460	480	495	515	530	550	565	605	620	640	655
590	290	305	325	340	360	380	395	415	430	450	465	485	500	520	535	555	570	610	625	645	660
595	290	310	325	345	365	380	400	415	435	450	470	490	505	525	540	560	575	615	630	650	665
600	295	310	330	350	365	385	400	420	440	455	475	490	510	530	545	565	580	620	635	655	670
605	295	315	335	350	370	385	405	425	440	460	480	495	515	530	550	570	585	625	640	660	680
610	300	315	335	355	370	390	410	425	445	465	480	500	520	535	555	575	590	630	645	665	685
615	300	320	340	355	375	395	410	430	450	465	485	505	525	540	560	580	595	635	650	670	690
620	305	320	340	360	375	395	415	435	455	470	490	510	525	545	565	585	600	640	655	675	695
625	305	325	345	365	380	400	420	440	455	475	495	515	530	550	570	590	605	645	665	680	700
630	310	330	345	365	380	405	420	440	460	480	500	515	535	555	575	590	610	650	670	685	705
635	310	330	350	370	385	405	425	445	465	485	500	520	540	560	580	595	615	655	675	690	710
640	315	335	350	370	385	410	430	450	465	485	505	525	545	565	580	600	620	660	680	700	715
645	315	335	355	375	390	415	430	450	470	490	510	530	550	570	585	605	625	665	685	705	720
650	320	340	360	375	395	415	435	455	475	495	515	535	555	570	590	610	630	670	690	710	730
655	320	340	360	380	395	420	440	460	480	500	515	535	555	575	595	615	635	675	695	715	735
660	320	345	365	385	400	420	440	460	480	500	520	540	560	580	600	620	640	680	700	720	740
665	325	345	365	385	405	425	445	465	485	505	525	545	565	585	605	625	645	685	705	725	745
670	330	350	370	390	405	430	450	470	490	510	530	550	570	590	610	630	650	690	710	730	750
675	330	350	370	390	410	430	450	475	495	515	535	555	575	595	615	635	655	695	715	735	755
680	335	355	375	395	415	435	455	475	495	515	535	560	580	600	620	640	660	700	720	740	760

VIRGINIA TECH METABOLIC SPEED PAC

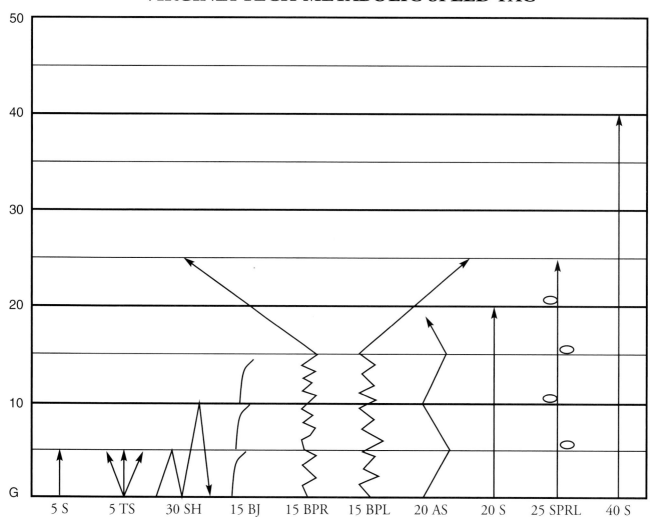

MOVEMENT DESCRIPTIONS

5 S - five-yard Sprint
5 TS - five-yard triangle Shuttle
30 SH - 30-yard Shuttle
15 BJ - 15-yard broad jump
15 BPR - 15-yard backpedal; turn and sprint 15 yards at 45 degrees to right.
15 BPL - 15-yard backpedal; turn and sprint 15 yards at 45 degrees to left.
20 AS - 20-yard alternating Shuffle (change every five yards)
20 S - 20-yard Sprint
25 SPRL - 20-yard Sprint; spin on right hand, then left (change every five yards)
40 S - 40-yard Sprint

	SET 1	SET 2	SET 3	SET 4	SET 5
1.	5 S	20 S	5 TS	Repeat Set 1	Repeat Set 2
2.	5 TS	15 BJ	25 SPRL		
3.	40 S	15 BPL	20 S		
4.	15 BJ	20 AS	15 BPR		
5.	15 BPR	40 S	15 BPL		
6.	20 AS	5 TS	40 S		
7.	20 S	30 SH	5 S		

Celebrate American Sports
in These Other New Releases from Sports Publishing!

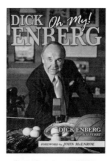

Dick Enberg: Oh My! 50 Years of Rubbing Shoulders with Greatness
by Dick Enberg with Jim Perry

- 6 x 9 hardcover • 250 pages
- 16-page color-photo insert
- $24.95
- Includes a bonus "Beyond the Book" DVD!

Michael Phelps: Beneath the Surface
by Michael Phelps with Brian Cazenueve

- 6 x 9 hardcover
- 230 pages
- eight-page color-photo insert
- $24.95

How About That! The Life of Mel Allen
by Stephen Borelli

- 6 x 9 hardcover
- 250 pages
- photo insert
- $24.95

Good as Gold: Techniques for Fundamental Baseball
by Frank White with Matt Fulks

- 7 x 10 trade paper
- 224 pages
- 100+ photos throughout
- $19.95 • (2004 release)

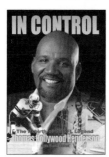

In Control: The Rebirth of an NFL Legend
by Thomas "Hollywood" Henderson with Frank Luksa

- 6 x 9 trade paper
- 370 pages
- $24.95

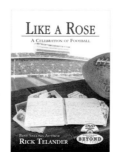

Like a Rose: A Celebration of Football
by Rick Telander

- 5.25 x 7.75 hardcover
- 160 pages
- photos throughout
- $19.95
- Includes bonus "Beyond the Book" DVD!

Tales from the Virginia Tech Sidelines
by Chris Colston

- 5.5 x 8.25 hardcover
- 200 pages
- photos throughout
- $19.95
- (2003 release)

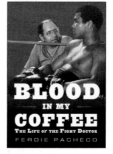

Ferdie Pacheco: Blood in My Coffee
by Ferdie Pacheco

- 6 x 9 hardcover
- 250 pages
- photo insert
- $24.95

The Teaching Professionals' Guide to Great Golf for Life
by Jim Linkin and Patrick Livingston

- 8.5 x 11 trade paper
- 156 pages
- photos throughout
- $19.95

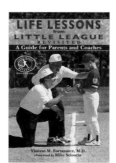

Life Lessons from Little League
by Dr. Vincent A. Fortanasce

- 7 x 9 trade paper
- 128 pages
- photos throughout
- $14.95

All books are available in bookstores everywhere!
Order 24-hours-a-day by calling toll-free **1-877-424-BOOK (2665)**.
Also order online at **www.SportsPublishingLLC.com**.